Introduction and Overview

This chapter is essential reading. In it I describe the contents and organization of the book and make suggestions as to how to get the most out of it. The book is intended for anyone determined on learning to be a professional teacher of children. If you are still reading, I assume that that is your purpose.

I have prepared the book with two important opinions in mind. The first is that the major objective of school teaching is to help children learn. This might seem rather obvious, but the fact is that some people – including many teachers – appear readily to forget it. Some teachers spend a great deal of time planning and preparing for activities without seeing them through to their consequences for learning. In this sort of approach children can be kept very busy, but unless learning is a deliberate focus for their activity it will not occur, or it will occur only incidentally.

Another distraction from learning takes the form of pseudo-social work. It is important that teachers take good care to provide for pupils' safety and security in school. Children who are distressed or otherwise insecure will not learn very much. But in some places the attention paid to the social aspects of schooling outweigh that paid to the academic aspect. A good social foundation must be laid, but if nothing is built on it, it serves very little long-term purpose. In this book you will find a persistent focus on children's learning.

My second guiding opinion is that good teaching is an extremely difficult job. Almost everyone seems willing and able to tell teachers how to do their work. Libraries are full of easy advice for teachers. Newspaper editors frequently find occasion to offer the benefits of their experience and wisdom on the matter of teaching. It is possible that bad teaching is an easy job. Good teaching on the other hand is exhausting and challenging even under the most helpful of circumstances. In fact circumstances are rarely helpful. Most teaching takes place in classrooms. These are by no means good natural learning environments. A classroom takes very careful and insightful management if it is to work in support of learning. In this book the difficulties of teaching are taken seriously. You will not find any trivial advice or easy tips – although you will find some tips. The focus of the authors is on identifying the complex circumstances which may defeat teaching, and on helping the reader to approach them in a constructive and well-informed way.

The best of teachers spend a lifetime learning to improve on their professional practice. My in-service classes for experienced teachers frequently contain significant numbers of teachers in their fifties who, after thirty or more years in the profession, still feel that they have a lot to learn and who are willing to spend their own time and money on doing so. For the thoughtful teacher good advice and good ideas can be had anywhere. Research on teachers has shown that even when shopping or on holiday they are on the look-out for ideas to promote children's learning and the quality of their learning environments. Attractive ideas are interpreted in the light of the teacher's fundamental principles of teaching and of accumulated class-room experience. Ideas are gathered from magazines, courses, newspapers, shops, other teachers and from books of all kinds. Reference books and 'teachers' books' are obvious sources, but there have also been a number of excellent novels, some depicting school life through the eyes of a child, which teachers have found particularly helpful in illuminating their understanding of classroom life and learning. Of course the quality of the idea is only as good as the quality of its treatment in the teacher's mind.

The chapters in this book are intended to help you prepare your mind for learning from and about teaching. As the book title makes clear, the authors write from a psychological point of view. Psychology is the science of mind. Research psychologists have a lot in common with teachers. They are interested in how people think, learn, remember, get on with each other, work and play. They are interested in people's feelings and attitudes, in what switches them on or turns them off and in what keeps them going when things get difficult. These matters are all of great importance to a teacher.

Teachers and research psychologists frequently work together to study teaching and learning in classrooms. They share a common objective in that they want to improve practice – however good it is. The pursuit of educational research has generated a lot of knowledge that is potentially useful to learning to teach. In this book a great deal of careful use is made of this research, whilst newspapers, shops and gossip are ignored.

In the following sections I take in turn each focus, learning, teaching and psychology, explaining how the book treats them and suggesting how the chapters can best be used to help you learn to be a better teacher.

Angela Lee

An Introduction to Teaching

An Introduction to Teaching

Psychological Perspectives

Edited by
Charles Desforges

BLACKWELL
Oxford UK & Cambridge USA

First published 1995

Blackwell Publishers Ltd
108 Cowley Road
Oxford OX4 1JF
UK

Blackwell Publishers Inc.
238 Main Street
Cambridge, Massachusetts 02142
USA

British Library Cataloguing in Publication Data

A CIP catalogue record for this book is available from the
British Library

Library of Congress Cataloging-in-Publication Data

An introduction to teaching: psychological perspectives/edited by
  Charles Desforges.
    p.   cm.
  Includes bibliographical references and index.
  ISBN 0–631–18726–X (alk. paper). – ISBN 0–631–18727–8 (pbk.:
alk. paper)
    1. Teaching – Psychological aspects.   2. Learning, Psychology of.
3. Educational psychology.   I. Desforges, Charles.
LB1027.I668   1995
370.15 – dc20   94-36287
                                                                      CIP

Typeset in 10½ on 12 pt Sabon
by CentraCet Limited, Cambridge
Printed in Great Britain by T.J. Press Ltd, Padstow, Cornwall
This book is printed on acid-free paper.

Contents

Focus on Learning

Children go to school to learn. If they are not learning, schooling is not working for them. Young humans have a natural capacity to learn. They learn very rapidly in their natural environment. School, however, is a place where children learn lessons rarely found in their natural environment. They learn science, history, geography and other academic subjects. They are expected to learn these subjects with a view to using their accumulated knowledge in later life. With its focus on the longer term and on somewhat abstracted knowledge, school learning is not at all natural. To cope with this, children need much more than natural capacities. They need to learn how to learn and how to manage their minds to make best use of them.

Knowledge may be useless, and it is certainly dangerous, if its application is not guided by a set of values appropriate to civilized living. Financiers and fraudsters know how to manipulate money. The different purposes to which they put their knowledge are strongly influenced by their values. Children are expected to learn a set of socially productive values in school. Values provide the framework for a fulfilling personal and civic life.

There are many different learning processes. Each has a key role to play in the acquisition of knowledge and values. Children need to develop a repertoire of learning processes if they are to make good learning progress.

In this book close attention is paid to natural learning, classroom learning, learning how to learn, learning academic subjects and learning values. This extended attention is based on the simple assumption that if teachers do not understand learning, they are unlikely to be very effective or efficient in promoting it.

Focus on Teaching

Just like learning, in many important respects teaching is a natural activity. Most of us are adept at showing, telling, describing and explaining in our everyday lives. Most of our natural teaching involves interaction with one person who, typically, asks us a question and seriously wants to know the answer. Normally, we have an easy, everyday familiarity with the topic in question whether it is how to bake a cake or how to repair a device.

There is nothing at all natural about teaching subjects and values to large numbers of children at once in crowded classrooms. Many of the pupils might not choose to be there. They might have no immediate interest, for example, in decimal fractions. They do, however, have lots of distracting interests. There are friends to talk to, games to plan. Classrooms are not natural learning environments. They are a device for cost-effective schooling.

Teachers do not have direct access to children's minds. Teachers can do no more than provide children with experience on which their minds may feed. Experience can be provided by showing, by telling and through various forms of work. The children must do the learning.

The art of teaching, then, is the management of pupils' experience, largely in classrooms, with the deliberate intention of promoting their learning. Managing learning has something in common with other forms of management. Managers should have clear objectives. They should deploy their resources to attain these objectives. They should collect evidence to monitor progress towards the objectives and, if progress is being thwarted, they should rethink and rearrange their resources accordingly.

Teaching as the management of pupil learning experience is a core theme in this book. There is a constant emphasis on setting goals for learning and on collecting evidence of learning.

Whilst all managers have something in common, specific management requires specific knowledge. Shop managers need a special body of knowledge relating to goods, prices, displays and customers. Teachers as managers need a special body of knowledge and special skills too.

Teachers need to understand the material they teach. They need academic subject knowledge. They also need a powerful grasp of the ways the subject can be taught and the materials for teaching it; the books, films, practical materials and field visits relevant to study must be critically appraised and their use fully understood. Detailed subject knowledge and curriculum knowledge are not treated in this book. These matters need extended and specialized attention. However, the general principles of subject knowledge and curriculum knowledge are treated in a way that can be used as a framework for further study.

Teachers need to know how classrooms work. Learning is especially sensitive to settings and contexts. It is easy to design environments which make people look stupid. Teaching consists of the management of learning experience *in classrooms*. A great deal of attention is paid in this book to how classrooms work and how to get the best out of them.

Knowledge finds its use through the application of skills. It is argued in this book that teachers promote the range of learning processes best when they have a repertoire of teaching skills. Several chapters are devoted to teaching skills covering showing, telling, describing, explaining, discussing and debating. Also covered are the skills of managing group work and of collecting management information on learning – the skill of assessment.

Just as teaching is about values as well as knowledge, so it is strongly influenced by values and knowledge. Teachers teach what they believe to be mathematics or history. Because some teachers have rather narrow or eccentric views of subjects, their pupils will inevitably receive narrow and eccentric experiences in those subjects.

Teachers also hold strong views about pupils and various subcategories of pupils. Working-class children, black children, female children have been considered by some to have inevitable weaknesses. Believing children to have limitations leads some teachers to provide limited challenges and, thereby, promote limited learning. Teachers' beliefs and values have a powerful impact on their planning, preparation and classroom interactions. The matter of teachers' values is persistently explored through the chapters here as a key theme.

A further key theme is the matter of teachers' learning. The major purpose of the book is to promote the development of teaching expertise. Teachers' learning is not different at the level of general principles from any other form of learning. To be successful, learner teachers need to apply deliberate attention to their experience. Experience alone is not a sufficient condition for learning. Experienced teachers are not necessarily good teachers.

Experience must be analysed, thought about, discussed, subjected to test if it is to provide a basis for improvement. As a persistent theme in this book, you are encouraged to collect evidence about your own performance as a teacher and to use that evidence as a basis on which to critique and advance your own skills.

In summary, a big theme of the book is the development of teaching competence through deliberate learning from reading, from practical experience and through discussion. The context of this learning is a range of knowledge, skills and values relevant to providing for and managing pupils' learning experience.

Focus on Psychology

Where has the material in this book come from? Why should you attend to it?

In the main the authors of this book have drawn on research conducted using psychological theories and methods. Psychology is frequently described as the science of mind. That is my view of it. In chapter 2 of the book you will see that no science can ever produce 'true' knowledge. Science provides us with ways of looking at the world. It has been well said that when you look at the world, what you see is your own mind.

Psychologists attempt to examine our ways of looking at the world and of interacting with it in our own terms. Like other sciences, psychology does not provide 'gospel truth'. The findings of psychology should be treated with caution and subjected to careful analysis. They are influenced, as in other sciences, by the researchers' values and theories. The authors of this book have 'come clean' on that issue. They make it plain that whether they are writing about direct teaching or managing group work or promoting autonomous learning, they have a view on what is important in this field and why: they express, one way or another, their value position.

One advantage of drawing on the research is that it allows you to look at the world of classrooms, teaching and learning on the basis of evidence carefully gathered and tested from a particular perspective. You can see the world as others see it. You must decide what to make of that. The authors have carefully documented their arguments so that you can check them out or otherwise follow them up. A second advantage of research is that it puts you in contact with the carefully documented experience of large numbers of teachers. You can see more experience in a single study than you might otherwise meet in a lifetime.

How to Use the Book

The purpose of the book is to help you use your practical experience to develop your teaching competence, that is to say, to increase your capacity to manage pupils' experience for learning.

The text of each chapter presents a way of looking at a concept or skill important to teaching. Each chapter carries an overview explaining the importance of the central theme and why it is an issue for a learner teacher. The overview also carries an outline of the chapter.

You should read the overview carefully as a framework in which to study the chapter.

Each chapter focuses on a specific issue. In practice, all these issues are interconnected in a seamless robe of experience. The focus of the author is a necessary writer's device. To help you draw the issues together, to reconnect them one to another, each chapter is followed by a commentary showing where the main links lie in the book.

Each commentary also contains a brief summary of the chapter and some guidance on relevant school-based work.

The commentary, including the guidance, might usefully be read before the chapter to alert you to what you will need to follow up on. It should certainly be read after the chapter as a framework against which you can check your understanding.

For each chapter then, a good procedure would be:

1   read the overview and commentary;
2   study the chapter;
3   re-read the commentary and check your understanding of the chapter;
4   follow up on the connecting themes indicated in the commentary.

Guides for School-based Work

The concepts and ideas in this book are intended to be applied to your professional practice. The suggestions for school-based work are central to your learning and professional development. They invite you to engage in the important learning processes of thinking, practical action, the collection of evidence, analysis, reflection, discussion and consultation.

I have provided suggestions rather than detailed specific plans and tasks. This is necessarily and deliberately to leave a lot to you to construct 'on site' as it were. It is necessary because the work has to suit you and your specific circumstances at your particular point of development. Classrooms vary enormously in regard to what is available, to pupil numbers and to a myriad of others factors relevant to any exercises you might undertake. Any attempt by me to set a tight framework or provide specific checklists and guidelines would be bound to be a bad fit to most circumstances.

Necessary or not, I have deliberately left the details to you. You will not learn very much if you do not take professional responsibility for your own learning. There are places where I could easily have provided you with detailed checklists (for teaching skills, planning for example). This would have saved you the bother of working on the relevant chapter. I have avoided this in the belief that any teacher who saves learners the bother of thinking is no teacher at all.

There is more to be said about the guidance of school-based work, however. It should invariably be negotiated with relevant heads, class teachers, supervisors and, where they advise it, with pupils and parents.

Everyone involved in your professional development has rights. The design of school-based work must conform to strict professional and ethical principles. As an example of a relevant issue, I frequently recommend the use of video or audio records. Other people should not be recorded without their permission, and the records should be kept confidential and used only for agreed professional purposes.

The ethical and professional issues involved in each suggested exercise that you undertake should be considered carefully and explicitly before starting. The tasks and projects I have suggested will not bring about easy or quick advances in professional competence. They provide only the first steps on a long road. Many, if not most, would bear frequent repeating with the aspiration to reach ever-increasing levels of competence.

The value of the work and the quality of your learning will be enhanced if appropriate evidence of your performance and of children's learning is collected and if you work in collaboration with other learner teachers to consider this evidence. There are chapters in this book which explain why that is so and how best to operate. In short, the whole book is about your learning. When you organize group work for yourself the principles of group work described here in chapter 8 apply to you. When you collect evidence about your professional learning the principles in chapters 16 and 17 apply to you.

Finally, from my point of view, the most important chapter applying to you is chapter 11, where autonomous learning is described.

This book is about teaching for a democratic society. Democracies need people who know their own minds, and teachers who can promote responsible learning. Chapter 11 might be a good place to start.

Part I

Basic Processes

1

What is Involved in Learning?

Geoffrey Brown

Editor's Overview

In this chapter, Geoff Brown introduces you to some ways of thinking and talking about learning processes. You already know something about learning and you would not be reading this if you were not a successful learner. Brown digs beneath our common experience to examine the terms in which psychologists have tried to understand learning as a basis on which to improve education and training. He shows that learning may involve

- making associations
- thinking
- problem solving
- information processing.

He emphasizes that these are ways of looking at learning, a set of intellectual lenses if you will.

We do not have to choose between these theories. Each learner is perfectly capable of all the processes Brown describes. Associating, thinking and problem solving are in each human being's intellectual repertoire.

Learning is stored in memory. Brown introduces an analysis of different memory processes. He emphasizes that if experience is to be usefully stored and easily retrieved, the act of memorization has to be deliberately worked on.

A key concept — metacognition — is introduced. Brown powerfully describes this as 'knowing your own mind' and emphasizes that successful learners acquire the capacity to control their own minds to meet their learning objectives.

Finally, Brown briefly discusses the matter of learning contexts. Contexts can make people look competent or stupid. Children are very sensitive and adaptive to classroom contexts, atmospheres and tasks. Teachers, Brown suggests, do not always have the control over the classroom context that they imagine.

The job of the teacher is a very complex one. It may involve presenting a model of acceptable behaviour to children and teenagers, encouraging and motivating them, and acting as a source of advice on a whole range of matters relating to their studies and their personal lives. Different teachers see their responsibilities differently in these respects, but it seems unlikely that any teacher would deny that central to the teacher's role is helping students to learn. Furthermore, if we wish to examine the practice of teaching, it seems essential that understanding teaching must address the nature of the complementary act of learning. This chapter will look at this issue.

There have been occasions when English primary schools have been criticized by parents for letting children play rather than making them work. It might have been that this was not the real reason for parental criticism, and that something quite specific was the source of their disquiet, but on the other hand it is worth reflecting on this commonplace discrimination of the difference between work and play. Traditionally schools are seen as places where children should work, and as a result of their efforts they will learn. Playing is seen as using time enjoyably, but unproductively. However, this difference between work and play does not survive close scrutiny. Few parents would dispute that their children learn the rules of games, or learn to enact certain roles in make-believe activities, or improve physical skills by taking part in sport. So learning of some sort seems to be going on. Furthermore, a potent marketing ploy in recent years has been to persuade parents that certain toys or pastimes have greater potential for encouraging learning than others. So if there is a difference between the activities of the classroom and the playroom it cannot be that learning only takes place in one, but maybe that what is learned is seen as of more value in one context than the other. Of course, a great deal of very valuable learning also goes on in contexts which are not designed for learning at all, as epitomized by the 'street-wise' urchin of innumerable films and novels.

It is also commonly observed that children do not simply learn all or part of what is intended by their teachers and parents. They pick up mannerisms and habits of which the adults may be quite unconscious. The resemblance between parents and their offspring is, of course, heavily influenced by inherited physical characteristics, but these are enhanced by a tendency to adopt similar forms of speech, postures and facial expressions. These are most probably learned, for, unlike the physical attributes, they apply to non-biological parents or care-givers too. What is particularly interesting about this phenomenon is that the learning may be quite unintentional. Teachers are increasingly conscious of what they refer to as the *hidden curriculum*, a reference to the less formal influences exerted by a school on the pupils' behaviours and attitudes to such things as rule conformity, punishment, tolerance and social responsibility. A school run on very authoritarian lines may be less successful in creating a sense of participant democracy amongst its pupils than one in which the school rules show that the staff practise what they preach.

So the process of learning is a fairly ubiquitous activity, and is not necessarily dependent upon some other person consciously adopting the role of teacher, nor on the learner setting out to master some skill or acquire some knowledge. This is not to say that the presence of a teacher may not exert a profound influence upon the direction and intensity of a learner's progress, nor that conscious intent to learn may not increase the learner's success rate; but these must remain issues open to question at this stage.

If we take the view that there is evidence of learning in the ways in which children change over time, and it does not seem a dramatic or controversial view to take, can we then define what we mean by learning? To assume that, because a notion is in common currency, it is widely understood and its meaning agreed may indeed be presumptuous. We frequently describe people as being intelligent, but may have little consensus on what that means. That the average child of 10 years of age is more capable of catching a ball than the average 3-year-old suggests that something has been learned in the intervening years. But we would probably not impute this same learning process to explain that the 10-year-old could lift heavier weights than the 3-year-old. In this case we would be much more likely to explain the difference in terms of the child's growth, and the development of muscles. Yet development of the nervous system could have influenced the acquisition of ball-catching skills, and the skills of balancing and weight distribution might have had a major impact on weight-lifting abilities. This illustrates one of the perennial problems of educational psychology – how to differentiate growth from learning. That may not seem like much of a problem. If change takes place, does it really matter? Sometimes it may not, but if we are embarking on a programme designed to help children acquire a particular skill, we need to build in safeguards to ensure that the expenditure of precious human and material resources is not being wasted. Maybe the change would come about anyway as the children get older.

Customarily we define learning as a process which brings about a relatively permanent change of behaviour which is not attributable to the maturational process or to state-altering chemicals such as drugs. Deciding that a change is permanent is not easy either, as psychologists and educators seldom monitor effects for longer than a year or two, and often for much less. If an investigation is looking for the effects of learning over hours or days there is the added problem of accounting for relatively transient changes in behaviour due to fatigue or lack of attention.

How Do We Explain Learning?

It will be helpful first to explore aspects of some traditional theories of learning. Not only will their shortcomings provide a yardstick with which to evaluate more recent developments, but no new theory appears 'out of the blue'; it always carries some legacy of the values and beliefs of earlier versions.

A theory is useful in so far as it helps us to understand some aspect of a learning situation. There will be limits to its usefulness, and circumstances in which it ceases to be helpful and should be discarded. In other words, a theory is a tool to aid understanding. It may be a versatile tool which we find helpful across a broad range of learning situations, or one with narrow applicability. Its credibility may be high if it uses as its raw material observations and descriptions of phenomena which we can readily accept, or with which we are already familiar. It may be more suspect if it needs us to make assumptions about a variety of features for which we have little or no evidence.

Before we examine these theories it is important to clarify what we can expect to find. It is not uncommon for the student to be perplexed by conflicting theories, asserting that either they must all be wrong, or one right and all the rest wrong. This is not necessarily the case. Consider an investigator embarking on a study of how children acquire an understanding of adult authority. Depending upon the researcher's particular interests and hypotheses, this may be done by investigating the role models presented by significant adults, and/or how the child's peers influence the effectiveness of the models. But the frequency and potency of particular models may be crucially influenced by the culture in which they exist, with some being deemed more acceptable than others. These preferred models may change over time, as the society changes its predominant views. Then again, children with particular attributes of intelligence, personality, social awareness or physical appearance may respond differently to a particular role model. If that does not seem complicated enough, we must not necessarily assume that the role model influences the child in a one-way interaction. The child's attraction to or rejection of the model adult may cause the adult to emphasize or tone down personal characteristics, or even to change them. In the face of this complexity most theories will take a specific context within which to work, and they must be seen in this context.

There are a few well-known theories of learning which form the bases of much contemporary research, and we shall examine these in turn. However, we should not assume that any particular recent study will necessarily follow one of the basic theories very closely, though the influence will usually be discernible once we know what to look for. It is perhaps better to visualize a continuum on which the extremes are exemplified by the 'classical theories' of Behaviourism and Cognitive Theory, but on which individual psychological studies will occupy some intervening position.

In discussing the various theoretical approaches it is not our intention to give a comprehensive account. That would take more space than we have available. The intention will be rather to focus upon the presuppositions which underlie the theory, and what its implications are for our understanding learning.

Behaviourism

Some of the earliest psychological investigations of learners relied upon the investigators either describing what they thought was going on in their own heads when they learned, or asking people to describe what they were experiencing. With the benefit of hindsight, it may not be such a bad system, but it undoubtedly runs considerable risks of distortion or deceit. On such grounds this procedure, known as *introspection*, was rejected by some American psychologists in favour of what they deemed to be a more rigorously scientific method of proceeding (Watson, 1913). This new method, *Behaviourism*, sought to reject any reference to internal mental states or processes which could not be observed or quantified, in favour of observable and measurable behaviour. It is sometimes said that behaviourists rejected the notion of internal mental states, but that is not so. What was asserted was that these states were not accessible to the investigator, nor was there any reason to suppose that laws which governed observable behaviour should not also govern activity in the mind (Skinner, 1964).

This approach to learning, exemplified by the work of Thorndike (1913), and Skinner (1938), is based upon a set of suppositions derived from early animal physiology and experimental investigations with animals in learning situations. It derives from an ancient notion called the association of ideas, and indeed an important and influential form of the theory bears that name, Associationism.

Ways of changing behaviour

It was observed by Pavlov in the latter part of the nineteenth century that a naturally existing reflex, such as a dog's response of salivating when anticipating the stimulus of food, could be manipulated by pairing the food with another stimulus such as noise. In time the dog would salivate when the noise was heard, even though no food was presented. This was described as a shift from an unconditional reflex (food–salivation) to a conditional one (noise–salivation). As this constituted a relatively permanent change in behaviour it was described as a learning process of a rudimentary kind, termed Classical Conditioning.

A complementary process known as Operant Conditioning was described by Skinner (1938). In this scenario an animal was observed to behave in a variety of ways (to display operands) in response to a stimulus situation. For example, if the stimulus was a constraining cage, a cat might display operands such a pawing at the walls and bars, scratching on the floor, climbing the walls or emitting loud noises. If any one of these led to release from confinement (that is, was reinforced), there would be an increased probability of that operand being repeated on another occasion. Over a succession of occasions all other operands would be extinguished and the successful one deployed immediately. Again, a relatively permanent change in behaviour had been effected, so learning had taken place.

On the basis of such experiments behaviourists developed the hypothesis that the fundamental process of learning was the elimination or establishing of stimulus–response bonds, by control of the environment and its potential for reinforcement. Figure 1.1 shows how the environment was controlled in these studies. Furthermore, behaviourists maintained that this process occurred in all animals, including man. The difference between a pigeon learning to distinguish between a triangle and a circle and a person learning

Figure 1.1 This shows, in a cut-away diagram, an example of a Skinner Box. Here all aspects of the environment can be carefully controlled. The pigeon learns that if it taps the big circle it gets corn out of the chute. Using these devices, pigeons were taught complex discriminations and patterns of behaviour.

Source: N. L. Munn. (1961). *Psychology: The fundamentals of human adjustment.* New York: Harrap, p. 387.

to drive a car was only in terms of the number of stimulus–response bonds implicated, and the complexity of their interrelationships. The laws which governed how the bonds were established, maintained, or broken were assumed to apply equally to all.

There is little doubt that humans and other animals can learn by this mechanism, and systems which successfully change behaviour are widely reported (see for instance Wheldall, 1987). It may not be the typical method by which learning does occur, however, and critics of the theory have described it as *reductionist* in its supposition that the learning of complex behaviour can be understood by analysing it into smaller elements and investigating each of these. They allege that complex behaviour crucially depends upon the relationships between the elements, and can only be understood in its entirety.

Possibly the most compelling argument in favour of behavioural approaches to learning was that offered by Skinner. He argued that everyday activities in home, school and the workplace utilize rewards such as smiling, praising and the giving of rewards to change people's behaviour. He maintained that the behavioural psychologist was not doing anything new, simply doing the same as people in normal exchanges, but more systematically and efficiently.

Skinner's use of behaviourist interpretation of learning as the basis of a system of instruction gave rise to the technology of *programmed learning* (Leith, 1964). The essential principles of programmed learning are that complex behaviour can indeed be reduced to sequences of smaller elements, and that machines could be designed to present these to the learner, invite a response, and reward success by moving the learner to the next element in the sequence. Confident claims were once made that this efficient technology would eventually render the human teacher redundant, but history has not borne out those claims.

In today's classrooms the observer is very unlikely to see evidence of programmed learning. There is much greater likelihood of seeing pupils rewarded by ticks, house points or praise from the teacher. There is also the possibility of seeing some form of *behaviour modification*, another adaption of behavioural principles to change pupils' actions. It is particularly common in helping children who have emotional and behavioural difficulties, and consists of controlling the environment in ways which ignore undesirable behaviours and reward more acceptable forms in a very systematic way. The rewards may be in the form of tokens which can subsequently be exchanged for some desired object or activity, and an agreement to operate under such a scheme may be the subject of a contract between the pupil and the teachers (Wheldall, 1987).

Yet the use of changes in observable behaviour as an indication that learning has taken place is the source of another concern. The philosophical reservations of Malcolm (1964) that internal mental processes might be very different in their nature from processes controlling action, were empirically demonstrated by experiments in which mental change appeared to have occurred without any change in behaviour (Tolman, 1932). This may be less of a criticism of current behavioural psychologists, some of whom would readily acknowledge the influence of mental processes. The current professional interest in *cognitive behavioural therapies* indicates by its very title a modified approach which acknowledges that internal mental processes cannot be ignored (Hughes and Hall, 1989 for example). Such therapies involve basic behavioural techniques, but acknowledge that a client's internal states of thinking and feeling must be taken into account.

Taking Skinner's argument, it might be legitimate to maintain that each of us uses behavioural techniques throughout the day, as we employ affection, approval, disdain, or rejection, to try to change the behaviour of people around us. Whether we can go beyond this, and argue that all forms of animal and human learning can be explained in behavioural terms is another matter.

Summary

- Activities or events which occur close together (are contiguous) tend to become associated.
- Activities which are reinforced (by a successful outcome or some other reward) are more likely to be repeated than those which are not. Conversely, non-reinforcement or punishment will lead to activities being discontinued.
- Immediate reinforcement creates the most rapid learning, but is susceptible to rapid extinction (loss of the learned behaviour) if reinforcement is discontinued. Using a schedule of periodic reinforcements takes longer to establish learning, but the learning is much more resistant to extinction.
- Artificial reinforcers such as prizes or tokens are referred to as *extrinsic motivators*. Learners who get reward from the satisfaction of having mastered an activity are said to receive *intrinsic motivation*. Both work, but there may be good reason for the teacher to prefer intrinsically motivated pupils.
- Contemporary behaviourists will sometimes use notions of thinking and feeling as well as behaviour in interpreting learning.

A Cognitive Approach to Learning

Much of the work using cognitive approaches to learning finds its origins in the work of Jean Piaget and his colleagues, often referred to as the Genevan School. Their model of learning is generally characterized as a *stage* theory, in that it suggested that the thought processes of the child developed through four distinct stages (Cohen, 1983). Such a view has received considerable criticism (see Brown and Desforges, 1979 for example), but it is not that aspect of Piaget's ideas with which we are principally concerned here.

Mental records of experiences

The Genevan School proposed that thought processes depended upon an ability to create, hold and modify internal representations of things which are experienced in the environment. For example, the newborn infant seems to react to whoever appears within its field of vision, and to be uninfluenced, as far as we can tell, by people who are out of sight. However, it is not long before the baby demonstrates by crying, or some other means of drawing attention to itself, that it resents the absence of the caregiver. In order to be aware that a significant person is absent, it must have developed some way of creating an image within its mind. This mechanism would also enable the child to judge that the face of another adult was unfamiliar as it did not match with stored representations of familiar people. So, in a sense, the child learns to be distressed by strangers. These internal representations are called *schemas*, and they will often be built up into quite complex patterns involving recognition, understanding, associated action and emotional reaction. Learning can then be defined as the acquisition of new schemas and their modification in response to new needs.

The process by which schemas are changed is termed *adaptation*, and it consists of two complementary aspects, *assimilation* and *accommodation*. When the learner meets a novel experience, an internal representation or mental image will be made of it, and the contents of the mind will be reorganized to build it into the store of knowledge. But that will rarely be a simple matter of assimilation, that is, adding to a store of knowledge. Usually the existing schemas will have to be adjusted to accept the novel experience, a process of accommodation.

How change takes place

The mechanism for change is termed *equilibration*. As a child begins to develop understanding, some of the important attributes which influence that understanding begin to acquire the relatively stable, balanced pattern of a schema. This allows some facility with problem situations, as the internal representations will have acquired *equilibrium*. This means that their interconnectedness will be seen as stable, and specific patterns of action will be associated with them.

Dealing with difficulties

Because of the complexity of our environment, no schema is likely to incorporate all the influential variables. There will be situations when action taken on the basis of a schema proves inadequate to some extent. This may lead to a state of uncertainty or disequilibrium as novel elements destabilize the pattern of understanding. A revised schema must be constructed, and this will be characteristic of a new stage in the learning process.

It is important to recognize how active the learner must be if restructuring is to take place. There are frequent occasions when our ability to handle new experience with our existing schemas does not work, but changes to the schemas are resisted. The learner may choose to ignore the information, as occurs when people select only those aspects of news which confirm their strongly held prejudice; or they may have to settle for uncomfortable disequilibrium if no obvious resolution is possible.

If a genuine cognitive transformation does take place, then learning will have occurred. Faced with similar circumstances again, there will be a revised schema with which to tackle it, and so the process may continue. This sequence is illustrated in figure 1.2. A crucial aspect of this model of learning is the emphasis on what the learner already knows. If it is the case that learning can be conceptualized as the restructuring of schemas in response to challenges presented by the environment, then ascertaining the quality of the student's present level of understanding becomes of paramount importance.

Hierarchical learning

Piaget's notion of a gradual ascent up a hierarchy of stages of thinking is an intuitively attractive one, and the term *hierarchical learning* is sometimes used to denote it. In Piaget's original theory the hierarchy was described as a universal sequence of stages which, for any individual learner, developed in concert across such diverse areas as speech, moral judgements, conceptualization of number, and so on. But we do not have to adhere to this broad notion. A hierarchy can be a description of systematic changes within a single area of experience, say, the child's concept of God, without any necessary implications for what else the child may understand. That is to say, a child's understanding of God may advance from a very simple 'old man in the sky' notion to a complex spiritual or theological concept whether or not the child develops higher-level understanding in other areas. Some care needs to be exercised, however, as a hierarchical structure may derive from qualitative differences in thought processes, but may also reflect the fact that this is how much of our knowledge is structured. A biological key is a familiar example of such structuring. At the level of greatest generality is the division into the plant and animal kingdom, at an intermediate level the distinction between

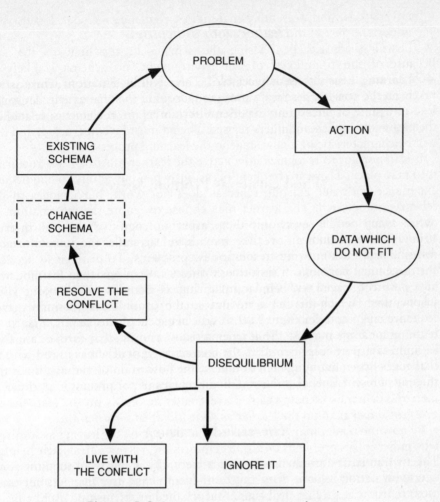

Figure 1.2 Learning as restructuring schemas.

animals with and without backbones, and lower still the separation of different species of, say, mice. Understanding this constitutes learning a hierarchy, but not necessarily hierarchical learning.

Summary

- Schemas are patterns of internal representations which people develop in order to understand the world around them.
- A schema will always have limitations, and new experiences may challenge the existing schemas. Finding out what type of schema the pupil

already has, and presenting material to challenge and develop it, is an important part of the teacher's job.
- Learning consists of revising the schema in the light of the new information.
- Learning does not take place if the effort needed to restructure is not made. A non-learner may choose to ignore conflicting experiences, select only those aspects of an experience which can be readily assimilated, or live with cognitive conflict.

The Learner as Problem Solver

What many feel is much more apparent in cognitive theories than in behavioural theories is an overall approach to learning as the *restructuring of thought processes* in order to tackle new problems. To distinguish between the theoretical positions in such a way does less than justice to the moderate views of contemporary behaviourists, but is perhaps not without some justification. During this century educational opinion has increasingly turned to addressing the relevance of what was being taught to pupils, that is, to learning for some purpose. That purpose is usually, in some form or another, to address a particular problem. Of course, there will always need to be a balance between knowing facts and knowing how to do something, but those theories which emphasize the restructuring of mental processes in order to meet the demands of new tasks, place greater emphasis on the learner as a *problem solver* than on the learner as an *acquirer of information*.

By now the reader may have realized that describing the learner as someone who either solves problems or acquires information is not particularly helpful. The two activities are intimately connected. The pupil who acquires some new information seldom does so to satisfy an acquisitive instinct, but more often to assist in solving problems. And to solve problems one usually needs to acquire some new information. In most real-life situations there is far too much information for any one of us to assimilate. What we do is to select, and our selection strategies will depend to some extent on what we feel we need to know, but may also be dependent on our preferred ways of operating.

Bruner and his colleagues (1956) demonstrated that, when faced with a difficult task, in which there was too much information to assimilate, people adopted characteristic methods of coping. Their experiment was an attempt to reproduce conditions in which a learner has to create a concept from an array of information which is much too extensive for it all to be dealt with at the same time. The procedure used a pack of cards, each bearing instances of four attributes, one, two or three squares, crosses or circles in either red, green or black, surrounded by either a single, double or triple border. From this pack cards could be drawn which were examples of a particular concept, such as 'all red cards with single borders', or 'all cards which have three figures or three borders, but not both'. An example of the set is shown in figure 1.3.

Adults were presented with a card and told that it was an example of the concept the experimenter had in mind. Their task was then to select other cards, and to inquire whether they too were examples, until the concept was discovered. The investigators were interested in the strategies the learners used. It was found that a person's preferred strategy was quite consistent over time, and each strategy had its own strengths and weaknesses. *Scanners* were those people who attempt to assimilate positive and negative examples in testing particular ideas. Some did this cautiously, testing only one aspect at a time, although in doing so they had to ignore information which might have been useful later on. Others attempted to test several ideas simultaneously, but they found the memory load very heavy. Others engaged in *focusing*, that is, taking a card which was a positive example and then

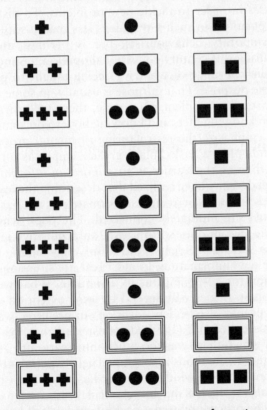

Figure 1.3 Cards used in an experiment on concept formation. This is the black set, but these cards were duplicated with red and with green figures, to make a total of eighty-one cards. Their use is described in the text.

Source: J. S. Bruner, J. J. Goodnow and G. A. Austin. (Eds.). (1956). *A study of thinking.* New York: Wiley, 33, p. 42.

changing one variable at a time. But the fourth group, called *focus gamblers*, changed several variables at the same time. If a card with several changed variables was predicted not to be an example of the concept, and that was confirmed, they had eliminated several variables in one go. But if their prediction was wrong, they would not know which of the variables accounted for the error. This gambling, or playing hunches, seems to be characteristic of many forms of human problem solving. It lacks the precise logic of the computer, but seems appropriate for organisms not blessed with the prodigious memory of those machines.

What is of interest is how and when people decide to 'cut corners' in seeking solutions. The expert probably does so as often as the novice, but there may be better bases on which to decide how, and when, to gamble.

Summary

- Many situations present us with more information than we can handle. We therefore tend to adopt strategies which limit the strain on our memory. Guessing or gambling on an outcome is one such strategy, and there may well be situations in the classroom when it is a sensible thing for the learner to do.

The Learner as an Information Processor

Psychological theories of learning which adopt an information-processing approach are modelled, to a greater or lesser extent, on an analogy between the human thinker and a computer. Some may find such comparison as 'dehumanizing' as behaviourists' reductionism, arguing that the computer is an inadequate model for the richness of human behaviour, and they may be correct. But if the analogy is reversed, and the computer is seen as the scientist's attempt to understand some limited aspects of the human mind by emulating its processes in a computer, that may seem more acceptable, and many psychologists have been persuaded that the effort is worthwhile. The effects have been twofold. The traditional computer used in commerce owes its success to the fact that it is vastly quicker and more efficient than a human at storing information, sorting it against specified criteria and making rule-governed connections between selected elements of it. The modern computer programmer is, on the other hand, at a decided disadvantage when attempting to model activities such as pattern recognition, spatial awareness, and creativity (Springer and Deutsch, 1981). There is extensive debate about the potential for success in these endeavours, but the optimists contine to seek computer simulations in attempts to log those features which may enable a computer to behave like a human.

A reciprocal influence has been the tendency to describe cognitive processes in the human as analogous to computer processes. These will become apparent as this model of human learning is explored.

Storing information

The best general-purpose model of human memory remains that developed by Atkinson and Shiffrin in 1968 (figure 1.4). It sought to bring together a number of experimental findings from psychological laboratories by proposing that memory consisted of three interrelated systems, each functioning according to different procedures:

- the *sensory register* being the most transient;
- *short-term* or *primary store* being more enduring;
- *long-term* or *secondary store* as the most permanent.

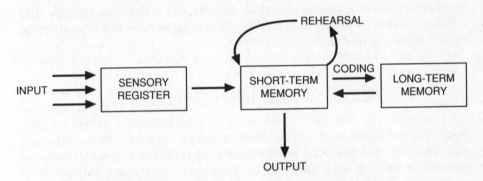

Figure 1.4 Atkinson and Shiffrin's memory model.

The sensory registers are stores dedicated to the reception of information from a particular sensory modality such as hearing or sight. Their capacity is limited, and items can be retained for little more than a second if they are not subject to further processing. This very brief stage does, however, give the brain time to make that decision, and whilst it functions as a holding device, some basic analysis of features and editing out of redundant information will occur.

Information which is selected for retention is then passed to the primary store. The original name of 'short-term store' was replaced because duration within this store proved to be rather difficult to ascertain. The reason for this is that one of our commonest strategies for remembering is to prevent the information from decaying. We do this by *rehearsal* which keeps the item within the primary store for an increased length of time. Saying a telephone number over to ourselves 'in our mind', or visualizing a particular pattern 'in our mind's eye' are examples of this. This change of name heralded a more profound change in psychologists' approaches to memory. Atkinson and Shiffrin's model suggested different memory structures within the brain. Craik and Lockhart (1972) shifted attention to the *levels of processing* to which the information was subjected, and whilst this approach is not without critics (see Baddeley, 1990 for a summary) it will be a more profitable model for us to adopt.

Primary memory has a very limited capacity of around seven elements. Paradoxically those seven elements, or chunks, can be individual letters or words. They can even be phrases, although there is then a typical reduction to about five chunks for the average performer. So a 'chunk' can be described as a unit of meaningful information for retention, but within limits. Whole chapters of books are meaningful, but few would claim retention of seven chapters, or even one.

The learner may often be subjected to a bombardment of stimuli, of which the amount passed into primary memory is in excess of its capacity. The analogy of a memory 'store' now offers us some possibilities of what might occur. There must be a possibility that the store will simply become full, after which no more would be accepted. Conversely the store may continue to receive incoming information, but only by eliminating that which is already there. Perhaps the least attractive proposition is that the contents will become a disorganized jumble of bits and pieces as the system breaks down.

Data from experiments which have subjected people (usually long-suffering students) to this information overload can be summarized by the *serial recall curve* (figure 1.5). This curve shows that the earliest items presented have been retained quite well, and this is termed a *primacy effect*. So early information is not displaced from memory. Yet there is also a marked level of recall of the very last items to be presented, a *recency effect*. It is the items in the middle of the presentation which fare least well. This has been interpreted to suggest that the curve is actually made up of two separate effects, one derived from items which were presented early enough to be transferred to the secondary store, and the last elements, which still resided in the short-term store.

Many researchers believe that the passive model of primary memory suggested by Atkinson and Shiffrin does less than justice to its influential role. It has an executive function, receiving information and then processing it for retention in the secondary (long-term) store. For this reason it has been referred to as *working memory*, and redefined as comprising a central executive system freely interacting with a system responsible for rehearsing verbal material, another devoted to visual and spatial information, and a fourth dedicated to auditory processing (Baddeley and Hitch, 1974; Salame and Baddeley, 1982). In this view the working memory is a very active system which significantly influences what gets transferred to long-term memory and how it is received there. It is, in a sense, a filtering and packaging system.

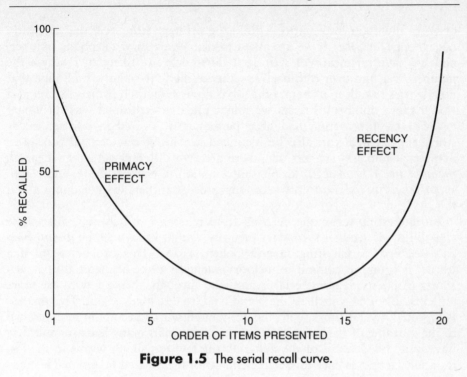

Figure 1.5 The serial recall curve.

Keeping a permanent record

The secondary memory is perceived as a relatively permanent store of exceedingly large capacity. To assess its total capacity is probably an impossible job because the amount it can store may always be amenable to extension if the contents and new material are better organized. Furthermore, much may be stored which we are unable to access. If we contemplate the vocabulary we usually use in speech or writing, it is only a small subset of the words for which we actually know the meaning. Being able to access the stored material on demand requires *recall*, a more demanding task than mere *recognition*.

Working memory is thought to process information into secondary storage by means of mnemonic strategies known as *control processes*, and it is at this point that the model becomes of particular interest to the student of learning. It seems highly likely that the constraints on capacity and speed which occur within the sensory registers and primary memory are constitutional, that is, governed by the characteristics of the nervous system. At later stages there appears to be much greater influence from conscious decision-making and the efficiency of the memory strategies adopted. This is an oversimplification, but will suffice for the time being.

Rehearsal has already been mentioned as a technique which we employ in order to maintain information within the primary store. Yet that is clearly not its only function. If we are asked to dial a particular telephone number, and we have no means of writing it down, we are likely to rehearse the number over and over to ourselves either audibly or silently, and hope that no one tries to talk to us before the job is done. However, if the same request was made a number of times we might find that rehearsal was no longer needed, the information had been permanently located in our secondary store. So *rehearsal* can also be identified as one of our control processes. Some psychologists suggest that there are two different sorts of rehearsal, *maintenance rehearsal* for keeping information in primary store, and *elaborative rehearsal* for transfer to secondary store, but there is some doubt about this.

An interesting technique deriving from rehearsal, which may offer some clue to how it accesses secondary memory, is that known as the *diminishing cue* (see Brown, Cherrington and Cohen, 1975). This can be useful if a learner is trying to commit to memory a lengthy piece of material such as a stanza of poetry. The material is first read through, then a few of the more anticipatable words such as 'the', 'and' and 'to' are blacked out. This process is repeated several times, with the obliterated words becoming more crucial to the meaning of the piece. After several rehearsals many learners find they have quite good recall of the material, the few remaining words in the last iterations acting as cues to sizeable chunks of memorized material. This may not be very different from what the behaviourists call the association of ideas.

The crucial decision in choosing a mnemonic strategy is to determine the characteristics of the material which are important. In the case of a piece of poetry the ordering of the words and the division into lines are important, and to lose either is to lose the poem. The same is true of the colours of the visible spectrum, where the sequence is important. However, sequence could be less important in trying to memorize the members of a government, or the meanings of individual nautical flags. Each of us might select a particular sequence which was meaningful to us, but not at all memorable to anyone else. Hence the emphasis is upon the *meaning*.

A common way to code material is to group it into segments to which we can ascribe some coherent meaning or pattern. Even a telephone number will probably be patterned, and may even have a rhythm when spoken. The number 622373 might become 'six . . . double two . . . three seven three' or 'sixty-two . . . twenty-three . . . seventy-three'. This is a very simple form of organization which works equally well for the colours of the spectrum, 'ROY G. BIV'. This *reduction mnemonic* has the added advantage of appearing to be a name.

Meaning is so important in storing information that a learner will often actually increase the amount of material in order to enhance it. This use of an *elaboration mnemonic* is well exemplified by the other familiar way of dealing with the spectrum, 'Richard of York gave battle in vain'. Here the brief list of letters is elaborated into seven words, but doing so vastly reduces the strain on remembering the sequence.

It will be clear from the above discussion that, whilst a great deal of information-processing research ostensibly focuses upon memory, there is no clear demarcation from processes of learning. The structure of our existing knowledge base has profound effects upon how we are able to deal with new information.

Paying attention

Earlier it was suggested that what we might refer to as the 'thinking end' of the information-processing system was in accessing secondary memory. Yet if that were wholly true it would be very odd indeed. It is difficult to imagine a system ultimately concerned with understanding meaning which was totally dependent upon prior systems which were relatively mechanistic and undiscriminating. From the hubbub of a party it is often surprising to find oneself singling out messages which have particular personal significance, such as one's name; a phenomenon referred to as the *Cocktail Party Effect* (Treisman, 1964). Such a phenomenon implies that at a very early stage, possibly in the executive of working memory, or even in the sensory registers, one important criterion which determines that specific information will be processed in preference to other competing stimuli is that the existing stored material exerts an influence in favour of that which is most meaningful. To accommodate this fact the pattern of information processing may be better represented by figure 1.6.

The experimental psychological investigations of attention are very diverse, and in some cases there is not sufficient detail reliably to inform our

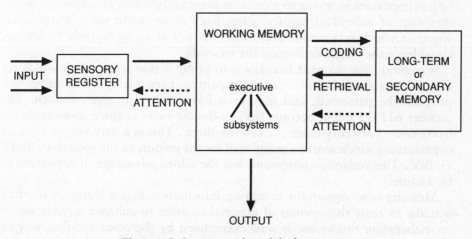

Figure 1.6 A revised model of memory.

understanding of everyday learning situations. This is compounded by two difficulties. In scientific studies there is considerable difference between those which define attention as selection of an item from competing items, and those which study tenacity on a single task. In classroom-based studies the danger is rather that invoking the concept has little explanatory power. That is, if learning does not occur, the failure may be attributed to a lack of attention, and if it does occur, attention is assumed to have been paid. In other words, stating that attention was not being paid is simply another way of saying that learning did not occur.

Knowing your own mind

It might be expected that young children would have less powerful memories than adults, even though parents and teachers are sometimes astonished at what their charges can remember. Investigations suggest that there is very little difference between young children and adults in the speed and capacity of their memory systems, but what does distinguish between them is their ability spontaneously to deploy appropriate strategies (Kail, 1984). The ability to reflect upon one's own mental processes, to deploy them in relevant circumstances, and to check one's degree of success are termed *metacognitive strategies* (Flavell, 1979).

Some studies have demonstrated that teaching aimed at improving children's metacognitive strategies, particularly metamemory, produces significant effects on learning outcomes (Brown and De Loache, 1978). It is also of interest to note that there is considerable similarity between the strategies employed by these investigators, and the advice offered by the authors of various 'How To Study' texts (see for example Rowntree, 1989).

Summary

- Memorizing is not a single process, but a complex of interrelated processes. The learner has some degree of conscious control over what is processed and stored.
- A limited amount of information can be held in primary (or working) memory, but permanent storage requires input to the secondary store.
- Rehearsal is a potent method of retaining material in memory.
- Creating a permanent memory of something is easiest if it has links with existing information in memory, that is, if it has meaning.
- The learner is most likely to pay attention to something which has meaning.
- One of the most powerful ideas of recent times has been that of metacognition. This means understanding how one's memory and thinking processes operate, and how to get the best out of them. Teachers can

assist learners by helping them develop effective ways of comprehending and memorizing information.

Learning as a Social Activity

So far we have been concentrating on the phenomena of learning as they impinge on a single individual. But apart from the occasional hermit, most of us learn a great deal in contexts involving other people, be they parents, teachers, friends or colleagues. Investigation of how influence works in these circumstances is difficult, for they are not usually amenable to experimental control, and it is not always easy to anticipate who will influence whom. If we were to investigate how particular teacher behaviours affected learners, we should have to allow for the possibility that someone who was effective with one child might be less so with another. This may be because the *individual differences* of children make some interactions easier than others, and differences need not only be in cognitive capacities such as memory or metacognitive strategy, but in *social competence* or *emotional stability*. One important argument against the use of punishment as a behavioural technique is that it arouses anxiety, which interferes with the learning process.

It should also be remembered that the manner in which the learner behaves may well have reciprocal effects upon the teacher. Whatever the balance of power or authority between two individuals, there will always be some degree of two-way interaction. Even the newborn baby can provoke considerable change in the behaviour of mature adults simply by smiling and gurgling. Teachers may secretly cherish the notion that they are totally in control in the classroom, but the teaching techniques they adopt, and the ways in which they organize their classrooms suggests shrewd assessment of previous reactions and anticipation of future reactions by their pupils. Learning is a complex set of processes, and it is very heavily influenced by the context in which it takes place.

Editor's Commentary

This chapter focused on fundamental learning processes. It was shown that learners have a repertoire of learning processes: learners can learn in many different ways. Also shown was that learning is context-sensitive: it is easy to make learners look bright or dull.

Learners can be given power over their own intellectual processes, including the processes of memory.

The implications of the ideas in this chapter are very far-reaching. They should be followed through in classroom observation and in several of the chapters in this book. The central questions are:

- How do we help children make the best of their natural intellectual processes?
- How do we help them to acquire deliberate control over their learning processes?
- What classroom contexts support learning most effectively?

As classroom exercises it would be useful to conduct very careful observations and conversations with children with the following questions in mind:

- What sort of work captures their attention most effectively?
- How do teachers focus children's attention on significant matters?
- What sorts of work help children make useful associations and connections in their knowledge and experience?
- What work best provokes useful problem solving, thinking, information processing?
- What techniques do teachers have for promoting children's memories of academic work?

Of course, these questions assume you know what attention, problem solving and thinking look like.

In relating this chapter to others it should be realized that different processes of learning may be enhanced by different processes of teaching. Teachers should develop a repertoire of skills and choose the particular skill best suited to promoting specific learning processes. This idea can be pursued as follows:

- Associations are best promoted through direct instruction, described in chapter 6.
- Thinking and problem solving are well promoted through discussion and group work, which are described in chapters 7 and 8.
- Methods of developing pupil autonomy are considered in chapter 11, whilst the teaching of strategic approaches to learning is introduced in chapter 5.
- The effect of context on learning is described in general in chapter 4. The particular effect of assessment on learning is introduced in chapters 16 and 17.

Remember! Learners are always actively learning something in classrooms. Learning is an active process. The key challenge for a teacher is to ensure that learners' activity is focused on making academic progress.

FURTHER READING

Bennett, N., Desforges, C., Cockburn, A. & Wilkinson, B. (1984). *The quality of pupil learning experience*. London: LEA.

> Although conducted some years ago, the research reported illustrates the use of a theory of learning to generate inquiry, and how that inquiry can be pursued within the real world of the classroom.

Butterworth, G. & Harris, M. (1994). *Principles of developmental psychology*. London: LEA.

> A very readable and up-to-date account of much of the psychology which underpins the educational process.

Greene, J. (1987). *Memory, thinking, and language*. Oxford, England: Blackwell.

> This elaborates on many of the issues covered in chapter 1, but with a particular emphasis on the crucial part played by language.

Grieve, R. & Hughes M. (Eds.). (1990). *Understanding children*. Oxford, England: Blackwell.

> A tribute to Margaret Donaldson whose work has played a significant part in the reappraisal of Piaget's theory. The diversity of the contributors' topics also illustrates well the remarkable range of studies to which the theory gave impetus.

Meadows, S. (1993). *The child as thinker*. London: Routledge.

> This provides an extensive review of contemporary studies of how children develop concepts and learn to think. It also focuses on what we know about children's understanding of a range of issues such as 'death' and 'mind'. Emphasis is given to the environmental factors and teaching practices which influence learning.

2

What is to be Learned in School?

Clive Carré

Editor's Overview

Learning is not only a verb. It is also a noun. Children go to school to learn something. The curriculum describes the content which children are expected to learn. It is, in most countries, laid down by local or national government. Unfortunately, what is laid down by well-meaning legislators is not so straightforward in the real life of schooling. In chapter 1, Geoff Brown digs beneath the common experience of learning processes to examine in more detail what goes on in learning. In this chapter, Clive Carré digs beneath the common sense of curriculum.

He shows that what teachers know about the subjects they teach has a crucial influence on how they teach and on how they respond to their pupils. The more teachers are familiar with the 'big ideas' of a subject and the more they know about how a subject works in accumulating and testing knowledge, the more they are able to represent the subject with integrity and to be responsive to their pupils' ideas.

You already have considerable experience in and knowledge about the academic subjects in the curriculum, but merely to know something and to know something for teaching are two different things. Clive Carré invites you to think about organizing your knowledge for teaching. He introduces a language for helping you do that. The ideas in this chapter are challenging. They are also fundamental to good teaching.

In most places in the world 'what is to be learned' is taken for granted; it is the curriculum, set down in statutory guidelines, some legislation more closely defined than others. In England and Wales, for example, the Education Reform Act of 1988 introduced the national curriculum, which specifies precisely what children must learn. Since the law tells teachers what to teach, it seems idle to raise the question of 'what is to be learned?' In this chapter I show that, notwithstanding the law, this is an important and fundamental question for teachers, and that it should be continually raised. The particular perspective you have about knowledge in teaching will influence what you do as a teacher; how you plan lessons, how you interpret curriculum demands and how you organize children's learning experiences. By way of an opening example, consider the following cases of student teachers' planning.

Choosing Content for Planning

As part of her course Anna had been introduced to ideas about the role of language in the curriculum, and had widened her understanding of children's fiction. The class she was going to teach was involved in rewriting and retelling stories. Having read *The trials and tribulations of Little Red Riding Hood* (Zipes, 1983), Anna was confident that the children would enjoy seeing the links between different literary versions of this well-known fairy tale. Here are her initial plans to teach English to a class of 11-year-olds:

1 Read a Chinese version of the story. Show illustrations. Discuss.
2 Divide into five groups. Boys and girls mix. Each group has different story of Little Red Riding Hood (include early oral version, nineteenth-century European and recent American fairy tales). Illustrations included.
3 Children make notes about how their version differs from the one they know.
4 Whole class discusses similarities and differences in their versions (guide children to consider structure and conventions of the fairy tale, and importance of pictures).
5 Give out sheet on which each group writes down answers to these questions:
   (a) Who are the main characters? Choose some words to describe them.
   (b) Who is bad?
   (c) Who saves Little Red Riding Hood, or how does she save herself?
   (d) How does the fairy tale end?
   (e) In what ways does the theme of the story relate to real life?
6 Groups report back to whole class. Use large sheet to combine different versions to show links.

Follow up: Rewrite the fairy tale in modern times, portraying Little Red Riding Hood as naive and gullible *or* clever and courageous. Produce puppet plays and invite 8-year-olds to see the new stories.

Can you infer what was in Anna's mind about what had to be learned? She felt that helping pupils learn about children's literature could proceed through a variety of language activities, enabling them to reflect on the fairy tale. She drew attention to the social and moral assumptions made by authors in different versions of the story, but did not neglect the knowledge of story structure and conventions. She believed that those aspects of content knowledge were more likely to be understood through the activities the children were being invited to do. In the process of discussing, analysing and responding she thought the children would probably become more competent readers, writers, speakers and listeners. She intended to use correct terminology, words such as 'fiction', 'text', 'plot' and 'character' at appropriate times. When I asked her what she meant by that word 'appropriate' she said that they should be used only after the children had some conceptual understanding of what the terms referred to. In that way the words actually helped the children to be users of language and share, more competently, their understanding.

Anna's planning was influenced by certain assumptions about knowledge, about what had to be learned. Content knowledge about language she thought important, and children needed to be introduced to correct terminology, but the processes of coming to acquire that knowledge, that is, using language, were her central concern. She certainly did not want to tell the children the rules of this genre (fairy tale category) at the beginning, to guide their reading and understanding of the texts. In her decision-making she was inadvertently echoing a current dispute in teaching English. Some think that writing is a technical process, and that in order to get better at it children need to be given rules and definitions about conventions of grammar, text organization and word usage before they write. Others believe that children are helped with the complexities of writing through seeing a purpose for the activity, and getting them to think *how* they go about the task, rather than concentrating on the final product. The practicalities of helping children's writing in this way, getting them to discover what they mean through the act of writing, using techniques of 'drafting' and 'conferencing' can be found for example in Graves (1983) and Cambourne (1988).

Here is another example of a student teacher planning for her first teaching practice, in science. Jane's class teacher had asked her to teach 'forces' to a class of 11-year-olds, and she had three sessions in which to do so. The school science policy provided some guidance as to what had to be taught at this level:

1 Understand that forces can affect the position, movement and shape of an object.
2 Know that more than one force can act on an object, and that forces can act in different directions.

For Jane, planning did not seem to be such a hurdle at all. She thought that what had to be learned by the children appeared to be fairly cut and dried. Her lesson included the forces acting on stationary and moving toys, defining and describing forces, and demonstrating that friction depends on the kind of surfaces in contact. She also set up some activities to teach skills. The children would use a force metre (a type of spring balance) to measure their arm muscle strength, their hand grip and leg thrust.

Jane thought that there were science facts to be taught and certain definitions to be copied down. The practical work was tightly controlled by Jane demonstrating an experiment to verify a statement about friction. The children's practical work was controlled too, to use apparatus to collect data in a clearly defined way. Jane was more concerned with 'putting over' the facts than with how the children might come to acquire them. She explained that she would feel guilty if the children went away with the wrong answers.

The planning decisions made by Anna and Jane rest in part on the assumptions they make about 'knowledge'. Anna saw her job as providing opportunities for children to make meaning. Interpretation and sense making, based on personal experiences, is the view that Anna would have of the way knowledge is built by learners. She might also believe that apart from individual contemplation, there is a social influence at play. Her planning included discussion activities, ways to help children connect with what others think, and ways to benefit from a confidence of shared understanding (a social construction of knowledge).

Anna's view of knowledge has been a characteristic of the primary school ethos for many years, generally described as process-based and child-centred. The Hadow Report (1931) urged for planning that was in 'terms of activity and experience rather than knowledge to be acquired and facts to be stored', and the Plowden Report (1967) suggested children's learning to be about 'individual discovery, first-hand experience and opportunities for creative work'. Both gave official sanction to the writings of Dewey (1916/1964), and the Plowden Report endorsed the work of researchers in developmental psychology such as Piaget and Bruner.

Jane made assumptions about knowledge different from this in her planning. She saw science as a clearly defined body of factual knowledge, with her most important consideration as the content to be transmitted, truthfully. This alternative view, which regards knowledge as static, unchallengeable and in general unchanging, assumes an independent, 'out-there' existence for knowledge. Such a view implies that knowledge has status of its own, a pile of facts separate and distinct from the response of the learner to it.

A brief introduction to Jane and Anna's planning indicates that making decisions about what is to be taught will, to a large extent, be influenced by the view of knowledge held by the teacher. Not only do you teach children; you model to your class what you think a subject is about, the nature of English, science, history and so on, and the nature of learning. Therefore how you view 'knowledge' will strongly influence what you do as a teacher. That is to say, it will influence what is to be learned. McDiarmid, Ball and Anderson (1989) discuss the link in this way:

a teacher whose understanding of the origins of the Civil War extends no further than being able to list 'slavery, states' rights, and Southerners' wish to preserve their lifestyles' may have little to draw on to help pupils understand the complexity and subtlety of historical causation of concepts such as 'states' rights'. Such a teacher would be unlikely to relate this idea to more contemporary events – say school prayer, AIDS legislation, abortion . . . or to assigning pupils to write a Bill of Rights for their school.

Some would view history in terms of factual knowledge. An alternative perspective is to see the subject as a set of procedures; history as process, based on questioning, reasoning and judgement. In the latter approach children can begin to understand that the causes of the Civil War have not been firmly established. Historical record is a process of continual reinterpretation. Further, a teacher may decide that historical knowledge of the past will make more sense to pupils if related to aspects of present-day citizenship; historical concepts can be associated with contemporary events, and with moral and social values. Such issues cross traditional subject boundaries.

How Do We Organize Past Experiences?

Most would agree that the knowledge individuals accumulate over time is not merely stockpiles of disconnected facts. We organize past experience and store it as memory. We have had to invent ways of talking about this knowledge structure. Its 'connectedness' or the way it is 'held' is given labels such as schema. Another way of talking about the knowledge structure is to suggest a distinction, originally recognized by Ryle (1949) between two fundamental types of knowledge.

1 'Knowing that' or propositional knowledge is often thought of as the 'stuff' of the subject, its facts and concepts. Children learn that 'light travels in a straight line', that 'King John signed the Magna Carta' and that 'square tiles tessellate.'
2 'Knowing how', or procedural knowledge is thought of as how we do things. For example, skills of measuring, and intellectual skills such as weighing evidence in history, or handling variables in a science investigation to make a 'fair test'.

When we talk about 'what is to be learned' it is easy to fall in with the labels of 'facts' and 'skills'. However, the distinction is not at all clear, and the components of the knowledge structure need further discussion.

Facts and propositions

Facts are generally accepted as those statements which most people would accept as correct, implying that they are true. Facts which children read about, for example, might include: a dog is a mammal, warm air rises, the angle in a semicircle is a right angle, Geoffrey Chaucer wrote *The Canterbury Tales*. If a fact is questioned as to its degree of truthfulness, then we are forced to reflect on the grounds upon which our claim to that piece of knowledge rests. It raises the question as to what it is to know a fact. Let me give some examples.

Aristotle (384–322 BC) thought that the earth was at the centre of the planetary system. Galileo refuted this belief and was brought to trial in 1633 for challenging the Church's proposition that 'the sun is immovable at the centre of the heaven.' The challenge, suppressed in Rome, was taken up in Europe, with eventual agreement of the science community that the earth moves around the sun. Clearly the 'facts' of this matter changed dramatically. On a shorter time span, when I was at school our chemistry chart of the periodic table showed 92 known elements. Present-day versions boast at least 105. What was regarded as a true fact at one time, on good authority, turned out not to be reliable. The 'fact' about known elements altered over about forty years. These examples raise the whole issue of what we believe may be firm knowledge, and what we take to be 'the facts'.

On what possible grounds can a claim be made that will guarantee the truth of a fact? A clue to an answer in science can be found in Bronowski's (1973) rebuff to the idea that physics would eventually give a true explanation of our world, and that scientists sought knowledge in an 'objective' way. Neither assertion is tenable. He says, 'There is no absolute knowlege. And those who claim it, whether they are scientists or dogmatists, open the door to tragedy. All information is imperfect. We have to treat it with humility. That is the human condition.' In pointing to the senseless task of equating 'truth' with 'certainty', Bronowski emphasizes that facts in science can only be true in the sense that most individuals accept and agree, for the time being, the interpretations of some scholarly community. Then, for practical purposes facts can be taken as more or less certain.

The scholarly community of historians feels equally sensitive about the body of facts in history, and questions the claims of history texts. What evidence do we have that Richard III murdered the two little princes of King Edward IV? How sure are we that King Alfred burnt the cakes? In what year did Rome fall? It is crucial in establishing 'facts' that historians carefully select and weigh evidence from the past, to be as certain as is possible about an event or a person.

Separating facts from propositions is merely a convenience, for there is no sharp division between them. Propositions link facts about a subject by stating relationships between them. So, the proposition that the Spanish

Armada set sail for England in 1588 can link to other propositions, for example that Queen Elizabeth I reigned from 1558 to 1603 and Drake reported victory over the Armada in July 1588. Other propositions about the persons and events help to provide ever-increasing relationships and meanings. Of course propositions may or may not be true, but they make up the large proportion of an individual's knowledge structure, much composed of the language of everyday chat.

The socially agreed, rather than fundamentally true, nature of facts and propositions can be illustrated by the map of the world. Its representation has over time been strongly influenced by social pressures and fitness for purpose. The deficiencies of the traditional Mercator map projection (e.g. Greenland appears three-quarters the size of North America and polar regions do not exist!) were corrected in the Peters projection, where surface areas are more accurately represented. However, the Peters projection has directional inaccuracies. Propositional knowledge about the relative sizes of countries and the position of Europe in relation to the rest of the world is governed by particular ways of representing the *same* data. Both maps work; the Mercator for navigation and the Peters for comparing land masses, but neither representation is an 'absolute truth'.

What can be said about cartography can be said of other subjects. A scientific parallel to the two versions of the world map can be found in the dual explanations of how light behaves. The traditional representation of light, as wave-like ripples, explains many properties of light. More recent experiments on light cannot be explained by this wave theory. A second theory explains light behaviour as if it were composed of particles. The two theories explain different phenomena, but neither the wave theory nor the particle theory is 'true' in any absolute sense. The two examples underlie the contingent nature of propositions, and the importance of social agreement which make them acceptable.

Concepts: the connectedness of knowledge

Although our knowledge structure acts as a whole, with all parts interconnected, there is physiological and psychological evidence which indicates that some parts are more tightly associated than others. The term 'concept' is used to talk about the way we make generalizations, mentally group a class of objects or events which have something in common. We tend to take for granted our ability to recognize a set; for example, we recognize apples from other fruits, and further, those characteristics which distinguish a Cox's apple from a Granny Smith. Recognizing common characteristics of a set, even when the members are not identical, is an important ability in understanding patterns and relationships. We do it instantaneously, without going through the characteristics in our head! In fact everything we see, touch or hear we try to place in particular sets; ordering things into 'likes' and 'unlikes' appears to be a foundation of human thought. While on the subject of apples, and shifting to a more abstract level, it took the genius of Newton to see the likeness between one falling from a tree and the arc of the moon's orbit around the earth; so was the now familiar theory of gravity conceived. The notion of concept and meaning are therefore closely related. We assign meaning to an object or idea by relating it through concepts to a class of similar ideas.

To communicate concepts requires language, chiefly in the form of nouns in propositions. The problem is that words have shades of meaning, and what individuals make of a word will depend not only on the context, but on their prior experiences. The meaning you hold for 'fruit' or 'mother' will depend on the particular sets of connections you've created over time (core concepts), and some will be quite arbitrary and personal (peripheral meanings). Therefore it is unlikely that any two individuals will have an identical understanding of a concept. In a classroom any number of different, idiosyncratic meanings can be found. Put another way, we don't see things as they are, but rather as we are. This has important practical implications, for teaching and for assessment. Frequently we have to rethink and adjust our personal understandings if they are inconsistent with what is generally accepted (see 'alternative frameworks' later).

As the set of connections which make up an individual's concept can be continually added to, almost without limit, one can only approximate to an understanding. The more abstract a concept, the more difficult it will be to say if anyone 'has' it. Consider those intimidating concepts which children are expected to develop in history and science: (1) change and continuity, causes and consequences; (2) adaption, energy, equilibrium, natural selection. Further, each of these concepts does not stand alone. Rather, each is interrelated with other concepts, into *conceptual systems*, the components of which often have a hierarchical structure.

The Nature of Procedural Knowledge

The way individuals form concepts and interconnect them into conceptual systems is the way we learn about the world. The result is propositional knowledge, the 'know-that' sense which includes the previously mentioned facts and propositions. The way we generate this propositional knowledge is through a number of procedures, collectively called *procedural knowledge*, which curricula label as processes or skills. Ryle's (1949) idea of 'know-how' was essentially the practical act of performing tasks. In education the notion of skill is not clear, as the following examples show.

In science, there are clearly defined practical skills which are necessary in investigations and which require careful muscular co-ordination: for example, in handling apparatus, taking readings from different scales, and various manipulative tasks. Intellectual skills would include, for example:

1   observing and inferring (if such a distinction exists);
2   various reasoning or cognitive strategies;
3   weighing evidence and drawing reasonable conclusions;
4   predicting;
5   asking questions, forming an argument, and correlating;
6   testing hypotheses (possible explanations) by experiment (fair testing).

Historians would also claim the importance of many of the above skills, with the exception of fair testing. In particular, questioning the validity of primary and secondary historical sources, reasoning and weighing evidence currently influence how lessons are planned in the subject. It is argued that the most effective way to gain historical knowledge is to teach it as the product of enquiry. Beliefs about what counts as a historical explanation have to be challenged, and children should be able to say, 'I don't believe that could possibly happen!' They need to examine how data were collected and interpreted, and the way disputes are resolved. In all subjects, there is a disservice to the discipline if procedural elements are not acknowledged, making explicit to children the nature of inquiry.

Many intellectual skills are thought to be generalizable across different subjects, as are communications skills. There is increasing emphasis on learners to show competence in oracy, literacy and social skills. Using talk and writing to communicate effectively, and using language to generate knowledge, is no longer seen as the province of English only (DES, 1975).

Despite the apparent differences between procedural and propositional knowledge, they are intimately associated, and are rarely, if ever, as clear-cut as suggested (Millar and Driver, 1987). The relationship between them is a complementary one. For example, in science, Qualter, Strang, Swatton and Taylor (1990) point out that to diagnose a fault in an electric circuit requires practical skills, but also an elementary understanding of electricity and the concept of a complete circuit. They also discuss the importance of theoretical ideas held by children and their ability to observe. Children often express what they know rather than what they see. Responses to the question, 'What are the similarities and differences between the ant and wasp shown in this photograph?' were analysed. They showed that children who were studying biology were more likely to include similarities and differences, which were not included in the photographs. Knowledge determines what you see, and influences the patterns you select and those you discriminate against. Thus whereas a geologist will pick out indicative features in a landscape, a non-specialist may see only undifferentiated masses of rock.

Summary

- Teachers have strongly held beliefs about the nature of knowledge and about what has to be learned in school.

- These beliefs have a direct influence on teachers' planning and classroom action and therefore on what children are expected to learn.
- We need a language for talking about knowledge as curriculum content.
- A distinction has commonly been made between 'knowing that' and 'knowing how', between propositional knowledge as facts and procedural knowledge as skills and processes.
- The status of knowledge changes over time. Theories and facts believed in one era may not survive into another era. Philosophers and scholars in academic subjects hotly contest how we can claim to know something.
- We describe our knowledge using common language, but words have private as well as public meanings: people understand events and concepts differently even when they use the same words.

Subject Matter and its Structure

A group of 7-year-olds, having finished their investigation, set about the task of explaining what they thought was happening when ice melted. They had some ideas about matter being made of tiny particles, and their representations consisted of coloured blobs of paint, rushing at speed, rotating, and colliding in excited states of dance.

'This isn't science', whispered one.
'Yes it is', came the reply. 'It's Friday, and we always have science.'

The certainty of children about what constitutes a subject is not matched by adult beliefs and criteria. Further, the distinction between what constitutes a subject at school level and an academic discipline is often blurred. Some philosophers think that subjects are distinguishable one from the other by the different ways of thinking within the discipline. Traditionally, subjects such as mathematics, science, English and history have been seen as distinctive, and have formed the basis of curriculum documents. The word 'discipline', in the control sense, means conforming to rules, proceeding in a way that is socially acceptable. Disciplines as subjects also imply rules of procedure, and ways of operating that are socially recognized and in accordance with subject norms. As a way of knowing, the discipline of history requires the historian to be selective, for not all events are of consequence; evidence needs to be weighed in order to provide an acceptable explanation. History is often described as essentially narrative, that is, telling a story, but in a controlled way. But it is unlike a literary novel in that any imagining must be based on empirical sources, on possibility, not unbridled fantasy (Rogers, 1979). Mathematics is distinctive. It has its own central organizing concepts and procedures. It has ways of checking consistency and has conventions about what constitutes a valid answer. Historians, mathematicians and other specialists learn the rules of behaviour in their subjects generally through imitation, picking up practical 'know-how' in a kind of apprenticeship, practising skills and using them in some accepted rigorous way. The process is part of the culture of their discipline.

'What is the nature of a subject discipline?' and 'how do subjects work?' are important questions. As I observed earlier, your view of subject knowledge will strongly influence what you do as a teacher, particularly in planning children's learning experiences. I want to examine this matter further through a consideration of the work of Schwab (1964) who suggested that academic disciplines could usefully be described as having substantive and syntactic elements.

Substantive Knowledge

Schwab described the *substantive structure* of a discipline as consisting not only of facts and major concepts, but in addition the way these are organized into frameworks, which themselves are used to guide inquiry. In physics, concepts of atom, electron, subatomic particles are understood in terms of an organizing framework called the Kinetic Theory. The model is an imaginative idea which we assign to unobservable atoms and molecules in order to explain how the world 'out there' behaves. The classificatory systems of chemistry and biology are other organizing frameworks which help explain what may appear superficially as a profusion of disparate bits of information.

To illustrate the importance that Schwab placed upon the way concepts are organized we can describe how two biologists might figure out how to investigate an ecosystem, that is, those interactions between physical features and organisms in an area such as a lake, field, or desert. One biologist may perceive the study as a collection of descriptive data about the plants and animals in the environment, and records of temperature, light or soil factors. The other may perceive the study in terms of energy flow through the various food webs, and collect data to reflect the dynamic nature of the functional whole.

Organizing frameworks act like personal theoretical lenses with restricted vision, modifying their owners' actions. The importance of this is that it points to their *role*. Substantive organizing frameworks are themselves responsible for guiding future research, by dictating the sort of questions researchers pose. The two biologists above perceived the ecosystem in very different ways, their particular frameworks allowing only certain types of problem to present themselves, and dictating the sort of hypotheses which might solve the problems.

Data collected from investigations may be meaningless unless there is some organizational framework to make sense of them. The discovery of pulsars is a nice example to illustrate this point. Jocelyn Bell Burnell when interviewed

(Judson, 1980), describes how, as a radio astronomer in Cambridge, she studied radio signals from outer space. As the tracing pen raced across the chart paper she noticed, totally unexpectedly, a series of small 'blips' on the recording. They were equally spaced, at about one and a third seconds, a bit like a flashing lighthouse. That is where the problem started. The pulses didn't make sense. She gradually discounted the idea that they were of human origin, that is, police radio, aeroplane or generator interference, because the pulses were so regular and were going round with the stars. It couldn't be a star, because they pulse at periods of some hours! And it wasn't the apparatus misbehaving either. Could it be signals from another civilization? Facetiously she labelled the radio source LGM-1 (Little Green Men), a name that stuck. After months of unrewarding discussion, a colleague of Jocelyn Bell Burnell suggested a framework which might provide an explanation for these radio waves: 'Way back in the 1930's, there were some theoreticians – with a great elasticity of mind, we felt – who had been studying different states of matter. They reckoned that there could be another stable state of matter so dense that a cubic centimetre, the volume of the tip of your thumb, would weigh a hundred million tons.'

What an incredible hypothesis. Such a massive body, with a density that could not conceivably be achieved on earth, stretches the imagination of most people. Yet such a body could be responsible for the observed rapid and accurate signals from space. I chose this example of a science investigation to show clearly how a new substantive framework was needed to make sense of data, for existing ideas were not enough; it acted as an explanatory focusing structure, or 'paradigm'.

One difference which Schwab emphasized, between humanities and science, is that in the former there may be rival frameworks or paradigms at the same time, whereas in the natural sciences there is only one dominant paradigm, culminating through successive paradigm changes. Only very occasionally is this *collective view* (say the paradigm of Aristotle's time) altered, by being challenged and overthrown by an alternative interpretation (present-day paradigm).

It is the collective agreement, as a necessary prerequisite to generating scientific knowledge, that provides a characteristic of science. It is not haphazard. On a broad canvas, writers such as Kuhn (1970) describe the meticulous social process at work which allows a personal 'Eureka!' to evolve to a point of public acceptance. Any new view is communicated through journals or lectures, where peer-reviewers accept or reject the new way of thinking. Gradually the new view becomes accepted by the scientific community, often against a background of criticism and conflict – cherished views are hard to abandon.

Bronowski (1973) gives a very human account of the way the theory of evolution was put forward independently by Darwin and Wallace in the 1850s. He describes the paradox posed for these naturalists, seeing the immense diversity of life, yet also seeing patterns of uniformity amongst animals and plants. Why the difference between neighbouring species? Darwin's five years on the *Beagle* only widened his experiences of diversity, yet remarkably there are hardly any diary entries to hint at his thinking, no organizing framework as a mechanism to provide such variety. After all, at that time, the Church's influence was that the Creator was responsible for species and the physical world.

At that time Lyell's famous *Principles of geology* suggested that the physical world undergoes change, governed by natural forces. Logic may have suggested that the same may be true for organisms. In 1839, a second key event in the story was Darwin reading Malthus's (1798) *An essay on the principle of population*. Darwin came to the conclusion that what Malthus said about populations multiplying faster than food, necessitating competition to survive, could be applied to nature. It acted as a selective force. New species survived from those best fitted to particular environments. The role of the Creator was unclear. Darwin had his theory. It may appear remarkable that he waited four years to write it down, but he was probably aware of the shock to society when his ideas became known. The controversy his new paradigm caused on publication of *The origin of species* in 1859 is well documented. The new paradigm became the accepted version, in spite of the Church's resistance to the challenge to Special Creation, and the unchangeability of species. Darwin's brilliant use of analogy, that is, artificial selection in domesticated populations and what might occur in nature, provided an explanation for evolution by descent with hereditary variation and natural selection.

The substantive organizational framework of Darwin has altered little since 1859, yet may itself be about to change. Kauffman (1993) works at the molecular level, and has provided a theory that explains how the essentially unlimited variety of biological complexities, in structures and functions, can be ordered. Using computer models of networks of interacting genes, he has shown that chaos does not reign in unlimited numbers of possible combinations; it emerged that only a relatively few different combinations were available in these networks. Kauffman demonstrated the existence of order from potential chaos, because the computer genes obeyed simple rules of regulation and interaction. The task now is to test the theory against evidence. I mention Kauffman's work briefly, because it is a good example of the tentativeness of scientific knowledge; creating ideas for new organizing frameworks emphasizes its continual reappraisal.

In disciplines such as literary criticism there are parallel concurrent paradigms, competing substantive organizing frameworks through which literary texts are interpreted differently. Thus, Ball (1990a) has pointed out that some disciplines have multiple frameworks, and she points out that 'no one "knows" the structures of mathematics.' In history, Rogers (1979) argues that procedures in analysing data are not always made clear, so 'differences of interpretation among historians mean that there is often no universally agreed and unambiguous information to be communicated.'

Syntactic knowledge

Besides the concepts and organizing frameworks of substantive knowledge, the structure of a discipline can be described syntactically. Schwab described *syntactic knowledge* as the ways and means by which propositional knowledge has been generated and established. It is the way in which new knowledge becomes accepted by a scholarly community, through various procedures of experimentation and verification. It therefore involves more than procedural knowledge and routine inquiry. Syntactic knowledge means the 'scientific method', or in history the investigative and interpretative procedures of inquiry, or in literature the analytical tools of criticism.

There are those who would think history to be about facts and would teach without a clear understanding of the role of argument, about handling evidence, checking that an event has significance, and about imagining in a historically valid way. Nichol and Mason (1991) introduce children to syntactic knowledge of history through questions based on pictures of the Bayeux Tapestry:

1 Do you think King Harold is the man below the word HAROLD? Or is he the man falling to the ground below INTERFECTUS: EST?
2 Harold was the last Anglo-Saxon king. The Anglo-Saxon army fought in a long line of foot soldiers. They carried shields, spears, swords and axes ... Are the three men on the left and the four on the right part of the battle line? The Normans fought on horseback.

The approach invites children to consider what it is to know something, and how valid that may be. In the case of King Harold, how reliable is the Bayeux Tapestry as a record, when it was woven some twenty years after the battle? Can we be sure that the soldier with an arrow in his eye is Harold? We can't be sure. As the tapestry is the *only* primary source we have from the Norman age, it is crucial that we ask questions about it, and weigh evidence carefully to become 'as certain as possible' about 'facts'. The emphasis upon handling historical evidence in this interpretive way, debating primary sources for inaccuracies and distortions, will encourage a healthy scepticism about how 'facts' come about.

Substantive Knowledge for Teaching

Content

There is a growing recognition that substantive knowledge shapes the way teachers teach; for example, Grossman, Wilson and Shulman (1989) report that content knowledge affects both what teachers teach and how they teach it. They cite for example one English teacher who, when teaching grammar, 'raced through a review of the homework, avoiding eye contact with students she thought might ask difficult questions . . . in stark contrast to this same teacher's style in teaching literature, which she knew well; in teaching literature, she emphasised open discussions and welcomed student questions and comments.' What other differences does the subject make?

Recent research from the Leverhulme Primary Project (Bennett and Carré, 1993) indicates a relationship of subject to teaching performance. Music specialists emerged clearly as better performers in music teaching than did science and mathematics specialists, in terms of more time spent on intellectual talk, and better planning and differentiation of classroom tasks. We suggested that the reasons for the importance of content knowledge in enhancing performance was that it enabled teachers to transform programmes of study and attainment targets into worthwhile and appropriate tasks, to frame accurate and high-quality explanations, and to diagnose accurately children's understandings and misconceptions.

In teaching mathematics for understanding, Ball (1990b, 1991b) argues that teachers in training have minimal mathematical understandings, and these are frequently rule-bound, like learning 'invert and multiply' as an algorithm for division of fractions. While many teachers could get the right answer to simple problems, they could not represent their procedures in pictorial form to assist pupils who might be in difficulty. Carlsen's (1991) study in science is particularly interesting, because he describes how differences in the same teacher's knowledge of different science content led to differences in opportunities for pupils to ask questions in those lessons. Hashweh (1986, 1987) also investigated the effect of subject-matter knowledge by working with teachers of physics and biology. He concluded that the more knowledgeable teachers were confident enough to reorganize the text and, if needed, add their own activities when planning lessons. Those teachers with less knowledge followed the text more closely and deleted sections that they did not understand; they maintained their own errors about the content (as their representations showed) even when the text contradicted them. It is clear that, without understanding science concepts, teachers are unable to diagnose the accuracy or adequacy of the content knowledge presented in texts.

In the light of the argument that a teacher's knowledge base should be adequate to ensure quality teaching, there is particular cause for concern when it is revealed that so many primary teachers have the same explanatory inadequacies and the same misconceptions as their pupils (e.g. Kruger and Summers, 1988, 1989; Kruger, Summers and Palacio, 1990; Carré, 1993; Carré and Bennett, 1993).

Organizing frameworks

It has been argued that the underlying structures of a subject have even more important implications for how and what teachers choose to teach. The most pertinent studies are based on a comparison of expert teachers' comments with those of novices. For example, in science, Chi, Feltovich and Glaser (1981) gave physics problems to experts and novices and found that the former categorized them by the underlying physics principles, their depth of knowledge and schemata of principles. Novices on the other hand categorized problems by their surface features, such as identical words or common features of the problems.

Wilson and Wineburg (1988) describe how the different knowledge of substantive structures of four teachers had a direct effect on their teaching of American history. For example one teacher, Jane, a history graduate, believed that history was not a stagnant set of facts, but rather saw it bound up in a context which affords meaning and perspective. In teaching the 'Roaring Twenties', Jane started by posing the extremes of 'flappers and their fellas', buying on credit and dancing the Charleston, and the oppressed blacks and poor farmers. She did this through slides and jazz music. She also included:

> readings from *The Great Gatsby* and *The Grapes of Wrath*, and a presentation
> of slides of the Dust Bowl. Students learned about social, cultural, political, and
> economic issues. They read primary and secondary source materials, studied
> photographs, analysed graphs and engaged in debate . . . In her classroom the
> past was a drama enacted rather than a script learned by rote.

Another teacher, Fred, was a political scientist, and for him facts and history were synonymous. In contrast to Jane, he lacked a wide knowledge of history, which resulted in his making 'sweeping generalizations across centuries, by linking American and French revolutions to the Civil War . . . Lacking knowledge of the contextual factors that make these events more different than similar, Fred blithely presenting *all* revolutions as close cousins.' A lack of history knowledge and of contextual factors made him blind to the inaccuracies he presented. The teachers in this study differed along a number of dimensions, including their understanding of the role of factual knowledge, the place of interpretation and evidence, the significance of chronology and continuity and the meaning of causation. What they taught was shaped by what they knew and did not know about history.

Syntactic Knowledge for Teaching

Grossman et al. (1989) highlighted the importance of the syntactic aspects of a teacher's knowledge in determining not only what, but how, student teachers taught: 'Novice teachers who lack knowledge of syntactic structures of the subject matter fail to incorporate that aspect of the discipline in their curriculum. We believe that they consequently run the risk of misrepresenting the subject matters they teach and seriously limit prospective teachers' abilities to learn new information in their fields.' They quote a number of cases to substantiate their view. In science, for example, they describe a teacher who, like many novices, thought science inquiry was about the techniques used in a laboratory. Contrast that notion with another who said, 'Science as enquiry is sort of the blanket or the twill in there with everything. That for me is the way everything should be approached.' In that statement is an implicit message that the conduct of his class would involve discussion about the importance of having ideas and testing them out. At a young age this would mean pupils initiating their own inquiry and involve asking questions like, 'What do you think might happen if we do this . . .?' or 'How could we think of a test for . . .?' I am not suggesting that in science teachers should engage in discussions on 'the scientific method', because there are serious doubts whether such a thing exists, in the sense of a set of procedures, or any prescribed set of rules for gaining or validating science knowledge.

In mathematics, too, teachers need to appreciate that the discipline is not merely a set of algorithms which have to be applied appropriately when specific problems arise. We have shown (Carré and Ernest, 1993) how primary teachers in training had inadequate understanding of both substantive and syntactic knowledge in mathematics. We also found that, whereas they appeared to be able to understand children's learning in routine tasks and could diagnose their errors, they could not do the same with non-routine tasks.

What Teachers Need to Know

Previous discussion has indicated the importance of substantive and syntactic knowledge in influencing how teachers' knowledge may inform their teaching. The seminal work of Shulman (1986, 1987) arguing for new methods of teacher training drew attention to the importance of subject matter and stimulated research in this area. His framework for a knowledge base for teaching included, amongst others, that teachers should have:

1   Content knowledge.
2   General strategies of classroom management.
3   Curriculum knowledge.
4   Pedagogical content knowledge.
5   Knowledge of learners.

In describing pedagogical content knowledge, 'that embodies the aspects of content most germane to its teachability' Shulman included 'the most useful forms of representation of those ideas, the most powerful analogies, illustrations, examples, explanations and demonstrations – in a word, the ways of representing and formulating the subject that make it comprehensible to others ... including the conceptions that students of different ages and backgrounds bring with them to learning.' This is an important statement, for it claims that a teacher's role emerges from an understanding of both subject matter and the ways children learn. The second issue now needs to be discussed briefly.

Knowing about Children's Knowledge Structures

Children come to school already armed with knowledge of the sort of concepts and ways of working that teachers plan to teach them. From the time we are babies we gather ideas about relevant science and about the physical world, through experiencing what happens when, for example, we push toys, tug on a kite or throw objects into the air. We develop personal theories about how things move, and develop practical understandings of weight, gravity and force. Our knowledge is represented as personal theories, and enables us to anticipate events and to build explanatory structures. This prior knowledge is often counter-intuitive to new knowledge that is learned about in school.

There is an extensive literature (Driver and Easley, 1978; Gilbert and Watts, 1983; Driver, Guesne and Tiberghien, 1985) which describes such children's knowledge structures in science, and draws attention to the importance of so-called 'alternative frameworks' and the effects of having them. It is evident that the ideas children develop to make sense of everyday experiences are, in general, sensible and plausible. For example, to many children gravity is strongly associated with the presence of air, and increases as the distance above the earth's surface is increased; the eye is thought to produce the light by which we see, and humans are not thought of as animals. Evolution is often thought of in Lamarckian terms; this naive view is that the characteristics of organisms (e.g. the bulging muscles of the blacksmith) developed in one generation can be passed on to the offspring. Many children think that plants get their food from the soil, even after lessons where photosynthesis has been studied, a view no doubt encouraged by advertisements where fertilizers 'feed' the plant.

Researchers have indicated that at all levels, from children of school age to graduates, and across different subject areas, personal understandings frequently run contrary to establishment views. Gardner (1993) gives a most readable account of 'misconceptions' in mathematics, but makes the point that the term may not be appropriate in this subject. In mathematics he suggests that 'most students suppress their intuitive knowledge about numbers and domains (like time or money or pizza) and instead try to follow rigidly applied sets of rules for solving problems. Only when the problem as set actually triggers the algorithm that has been mastered will students get the right answer.'

What is the practical importance of these findings? In science, Driver (1989) clearly points out that 'what pupils learn from lesson activities, whether these involve talk, written text or practical work, depends not only on the task set but on the knowledge schema that pupils bring to the task.' So merely knowing about the existence of their prior knowledge is not enough. Strategies are needed to help children *restructure* their understandings, as discussed in Carré and Ovens (1994). What has to be learned may have to be relearned, and overcoming those intuitive and obstinately peristent knowledge structures is no easy matter.

Summary

- There are different ways of talking about knowledge for teaching.
- What you know, and how you think about it, strongly influences how you teach.
- Knowledge is commonly represented as 'concepts', 'facts' or 'skills', but there is considerable dispute about the status of these terms.
- The curriculum is generally organized into academic subjects or disciplines.
- Disciplines may be said to comprise substantive and syntactic knowledge.
- Substantive knowledge refers to the concepts and 'big ideas' or 'organizing frameworks' of a subject.
- Syntactic knowledge refers to the processes by which knowledge is accumulated and tested in the subject.
- Confident, valid and flexible teaching requires teachers to be familiar with substantive and syntactic knowledge of a subject.
- Children always have common-sense ideas about a subject. These influence what they learn from a lesson. Teachers must consider children's conceptions in planning lessons.
- Teachers also need to know the best ways of representing the ideas in a subject to their pupils.

Editor's Commentary

This chapter focused on the structure of academic subjects, on their content and on the processes by which knowledge is accumulated in a discipline. The technical language of the chapter is less important than the big ideas it contains and the questions it raises.

The central questions are:

- What do you know about substantive and syntactic structures of subjects?
  - How can you find out about what pupils know about the subject before you teach them?
- How can subjects best be presented to pupils so that they meet authentic experience in the discipline?

If you have understood this chapter you will appreciate that these questions will occupy your lifetime's work as you develop your practice because the academic subjects do not stand still. However, you must start somewhere. Useful school-based exercises are:

- Observe teachers and discuss with them how they find out what children already know about topics to be taught.
- Attempt some diagnostic work with children using teachers' and your own ideas.
- For a subject in which you feel confident, examine how different reference and school books represent the same topic or idea. Try out these representations and discuss with children what they made of them.

Of course these exercises should be carefully planned with teachers. Detailed records, including tape recordings where appropriate, should be kept if you are to learn from your experience.

The ideas in this chapter should be linked with those in other chapters. The organization of children's classroom experience should be designed to promote academic attainment. This central idea can be pursued as follows:

- The relationship between classroom experience and learning is examined in chapters 4 and 5.
- The organization of curriculum experience is discussed in detail in chapter 9.
- The assessment of academic progress depends on what is meant by academic progress. This matter and its implications for assessment are discussed in chapters 16 and 17.

FURTHER READING

Ball, D. L. (1990). The mathematical understandings that prospective teachers bring to teacher education. *The Elementary School Journal, 90* (4), 49–66.
    In discussing the mathematical knowledge of preservice teachers, the article portrays the complicated process facing them to represent mathematics effectively. The author gives a clear indication of the importance of teachers' understanding of substantive and syntactic knowledge of mathematics, to enable their teaching to be valid from the point of view of the subject and at the same time appropriate to the learners.

Driver, R., Guesne, E. & Tiberghien, A. (Eds.). (1985). *Children's ideas in science.*
   Milton Keynes, England: Open University Press.
      This book includes chapters on children's beliefs about the natural world and
      how their 'alternative frameworks' conflict with accepted scientific theories
      taught in school. Topics include many which are fundamental to learning
      science, such as light, force, heat, kinetic particular theory and motion.
Reynolds, M. (Ed.). (1989). *Knowledge base for beginning teachers.* Oxford, Eng-
   land: Pergamon Press.
      This book focuses on the idea that teaching has a distinctive knowledge base,
      and the chapter authors make its structure explicit, particularly for the beginning
      teacher. There are chapters on general knowledge about teaching, and also on
      subject-specific knowledge, including discussions of the teaching of reading,
      writing and arithmetic. Of particular value is chapter 3, which articulates the
      dimensions of a teacher's subject knowledge and underpins the arguments with
      clear reference to the research literature. Chapter 17 deals with the role of
      representations in teaching subject matter and does so with reference to teaching
      different subjects, including history, mathematics and science.
Rogers, P. (1979) *The New History: Theory into practice*, Teaching of history series,
   No. 44. London: The Historical Association.
      This pamphlet is excellent introductory reading on the nature of historical
      knowledge, its distinctive features being discussed critically in relation to
      classroom practice. Questions such as, 'In what sense, if any, can children
      become "mini-historians", and at what age and ability level?' are answered in
      terms of the activities in which children might be engaged, and a teacher's
      understanding of historical knowledge.

3

Development and Learning

Richard Fox

Editor's Overview

We cannot teach everything at once. The curriculum must be sequenced and paced to progress in good order and at the most profitable rate for children. The problem is, how can we get the order and pace right? In this chapter, Richard Fox looks at this question from the particular point of view of developmental psychology, which is the study of the relationship between the growth of competence and age. He defines the key concepts of

- learning
- instinct
- development
- maturation.

He shows that children are naturally good at thinking and learning in familiar settings and that they make natural or 'emergent' progress in understanding literacy and mathematics through their everyday experience of print and number.

He also shows that the effect of instruction on these emergent powers depends on whether the instruction maps on to the child's attainment. If instruction is too easy it wastes the child's time and may be boring; too difficult, and it may lead to the child becoming alienated. The important concept of 'readiness to learn' is raised, and the question, 'should we wait for or prepare for readiness?' is considered.

The general trends in intellectual development in age are described. The idea of 'locus of concern' is introduced. This describes the range, which increases in time, space and abstraction as children get older, across which children can successfully apply their thoughts. The child's locus of concern, however, is not influenced by age alone. It is also influenced by knowledge and experience.

Teachers and Child Development

Primary schooling is associated with a period in children's lives of rapid growth and development, physically, socially and intellectually, and primary teachers are centrally concerned with aiding this process of development and with channelling it towards worthwhile goals. If, in particular, there is a natural or predictable order to the way in which children develop their knowledge and understanding of the world, then it seems clear that teachers should know about it. Such common developmental pathways might be associated with biological changes in the growing brain, making more powerful forms of thinking available to children as they grow older. Or they might simply relate to the nature and organization of the subject matter and how it is taught.

One point of schooling is to enlarge the child's horizons, via a broad and balanced curriculum. Another perhaps is to speed up learning, to make it more efficient and effective than it would be without schools and teachers. Since one cannot teach, or learn, everything at once, teachers inevitably have to sequence tasks and activities within a curriculum. They should try to do this so as to fit teaching to the nature of children's emerging understanding. Teachers have to make frequent judgements about the pace at which new ideas and challenges are introduced, and they need to predict the difficulties which children are likely to have. Teachers who know something about both what steps of progress children are likely to take next, and also what obstacles they are likely to stumble over, are much better placed to set relevant tasks, to ask helpful questions and to provide explanations at the right level of difficulty. They are more likely to notice significant advances, when observing and listening to children, and they are better able to predict what things children of different ages will find interesting.

In judging the pace of work, teachers strive to avoid the twin perils of on the one hand failing to provide sufficient challenge and interest, so that children become bored, and on the other of forcing the pace too fast, so that the children's confidence and understanding both start to collapse. There is certainly a danger of children becoming bored, but boredom can result from either a lack of intellectual challenge or a failure to understand.

The extent to which our school-based knowledge often turns out to be superficial, liable to error, inflexible and easily forgotten might prompt us to wonder if we would not often do better to 'make haste slowly' by taking the curriculum at a pace which allowed a far more thorough understanding to become rooted in pupils' minds. The order and pace of teaching in turn seem to depend on some estimate of the difficulty of the subject matter and the intelligence of the learner. Yet how can we define 'difficulty'? And how does intelligence itself change with age and experience? Children understand arithmetic before algebra, and they might understand pictures before they understand print, but why should this be so? Such questions set us off in the direction of trying to discover more about how children's minds develop.

How are Learning and Development Related?

In the past twenty years or so, research into children's thinking and understanding, their 'cognitive development' has led to major changes in psychologists' ideas about young children's mental capacities and how they can be helped by teaching. Whereas, formerly, there was a considerable measure of agreement that there existed general, age-related, stages in the development of human thinking, now there is a general scepticism about whether any such stages exist. Formerly, there was an attempt to fit teaching to what was perceived as a natural 'blueprint' of development. Now there is more emphasis on the power of teaching to bring about learning and development.

De Loache, Sugarman and Brown (1985) noticed that with increasing age and experience, young children gradually developed increasingly effective strategies when given a set of plastic 'nested cups' to play with. The youngest and least experienced tended to try to fit pairs of cups together at random. If two cups would not fit, the child tried using brute force, pushing harder to make them fit. When this failed they tried a different pair of cups. A second strategy was to keep hold of one cup and to search for a better partner for it, but if this failed, the child was likely to drop these cups and start again. Older and more experienced children had developed two further strategies: sometimes they reversed two cups, trying to fit 'a' inside 'b' rather than 'b' inside 'a'; sometimes they were able to take a cup and insert it between two other cups in the correct point in the sequence.

These two strategies, of reversing cups and of inserting a cup between two others, certainly helped children to succeed at the task, and seem good evidence of 'development'. Overall, the less successful children tended to experiment at random with cups, whereas the more successful seemed to have begun to think about each cup in relation to the whole series. But are such developments the result of growing older and of having more 'brain power' to use in solving the problem? Or were the more advanced strategies simply the result of learning through experience, which could be gained at any age?

The meanings of 'learning' and 'development' can be difficult to distinguish. Learning is used as a more general term, being applied to any example of an enduring change in knowledge, or skill, which results from experience. In this sense learning (from experience) is contrasted with instinct (a biologically built-in way of responding to a problem). 'Learning' is also used to describe short-term specific gains in knowledge, whilst 'development' is reserved for longer-term, broader changes in knowledge, skills, attitudes or indeed other mental states. Thus we talk of learning the two-times table but of developing an understanding of multiplication; we talk of learning to spell a word but of developing literacy. These short- and long-term differences in meaning are only relative, however, and suggest that development is simply the sum total of individual bits of learning. On this view there is nothing more to cognitive development than a history of episodes of learning.

Sometimes, however, 'development' carries an extra layer of meaning. Those who use it may do so to emphasize the fact that children are active participants in the business of learning, who spontaneously work out their understanding of the world rather than having to be prodded into learning things by external forces. In this view, development is held to be at least partly a self-regulating affair, increasingly under the child's own control, and is contrasted with a view of children as passive beings, shaped by their learning environment. Sometimes a further step is taken, linking this notion of self-regulating development to a theory about age-related biological growth, from immaturity to maturity. Perhaps the self-regulation is really based upon the underlying growth to maturity of the brain and the nervous system.

The central instance of this sense of the term is physical development. Without any doubt the physical development and growth of normal children follows a predictable course which is the outcome of an interaction between internal, genetically controlled changes, and external, environmental influences such as diet, health and exercise. There are, for instance, clear stages of developing maturity in children's bone structure, body shape, skilled movements and reproductive organs. The question is whether, and how far, such maturational stages of development apply to the mind, as well as to the body, whether children's thinking, like their strength and agility, is partly under biological control. To the extent that it is, development has to account for maturation as well as learning. A developmental account of children's progress in understanding the world will then contain more than simply accumulated episodes of learning.

The Role of Maturation

There is abundant evidence of growth and maturation in the nervous system during childhood, on which we know that thinking and learning depend. It is still far from clear, however, exactly what limits or opportunities such changes produce, in terms of the pace and direction of human learning. In considering how important maturation is, or is not, it may help to think of four distinctive points of view, each allowing it a greater or lesser contribution to development.

Position 1: Maturation plays no significant role. Development is nothing but an accumulation of learning experiences.

Position 2: Learning is the basic process which leads to development. The pace of learning, however, especially in early childhood, is constrained by the pace of the maturation of the brain.

Position 3: Development reflects the underlying process of maturation, which precedes and leads to learning. Maturation thus makes learning possible within a certain range.

Position 4: Children's cognitive development reflects a natural process of the unfolding from within of the mind's potential powers. Given any minimal experience of the world, normal development will naturally occur.

Of these four possible positions only (4) is utterly out of favour at present. Position 2 would probably command the support of most contemporary psychologists, though (1) and (3) would also have their champions.

Position 3, which accords a strong role to maturation has often been linked to the theory that all children pass through a universal series of stages of development, which govern the kinds of thinking they can effectively manage. This was the view of Piaget, a pioneering researcher into cognitive development. Piaget held a view of children's development in which he sought to go beyond accounts which attributed everything to experience (position 1) or everything to maturation (position 4). He argued that there are four principal sources of influence affecting the developing mind: biological maturation, experience of the natural physical world, experience of interacting with people and, lastly, the child's own internal, reflective, thought. For Piaget, these influences combined to produce four stages of developing thought, each involving a reorganization of knowledge and each successively enabling more powerful kinds of thinking to emerge.

Since the 1960s and 1970s, a powerful critique of Piaget's stage theory has gradually emerged, as it has been demonstrated time and again that in familiar contexts, with simple versions of problems, young children are capable of all the types of thinking which Piaget thought developed only at later ages. A radical alternative view has gradually taken shape: there are no major qualitative changes in children's thinking abilities. They simply acquire more and more knowledge, which they apply more and more efficiently (i.e. position 1 above). But does this view simplify too much? Perhaps it only solves the problem of maturation by ignoring it.

Summary

- We cannot teach everything at once: the curriculum has to be sequenced and paced.
- Psychologists and teachers have considered whether there is a natural sequence and pace to learning, whether, in a sense, learning can be matched to natural developmental processes.
- This raises the question of what we mean by natural development or maturation, and several views of this have been described.

Early Learning

There is now little doubt that even in the first few days and weeks of life children demonstrate the beginnings of the crucial processes of intelligent problem solving and rational thought. They notice similarities and differences, recognize patterns, anticipate sequences of events and try to exercise control over their environment. Thus, to take but one example, infants in the first two days of life have been shown to be capable of controlling the rate at which they suck on a specially adapted rubber nipple in order to activate a recording of their mother's voice (DeCasper and Fifer, 1980). These babies, in other words, were able either to slow down or speed up their rate of sucking when this led reliably to a tape of their mother's voice, as opposed to a stranger's voice, switching on. Although infants are born in a relatively immature and vulnerable state they are clearly active learners from day one.

By the age of 4½ years, when many children start school, children are already intelligent and knowledgeable members of their culture. They can understand and use the major types of spoken sentence, recognize and use concepts, understand simple analogies and metaphors, search for the causes of events and interpret the intentions and beliefs that lie behind typical human actions. As an example, consider the ideas involved in the following conversation between a parent and an American child of 4 years 2 months, who had seen several videos of Judy Garland films:

Child: Did Judy die because she was old?
Parent: No, she wasn't very old when she died.
Child: Then why'd she die?
Parent: She got sick.
Child: Why'd she get so sick if she wasn't old?
Parent: I think because she didn't take care of herself. I remember reading that she ate and drank all the wrong things, things which weren't healthy.
Child: Why? Didn't she know what was good to eat?

Parent: I think she did but I read that she was sad and I guess she didn't think about taking care of herself.
Child: She was sad? What made her so sad like that?
Parent: I don't know, but it makes me sad for her.
Child: Me too. Why was she so sad? Why wasn't she happy and proud that she had made all those beautiful movies?

(Shulman, 1991, p. 16)

In this exchange the child shows that she knows that there are causes of death, that old age may be accompanied by ill-health, that health depends partly on knowing what one should eat, that sadness (depression) has causes and that success and achievement normally produce feelings of happiness and pride. Her general knowledge and the way she pursues a line of questioning are impressive. We underestimate 4- and 5-year-olds at our peril. In spite of this exciting evidence we now have of children's early competence in thinking, however, we should not lose sight of the tremendous progress that they will make in the primary years between 4 and 11.

The Idea of Readiness to Learn

The idea of cognitive development has often been associated with the idea of readiness to learn. This suggests that the introduction of various kinds of learning, such as reading and mathematics, should be delayed until a child shows clear evidence of 'readiness'. Treated too dogmatically, the notion of readiness can do considerable harm through leading teachers to underestimate what young children can actually achieve. 'Readiness' suggests a particular moment in time, or at least a sensitive period, before which no useful teaching or learning can occur. Generally, however, imaginative parents and teachers can find ways of introducing such things as reading, counting and scientific enquiry, which make sense even to 3-year-olds and which they enjoy. Readiness is perhaps more usefully thought of in terms of a gradient of difficulty with respect to a problem, such that simpler forms and familiar contexts have to be used at its beginning.

The enduring power of some idea of readiness to learn is illustrated in an anecdote told by Jenson (1973). He tried to teach his 5-year-old daughter how to play chess, and being a very systematic psychologist he went to a lot of trouble to give her carefully thought-out lessons. The little girl was keen to be able to play and was able to learn in a few sessions all the names of the pieces and their various legal moves. The object of the game was carefully explained and demonstrated to her, and then father and daughter sat down to play. A proper game did not emerge, however, in spite of further teaching and encouragement. The child was quite unable to plan and co-ordinate her separate moves in any purposeful way. Soon her interest waned, and, for fear of spoiling the game for her, Jenson abandoned the project. A few weeks later, however, he taught her to play draughts (checkers) and this time his daughter learned to play and enjoy the game without any great difficulty.

Jenson attributes the very different outcome to the difference in complexity between the two games. He argues that his daughter was sufficiently mature, intellectually, to integrate the rules and strategies of draughts, but not of chess. This, he feels, is an example of 'readiness' in that either maturation, or her state of knowledge, or both, meant that his daughter could not make sufficient progress with chess to sustain her motivation. His explanation is strengthened by the fact that almost a year later he and his daughter returned to chess, whereupon she easily learned to play and was soon demanding games with her father as soon as he came home from work.

The risks of ignoring the concept of readiness to learn entirely seem obvious: children who are pressed to continue to learn something in which they show no interest, when they are persistently failing, and especially if there is no necessity for them to learn it, are going to experience repeated frustration. This may lead them to avoid this subject whenever possible, and even to avoid the person who persists in trying to teach them. But introducing children to new ideas and experiences and encouraging them to struggle with new problems and challenges is not at all the same as 'pushing' them too hard.

The key to sensible decisions in this area seems to be a sensitivity to the child's waxing and waning interest and engagement with a problem. With young children, the wise adult persists so long as the child can make some progress, given gentle encouragement and repeated help. If this is not succeeding, it is probably time to back off for a while or to think of a means of simplifying the task. With older children, where the subject is of vital importance, as is currently the case with literacy at about the age of 6 or 7, it may be necessary to persevere, but again great efforts should be made to modify the task so that progress is guaranteed.

Emerging Knowledge

Readiness is an idea which has been applied to the teaching of reading in the hope that careful timing would lead to optimal rates of progress. However, 'reading readiness tests' had too fixed an idea of what learning to read involved, and were not always good indicators of what a child could actually achieve with a book (Beard, 1992). Most 3-year-olds are beginning to take an interest in the print they see around them, at home, in shops and on television, and this is perhaps the nearest clue to 'readiness'. Sulzby (1988) has studied such 'emergent reading' and shows how an understanding of literacy can emerge from everyday encounters with books and print.

Sulzby asked 2- to 5-year-olds to show their emerging understanding of reading by retelling a familiar story book, with illustrations, to an adult. She was able to identify a sequence of levels of progress towards independent reading, which may be summarized, in slightly condensed form, as follows:

(1) Labelling and commenting: the simplest kind of response: labelling objects in the pictures while turning the pages of the book, and making isolated comments about them (thus: 'there's the balloon man . . . that's the sun . . .').
(2) Following the action: a running commentary on separate pictured actions (thus: 'kissing him . . . see? . . . she's putting him to bed. She's going to [make] his bed . . .'). Up to this point no organized account of the story has emerged.
(3) Dialogic and monologic storytelling: a version of the story is told, but uses ordinary conversational language. The child may use 'voices' for the characters, or make conversational comments. Then a complete 'monologic' retelling may appear, still reliant on the pictures and containing features of oral informal speech (thus: 'This is his house and he is going to sleep. He was reading a book. And he was going to bed and then after that he was reading the book and he saw pictures of the mountains up here . . .').
(4) Reading and storytelling mixed: the language of retelling the story starts to accommodate to the actual words of the text. 'Book-like' versions, with repetitive patterns and actual phrases remembered from the text, are produced (thus: ' "Help! Help! Get me out of here!" said the baby bird . . .'). Then come verbatim retellings, with substantial stretches of the actual text included.
(5) Attempts governed by print: some children may, for a while, refuse to retell the story on the grounds that they can't read it 'properly'. Then some of the fluency of the oral retelling may be abandoned in order to engage more and more accurately with the words of the text itself. Children try to sound out letters or recognize individual words, working these aspects of 'real reading' into the retelling of the story.
(6) Towards independence: different aspects of reading, including word recognition, letter–sound relationships and predictions of what will happen next may be attempted, but often these strategies are imbalanced. Reading is effortful and dependent on frequent adult help. From this point on, however, the child, who may well by now be being taught to read, increasingly combines the multiple cues to meaning and works towards complete independence as a reader.

Sulzby's research provides a good description of the typical course of developing understanding. The child's level of emergent reading stays stable across short periods of time but involves gradual elaborations and innovations which lead eventually to independent reading over a longer time period.

Feldman (1980) describes a very similar pattern of ragged, stage-like progression, with minor advances and retreats, in a study of children's developing ability to draw a map. Feldman asked children aged between 10 and 13 years to draw a map of a model landscape, with buildings, roads, hills and a lake. The most primitive maps were very like pictures, with only parts of the landscape included and with the size and relative position of the various objects and features often being wildly inaccurate. The most mature

maps preserved the scale and relative position of different features, used a
consistent plan, or bird's-eye, viewpoint and conventional symbols to represent objects, for example, trees. Advances in the various dimensions of map
drawing, such as accurate scale and plan viewpoint, occurred in a piecemeal
fashion. A plan view of roads, for example, generally appeared long before a
plan view of buildings.

Children appeared to spend periods of time consolidating their map
drawing at a particular level before moving on to elaborate its features.
Elaboration, building on a well-established base level, then led on to
occasional innovations, such as using a symbol to represent an object or
attempting a more accurate scale. Innovation in one area would gradually
spread to other areas until a more advanced overall level of map drawing, as
scored by the researchers, would be achieved. Then the new level would be
consolidated once again.

Both Sulzby's study of early reading and Feldman's study of map drawing
show a slow process of developing knowledge and skill, resulting from
repeated engagement with a problem over a period of several years. Each
study shows a developing series of levels of understanding, or mastery, of a
problem, with periods of consolidation, elaboration and then innovation.
The detailed nature of the steps in developing competence have to be worked
out through careful observation in each separate domain, however. Rather
than providing a unified overview of cognitive development, such research
establishes some common pathways taken by learners through particular
areas of knowledge. Rather as with individual pathways through a wood,
there are both common pathways or routes, and also some individual
variations. The course of development is shaped in each case by the nature of
what is being learned, and by the cultural context in which the learning
occurs. What needs to be considered next is the particular influence of
teaching on such developments.

The Influence of Practice and Instruction

Siegler (1978) has investigated children's understanding of a balance beam,
like a see-saw, which had four pegs fixed on each side of a fulcrum. In a
given trial a number of (uniform) weights would be hung on a single peg on
each side of the beam. The beam would be held level while the child was
asked to predict whether, on release, it would tilt to the left or right, or stay
balanced. Then the beam was released so that the child could see the
outcome. Siegler studied children's understanding of this problem over a
wide age range from 4 to 17 years. He also studied how independent practice
and teaching affected children's success. In general, 3-year-olds were unable
to do more than guess at random in this situation, whereas some 4-year-olds
and most 5-year-olds started to succeed, provided that only the number of

weights hung on each side was varied. The distance of the weights from the fulcrum also matters, of course, but the 5-year-olds persistently ignored this. Even with further practice with the beam these children made little progress. But when Siegler tried deliberately teaching them to pay attention to the distance factor, their understanding in many cases advanced rapidly. Instruction thus had a powerful effect.

In the age-range 7 to 12 years, children started to be able to cope with problems in which both weight and distance were varied, provided that only one or the other was unequal. If both the number of weights and the distance from the fulcrum were unequal, and tending to produce opposing effects, children started guessing once again. Eight-year-olds, however, were able to make advances on the problem simply through engaging in independent practice. It seems that their initial knowledge was sufficient to make practice effective even without instruction. By 12 or 13 years, some children were able to co-ordinate weight and distance variations of all kinds, thus solving all the problems presented. Even at the age of 17, however, some young adults continued to make mistakes. Presumably they had not managed to work out the general rule which generates the correct answer in every case.

Siegler found that practice, verbal hints and instructions were all useful to children in this context, but their effects were dependent on the child's initial level of understanding. Thus a teacher would find helpful both a knowledge of the typical sequence of advances made in understanding this problem – the likely 'paths through the wood' – and also a sensitive observation of each child's current state of knowledge. Teaching and independent practice both facilitate development, but in different ways. Teaching seems to help most in introducing new problems, new ideas and skills, and in supporting, or scaffolding, children's early attempts at understanding. Practice seems to function best when it permits the consolidation and elaboration of early understanding. Whether they are learning from instruction, from imitation or from practice, children always need feedback which tells them what is going right and what is going wrong, as well as encouragement to believe in themselves and to persevere.

Summary

- Young children have remarkable competence at thinking and learning in familiar settings.
- They appear to have the same basic processes of logic and creativity as adults.
- There is evidence of emerging competence with spoken and written language and with mathematics.
- The effect of teaching on this competence can be positive or negative: it depends on sensitive timing by the teacher.

- There appears to be a 'right time' to teach something: this has been called 'readiness'.
- The current view is that readiness should be prepared for rather than waited for.

General Trends in Developing Cognition

Developing knowledge, as we have seen, is the outcome of learning, albeit learning which is constrained, to some extent, by the pace of biological maturation. The learning which is actually possible for a child at a given time is governed by a number of factors, including, pre-eminently, his or her existing knowledge. Other factors include the ability to manage and apply that knowledge and a willingness to engage with the problem at hand. Children encountering problems, whether in everyday life or in the classroom, respond in the light of their existing knowledge, which includes what they understand the problem to be, how important they rate its solution, what help they think is available and whether or not they feel confident of finding a solution.

In the wake of lessening confidence in general stage theories of cognitive development, notably Piaget's, there has been a tendency to avoid grand theorizing in recent years. Donaldson (1992), however, provides an interesting exception. She suggests a framework for understanding at least some of the ways in which children's thinking, and their interests, tend to develop, by considering how they are able to locate their mental life within space and time. Initially, Donaldson argues, infants live exclusively in the 'here and now', dominated by their current physical and mental state and by the immediately present environment. Their thoughts and feelings coincide with their perceptions and actions, with almost no ability to conceive of the past or the future, or of places other than where they currently are. By the age of about nine months, however, infants begin to show in various ways that their 'locus of concern', to use Donaldson's terminology, is beginning to expand, to permit a focus on events in the past and future, and on people and places not immediately present. This broadening of outlook entails a partial splitting off of thinking and feeling away from immediate perceptions and actions. No longer so dominated by the perceptual present, the child's memories and anticipations begin to provide a more stable and independent basis for choice, decision-making and action.

The child's ability to begin to make sense of things in terms of past experience and plans for the future, to consider 'there and then' as well as 'here and now', becomes established during the second year of life. Both time and space are becoming gradually expanded in the child's mental outlook, from the original limits of the immediate here and now. A further important advance occurs between the ages of 3 and 4 years, with a shift in the possible locus of concern away from specific happenings and towards more general issues. Thus a toddler may show a great interest in when some particular jam tarts are ready to eat, but the 4-year-old may add to this interest a curiosity as to what actually happens to jam tarts when they are put in the oven. To give another example, a 2-year-old, encountering a dead bird in a field, might ask what it is and comment: 'Bird dead'. A 3- or 4-year-old will sometimes pause and ask: 'Why do birds die?' In short, children start to ask questions of a very general kind, in order to find out how the world works. They also observe, listen (sometimes!), try things out, play and argue. In all this, emotion and thought go hand in hand. Children's acquisition of knowledge is bound up with their hopes and fears, their excitement and disappointment, joy and grief. Often children are still pursuing their own immediate concerns and interests, for much of the time, but the point is that they can now occasionally change gear to a more general kind of inquiry, which takes them beyond matters of self-interest towards a concern with the general nature of the physical or social world.

One further important development in intellectual power deserves to be mentioned. Throughout the period roughly between 3 and 9 years, children can understand quite abstract ideas and relationships, but only if they occur within either a real or an imagined context which already makes sense to the child. Thus children have great difficulty with rather abstract logical problems of the sort: 'If Jane is taller than Susan and Susan is taller than Laura, who is shorter than Jane?' If they can see three dolls of different sizes, however, or even if they are encouraged to imagine the three girls visually, they do much better at such logical puzzles, as indeed do adults. Embedding a problem within a familiar context thus provides our reasoning powers with a crucial kind of support.

Some children, towards the end of the primary phase of schooling, begin to be able to make an occasional shift away from this normal dependence on context. They begin to take an interest in very abstract patterns of relationships, generally using symbolic notation. Thus, if one gives children sets of coloured counters, or cubes, of say four different colours, one may ask the question: how many pairs can you make, so that each pair contains a different combination of colours? Typically, children can make some sense of this, but they do so largely via unsystematic trial and error. As a result, after collecting a number of pairs, 7-year-olds may think they have found all the pairs, but they have no strategy for checking whether they have missed some. Between about 7 and 9 years, children may be uneasy as to whether they have definitely found all the possible pairs or not, but are still unlikely to know how to make sure. From about 9, some children attack the problem more systematically, for example by setting out a matrix of rows and columns of the colours. They may be able to show why they are sure that they have found all the combinations. What is more, some children may even be able to find the general pattern of numbers of combinations which results from combining things two at a time, from sets of different sizes.

At this point the child may no longer require the counters at all. He or she begins to operate within the world of mathematics, in a way which transcends any particular instantiation of the actual world. As Piaget put it, the actual world comes to be thought of as simply one of many possible worlds. This sort of development of the systematic exploration of quite abstract systems and possibilities may only turn up rather rarely in primary classrooms, but it has considerable implications for a developing understanding of both science and mathematics, and perhaps other subjects, too.

Whether Donaldson's particular formulation of general trends in cognitive development stands the test of time remains to be seen. It should perhaps be treated as a challenge to investigate how, and in what contexts, children think within more or less expanded perspectives of space and time, articulate questions and answers at more and less general levels, and think with more or less support from familiar contexts. Besides looking for such broad unifying trends in cognitive development, across different areas of knowledge, it may also be profitable to think of development in terms of repeated cycles of problem solving, and it is to this that we turn next.

Development within Problem Solving

There seem to be some very general stages of problem solving, which relate to the learner's initial degree of knowledge. We could describe these stages as:

- initial investigation
- partial understanding
- consolidation
- elaboration
- renewed innovation.

With little or no knowledge of a problem, children, and adults too, make relatively blind trial and error attempts at solution, which typically involve looking for familiar patterns, engaging with isolated elements and often encountering failure and frustration. Partial understanding leads to partial solutions, which may work only with much time and effort, or which ignore troublesome parts, or cases which do not fit. A complete or satisfactory solution often leads to a new understanding of the nature of the problem, and how it relates to other problems. Further practice may then lead to a routinized solution or to the discovery of alternative solutions. Routinization may involve a combination of moves, such as describing the problem and its solution in words and concepts, memorizing key facts, honing skills or learning to apply rules. Development can thus be described in part in terms of repeated progress through the problem-solving cycle, from no understanding to routine solution.

Brown and Reeve (1987) gave 4- to 7-year-olds the problem of assembling a model train track, from eight pieces, some straight and some curved. This was an open problem for the children in the sense that they had not encountered it before. The nature of a solution was clear however: the pieces had to be clipped together to make a continuous track. In this open situation the same types of strategy which we encountered above with the nesting cups problem for 2- to 4-year-olds emerged once again in the actions of these older children. The least successful tended to fit sections together at random until the arrangement became impossible to continue. They then attempted to force sections together, or abandoned one piece in favour of another, or took the whole assembly apart and started again. More successful children tried reversing two pieces or inserted pieces into a partly arranged complex. Once again, they seemed to consider the relationship between the parts and the whole. The most successful moved on to innovation, finding not one, but two ways of constructing the track.

A similar pattern of developing strategies can also be found in children's progress in learning to revise drafts in writing (Graves, 1983). Initially they tend to be at a loss as to what can be changed, or make only sporadic local corrections, changing a spelling or substituting one word for another. Later they revise by adding sentences to the end of a piece, or else abandon a draft and start again. Finally they learn how to insert and reorder not only words, but sentences and whole sections of text. In each case, with the nesting cups, the train track and the revision of writing, we see different strategies emerging which relate to the child's degree of understanding. The use they can make of practice, and of instruction, will again vary with the progress they have made, and again teachers can try to assess this, in order to make either teaching or practice more focused and useful.

Conclusions

Teachers repeatedly need to assess the developmental status of children's knowledge of a problem. Children navigate through a problem area, as Brown and Reeve put it, within a 'band width of competence' needing much support in the early stages and more independence later on. Levels of understanding may need to be consolidated until well established, freeing the learner's thinking capacity to attempt to elaborate parts of a solution, to try a limited innovation or to integrate understanding across different areas. Children's readiness to profit from practice or instruction may thus be likened to what Vygotsky (1978) called 'the zone of proximal development' (cf. chapter 7). In this zone, children can make progress in learning, but only with assistance. Teaching operates by attempting to support children's partial solutions, suggesting new strategies or providing helpful feedback about the child's current efforts. Later in the cycle teaching will consist of setting problems for independent practice and encouraging a clear understanding of how a solution was reached.

Development cannot be understood except in relation to the surrounding cultural context in which it occurs. Yet cultures change, and each child develops to some extent a unique version of the culture, in terms of knowledge and values. Whilst Vygotsky emphasized the importance of social interaction, including teaching, in facilitating development, it is worth noting, in concluding this chapter on development, that children are also capable of active problem solving by themselves. They often play with materials or with language, set themselves challenges, discover problems, try out solutions and talk to themselves about their current knowledge and about how they imagine things might be. Children can thus create their own zones of proximal development and navigate within them, through playful activity and through reflective thought. The challenge to teachers is to understand children's learning well enough, in terms of both its social and individual dimensions, to be able genuinely to facilitate it.

Editor's Commentary

Young children are very competent thinkers but they cannot do everything an older child can do. What is the nature of their limitations? Do they have biological limits on what their minds can cope with, and, if so, do we have to wait for them to get older before we teach certain topics? Or do they simply lack experience and knowledge? In which case how can we help them to acquire experience most easily?

These are difficult but unavoidable questions. There are no simple answers. Important concepts in talking about these matters are

- readiness
- locus of concern
- zone of proximal development
- learning
- development.

Nowadays the majority of psychologists take the view that carefully timed sequenced and paced teaching provides for learning which promotes broad development.

These ideas may be pursued by the following school-based exercises:

- Discuss with teachers their view of 'readiness to learn'. How do they assess readiness in a particular instance (e.g. reading readiness)? And how do they prepare for readiness?

- Examine, for at least two curriculum areas, how work is sequenced for children. Why are topics met in a particular order? Is it merely tradition or is there a developmental rationale? If so, what is it and what evidence is it based on?
- Before teaching a particular topic in the curriculum, discuss with teachers how you might assess specific readiness to learn. Try out their advice and discuss the experience with willing mentors.

Teachers cannot consider learning and development in isolation: their job is to link the developing child to the curriculum. Consequently it is important to make connections between the ideas in this chapter and those in others as follows:

- The idea of readiness should be linked to the ideas of subject structure and representation and of children's perspectives on knowledge. These are pursued in chapter 2.
- The idea of sequencing instruction is considered in detail in chapter 6.

FURTHER READING

Child Development is a huge area of research and there are many good introductory textbooks available. One straightforward example is:

Bee, H. (1989). *The developing child* (5th ed.). New York: Harper & Row.

A more specialized, but excellent, text is:

Flavell, J. H. (1985). *Cognitive development* (2nd ed.). Englewood Cliffs, NJ: Prentice Hall International.

A good collection of recent research articles is:

Woodhead, M., Carr, R. & Light, P. (Eds.). (1991). *Child development in a social context*, vols. 1–3. London: Routledge.

A readable account, oriented towards parents, is:

Shulman, M. (1991). *The passionate mind*. New York: Free Press.

Part II

Contexts for Learning

4

Learning in Classrooms

Anne D. Cockburn

Editor's Overview

Most school learning takes place in classrooms. In this chapter, Anne Cockburn draws on educational research to describe how complex classrooms are: they are by no means ideal learning environments even when managed by competent teachers.

She shows that although people in classrooms are generally very industrious, much of the work that they do is not conducive to learning. She introduces a number of important ideas to help explain how this problem comes about. These include

- the public nature of classroom life
- the pressures on teachers and children to adapt
- the role of praise and assessment in adaptation
- the classroom as a production line
- the problems of designing work which meets the academic needs of diverse learners.

Anne Cockburn's argument is that we must understand how classrooms really operate if we are, as teachers, to make the most of them as learning environments. Classroom work is not at all what it seems at first sight.

Introduction

What goes on in classrooms in the name of learning? A surprisingly deceptive question with perhaps an equally surprising answer. We still do not really know. Certainly we know that considerable learning does go on in classrooms. The majority of children start formal schooling at 4 or 5 and, within a few years, the majority can read, write and manipulate numbers with relative ease. Very occasionally you can almost 'see the cogs turning' in someone's brain as they grasp a new concept ('Oh, I see what you mean . . .'), but usually there is nothing to hear or observe. Indeed Desforges and Cockburn (1987) noted that teachers were 'fascinated' and 'sometimes mystified' by their pupils' ways of learning,

> 'I don't know how they learn . . .'
> 'I wish I knew how they learn. I haven't got a clue. When we get stuck on something you can almost see them thinking and I'd love to know what is going on in their heads.' (p. 29)

We may have little knowledge of how exactly children learn in classrooms but, over the last thirty years, we have gained considerable insights into classroom processes. And with these, has come a greater understanding of teachers, pupils and learning within the classroom setting. Most strikingly we have begun to appreciate that, although at first sight classrooms appear to be exceptionally busy and productive environments, this impression often masks the reality of classroom life. Teachers and pupils are undoubtedly busy but, to the untrained eye, what seems to be going on may, in fact, be rather different from what is actually occurring. It is the aim of this chapter to highlight some of these differences so that you can gain more insight into your own practice and life in classrooms.

We shall begin by focusing on aspects of classroom life as described in several research studies. From these we will consider some of the wide variety of thoughts and behaviours which might be occurring in classrooms with a view to providing you with a broader picture of the educational process and your role in developing pupil learning.

Classroom Close-ups

The following are cameos of children at work as reported by Cockburn (1986) and later used by Desforges and Cockburn (1987):

> Mrs T. took Eleanor's group of seven year olds methodically through a batch of five workcards (i.e. she discussed every question and answer). Several minutes

later Eleanor was seen to be rapidly recording her answers without any reference to the unifix cubes she had been instructed to use ... When asked how she was doing these sums Eleanor replied, 'Well Mrs T. has just told us them (i.e the answers) hasn't she?' (p. 113, first parenthesis added)

Six year old Joanna ... spent several minutes puzzling over sums of the following type:

$$\begin{array}{r} \text{add } 6 \\ 2 \longrightarrow \end{array}$$

She then turned to Nicola's book ... (p. 114)

Seven year old Kerry was given the task of adding tens and units with carrying. She had been shown the technique of adding the units, jotting down the carrying figure and then adding the tens including any carried. She ignored this in favour of her own strategy which involved working in her head, adding the tens, adding the units, adjusting the tens as necessary and writing down the final answer. With this method she achieved 100 per cent success. (pp. 117–18)

When Eleanor and Joanna's teachers saw their work they were pleased and rewarded the girls with a tick and a smile, In neither case had the child done the work as intended. Nor indeed had Kerry but, unlike the others, she had actually been mathematically engaged with the task she was undertaking. In response to her efforts her teacher commented, 'Good, but could you just put the ones down there because one day you might forget them' (Cockburn, 1986, p. 118) You can appreciate the teacher's point of view, but what behaviour strategies were actually being reinforced when the girls presented their work to their teachers?

Were such findings particular to mathematics sessions? Consider Bennett, Desforges, Cockburn and Wilkinson's (1984) observations of 'free writing' tasks which were typical in the classes of 7-year-olds they observed. The usual format of the lessons was for the teacher to introduce a topic such as a recent television programme, 'volcanoes' or 'spiders', with much energy and enthusiasm. The salient features were discussed and key words were put on the blackboard. The children were then asked to write their own account, making it as exciting and dramatic as possible. Bennett et al. (1984) considered the range of work produced. At one end of the spectrum,

The children typically had limited memory for the stimulus of writing. They were slow to get to the task and the preliminaries of writing the date took up much of the time available. Performance on the task was slow; less than one word per minute ... They made persistent demands on the teacher's time ... Error rates were high even when copying words from the blackboard or from their word books. Despite this the children had every appearance of working hard. (p. 50)

In other cases the researchers observed,

The responses of these children were generally rapid and concentrated. Some produced 200–300 words in less than 45 minutes. In terms of quantity there seemed little scope for improving facility and, to that degree, further practice seemed unprofitable. More noteworthy was that the stories lacked organisation, structure and punctuation. (pp. 51–2)

In both situations the children seemed quite happy in their work. Their teachers' evaluations of the writing focused on aspects of effort, neatness and quantity. Rarely – if ever – was the content of the story mentioned. In other words, the teachers presented the tasks as if they were exercises designed to encourage creativity and imaginative writing. These qualities were rarely mentioned again. Instead the teachers tended to focus on presentation and story length when marking the work. Such tasks were very much part of the children's experience and there was little variation in the manner in which they were presented. What then do you think the pupils would be learning about the experience of writing? Would they see it as an opportunity for creativity and free expression as some of their teachers had originally intended?

A Step Back

Take a step back from the detail of classroom life and you can begin to appreciate the context of these activities. It has been suggested, for example, that, on average, teachers have 1,000 interpersonal exchanges each day (Jackson, 1968). Indeed, on the basis of work with fifty-eight primary teachers, the ORACLE team concluded that teachers spend 80 per cent of their classroom time actively interacting (Galton, Simon and Croll, 1980; Galton and Simon, 1980; Simon and Willcocks, 1981); 15 per cent of the time they are interacting with the whole class but, typically, 56 per cent of their time is spent interacting with individuals.

This may sound a lot but, in reality, it means very little time for each child, given that you may have thirty in your class. Moreover the interactions tended to be instructional, monitoring or routinely supervisory rather than probing, open-ended, higher-order questions. In other words, the teachers generally focused on behaviour and how to complete the task rather than on asking searching questions designed to encourage their pupils to think deeply about the work in hand.

Surveying primary schools in Leeds, Alexander (1991) noted that, in common with several other studies, there was a widespread commitment to 'group work, multiple curriculum focus teaching (different groups of children working simultaneously on different areas of the curriculum), thematic curriculum planning and delivery' (p. 4). Typically therefore a teacher selects a topic such as 'Houses and homes' or 'Colour and light' and devises a range of activities around the theme ensuring that as many curriculum areas and attainment targets are covered as possible. Alexander (1991) noted that there was a general tendency for these experiences to be 'dominated by writing and reading' (p. 3).

It is likely that many of these tasks will be practice tasks. Bennett et al. (1984), for example, noted that almost 60 per cent of tasks given to 7-year-olds involved going over familiar material; 25 per cent of the tasks introduced new ideas, procedures and skills and about 7 per cent required the application of problem-solving or restructuring (discovery) skills.

Approximately a third of the pupils' time will be spent in whole-class lessons (Alexander, Rose and Woodhead, 1992). The younger the children, the more likely they are to be sitting in groups rather than in traditional rows. That does not mean to say that they will be working collaboratively on a task. Rather a classroom 'group' most often means that children are working independently on a task which may, or may not, be the same as their colleagues' (Bennett, 1987; Tizard, Blatchford, Burke, Farquhar and Plewis, 1988). Much of the talk tends to be task-related, but Bennett et al. (1984) noted that, on average, 25 per cent has nothing whatsoever to do with work.

Taking Another Step Back

Schools and schooling are part of our everyday life for so many years that we rarely, if ever, step right back to consider them objectively. When we do so, we begin to see that there are several, often unexamined, demands made upon the individuals working within the system. Jackson (1968) draws attention to six of such demands which may have important consequences for the relationship between education and schooling. The first point is that, whether they like it or not, children have to attend school.

> In this regard students (i.e. pupils) have something in common with the members of two other of our social institutions that have involuntary attendance: prisons and mental hospitals. The analogy, though dramatic, is not intended to be shocking . . . Yet the school child, like the incarcerated adult, is, in a sense, a prisoner. He too must come to grips with the inevitability of his experience. He too must develop strategies for dealing with the conflict that frequently arises between his natural desires and interests on the one hand and institutional expectations on the other. (p. 9, parenthesis added)

Second, Jackson (1968) notes that classrooms are unusually crowded places. Although we may sometimes find ourselves in a crowded theatre or bus, 'only in schools do thirty or more people spend several hours of each day literally side by side' (p. 8). This is not an easy situation if you prefer to be alone or with a small group. Moreover, although the children quickly come to know each other at school, they are not encouraged to talk about their daily lives but rather to pursue the work they have been assigned.

The third feature of classroom life arises, at least in part, from the number of participants: the day is full of interruptions. For example,

> During group sessions irrelevant comments, misbehaviour, and outside visitors bearing messages often disrupt the continuity of the lesson. When the teacher is working individually with a student . . . petty interruptions, usually in the form of other students coming to the teacher for advice, are the rule rather than the exception . . . Students are expected to ignore these distractions or at least turn quickly back to their studies after their attention has been momentarily drawn elsewhere. (p. 16)

Interruptions also occur due to timetabling arrangements. Thus a picture may be half-finished or an understanding may be evolving just as it is time for break or assembly.

Delays are another feature of classroom life. There are many reasons for delays, but you only need to observe children for a short time to see how much waiting they do in lines, waiting for their work, waiting for a colleague to answer a question before the lesson can move on, and so on.

The fifth feature Jackson (1968) discusses is the denial of desire.

> The raised hand is sometimes ignored, the question to the teacher is sometimes brushed aside, the permission that is sought is sometimes refused . . . it is probably true that most of these denials are psychologically trivial when considered individually. But when considered cumulatively their significance increases. And regardless of whether or not they are justified, they make it clear that part of learning how to live in school involves learning how to give up desire as well as how to wait for its fulfillment. (p. 15)

And, finally, schools are basically evaluative settings and, as Jackson (1968) states, 'It is not only what you do there but what others think of what you do that is important' (p. 10).

Given all these constraints, it is perhaps surprising that anyone does any work, let alone learns anything, in a classroom setting, but indeed they do, as I indicated earlier. To a great extent this learning progress is due to teacher expertise, but the children also have a major part to play, although it may not always be in the way we would like or in the way we might imagine. In the next section we will examine the role of the pupil in classroom learning.

Becoming a Classroom Learner

James (1899) once graphically and amusingly described the classroom situation concluding, 'The mind of your enemy, the pupil is working away from you (the teacher) . . .' (p. 10, parenthesis added). In some cases this may well be a conscious rebellion on the part of the children, but research evidence suggests that pupils' classroom behaviour has largely arisen more naturally and may be seen as an intelligent adaptation to the classroom environment (Doyle, 1977).

From a very young age children construct meaning from their world and make deductions. It is not long before babies learn that if they cry someone will generally rush to attend to their needs. As they grow older, children continue to observe, listen and make deductions. Thus it is not uncommon for young children to apply their limited knowledge of the English language and come up with 'I goed . . .' 'We saw some mouses' and so on. In other words children are powerful pattern recognizers. The pupils I described earlier in the chapter were simply continuing previously established trends in their thinking. That is to say, they were imposing patterns – albeit not always desirable ones – on their experience. As a teacher you may find that such deductive behaviour is so unpredictable that it makes teaching extremely difficult. But it can also be seen as a challenge and, if you can encourage and capitalize on it, you have a real chance to nurture your pupils' independence and creativity. There are, however, other factors at work.

Dunn (1989) notes that from an early age children are very aware of other people and the impact of their behaviour. Ward and Rowe's (1985) observations demonstrate

> Several 4-year-olds working round a dough table. Each was working independently of the others. And each worked on his or her unique project. One made a ring and offered it to the play leader. She said, 'How lovely' and kept the ring on her finger. All the other children immediately abandoned their projects, made dough rings and presented them in the same fashion. (p. 3)

In other words, on discovering what they perceive their teacher wants, many pupils will endeavour to produce it. Indeed Marx and Winne (1981) noted that some primary pupils were so keen to divine what their teachers wanted that they 'picked up' messages from their teachers when, in fact, no such messages were transmitted. As King (1978) illustrates with reference to Clever Hans, the horse who could supposedly do addition sums,

> On one occasion I observed a girl 'counting' in the same way as the famous 'talking' horse, Clever Hans. 'Teacher asks Denise to count off six on the number cards pinned to the wall. She looks at the teacher not the cards, playing a finger on each card, following the teacher's nods and smiles; she pauses at five but goes on to six with a few more signals, which then stop, and so does she.' (p. 41)

Both now and in the past, you too have probably tried to please your teachers by working out what they want. And this desire may well have overridden your desire to learn about a subject. Doyle (1977) described this as 'exchanging performance for grades': 'What do I need to do to pass this essay?', 'How can I make Mr Jones praise me?' and so on. In other words, what can you do to get the desired reward be it an 'A' or a pat on the back? This type of motivation can induce you to work but, as we will discuss, does not necessarily guarantee learning.

Summary

- Classrooms are busy places; they are crowded and subject to many interuptions and delays in the work programme.
- Teachers are outnumbered, and although they spend a great deal of their time with individual children, they do not focus their attention on learning and understanding: they manage learners rather than learning.
- Not surprisingly, children often complete their work in ways not intended by the teacher.
- There is a preponderance of routine practice work.
- Children try very hard to please their teachers to gain their praise.
- Teachers often praise activities that have little to do with learning.
- Teachers and children have to adapt to this environment.

Work and Learning

It appears that schools may, in fact, exacerbate the above effects by stressing the importance of work. On arrival at school, for example, there is generally a great emphasis on 'work': 'Let's get down to work'; 'When you have finished your work you can . . .'; 'For homework tonight I would like you to . . .', and so on. Marshall (1988), however, argues that this encourages people to think in terms of a production line model where the product (e.g. a drawing or a story) is of paramount importance and the method of producing it is almost seen as irrelevant. Eleanor and Joanna at the beginning of the chapter, for example, presented a product and 'were paid for' their work with praise, but there was no mention of the processes by which they achieved the end result or of any learning that they might or might not have achieved, unlike Kerry, who actively thought about her tens and units, produced a less exemplary product in the teacher's terms and was 'paid' accordingly. Bennett et al. (1984) summarized this phenomenon so commonly seen in infant classrooms, 'Production pleased the teacher who cheered the child' (p. 63).

Desforges (1993a) suggests that the assessment system is essentially the clearest indication of what a teacher expects of her pupils and, if you recall, pupils are very keen to do what their teacher seems to want. As the following account illustrates, however, hard work and specific rewards do not guarantee appropriate understanding and learning.

The children in Mrs W's class were most industrious workers and cheerfully completed the tasks she presented. Over several weeks the focus in mathematics had been the development of counting skills. When Mrs W. asked her reception class, 'Why do you think we need numbers?', however, the following seemingly bizarre conversation took place,

Michelle: We need to count the numbers.
Simon: We need to draw the numbers.
Mrs W.:   Why do we need to draw the numbers?
Lisa: So we can copy them.
Mrs W.:   But why do we need numbers at all?
Lisa: So we can colour them in.
                    (Cockburn, 1986, p. 209)

In almost any reception class you will indeed see children counting, drawing, copying and colouring in numbers ... I am not condemning the many intermediate tasks required to give children experience in working with numbers. I am simply suggesting that, as practising teachers, it is perhaps important that you draw your pupils' attention to the longer-term aims of their work from time to time. This would focus the children's attention on the importance of learning to count in order to meet their needs and thus encourage them to apply themselves to committing numbers to memory. In other words you would be stressing the ultimate goal you were striving for and for which praise would be awarded. Indeed Desforges (1993b) argues: 'Children work hard in classrooms. Unfortunately, hard work is not necessarily associated with mindful learning ... the overarching characteristic of learning is the deliberate and committed pursuit of new competencies ... quality learning is mindful of the goal of learning; the goal is not incidental' (p. 3).

Before we move on to consider classroom situations where children are actively learning, it is important to stress that it is not necessarily always teachers' reward systems which encourage production at the expense of learning. For example, some behaviours are exacerbated by the situation in which pupils find themselves. In some subjects, for example, an element of competition may be observed. In part this may be due to the way the tasks are presented. It might also be due to the personal characteristics of some pupils. For example, on visiting an infant class at work on a mathematics scheme, very soon you are likely to hear something similar to Desforges and Cockburn (1987):

I did eight pages today and I got them all right.

I've only got six more pages to go.

I started there and I've done this page and now I'm on this page and I've only got one, two, three, four, five more pages to go.

I've got to get on so that I can get on to book six. (p. 101)

You might suppose that the teachers concerned put great pressure on these children to do as much mathematics as possible. 'On the contrary they persistently emphasized steady work and had to remind the children they were to do only as many exercises as they had been told' (ibid.). Had the books and pages not been graded and numbered perhaps things might have been different.

In brief, it can sometimes be helpful to view classrooms in terms of a production line model where the participants see the product of each individual task (e.g. a page of sums or a colouring) as the most important aspect of their work. With a change of effort and focus mindful learning might become a more prominent part of their schooling.

Active Classroom Learning

Is it possible for a teacher to teach something, ask and reward her pupils for a clear and specific response which encourages understanding and mindful learning and achieve 100 per cent success? Let us consider some work by Driver (1983):

A class of 13-year-old pupils had completed a 6-week sequence of work on 'molecules in motion'. At the end they were given some homework to use the idea of kinetic theory to explain a range of phenomena, including the expansion of mercury in a thermometer when it is heated. The following responses were among those that were given (by the children):

Mercury rises up a thermometer tube to get away from the heat. As soon as it has done (this) it stays till the heat has gone.

Mercury rises when it is heated because of a substance in the mercury that when heated is pushed up the thermometer.

Mercury rises up a thermometer when it is heated because it gets hot and the particles move away from the heat and up the thermometer.

Mercury likes to be cool so when it is heated the particles are trying to get away from the heat, so they move up as it's the only place it can go.

When mercury is heated it pushes the particle further away, thus the mercury's mass becomes bigger and it climbs up the thermometer giving a temperature reading.

Heat is making the particles expand, they now need more space to move and so they push upwards making the mercury rise as well. (p. 43, first parenthesis added)

Here we have a real case of active learners. As Desforges (1993a) observes, 'Children it seems, are well endowed as thinkers. In whichever domain we examine we see evidence of children taken by meaning. This is not necessarily *our* meaning or *the* meaning but *some* meaning as they engage with their environment' (p. 11). Nevertheless how did such a variation in responses arise? After all, the children had all received the same six-week programme. Examination of some younger pupils at work gives some insight into the range of responses.

Consider the work of first school pupils, Gavin and Michael. Gavin was given the following workcard:

> Make 5
>
> △ △ △
>
> Make 7
>
> ○ ○

In response to the instruction 'make 5' he drew a big circle round the three triangles and two small circles (Desforges and Cockburn, 1987, p. 69). Four-year-old Michael had become very familiar with the task of joining up dots to form letters of the alphabet such as ⦂∴. He was presented with a work sheet which began:

> 1   2   3   4   5
>
> •   •   •   •   •

'and his teacher required him to copy the numbers starting at the dot in each case. Michael joined up the dots' (Desforges and Cockburn, 1987, p. 68).

In neither case was the teacher impressed by the child's responses, and yet both children had used their intelligence. Their failure to respond in the standard manner expected by their teachers was almost certainly because they were making use of previous experience: in Gavin's case to follow instructions and in Michael's case to utilize a strategy his teacher had already taught him in another context.

Returning to the work of Driver (1983) described above: the children were given information on molecules in motion and then asked to apply it. In so doing – just as Gavin and Michael – they had to interpret the material presented, which, as they were free-thinking, unique individuals, led to a range of responses.

An example by Easley and Easley (1983) illustrates the type of responses children typically make when interpreting their work. Easley and Easley describe three Japanese children who were asked how many apples would be left if they started with a dish containing three and took two out. One child interpreted the work within the context of school learning, saying that one would be left and demonstrating the 'taking away' process. The second child analysed the material presented in terms of the situation and replied that all the apples would be left, pointing out that there was one in the dish and two others in the teacher's hand. And the third child applied learning from another context saying that it was an inconceivable problem because his mother had told him that he must never take more than one apple at a time.

Thus, it would appear, as Desforges (1993b) concludes, 'Sense making, for each child, is determined by their view of the relevant context' (p. 7). As a teacher, it may sometimes be difficult for you to ascertain within which context a child is interpreting a task, but preliminary findings of Desforges and Bristow (1993) suggest that pupils are more likely to apply 'out of school knowledge' (p. 38) in science tasks than in mathematics tasks.

Certainly it is acknowledged that effective learning frequently takes place when one can relate to a child's knowledge and understanding (Froebel, 1887; Montessori, 1912; Steiner, 1926). This, however, may be easier said than done. Consider a straightforward dialogue such as the following in a reception class,

> Paul was doing some work on floating and sinking when his teacher presented him with one of those plastic, practice golf balls with holes in it.
>
> Teacher: If we put this into the water do you think it will float or sink?
> Paul: Sink.
> Teacher: Why?
> Paul: Because the water will go in the holes.
> Teacher: What do you think would happen if I wrapped it up in cling film?
> Paul: What's cling film?
> Teacher: It's the stuff you wrap your sandwiches up in.
> Paul: It would sink.
>   . . .
> Teacher: Why do you say that?
> Paul: Because the weight of the sandwiches would have weighed it down.
>   (Cockburn, 1992, pp. 19–20)

Again, here is a child who was thinking in a reasonable and logical manner but, if such crossed wires can occur in such a short dialogue, what hope has a teacher with thirty such brains translating everything she says into their own personal understanding? And yet Fisher (1990) points out: 'If a child's intuitive ideas remain unquestioned and unexamined they can hamper the development of understanding in science and other areas of a child's experience' (p. 220).

As a teacher you will need to be aware that each and every one of your pupils will have a wide range of experiences which they may call upon and apply to the task in hand. If they misuse them then future academic progress may be endangered.

Matching and Task Presentation

Consideration of the above suggests that, for appropriate learning to take place, a teacher needs to appreciate each pupil's understanding and knowledge and then provide tasks which acknowledge these and stimulate opportunities for further learning. Indeed Ausubel (in Ausubel, Novak and Hanesian, 1978) concluded: 'If I had to reduce all of educational psychology to just one principle I would say this: the most important single factor influencing learning is what the learner already knows. Ascertain this and teach him accordingly' (p. iv).

How successful are teachers in providing tasks which encourage appropriate learning? Returning to the work of Bennett et al. (1984), of 417 tasks observed, 43 per cent were matched to the children's learning needs in mathematics and 40 per cent in language. In other words, two out of every five tasks presented were considered highly suitable for the individuals for whom they were designed.

Interestingly levels of matching were approximately the same whatever a pupil's position in class (i.e. 2/5 tasks were matched). In cases of mismatch, however, high-achieving pupils were far more likely to be given tasks which were too easy and low-achieving children were more likely to be given tasks which were too hard. Those in the middle were sometimes given tasks which were too easy and sometimes given tasks which were too hard. What does this suggest? How might the pupils be affected?

Further analysis of the data showed that success in matching tended to be higher in new tasks rather than the more familiar practice tasks.

Considering tasks along another dimension provides further insight into classroom teaching and learning. Prior to each mathematics task, Desforges and Cockburn (1987) asked teachers their intended aims. These were then classified in terms of procedural tasks (i.e. those requiring pupils to carry out standard calculations or specific procedures such as '3 + 1 = ') and conceptual tasks (i.e. those requiring the application of mathematical understanding. This might involve a problem such as, 'If I had three sweets and Betty had two, how many would we have altogether?') Some 80 per cent of the teachers' aims for tasks included a conceptual component, and yet 96 per cent of the time teachers actually taught procedures. In other words teachers frequently intended that their mathematics tasks should further, for example, their pupils' understanding, and yet, almost without exception, they focused the children's attention on how to follow a specific set of rules. Why? Why did these experienced teachers have so little success in translating the conceptual component of their aims into practice? Does it matter? The answer depends on your philosophy, but I would argue that many of the routines one is taught as a child are not required in adult life. Personally I would rather understand basic principles so that I can adapt my knowledge to suit situations than try and dredge up long-forgotten formulae and apply them – perhaps incorrectly – to a possibly inappropriate situation.

Returning to the teachers: if they said that they were striving for pupil understanding why did they not present their tasks in an appropriate manner? Part of the reason lies in the wide variation in pupils' previous knowledge, understanding and interpretations of the work as discussed above. This may further be illustrated by considering a lesson on spheres with a class of 7- and 8-year-olds.

> Mrs G. set out to introduce her third year infants to the names of three-dimensional shapes. She had the children sitting in a circle on the carpet. They had established that a globe was sphere-shaped. A globe had been passed round. Its spherical properties had been pointed out and felt.

> Mrs G.: . . . Now can anyone else tell me something that's a sphere? Adam? (who has his hand up)
> Adam: Square

> At this point Mrs G. recalled, 'I was ever so surprised he said that . . .'
> Seconds later, in giving a further example of an everyday object that is a sphere, Ben offered 'Half the world.' Mrs G. noted

>> . . . oh, dear! I cannot get into that now . . . I decided to pass over his suggestion for the sake of the rest of them.

> There followed a ten-second period of acceptable responses for sphere-shaped objects and then Samantha suggested, 'a circle'. Mrs G. thought.

>> Help! This is going to be a lot more difficult than I thought. (Desforges and Cockburn, 1987, p. 113)

Another part of the answer for teachers' lack of success in promoting a conceptual approach lies in 'comfortable ways to learn'.

Consider how you typically come to understand ideas and concepts. Do you try things out practically (e.g. 'playing' with a new computer), discuss the issue with others or mull it over for some time? Depending on the subject matter, a combination of all three often proves most effective. Indeed Haylock and Cockburn (1989) consider that 'Mathematical activity involves the manipulation of concrete materials, symbols, language and pictures . . . connections between these four types of experience constitute important components of mathematical understanding' (p. 13). But following her observations of a wide variety of mathematics lessons, Cockburn (1986) noted: 'When practical work or discussions were in progress they [the children] tended to wriggle. As soon as their teachers focussed on specific tasks, however, they generally seemed to settle down and become more attentive' (p. 205).

Gelman and Gallistel (1978) also observed that if young children were presented with tasks beyond their capabilities they became less co-operative. Davis and McKnight (1976) went so far as to suggest that pupils will subvert a task which makes unfamiliar demands on them. In response to a concern that so many ninth-grade algebra teachers presented their pupils with routine textbook exercises, the researchers took over the teaching of a maths class with a view to developing pupils' mathematical understanding. They met with considerable resistance from the children and commented: 'One thing was clear from all this: it is no longer a mystery why so many teachers and so many textbooks present ninth-grade algebra as a rote algorithmic subject. The pressure on you to do exactly that is formidable!' (p. 282).

Adopting the children's perspective, Fisher (1990) presents the following suggestion:

> Related to fatigue is the problem of overload. This may be the result of the child being asked to do too many things at once. In writing for example they may be expected to get their ideas right and in good order, and at the same time to attend to punctuation, grammar, spelling and handwriting . . .
>
> One cause of conflict may be confusion in the child's mind about what he is being asked to do. Ambiguity can be stressful. 'What are we supposed to be doing?' 'How do we begin?' 'What's it all about?' There should be a clear focus on the process involved or the task to be achieved. (p. 242)

In other words it may be that children resist sessions which, in their view, do not have clearly defined aims which enable them quickly to translate performance for grades.

Returning to the production line model: although teachers are good at matching work to children's needs, both they and their pupils tend towards tasks which have an immediate and obvious product (e.g. a story or a diagram) rather than striving for longer-term, less obvious, goals (e.g. an understanding and appreciation of the concept of a number). Despite this, learning does take place, but there is almost certainly much effort and potential wasted.

Your Challenge as a Teacher

Every child, teacher, school and classroom situation is different. People's behaviour can never be entirely predictable. This makes your job as a teacher exceedingly difficult but by no means impossible. Indeed if you can see it as an intellectually demanding and stimulating challenge, so much the better. There is no one way to teach, but there are several factors which can increase your chances of success as a teacher. Many of these will be discussed in subsequent chapters.

The important point to remember is that classroom life is rarely how it appears at first sight and that, as a successful teacher, you should endeavour to maximize the link between classroom work and pupil learning. To do this you need to adopt a research-like stance to your teaching. In other words you need to gain as much insight and understanding of classrooms, pupils, work, learning, yourself and the relationships between them as possible. Fail to do so and you will remain blind to the reality of classroom life and your success as a teacher will be diminished.

The key is certainly to read books such as this but, equally important, it is vital to observe and analyse what goes on in your and other classrooms as objectively as possible. Stand back from the action now and again, and observe how your pupils are actually spending their time: are they actively engaged in learning or are they working towards a final short-term product with little thought of the process? Do they respond better to some types of tasks than to others? What do they do when they encounter a problem? Equally important, how do you behave? Do you endeavour to encourage understanding? When, and what, do you praise?

Finally, classrooms are extremely complex environments. There is no magic formula or ideal way to teach. Indeed, Bolton (1989) points out: 'The more successful we are in specifying the causes of a particular action, the less generally applicable are the conditions we discover, for they will be peculiar to the person at the time of action.'

In brief, therefore, a crucial process throughout is for you to reflect on your reading, observations and practice and use the information to create and refine opportunities for classroom learning.

Summary

- Children and teachers work very hard in classrooms, but the work often does not lead to learning.
- This is partly because children seem to see classroom work as a production line: their goal is to complete their quota on time. Because they focus on work management, they frequently miss the deeper conceptual purpose of their activities.
- Much of the work in classrooms would not in any event promote learning. This is because
  - a significant proportion of it is too easy or too difficult for the children;
  - some of it is poorly designed and does not require the sorts of effort teachers intend.

- These problems arise because teachers are immersed in a welter of events and information. Teachers do not spend much time diagnosing children's attainments. Diagnosis is extremely difficult to carry out in classrooms.
- Children do not help: tasks which are demanding of learning often cause classroom management problems.

Editor's Commentary

This chapter raises some fundamental questions about classrooms as places for learning. It should be emphasized that the teachers whose work was reported here were considered by their peers to be exemplary. It seems that some classroom management processes actually work against children gaining a deeper understanding of academic subjects. If classroom work is to lead to children gaining such understanding, then several questions have to be answered. These include:

- How can teachers in busy classrooms obtain reliable and valid information about children's understanding and attainment?
- How can classroom work be designed so that it is conducive to learning progress?
- How can the common children's metaphor of classroom work as production line work be changed to one which is more appropriate for higher levels of understanding?

It is important that you do not take life in your classroom for granted. Evident busyness and a good working atmosphere are very pleasing to a young teacher, and these factors frequently fool parents and headteachers into believing learning is taking place. But is it? The themes in this chapter can be pursued in the following areas of school-based work:

- Take time to observe a range of children carefully as they carry out your work. Talk to them about the work. Do they interpret it the way you intended?
- Use some of the references in this chapter to find out how to carry out diagnostic interviewing. Carry out this technique on a range of children across the curriculum. Is their work too hard, too easy or about right for them?
- With their agreement, observe some teachers and keep a record of how they use praise. What do they praise? How is this related to children's learning?
- How do teachers assess children's work? How helpful is the assessment in improving the child's understanding?

The ideas in this chapter are closely linked to concepts in other chapters. The style of classroom management and the role the pupils are expected to play have a critical influence on the quality of learning experience. These themes are considered as follows:

- The management of order in a classroom has a particular impact on learning. This is discussed in chapter 10.
- The more autonomous pupils are, the more they strive for understanding. This matter is considered in chapter 11.
- Assessment in the classroom can defeat or enhance understanding. The technicalities of good quality assessment are described in chapters 16 and 17.
- Well-managed group work is recognized as a forum for higher-quality learning. The nature of such work is described in chapter 8.
- Ways in which children can be given greater strategic control over their learning are described in chapter 5.
- Ways of thinking about and meeting the needs of a wide range of pupils are considered in chapter 12.

FURTHER READING

There are several books and articles which would provide useful follow-up reading but the four below will cover many of the key issues between them.

Bennett, S. N., Desforges, C. W., Cockburn, A. D. & Wilkinson, B. (1984). *The quality of pupil learning experiences*. London: Erlbaum.

In this book Bennett and his colleagues provide a detailed discussion of the language and mathematics tasks first school teachers set their pupils. They also describe how to conduct interviews with your pupils to ascertain whether the work they are doing is appropriate.

Desforges, C. W. and Cockburn, A. D. (1987). *Understanding the mathematics teacher*. Lewes, England: Falmer Press.

This is a detailed study of seven first school teachers and their pupils during mathematics sessions. It provides in-depth analyses of classroom processes and gives valuable insights into many facets of teaching.

Fisher, R. (1990). *Teaching children to think*. Oxford, England: Blackwell.

A stimulating and readable book which considers the nature of thinking and thinking skills.

Marshall, H. H. (1988). Work or learning: Implications of classroom metaphors. *Educational Researcher*, 17, 9–16.

This is an important article which explores the distinction between work and learning, which is often a hidden aspect of classroom life.

5

Learning Out of School

Charles Desforges

Editor's Overview

In school we plan to teach children usable knowledge. There is a big difference between knowing something and being able to use that knowledge appropriately in any context. It turns out that people have a lot of difficulty using the knowledge they acquire in schools. Teaching knowledge utilization is a major challenge for teachers.

In this chapter I analyse this problem and suggest what teachers might do to solve it. I show that there is a chain of circumstances which link knowledge acquisition to knowledge utilization: if any link in the chain fails then knowledge will not be usable.

I show that teachers have to work deliberately to ensure that pupils acquire

- a lively knowledge base
- applications strategies
- positive 'can-do' dispositions.

I compare school learning with out-of-school learning and show how important teamwork, the use of cognitive tools and the use of the situation are in the latter context for learning.

Finally I discuss the long road of professional development involved if teachers are to rise to the challenge of teaching knowledge utilization.

At first sight it may seem strange that in a book on teaching we consider learning out of school. I intend in this chapter to show that, rather than being an aside or a distraction, understanding learning out of school has important implications for planning learning in schools. An obvious starting point in drawing the links between learning in and out of school is the recognition that a central objective of schooling is to prepare children for their lives after school. Material we teach in school is expected to be usable in a range of contexts in pupils' domestic and working lives. Teachers attempt to teach knowledge and skills which are usable. Furthermore, they try to teach general skills of learning and adaptability so that their pupils will be able to learn in situations which may materialize in their adult lives.

Any serious attempt to teach knowledge utilization is more likely to be successful if the teacher understands the contexts in which that knowledge is likely to be applied. Of course this cannot be done at any degree of specificity. It is extremely difficult and indeed probably unwise to anticipate the working lives and conditions of today's school children. My primary school teachers, for example, could not possibly have imagined the growth of miniaturized information technology and the massive impact which this has had on everyday and working lives. It is equally unwise for schools to prepare children for particular jobs. Most of the skilled trades which were prevalent when I was a child have simply disappeared from the industrial scene.

The issue of knowledge utilization is not centrally a matter of teaching children specific skills of knowledge application. It is a matter of helping them in a general preparation to be adaptive learners. This, as I shall show, has proved to be a very difficult objective to attain. And yet, somewhat paradoxically, I shall also show that before children come to school they seem to be quite naturally adaptive learners.

In this chapter I will discuss children's learning out of school, compare school settings with out-of-school settings, and consider how best teachers might prepare children to be adaptive in the utilization of school knowledge.

Children before School

In many respects the achievements of the pre-schooler are staggering. They are most clearly seen in their mastery of the child's home tongue. A language is an extremely complex and abstract communication system. Yet the 5-year-old's grasp of this system is very similar to that of an adult speaker. Children starting school have a large, active vocabulary. They understand and can use syntactical structures such as plurals, possessives, tenses, active and passive moods and negatives. They communicate effectively with adults and with their peers. It is common experience that 4- and 5-year-olds 'talk down' to babies or pets. This capacity for shaping a message for an audience has been explored in laboratory settings. Gelman and Shatz (1977), for example, asked a sample of 4-year-olds to introduce a new toy to younger children and to adults. The 4-year-olds used longer sentences and more complex grammatical constructions when they spoke to the adults that when they talked to 2-year-olds.

Pre-schoolers are very creative with language. Chukovsky (1963) (reported in Smith and Cowie, 1991) recorded 4-year-olds generating rhymes:

> I'm a flamingo
> look at at my wingo.

And they enjoy the incongruities of language. Again, Chukovsky recorded the 5-year-old who said to her mother, 'I can play the piano by ear' – and then, laughing, banged her ear to the keyboard.

The 5-year-old's grasp of the complex and abstract system of language is powerful, purposive and creative. It has been acquired extremely rapidly. It is important to consider how this learning may have been achieved. Some of the best insights into this process come from the study of children's errors as they use spoken language. These show that children play a very creative role in learning. They do not merely reproduce what they hear. They say 'foots' instead of 'feet', 'sheeps' instead of sheep and 'runned' instead of 'ran'. Since it is extremely unlikely that they ever hear these constructions, we may conclude that they are inventions or overgeneralizations of regular patterns. Overgeneralizations are also seen when children, for example, apply the word 'dog' to many or all, four-legged small mammals (cats or sheep for example).

But as young children appear to be active in creating patterns or overgeneralizations, they seem to be equally active in repairing the errors generated in this way. Clarke (1990) has reviewed studies which show these active 'repair' processes. For example, at about 2 years of age children begin to ask incessantly for the names of things. Once this process starts, children begin to refuse to name things for which they do not have the words. Additionally, they stop overextending the words they already have. For example, when they meet the word 'sheep' they stop using the word 'dog' for sheep – although they may still use the word 'dog' for cats.

Other studies emphasize young children's creative capacities. With an initially small vocabulary they talk about many things. Clark (1990) exemplifies how they do this by coining terms. She records cases including a 2-year-old who invented the term 'penny-teacher' for a teacher at Sunday School who took the collection, and the child who invented 'oil spoon' to distinguish it from the 'egg-spoon', the former being used to take cod-liver oil.

In contrast to coining, young children will reject words if they already have a serviceable label. As Clark (1990) notes, 'if an adult asks of a two year old's toy bear, "Is that your toy?" a typical response is, "No, it's a bear"' (p. 15). A moment's thought and readers will be able to build their own catalogue of young children's inventive language use.

Overall we can see, in the way young children learn their home tongue, processes of creativity, invention, categorization and the application of logic to decisions. For example, we may assume the implicit reasoning; *if* there are more than one you add -s; *therefore* one foot, two foot*s*. Young children appear to learn their home tongue through the application of natural capacities to see or create patterns and hypotheses about language. They also appear to have the capacity to apply logic to testing and revising their own creations.

Pre-schoolers' achievements are by no means limited to learning their mother tongue. Many studies have shown that they have made considerable progress in understanding mathematics as well as language. Carpenter and Moser (1982) showed that 4- and 5-year-olds could work out word problems providing the quantities were small. For example, when asked, 'If you had three sweets and I gave you two more how many would you have altogether?', most 5-year-olds had no problem in giving the correct answer. They had similar success with substraction word problems in the same number range. In one of my studies I explored young children's understanding of sharing as a mathematical process (Desforges and Desforges, 1980). I gave them, for example, three dolls and six Smarties and asked them to share out the Smarties to make it fair to the dolls. Three-year-olds found this easy, dealing out the Smarties like playing cards. I then gave them two dolls and seven Smarties. Again, they found this easy. They insisted that I, or preferably they, had the spare Smartie. When I pressed them, however, they said that they would need an extra Smartie or they would have to cut up the Smartie into equal pieces. The children had a clear, practical grasp of apportioning quantities.

Another instance of children's acquired sense of quantity was revealed in a series of studies by Gelman and Gallistel (1978), who showed how children gradually made sense of the business of counting. At first they seem to treat counting as a naming game, i.e. the numbers simply name objects – but in a specific order. Later they realize that counting is related to quantity. You count by pointing out each item in a set and saying its number name. This intellectual realization comes before they sort out the physical skills of organizing their pointing behaviour. For example, when asked how many dots there are in a 3×3 matrix, 4-year-olds know that counting will give the answer, but they frequently point off the items in such an unsystematic way that they get the count wrong.

In mathematics as well as language, there is ample evidence that children make sense of their experience in the world. And just as with language, young children have been shown to be creative with quantity relationships. Groen and Resnick (1977) taught 4- and 5-year-olds to add up by a process of 'counting out and counting all', i.e. to add three to four you set out three objects, then set out four objects and then count the lot. The researchers then gave the children lots of practice with these sums using small quantities. It quickly became evident that the children had invented faster ways of getting to the answers. Their initial common invention avoided putting out the first quantity. The children put out the second quantity and counted that on from the first given number. For example, to add one+five they put out five objects and counted on from one. The second elaboration from the children involved avoiding putting out the larger quantity. The children put out the smaller quantity and counted on from the larger, i.e. to calculate 'four+two' they put out the two and counted 'four, five, six'. In these ways they invented economical methods to replace the taught procedures. The second invention rests on the assumption that $x+y = y+x$, i.e. that it does not matter in what order you add up the numbers. I am not claiming here that the children had invented a general law of numbers. Rather I am saying that, from the experience of their practice they had spotted a relationship and made pragmatic use of it. That is to say, that from the study of Resnick and Groen we may infer that the children had seen that, say two+three gives the same answer as three+two, and in the task they had been given they worked out how to make good use of that observation.

Given their achievements with language and quantities, it will hardly come as a surprise to note that young children are adept at applying their natural learning capacities to their social surroundings, to the feelings, intentions and desires of those in their family circle and to the social rules and knowledge which govern or guide our behaviour. Until recently these matters had not been extensively studied in private family settings, where children's achievements would be most in evidence. Increasingly however, researchers are building a detailed understanding of the ways in which children engage in social life, learn to understand its rules and endeavour to manipulate the possibilities. Dunn (1989) has reviewed some of this work and points out that, 'from early in the second year children respond to expressions of distress, annoyance or frustration in their parents with practical attempts to comfort, support or help – attempts that become in the course of the second and third years increasingly effective and sophisticated' (p. 70). In the third year chiildren increasingly ask questions about people's inner states of mind. 'A new curiosity about why people behave or feel the way they do is born' (ibid.).

Young children reveal their grasp of social understanding in several different ways. By the third year they invoke social rules in disputes, whether it be to justify their own actions or to get a sibling into trouble. At the same age they are selective about which jokes to tell whom. With their siblings they joke about 'scatological or disgusting issues' whilst with their mothers they 'tease about whether they love them' (Dunn, 1989, p. 72). The ability to invoke rules or select jokes indicates not only an understanding of rules as such but also a grasp of the logic of application. For example, their implicit logic of joke censoring might be seen to run as follows

Mummy does not like disgusting statements;
This statement is disgusting;
Therefore I will not express this statement to Mummy.

Since children can hardly be born with a knowledge and understanding of specific social rules, we are left to assume that they learn them very rapidly and then apply them as appropriate.

It would be very easy to extend this catalogue of the learning achievements of very young children. There is increasingly documented evidence of their capacity to make sense of their physical and social world, of communication and symbol systems and of social rules and relationships, and of their ability to utilize this knowledge to meet their purposes.

Torrey (1973) reported a case of an American pre-schooler who evidently taught herself to read. The child lived in most unpromising material circumstances. Adults in her environment denied teaching her. Researchers assumed that she had taught herself, evidently from watching television. Clark (1976) has reported in detail on several cases of precocious reading achievements. In some of these instances the parents had a deliberate policy to teach reading. Even so, fluent reading at age 3 is impressive. In other cases in Clark's study, however, the children had made progress in the face of parental disinterest or even against their parents' expressed wishes.

In parallel with beginning reading, many young children take an interest in writing. Gardner (1980) has shown that from the age of two some children categorize certain activities as 'writing' and, in a scribble, try to imitate the flow of script. Whilst the limitations of the writing of pre-schoolers are perfectly obvious, their achievements should not be underestimated. They have started to impose sense on an exceedingly abstract symbol system. They make progress in regard to social conventions and to specific symbols. Occasionally their achievements are outstanding. Bissex (1980), for example, has documented the progress of her own son as he, effectively, taught himself to write.

Summary

- The breadth of young children's attainments is impressive. Children are not specialists. The children who learn to speak their home tongue are the same children who are understanding and manipulating their social world and coming to a grasp of quantities and their relationships. Implicit in these achievements are capacities for curiosity, creativity, invention, exploration, logic, organization and purposeful knowledge application. And these capacities are evident in the great majority of pre-school children. They do not appear to be the special gifts of a select few.
- Of course it needs to be emphasized that these attainments should not be overestimated. Richard Fox in chapter 3 has discussed some of the limitations on early learning related to development. And there are huge differences between individuals in the scope and speed of their learning in any domain. Suffice it to say that there is plenty of evidence to show that pre-schoolers have the potential at least to be adaptive learners.

Learning out of School

School-aged children obviously learn a great deal out of school hours. From learning to ride a bike to acquiring highly efficient skills on the latest computer games, their achievements are obvious and comprehensive. For the purposes of this chapter, however, I want to focus on achievements which are very similar to those acquired in the school curriculum. In particular I will focus on mathematics, where there is increasing evidence that children with very little schooling acquire some impressive computational competence.

Studies have shown that children acquire competence in domestic or commercial transactions, the latter in particular in countries where children have to be money earners at an early age (Saxe, 1988). Some of the most carefully documented of these studies have been conducted on young street traders in Brazil (Nunes, Schliemann and Carraher, 1993; Saxe, 1988; Carraher, Carraher and Schliemann, 1985).

As Saxe (1988) stresses, street trading in Brazil is an economic necessity for a large number of urban youngsters. Trading involves purchasing the goods from a variety of wholesalers, pricing the goods to sell in various units (i.e. single items or multiple item packs) and selling, which involves calculating the price of complex purchases and the change due to customers. An added complication is that Brazil's inflation rate at the time of these studies was 250 per cent per annum. Selling had to make not only a straight profit but a profit which allowed for the inflated costs of restocking.

As Nunes et al. (1993) point out, street traders have to perform a large number of calculations, usually without recourse to pencil and paper and involving multiplication, addition and substraction. Nunes and her colleagues studied several of these children in the working environment of their street stalls. Of the children studied, only one had had more than four years of schooling. The children's capacities were tested in normal trading transactions for example.

Customer/researcher: How much is one coconut?
Trader: Thirty-five.
Customer: I'd like ten. How much is that?
Trader: Three will be one hundred and five; with three more that will be two hundred and ten [pause]. I need four more. That is . . . [pause] three hundred and fifteen. I think that's three hundred and fifty.

In all, sixty-three problems were set in this way to five young street traders aged between 9 and 15. Collectively they got sixty-two of these correct – a success rate of 98 per cent.

In a study by Saxe (1988) it was shown, perhaps not surprisingly, that older children were more accurate in their calculations than younger children for a given level of schooling. But for a given age, amount of schooling made little difference to the accuracy of calculating with money bills. It should be emphasized that these calculations involved very large numbers because of the effects of inflation. A box of candy, for example, at the time of the study cost 20,000 cruzieros.

These studies show the very considerable power of youngsters to learn and apply complex mathematical procedures to a very high degree of accuracy. When these achievements are added to those of pre-schoolers as catalogued in the previous section, it might lead us to expect that teaching children to acquire and utilize knowledge should be extremely easy. In fact, nothing is further from the truth.

Knowledge Utilization

In the event, people have very great difficulty in utilizing knowledge learned in one context on problems met in another context. Employers frequently complain that young workers cannot solve apparently simple problems met in the workplace. These limitations are well documented. In one national mathematics survey, for example, it was found that 80 per cent of 12-year-olds could quickly and correctly divide 225 by 15. However, only 40 per cent could solve the problem, 'Suppose a gardener had 225 bulbs to place equally in fifteen flower beds, how many would be put in each bed?' Most of the failing pupils did not know which number operation to use, although they were capable of conducting the routine once the appropriate procedure was named.

These difficulties are somewhat surprising. Detailed studies increase the puzzle. In one study, by Säljö and Wyndhamn (1990), some Swedish 12- and 13-year-olds were asked to find the cost of posting a parcel, given the package, some scales and a simple post office postage chart showing, for example, that items not exceeding 20 g could be sent for 2 Kroner, those not exceeding 100 g could be sent for 4 Kroner and so on. All the pupils were good readers and capable of basic skills in mathematics. Some were accomplished at mathematics. Nevertheless many of them failed to find the correct postage rate and most of them had a great deal of trouble with the task. The higher the academic attainment of the pupils, the more roundabout were the problem-solving procedures. Classroom knowledge of mathematics was imported into this apparently simple practical problem. Some pupils, for example, plotted a graph of the postage chart and made careful interpolations of it. They clearly had considerable difficulty in knowing which, if any, aspects of their schooling knowledge could be applied to the 'real-world' problem.

The Brazilian street traders in the Nunes et al. (1993) study had a similar difficulty, only, as it were, in the reverse direction. Following their 98 per cent success in calculations at their stalls Nunes et al. set the children a formal arithmetic test on which the items were exactly the same as those met in the street, only reduced to the arithmetic operation. For example, instead of asking on the street, 'What is the cost of ten coconuts at thirty-five each?' the trader was given pencil and paper and asked 'What is ten×thirty-five?' On these tests the children had a great deal more difficulty. Their average score fell from 98 per cent on the street to 37 per cent in the 'school test'.

At first sight the Brazilian and Swedish children have reverse problems. The Brazilians did not appropriately apply 'real-world' maths to 'school' problems, whilst the Swedish children tried to apply 'school-maths' inappropriately to a 'real-world' problem. However, the issue could be expressed another way. We could say that both groups of children failed to apply knowledge learned in one context to a problem set in another context. The expectation generally held by teachers is that problems may be said to have a core or a family resemblance. If the core skill is attained, pupils should spot similar problems in their resemblances and be able to solve them. In the Brazilian case, for example, the core operation at the heart of both the street and the classroom problem was the multiplication of ten×thirty-five.

There is a very great deal of evidence that calls into question this view of knowledge utilization. Problems, it appears, may be defined at least as much by their context as by their so-called core attributes. Also, it seems, when we learn something, the context in which we learn it becomes an important part of what we learn. It is no simple thing to separate what we know from the context in which we learn it. Some psychologists (e.g. Brown, Collins and Duguid, 1989) argue that knowledge is fundamentally 'situated'. This means that knowledge is an inseparable part of the activity, context and culture in which it is generated and used.

This view means that material taught in the classrooms is embedded in the culture of the classroom work. Recall that Säljö's children, when presented with a straightforward problem, immediately reached for their graph paper. We might infer that the problem as they saw it was determined much more by the demands of their maths lesson than the demands of the postal service. The children, it appears, had learned classroom working practices rather than a capacity to search for a core attribute of the problem.

In one of my research studies I attempted to explore how young pupils used their knowledge to learn. In maths, science and English, pupils were taken forward in some work until they met, by design, a point of difficulty. They were then given a learning pack to help them forward. The pack consisted of practical apparatus, work cards and text which explained the way ahead. Whilst all the children were good readers and readily used the text in science and English, they almost completely ignored it in mathematics. In their view and experience, reading was not relevant to learning in mathematics (Desforges and Bristow, 1995). Their view of what counted as applicable knowledge was clearly framed by their classroom experience.

If classroom working practices and context impose limitations on children's capacity to utilize knowledge on real-world problems we might expect to find it very difficult to teach children how to apply school knowledge. This is indeed the case. Teachers have commonly used a variety of methods to promote pupils' knowledge application. These approaches have included project work, investigations, problem-solving exercises, teaching problem solving, and more generally, teaching strategies for thinking and learning (Nickerson, Perkins and Smith, 1985). Despite these efforts it is difficult to find any evidence of generalized learning achieved through these means. This conclusion is evident in reviews of research from many subject areas including mathematics (Kameenui and Griffin, 1989), science (Halpern, 1992) and economics (Voss, 1987). If teachers are to help children make the most of the knowledge they acquire in classrooms, clearly a greater understanding of the problem will be necessary.

Understanding Knowledge Utilization

To increase the likelihood of successful knowledge application it is necessary to explore in a little more detail how, at the level of the individual learner, knowledge application breaks down. Second, it is important to understand the key differences between the context of the classroom and the context of out-of-school demands. Third, it is essential to grasp how teachers might develop their professional skills in this aspect of teaching.

In regard to individuals, Prawat (1989) has provided a useful framework for understanding what might go wrong when pupils fail to apply knowledge. Knowledge application might fail, argues Prawat, when

- the pupils do not possess the knowledge they are assumed to have, or
- the knowledge has been acquired but its relevance to a new problem is not seen, or
- the relevance of available knowledge is seen but an application strategy is not available, or
- the strategy is available but the learner lacks the self-confidence or attitude to make the effort to succeed.

Each of these points may be seen as a link of a chain. If the chain breaks at any point, knowledge application will fail. Each link is worthy of consideration.

When children fail on a novel problem we often assume, because the relevant part of the curriculum has been covered, that we have a failure of knowledge application on our hands. It might in fact be that the children simply do not have the knowledge in the first place. It is one thing for teachers to cover a curriculum. It is another entirely for the pupils to have securely learned the concepts and skills covered. Modern curricula are very wide and teachers are most anxious to cover the whole scope. Coverage rather than learning is a central expressed anxiety for many teachers (Desforges and Cockburn, 1987). It seems obvious, but one of the most important factors in failure to apply knowledge is failure to grasp the material in the first place.

The second link is equally commonly broken. Pupils learn basic skills and routines but they do not learn to see their relevance to novel situations. Recall the pupils who could not see the relevance of their division skills to the gardener's problem cited earlier. This link is broken because too much time is spent on routine practice tasks in the basic concepts, and not enough time is spent on learning how to recognize their relevance to new problems. Bennett, Desforges, Cockburn & Wilkinson (1984) for example, observed very large numbers of routine practice tasks and low proportions of problem-solving tasks in a sample of English primary schools. Through practice, knowledge may become compartmentalized and therefore difficult to apply.

In regard to the third link, the appropriate knowledge is possessed, its relevance is seen but a way of using the knowledge in the particular problem does not come to mind. By way of illustration I can call on plenty of personal experiences. In one instance I was helping a farm labourer to build a barn in a remote area. We dug the footings for one wall and needed to mark out a right angle to dig the next trench. We had no surveying equipment. I recalled that you can make a right angle triangle using sides in the ratio three to four to five. I could not, however, for the life of me think how to do that on a wild hillside. Knowledge application needs a breadth of general experience or some considerable inventiveness or imagination if it is to be successful. In regard to the barn you may be reassured – and certainly the farmer was – to learn that the labourer had anticipated the problem and brought up twelve lengths of bailer twine with which we fashioned the triangle we needed.

The final link in the chain refers to the personal adjustment of the learner in regard to problem solving. Some people are a lot more determined than others that they will solve problems presented to them. Some pupils become very anxious in the face of a problem, or they feel 'useless'. Some common responses to problems involve either impulsiveness (to get it over with) or avoidance. These unconstructive attitudes seem to be learned. Some children are perfectly confident in one subject and completely defeatist in another (Bristow and Desforges, 1992). This suggests that such attitudes are not natural properties of people. Rather, they are learned responses to previous experience.

Summary

- Although children appear to be naturally adaptive learners, on closer inspection research shows that they (and adults too for that matter) have

great difficulty in utilizing in one setting knowledge acquired in another setting. The learning setting is difficult to disconnect from the learning.
- Attempts to teach knowledge utilization have not been very successful. Any new approaches will have to be built on a better understanding of what is involved in knowledge utilization.
- Knowledge utilization may be seen to involve a chain of processes. If any link breaks, utilization will not occur. Teaching knowledge utilization means strengthening the links.

The links are:
- acquisition or initial learning
- seeing relevance
- having 'on-site' knowledge
- being determined to succeed and possessing good self-management skills.

Teaching Knowledge Utilization

A great deal can be done to strengthen the links in the processes of knowledge application and to minimize the problems indicated above. Three closely connected streams of teaching need to be enacted. It is necessary, simultaneously, to teach

- an active knowledge base
- application strategies
- a positive disposition.

Promoting an active knowledge base involves getting pupils to see the connectedness of ideas and concepts. This can be achieved through activities involving compare-and-contrast work, through brainstorming and through concept mapping. For example, pupils might attempt to compare and contrast the Romans and the Vikings seeking out what they had at difference or in common. A class might attempt to draw a diagram, or concept map, of the properties of an insect and compare it with their concept map of a mammal, for example.

Other ways of fostering lively interaction with ideas include debating, arguing, defending an unpopular case or giving explanations to other pupils. All these ideas have the objective of demanding from pupils that they not only know something but that they give a great deal of attention to what they know, how they organize what they know in their minds and how they relate what they know about one matter to what they know about other matters.

Brainstorming in particular, helps to promote a lively knowledge base. If the youngsters working on Säljö's parcel problem had been asked to list and compare all the different ways of finding the cost of posting a parcel, then perhaps they would not have such trouble with the postage chart.

Knowledge application strategies are deliberate intellectual processes used to guide work towards a goal. They come in different guises. They are sometimes called study skills or work skills or problem-solving processes. Whatever they are called, they are intended to help the individual organize knowledge to reach a particular point, whether that be to solve a problem or learn a new technique or understand an idea, for example. All strategies have factors in common. They involve

- defining the problem
- considering alternative solutions
- planning a way ahead
- monitoring progress
- evaluating progress.

Deliberate control over strategies does not come naturally or easily. It has to be taught and practised. Good advice on how to go about this can be found in Prawat (1989) and Pressley, Goodchild, Fleet, Zajchowsky and Evans (1989). In essence, teaching strategies is much like teaching anything else. Kyriacou (chapter 6) has set out clearly the steps needed for effective instruction.

Unfortunately, as my earlier analysis indicated, having a rich knowledge base and the grasp of some effective applications strategies is not enough if the pupil, when faced with a challenge, is defeated or otherwise overwhelmed by anxiety or rejection. Pupils need to learn how to work through these states and moods if they are to be effective learners. They need to learn that such reactions are not at all uncommon. The difference between an effective learner and a defeated learner is not what they feel but what they do about what they feel. This is an exceptionally difficult problem for a teacher but it is a teaching problem. Defeatism and dependency are not inbuilt features of a personality. They are learned reactions to situations. It follows, therefore, that pupils can learn to pause, keep calm, reflect. Space does not allow an extensive treatment of the methods available to teach these responses. Prawat (1989) has reviewed some of these. Detailed accounts of techniques are described and evaluated for reading by Block (1993) and for writing by Graham and Harris (1993). And Nolen (this volume, chapter 11) provides detailed consideration of the personal and emotional development necessary if learners are to support themselves.

Context

Clearly a lot can be done by teachers to promote knowledge utilization in the classroom. But you will recall that people have a major problem in applying what they learn in one context to problems faced in a different context. How will classroom knowledge utilization compare with knowledge utilization expected elsewhere? And what can teachers do to help pupils bridge any gaps?

In order to make progress with these questions it is necessary to understand more about the major contextual differences which pupils might come across. Resnick (1987) has offered a useful analysis of the differences expected of learners in and out of school.

She has identified three major differences. These are summarized below:

In school	*Out of school*
individual cognition	shared cognition
pure mental activity	use of cognitive tools
generalized learning	situation-specific competence

In a work setting, the predominant activity takes place in teams. Whether it be sailing ocean liners or servicing cars, a large number of people are involved and each has to interact productively with others if effective work is to ensue. In schools, teamwork is the exception. In the main, pupils are expected to work to a large degree in isolation, and particularly so at the point of assessment.

In the workplace a large number of cognitive tools are available to support or take the load off thinking activities. Computers, standard tables (e.g. for deciding pricing or material usage) and checklists (e.g. as used by pilots) are the norm. These devices are intended to provide intellectual support for workers and to free their attention for more important concerns. Industry and commerce have, throughout their history, worked to produce such supports which are properly called 'cognitive tools' since, just as a physical tool (e.g. a hammer) makes physical work easier, cognitive tools make intellectual work less burdensome.

In contrast to industry and commerce, schools generally show resistance to the use of such devices. Pupils are, in the main, expected to work things out for themselves. There has been, and still is in many places, strong resistance to the use of computers in schools on the grounds that they will make children lazy and incompetent. One immediate effect of such an attitude is that pupils spend a great deal of their mental energy focusing on the details of intellectual processes, and this leaves them little spare attention to focus on the broader problem. Again, the isolation of pupils from cognitive tools is particularly evident in examinations and other assessments. In consequence, even where cognitive tools (and here we can include directories, guides, dictionaries and tables of important formulae) are available in schools, pupils must focus their attention on how to do without them precisely in important situations, where industry and commerce would deem them to be most relevant.

Another aspect of this difference is a focus in schools on abstract symbol manipulation, to be contrasted out of school with the use of the whole physical context to support reasoning. Resnick (1987), by way of illustration, describes the case of some Weight Watchers using everyday arithmetic in recipe calculations. In the particular instance quoted, a recipe for four people had to be converted to make three meals. The recipe demanded, for four, two-thirds of a cup of cottage cheese. How to get three-quarters of two thirds? In school we are taught how to multiply fractions using rather esoteric procedures. Instead of this, Resnick reports, the cook used a measuring cup to get two thirds of a cup of cottage cheese and then patted this into a pancake which he then divided into quarters. The cheese itself became part of the calculation process.

Resnick further cites the case of children in a class being told that they had certain coins, specifically 25 cents, 10 cents, and two 1-cent pieces, and then being asked how much more they would need to buy a 60-cent ice-cream. In real life this problem would probably lead to a search through the pockets for a 'round change' coin (such as another 25-cent piece in this instance). Some pupils in the class tackled the problem this way, arguing that if you ignored the two 1-cent pieces you could get the ice-cream with another 25-cent piece. One girl however did a straightforward classroom substraction calculation and, correctly, announced that what was needed was an extra 23 cents. When her answer was ignored by the class, she added that you could get a 25-cent piece, get some change for it and then use 23 cents of it to complete the sum for the ice-cream. The point here is that, yes, you could do all this, but in real life you never would. You would let the seller worry about the change. Resnick argues, 'Out of school, because pupils are continuously engaged with objects and situations that make sense to them, people do not fall into the trap of forgetting what their calculation or reasoning is about ... actions are grounded in the logic of immediate situations. In school, however, symbolic activities tend to become detached from any meaningful context' (1987, p. 15). Of course this detachment makes symbols very powerful but if they cannot be later embedded in particular contexts they become unusable.

This idea raises Resnick's third point of contrast between settings in and out of schools. Schools specifically attempt to teach theoretical principles and symbol systems with the widest possible applicability. That is the whole point of schooling. The problem is that knowledge is always used in very specific settings where practical contingencies invariably make a difference. Workers tend to develop particular ways of doing things. For example, in a study of expert radiologists reported by Resnick it was shown that they did not interpret X-rays using the methods taught in medical textbooks. They developed their own on-site ways of looking at prints.

I am not arguing here that general skills are useless and only situation-specific skills matter. Situation-specific skills clearly have their serious limitations as indeed the name applies. They are not at all transferable. I am simply describing a researcher's view of the key differences between learning in school and applying knowledge out of school. What are the implications for the teacher?

At one level, the response is obvious, albeit rather vague. In school we need to teach pupils to capitalize on their capacity to be adaptive learners. Resnick's point is that 'As long as school focusses mainly on individual forms of competence, on tool free performance and on decontextualized skills, educating people to be good learners in school settings alone may not be sufficient to help them become strong out-of-school learners' (p. 18).

Resnick suggests that teaching for adaptive learning in schools requires planning for learning which reproduces the features of out-of-school knowledge use. To repeat these features, such planning would need to require from pupils, teamwork, the use of a broad range of cognitive tools and the solution of large problems which have the characteristics of real-world challenges, i.e. problems which are messy and complex and are embedded in a context which is part of the problem and may be part of the solution process. This recipe for teaching knowledge application should be added to the direction given in the previous section on teaching strategies. The whole business is clearly very challenging for teachers.

Professional Development in Teaching Knowledge Application

I have shown that teaching knowledge application and strategic or adaptive learning in schools is exceedingly difficult. It is, however, the very essence of what schools are about. The teacher's central task is to teach powerful ways of knowing and doing, which can be applied out of school. It is a daunting task. And research shows just how long it takes and what persistence is involved if teachers are to develop the appropriate competencies for strategy instruction. Duffy (1993) reports a study lasting several years of a group of teachers who were determined to develop strategic literacy skills in young pupils, that is to say, they wanted their pupils to have explicit thoughtful control over their reading skills which would help them adapt their attack when they had problems. An example, provided by Duffy, of such a pupil at work involved one who substituted the word 'curtain' for 'current' in the following sentence: 'They were careful to avoid the strong current which might carry them away.' The young reader quickly ran into trouble and returned to correct his error arguing, 'There wasn't anything to carry them away. A curtain could not do it, so I went back . . .'

It took several years for the teachers in Duffy's project to be able to inculcate such strategic thinking about reading into their pupils. The teachers initially had a great deal of resistance to the very idea of strategy instruction, arguing that either it was not necessary or that it distracted them from making quick progress through the reading schemes. Some of the teachers did not have any explicit strategies themselves, a fact which necessarily imposes limits on what can be taught.

Once the teachers became aware of strategies, they went through a phase of using them to help them question children, but they did not let the children know about these techniques. It seemed they wanted to keep control over the strategies. A third phase in teacher development involved the explicit teaching of strategies, using some of the teaching techniques I described earlier. Unfortunately they focused their teaching too narrowly, with an emphasis on specific pages of the reading schemes and with the result, as reported by Duffy, that, 'the students almost always could name the strategy and make a vague statement about its importance; however, they could seldom describe the stragegy's function, when it would be used, how it would help them . . . or how they would apply it' (p. 14).

In the fourth stage of professional development in strategy instruction identified by Duffy, teachers began to teach strategies at the point of need and, significantly, they modelled strategies by thinking aloud as they themselves used a strategy in a text. As Duffy points out, 'In doing so, they illustrated for students that using a strategy is not a matter of following procedural steps in a rigid manner but is, rather, an adaptable, flexible, trial-and-error process' (p. 15). Even at this level of achievement, however, the students were not conscious of why they were learning strategies, and they assumed they were for use only in the reading scheme books. In consequence, these children continued to see strategies as merely an aspect of schoolwork which had no real-world application. What else could the teachers do?

At this point, according to Duffy, some of the teachers despaired of ever teaching pupils the free and flexible use of strategic approaches to literacy. Duffy calls this stage of professional development, the fifth in his scheme, 'the Wall' in reference to the notorious experience met by marathon runners as their blood sugar runs out! At this stage, the teachers continued to request lists of strategies to teach in the hope that if they taught more they might increase their effect. What they had difficulty facing was that, if they wanted their pupils to transfer their learned strategies to out-of-school reading, then they would have to import 'real-world' reading into the classroom. This, argues Duffy, posed these teachers with a problem of control: 'because they used schoolwork to maintain a smooth classroom activity flow, they could not imagine how to maintain this flow (and, therefore, classroom order) if they abandoned schoolwork in favour of real reading' (p. 115). One of Duffy's teachers said, 'I can't have twenty kids all going in different directions.' This problem is discussed in chapter 10 (this volume).

The teachers in Duffy's study only got over 'the Wall' when they accepted that teaching strategies involved more than teaching lots of strategies. There is an extra dimension to the problem. It is that literacy itself has to serve some real-world purpose to the children. It has to be a useful tool to advance their own interests. As one teacher said, 'The interest comes first – what they want to do and how they want to do it!' It was important that the pupils have a goal in mind or a real problem to solve, and hence an overriding purpose in reading in the first place. Thus, authentic activity is a keystone to strategy teaching: it is what gives learning, and hence the strategy, meaning.

Having realized this, teachers pass through several more phases in their professional development in regard to strategy instruction which promotes pupils' capacity to apply their knowledge. For my purposes, the key points to note are that teachers can expect a long period for their own learning if they are to become proficient at inculcating knowledge application skills in their pupils, and that this development involves every aspect of classroom management as well as straight teaching skills. Knowledge that can be transported beyond the classroom has to be embedded in authentic activity brought into the classroom as a context in which to teach strategies.

Summary

- Children before school show strong evidence of being able to apply their knowledge to many settings. Paradoxically perhaps, learning in class-rooms proves very difficult to apply in settings out of school. Despite a long history of efforts to teach knowledge application, most methods to date have failed. Strategies can be taught, but then they do not typically travel beyond the classroom.
- There are important differences between in-school and out-of-school contexts, including especially the way context is used in problem solving and learning. Schools endeavour to decontextualize learning: out of school the context is a significant learning resource. Schools are set up to teach powerful general processes, but pupils must also learn how to recontextualize these in particular settings.
- Some studies suggest that teachers should teach strategies in the context of authentic activity. This technique looks promising, although it takes a great deal of professional maturity on the part of teachers before they develop the skills of classroom management which sustain both classroom order and authentic activity.

Editor's Commentary

In common with chapter 4 I have attempted in this chapter to add to your understanding of classrooms as learning environments. The particular problem I have described is that of teaching knowledge utilization. Teaching usable knowledge is the central purpose of schooling: it is a teacher's most difficult challenge. I have explained why that is and what might be done about it.

Whether you succeed or not depends on your commitment to teach deliberately certain strategies and dispositions. It also depends on whether you can manage authentic work in your classroom without, as so many teachers fear, losing order. Authentic activities involve real-world, messy problems, teamwork, flexible timetables and schedules, and the use of cognitive tools in support of learning.

The issues raised in the chapter can be followed up in the following school-based work:

- Discuss with teachers and observe their practices in regard to how they attempt to teach knowledge utilization.
- When you have taught something, assess, across a range of settings, how far your pupils can use their learning. Discuss this question with them.
- Design and enact a set of authentic teamwork activities to create opportunities for pupils to utilize knowledge. Carefully evaluate what you as a teacher learn from this experience.

The ideas in this chapter should be carefully linked to the discussions in related chapters. Several issues are raised but especially noteworthy are

- deliberate teaching, which is discussed in chapter 6
- classroom management, which is discussed in chapters 4, 10 and 15.
- pupils' dispositions and attitudes, which are discussed in chapter 11.

A major last point to re-emphasize is that good teaching does not come easily. Suggestions for good practice here cannot be properly tried in a week. Professional development in quality teaching is a lifelong task.

FURTHER READING

Gardner, H. (1993). *The unschooled mind*. London: Fontana.
　　Gardner shows just how powerful are the minds of children. He also shows how the normal institutional practices of schools constrain these powers. He provides extensive advice on how teachers can rise above these constraints in providing for learning. He places particular emphasis on treating children as apprentices to real-life learning.

Newman, D., Griffin, P. & Cole, M. (1989). *The construction zone: Working for cognitive changes in school*. Cambridge, England: Cambridge University Press.
　　Newman and colleagues extend the idea of apprenticeship and offer a range of practical advice on how it might work in science, social science and mathematics.

Farnham-Diggory, S. (1990). *Schooling*. Cambridge, MA: Harvard University Press. This book starts with a clear summary of research on children's learning. This is followed by detailed accounts of successful approaches to teaching based on latest theory. There is a special emphasis on science, technology and basic skills.

Part III

Teaching and Classroom Management

6

Direct Teaching

Chris Kyriacou

Editor's Overview

We have seen earlier that learning involves a range of processes and goals and that good teachers should develop a repertoire of teaching skills in order best to promote different learning processes.

In this chapter, Chris Kyriacou focuses on one teaching skill, that of direct instruction. He emphasizes how and why direct instruction works, when it should be used and when it might not be used. He describes in detail several different types of this form of teaching.

The chapter contains a large amount of 'how to do it' advice. Most teachers use direct teaching extensively. The professional challenge is twofold. First, we need to make sure we use the right tool for the job, only using direct teaching in appropriate circumstances. Second, we need to work up the skill of direct teaching paying special attention to all its component parts. The chapter provides guidance on these matters.

At its simplest, direct teaching can be defined as teaching in which the teacher is telling pupils or showing them what he or she wants them to know or to be able to do. The most extreme example of direct teaching is a lecture to a whole class. Other terms in common use for this approach are 'direct instruction', 'explicit instruction', 'didactic teaching' and 'active teaching'. However, it is important to note that such terms have been in use over a long period and have been defined in various ways by different writers (see Rosenshine, 1987; Slavin, 1991). We shall also see below that direct teaching is actually a broader and more sophisticated approach than the simple definition given above implies.

The Nature of Direct Teaching

In order to consider the nature of direct teaching we need first to put the term in a wider context. We need to think about how direct teaching relates to notions of pupil learning and effective teaching, how direct teaching can be distinguished from other approaches, and what key psychological considerations are involved in direct teaching.

Direct teaching and pupil learning

Pupil learning may be judged in terms of the development of pupils' knowledge, understanding, skills and attitudes. Knowledge in its simplest terms refers to facts (e.g. knowing the capital of France, which letters are vowels, the date Columbus discovered America). Understanding refers to the meaningful interrelationship between items of knowledge. For example, I might know that the Second World War started in 1939, but that might be a simple act of memorization. To have understanding, I need to be able to relate that fact to other knowledge, such as what a war is, the origins of wars, the countries involved and why that war started in 1939 rather than sooner, or later or not at all. It is only when separate items of knowledge are related to each other that we get any sense of understanding. 'Skills' refers to the pupils' performance in carrying out certain tasks (e.g. handwriting, reading aloud, developing a line of argument, finding information about a topic in a textbook). The essence of a skill is that it is an identifiable component of doing a task that can be developed and improved. Skills include intellectual skills, social skills and physical skills. Finally let us look at attitudes. Attitudes regarding learning have two main aspects: first, the development of positive attitudes by pupils towards the topic, subject area or activity and to education and schooling in general; and second, the development of positive attitudes by pupils towards themselves as individuals, and more specifically as learners (i.e. developing a positive academic self-concept).

This distinction between knowledge, understanding, skills and attitudes, enables us to think more clearly about what type of learning teachers are trying to foster, whether it be judging a particular lesson or activity within a lesson or judging a whole course or programme of work. It is, however, important to note that these four terms are used in many different ways by different writers and also overlap in complex ways. For example, knowledge about where to find books in the school library might be considered to be a 'study skill' rather than an item of knowledge, just as a positive attitude towards a subject may arise as a by-product of understanding and enjoying the work involved.

Direct teaching and effective teaching

Having defined learning in terms of four types of learning outcomes, we now need to think about how to judge whether the types of activities teachers can use to bring about the pupil learning are effective. In essence, 'effective teaching' refers to the extent to which the teacher employed learning activities successfully to bring about the intended learning outcomes for the lesson or programme of study (L. W. Anderson, 1991; Kyriacou, 1991). For example, if we focus on a particular lesson dealing with the topic of 'square numbers', we will usually find that there is a range of learning outcomes intended. The teacher may want pupils to know what square numbers are (knowledge), to understand the nature of square numbers (understanding), to be able to identify and test whether a given number is a square number (skills) and to do all this in a way that helps develop pupils' positive attitude towards mathematics as subject and towards themselves as learners (attitudes). Any given lesson may have a greater emphasis on one or more of these four types of learning outcomes, but the vast majority of lessons in schools will involve a mixture of all four most of the time. Some lessons, however, or particular activities within a lesson may well be targeted on a single type of outcome.

In judging effective teaching of a particular part of a lesson, the whole lesson or an extended programme of study, we need to ask four key questions:

1   What learning outcomes were intended?
2   Were the learning outcomes appropriate for meeting the pupils' needs in the context of the aims of the particular programme of study?
3   What learning activities were used by the teacher?
4   Did these activities successfully bring about the intended learning outcomes?

If the learning outcomes were appropriate (taking account of the pupils, the course of study and the context of the school) and the activities successfully achieved these outcomes, we can say the teaching was effective.

The direct teaching approach

We can now turn our attention to the notion of direct teaching. In fostering pupil learning, the teacher has a host of diverse activities from which to choose. These may include lecturing, setting a written task, showing a video, making use of a computer, going on a trip outside the school, getting pupils to write an essay.

Generally speaking, we can arrange such activities on a continuum based on the extent to which the teacher is directly involved in the activity. An example at one extreme, where the teacher is 100 per cent involved, would be when the teacher is explaining something to the whole class. An example at the other extreme would be an activity where the pupil reads a comprehension passage and then answers some questions listed at the end of the text. To the extent that the teacher is directly interacting with pupils (talking and listening), we can refer to this as *direct teacher involvement*. To the extent to which the pupils are carrying out a task without the teacher being involved, we refer to this as indirect teacher involvement.

It is important to note that in order to place any given learning activity along this continuum we need to consider when and how the teacher is involved in the activity. Some activities such as 'explaining' will unequivocally be an example of direct teacher involvement. An activity such as silent reading by pupils will be an example of indirect teacher involvement. However, an activity such as carrying out a science practical may or may not involve a high degree of direct teacher involvement, depending on how the teacher approaches such tasks.

In addition we also need to look at what the teacher says and does during such interactions with pupils. If the teacher has a clear idea of the knowledge and understanding he/she wants to develop, he/she can directly transmit these to pupils by informing and explaining. In the case of skills, the teacher can directly show, demonstrate or 'coach' the skill. In the case of attitudes, the teacher may draw attention to those attitudes he/she expects to be displayed or developed. The notion of the *direct transmission* of information is an essential component of the direct teaching approach. If the teacher, however, gives advice and guidance to help shape the learning experience but still leaves the pupils to 'discover' the knowledge or understanding, or develop skills and attitudes through their own further efforts, this is commonly given the contrasting term of 'indirect' (or 'inquiry-oriented') teaching.

Direct teaching refers to the use of learning activities which typically involve *direct teacher involvement*, participation and interaction with pupils, in which, through the use of informing, describing, explaining, questioning, modelling, demonstrating and coaching the teacher *directly transmits* the knowledge, understanding, skills and attitudes that he or she wishes to develop. A lesson based on the direct teaching approach will usually have the following five main stages (Good and Brophy, 1991; Rosenshine, 1987):

1   The teacher sets clear goals for the lesson.
2   The teacher teaches through exposition of what is to be learnt.
3   The teacher asks questions to check pupils' understanding.
4   There is a period of supervised practice.

5 The teacher assesses pupils' work to check that the goals have been achieved.

These stages have been identified by so called 'process–product' studies of effective teaching. In such studies, researchers have observed lessons and focused on different features of the teacher's behaviour and lesson structure and organization (these are the process variables), and then looked to see which of these features were more evident in lessons where pupils appeared to have learnt more as measured on standardized tests of educational attainment (these are the product variables). A host of such process–product studies reported since the 1960s has built up a picture of the most effective lessons as being characterized by direct instruction organized in terms of the five stages outlined above (e.g. see Cruickshank, 1990; Slavin, 1991). However, there are some important reservations to note, and these will be highlighted in the final section of this chapter.

The psychology of direct teaching

Whilst there is a host of important psychological features involved in teaching and learning, there are three that are particularly important in the context of direct teaching. The first of these is the clear specification of the *learning objectives*. At its most sophisticated, direct teaching is based on a careful matching of direct teaching to a consideration of specific and clearly described learning objectives (Biggs, 1990; Gronlund, 1991). To some extent the National Curriculum is an example of an attempt to make clear such learning outcomes by specifying attainment targets and their constituent levels. In the United States an approach termed *mastery learning* is based on requiring pupils to achieve a set of learning objectives at one level before they can progress to the next level (Anderson and Block, 1987; Kulik, Kulik and Bangert-Drowns, 1990).

The second important consideration is that of *cognitive matching*. All pupil learning must inevitably take account of and build upon what the pupil already knows, understands and can do. 'Cognitive matching' refers to the teacher being able to judge what is the optimal level of further learning that can be achieved, and then organizing the learning activity to achieve this further learning. Of particular interest in recent years has been the increasingly major influence of the writings of Vygotsky (Smith and Cowie, 1991: Sutherland, 1992) and the notions of the *Zone of Proximal Development* (the distance between a child's actual developmental level and the potential level of cognitive development that the child can achieve with help) and of *scaffolding* (the way a teacher can support and shape the child's development of understanding through appropriately prompting and directing attention to key features of a learning activity).

The third important consideration is that of *academic learning time*. Many researchers have argued that one of the most important variables in accounting for why some teachers are more effective than others is that the more effective teachers are simply able to maximize the amount of time in which pupils are engaged in successful learning activities. Advocates of direct teaching have argued that direct teaching can be particularly effective in maintaining high levels of academic engaged time, and research studies of direct teaching have thus tended to focus on those features of direct teaching which help maximize academic learning time (Berliner, 1987; Cruickshank, 1990). These include clarity of teacher's instructions and explanations, emphasis on engagement in academic tasks, active involvement by a teacher in learning activities, and highly structured lessons.

Direct Teaching Methods

Since the 1960s, there has been a steady increase in the advocacy and adoption of a diversity of teaching methods in primary and secondary schools. At the present time, the variety of teaching methods used by teachers is typically much greater than it has been in the past (Kyriacou and Wilkins, 1993). Despite this, direct teaching methods continue to be the most important and widespread approach adopted by teachers (Kyriacou, 1986, 1991). Direct teaching methods can usefully be grouped together under the following headings:

1 Informing, describing and explaining.
2 Demonstrating, modelling and coaching.
3 Asking questions.
4 Monitoring practice and active intervention.
5 Direct teaching by proxy.

Informing, describing and explaining

Studies which have explored teachers' and pupils' views about good teaching almost all report the characteristic 'the teacher is able to explain clearly' amongst those highly rated (e.g. Brown and McIntyre, 1993). Indeed, a teacher explaining something is almost certainly the most widely held image of what teaching means. As such, it is not surprising that writings and research about teaching have focused much attention on the key characteristics of effective teacher explaining (Ornstein, 1990; Wootton, 1992; Wragg and Brown, 1993a). Particular attention in the analyses of effective teacher explaining (and questioning: see below) has been reference to the need for adequate scaffolding (i.e. how well the teacher assists the pupil in learning from the explanations given) (e.g. see Roehler and Duffy, 1986).

Exposition by a teacher, whether it be informing, describing or explaining, typically ranges from just a few minutes in length to a mini-lecture lasting about half an hour. In many cases, however, exposition will not consist purely of a teacher talking and pupils listening or making notes. Rather, the teacher will intersperse the exposition with questions to pupils to help maintain their interest and involvement, and to check that they follow and understand what has been said. Teacher exposition falls into two main categories. The first is, exposition that transmits the topic itself, such as explaining how various geographical and economic factors influence the location of early settlements, or why a balloon makes a loud noise when it has burst. The second category is exposition that alerts pupils to important features of the topic or task they are about to study of which they need to be aware if learning is to proceed effectively (for example, pointing out that in calculating the length of a side in a right-angled triangle they must make sure that if the missing side is the hypotenuse, the formula is arranged differently than if it is one of the other two sides missing). In practice, many explanations at the beginning of a lesson combine both these categories. Ausubel (1968) has argued that teachers should alert pupils at the start of the lesson to ways in which the content and tasks relate to their previous learning in order to make the new learning more meaningful and thereby more effective. In particular, he advocates that teachers should provide pupils with superordinate concepts for organizing the ideas that will be covered in the lesson, which he has termed *advanced organizers*. Advanced organizers are basically key ideas that provide a framework for pupils to make sense of the learning activity. For example, if pupils were considering material which related to the cause of a particular war, it would be helpful for the teacher to alert them to the fact that there is an important distinction to be made between the context that made the outbreak of war more likely (e.g. political unrest at home, concern over trade disputes, territorial ambitions) and a precipitating event (e.g. the other power invading a third country, the death of a monarch). Such a distinction can help pupils categorize the historical evidence more effectively and consider the difference between asking 'why?' and 'why then?' Ausubel also advocates the use of an end-of-lesson review in which the teacher and pupils review what has been learnt and link this to previous and future learning, as this also helps pupils develop a framework for their learning and provides an early opportunity to correct any possible misunderstandings. Many models of direct instruction emphasize the importance of the need for teachers to brief and debrief pupils before and after tasks to maximize learning.

Research on teachers' explaining has highlighted a number of features that increase its effectiveness:

- Clarity: the most important feature of any explanation is that it is clear and at the appropriate level for pupils to understand.
- Structure: the explanation is structured carefully so that the major ideas

and concepts are broken down into meaningful segments, and these are then sequenced together logically.

- Length: expositions should be brief, typically lasting no more than ten minutes in primary schools or twenty minutes in secondary schools; pupils will find it hard to maintain attention for longer periods unless the exposition is interspersed with questions and other activities.
- Maintaining attention: the delivery should involve variation in emphasis, tone and pitch; eye contact with pupils should be maintained and spread around the classroom, and body language should convey interest and enthusiasm.
- Language: the teacher avoids use of overcomplex language or terms that are not familiar or understood, and explains any new terms that pupils will need to know.
- Use of examples: the explanation makes use of examples, analogies and metaphors, particularly from everyday life or ones that directly relate to pupils' experience and interests.
- Checking understanding: the teacher looks at pupils' faces for signs that they may be puzzled, uses questions to check understanding before moving on, and gives pupils an opportunity to ask questions.

Demonstration, modelling and coaching

One of the most important roles that a teacher plays is that of providing a model for the type of thinking and behaviour that pupils are required to follow. Everything a teacher does in approaching the subject, topic or task is to a large extent a model of greater expertise, whether it be in carrying out a science practical, reading aloud from a book, doing a mathematical investigation on the board, or showing pupils how to throw a cricket ball. As such, an important aspect of direct instruction involves a consideration of how teachers can demonstrate, model and coach pupils to best effect (Good and Brophy, 1991).

Many teachers take for granted that pupils possess the study and learning skills necessary to undertake the academic tasks set, or assume that they can easily develop such skills by trial and error. In fact, a number of writers have pointed out that pupils are often unable to undertake tasks successfully simply because they lack such skills (Nisbet and Shucksmith, 1986). As a result, teachers now typically spend more time in lessons checking that pupils have the appropriate study and learning skills, and explicitly devote time to developing these where necessary. Indeed, the teaching of study and learning skills is one of the fastest-growing areas of development in schools. An example of an area where this is particularly evident is that of revising for tests and examinations, where it is often assumed that pupils can adequately manage their time to prepare, and have developed effective procedures to revise topics. In reality, many pupils are unable to do this effectively, so that direct instruction of revision strategies has proved to be very beneficial (Maclure and Davies, 1991).

Being a good model, however, does not mean that the teacher has to be perfect and should know everything there is to know about the subject. Indeed, it is often educative to point out to pupils that there are things you do not know, as this conveys that there are still things to be learnt, understood and discovered about the subject, even for those who have studied it for many years. Nevertheless it is important to act with integrity. For example, if you have made a mistake in explaining a procedure, you should admit this straight away and correct the mistake. As a model, you need to be honest about what you know, what you do not know, and areas where you are uncertain.

In addition, the teacher should convey interest in and enthusiasm for the subject. Displaying interest and enthusiasm is infectious. In contrast, if the teacher sounds bored and appears to be going through the motions of teaching with little interest, this will make it harder for pupils to sustain their interest and involvement in the lesson. Being a good model can be enhanced by the surroundings, by displaying colourful posters and examples of pupils' work on the walls, to convey the impression that the work in hand is interesting and worthwhile.

Another important aspect of modelling is to show pupils how a task can be broken down into parts, and then to help pupils successfully to undertake such parts. A nice illustration of this is a primary school teacher who demonstrated on the board how to write a poem. She first elicited from pupils a possible topic for the poem, then elicited some ideas about one of the topics, decided on a rhyming scheme, and then drafted, and redrafted a short poem on the board, getting further ideas from pupils as she went along. Such an experience gave pupils an insight into what was involved in writing a poem.

In some subject areas, the way a teacher demonstrates how to approach a task or to lay out work is meant to be an exemplar for pupils. Indeed, teachers often say they want the task approached or the work presented in the way shown. Such instruction helps pupils get a clear understanding of what is required by the task set. In teaching a foreign language, the role of the teacher as model is taken even further, as the teacher's use of the language typically constitutes the main tuition in the foreign language. Here the teacher needs to highlight, through emphasis and repetition, the key features of the language that pupils need to notice to develop their competence (Peck, 1988), a process that in the early stages of learning has much in common with the way parents try to shape and extend the language used by young children. The teacher's role as model is also very evident in tuition in playing a musical instrument and in skilled performance in sports, where the quality of teacher modelling and coaching has a major impact on the quality of the pupil's later performance.

Asking questions

There are few professions to compare with teaching in which a person asks so many questions to which he or she already knows the answer! Asking questions is one of the key skills of teaching, and has been the subject of much research and analysis (Brown and Wragg, 1993; Dillon, 1988; Morgan and Saxton, 1991).

In looking at different types of questions, an important distinction is made between asking *closed questions* (where there is one clear and unambiguously correct answer) and asking *open questions* (where many different answers can be considered to be correct or acceptable). Another important distinction is made between asking *lower-order questions* (based largely on the recall of factual information) and *higher-order questions* (which require pupils to engage in careful thought and critical analysis before answering). Research on classroom teaching indicates that the majority of questions asked by teachers are closed and lower-order. Morgan and Saxton (1991) have argued that teachers should make use of more open-ended and higher-order questioning to stimulate pupils' thinking and understanding.

Research has also indicated that when teachers ask open and higher-order questions it is important to give pupils some time to think before assuming the pupil is unable to answer. Allowing pupils an adequate length of *wait time* seems to lead to a better quality of answers (Cruickshank, 1990; Slavin, 1991).

Also important in asking questions is matching the question to the level of pupil understanding. A particular pitfall for teachers is to have too strict an idea of a correct answer in mind, which can lead to rejecting as incorrect a pupil's answer that in many respects was correct. Pupils often spend a lot of time trying to work out what type of answer the teacher wants to hear. In contrast, many writers advocate that teachers should spend more time thinking about what a pupil's answer indicates about the pupil's current understanding, and build up from there. This idea of building up from the pupil's understanding lies at the heart of the *constructivist* view of how pupils learn, which focuses on how pupils actively construct new understanding by relating learning experiences to their previous understanding (Gipps, 1992).

A very important task for teachers is that of *differentiation*, which refers to being able to present learning activities which cater adequately for the different levels of ability between pupils in the same class. Kerry (1993), in a study of developing teachers' classroom questioning skills, argues that the effective use of questions (both oral and written) lies at the heart of the teacher's ability to achieve differentiation, since skilful use of what, how and when questions are asked can provide very different levels of challenge and cognitive demand to the pupil, and can also allow pupils to engage with a question at a level appropriate to their needs.

Another important aspect of asking questions is the need to provide *positive reinforcement* whenever a pupil has answered a question. This involves not only giving praise (e.g. saying 'good' or 'well done') when the answer is correct, but also being supportive and encouraging when it was nearly correct or the pupil has made an effort. Regular use of praise will help pupils become more confident in trying to answer questions. In contrast, being hostile or, even worse, shaming a pupil for a poor answer is likely to inhibit pupils and alienate them from further involvement. Much has been written about the skilful use by teachers of reinforcement in the classroom to promote learning (e.g. Wheldall and Glynn, 1989). Effective handling by a teacher of question-and-answer interactions with pupils is probably one aspect of teaching which most powerfully contributes to establishing a classroom climate in which pupils feel positively about themselves as learners and are motivated to participate actively in the academic tasks which take place.

Finally, research indicates that another important aspect of asking questions is to ensure that they are distributed around the classroom. This involves avoiding blind spots, avoiding only asking pupils whose hands are raised or who are likely to give a correct answer, and not ignoring those who avoid eye contact.

Monitoring practice and active intervention

A feature of the direct instruction approach is a period of 'guided' or 'assisted' practice. The phrase 'practice makes perfect' is widely used, but in fact it is *practice plus feedback* that makes perfect, particularly if that feedback is quick and helpful, and comes from a teacher who is sensitive to the type of feedback that will be most useful. In the early descriptions of direct instruction, the emphasis in feedback was simply that it should be quick and corrective. In this case, providing an answer book to check answers would satisfy this requirement (as in programmed learning texts – see later). However, with an increasing acceptance of a constructivist view of pupils' learning, in more recent discussions of the role of feedback in direct instruction, the emphasis has been much more in terms of providing scaffolding, in which the teacher carefully engages with the pupil to help advance the pupil's understanding (see L. M. Anderson, 1989). An example of this is a study by Mercer and Fisher (1992), who explored how teachers can effectively intervene to help pupils learn when using computer-based activities. Their analysis of the support teachers offered illustrates how, if this is done effectively by scaffolding, it can enhance the experience inherent in the software package, and indeed can help overcome shortcomings that would otherwise arise from pupils using the software package without teacher intervention.

Another important feature of monitoring practice is that intervention should be active. It is easy for teachers simply to circulate around the room, only offering help when pupils appear to be having problems. Unfortunately, some pupils with problems do not ask for help, and instead move on to the next question or task or try to give the appearance of working whenever the teacher is nearby. In addition, pupils often fail to recognize they have made errors as they proceed. In these circumstances, it is important for teachers to interrogate pupils actively whilst they are working (rather than waiting for pupils to ask for help), and to check their work and ask them questions to check their understanding. Such active intervention enables problems to be identified at an early stage and ensures that tuition is distributed across all pupils, both the successful pupils and those having problems (and in the latter case both those seeking help and those who do not).

Activities which enable regular practice of what has already been learned is also very important. Time needs to be set aside during a programme of study to ensure that pupils are regularly tested and that they rehearse previous learning. It is certainly a mistake to assume that pupils who have learnt something well will be able to recall and use that learning later when required. All learning needs to be used frequently if pupils' facility with it is to be assured. Within direct instruction there are three things teachers can do to help establish the effectiveness of learning and thereby facilitate later recall.

- First, they need to make the new learning as meaningful as possible, by relating it to previous learning and understanding, which may involve the use of advanced organizers.
- Second, there is need to ensure that the learning is 'well learnt' through appropriate practice. Such practice involves not simply repeating the same learning, but also using a variety of examples where that learning is relevant. For example, in learning how to divide numbers, practice should include not simply doing a series of division sums but also dealing with a variety of problem-solving situations where division occurs.
- Third, the teacher needs to teach pupils various tricks that help recall and performance. This may range from simply devices, like spotting clues (for example, the letter S looks like a snake and a snake makes a hissing noise), to quite sophisticated mnemonics that enable a pupil to recall a list or formula.

It will be evident from the consideration here that the period of practice within the direct instruction approach is not just a simple matter of working through an exercise which displays what the teacher has demonstrated or explained at the start of a lesson.

Models of direct instruction include a period of review at the end of a lesson or activity in which pupils are debriefed about what they have learnt. This enables pupils to assess their performance and learn from mistakes, and enables teachers to check whether their teaching has been successful (Brophy and Alleman, 1991). More recently, however, an extended version of this, termed *reviewing* has been widely advocated. Reviewing refers to teachers spending some time with pupils at the end of a sequence of lessons, asking pupils to review their own progress and to identify aspects of their work they feel they have done well, any difficulties they have encountered, and what they feel they have learnt over the period being reviewed. Reviewing seems to be effective in helping pupils to consolidate their learning by being more aware of the learning outcomes that have occurred. Much of this has been stimulated by the development of new forms of recording pupils' progress through profiling and records of achievement, which encourage pupils' self-evaluation and, to some extent, the negotiation of targets for their own learning (Pole, 1993).

Direct teaching by proxy

Whilst direct teaching normally involves the teacher being directly involved in the learning activity, there are some activities where this role is transferred to another person or is embodied in a sequenced set of material or technology. The first category includes activities such as parental or peer tutoring, where a parent or pupil is given the teacher's role in tutoring a pupil within tightly confined guidelines. The most common examples of such tutoring involve reading, and to a lesser extent help with number work in the primary schools (Topping and Lindsay, 1992). Such schemes appear to be very successful, and clearly offer an opportunity to boost pupils' academically engaged time and to provide close individual attention.

The second category refers to the use of programmed learning texts and highly structured learning sequences based on computer software packages and other forms of instructional technology (see Ellington, Percival and Race, 1993; Eraut, 1989; Ornstein, 1990). Such schemes typically provide in visual form the teacher's explanation or demonstration together with an opportunity for practice. Incorrect response involves a feedback loop which either provides a further explanation or demonstration (sometimes linked to the nature of the incorrect answer) or returns the pupil to the original explanation or demonstration. Some courses have been based cleverly around video packages. A number of particularly sophisticated versions of direct teaching by proxy involve learning a foreign language. In effect, such schemes exemplify a mechanistic and prespecified form of direct teaching which takes pupils through an experience which simulates the five main stages of a typical lesson based on the direct teaching approach outlined earlier. Whilst the pace of the activity is under the pupils' control, there is little if any other form of room for manoeuvre or control passed over to the pupil within the context of the programmed course.

The development of materials using a variety of instructional technology, ranging from programmed learning texts to video-cassette packages, is particularly well developed and more frequently used in further education colleges than in schools. A number of authors have thus produced guides for their effective use within the further education context (e.g. Walklin, 1982). This is even more the case within the further education sector for courses of vocational education and training, where a precise analysis of how such instructional technology can contribute to the delivery of precise learning outcomes is clearly described in the programmes of study typically required for course validation. Walklin, for example, illustrates how a skills analysis for a job can be used as a basis for specifying precise learning outcomes, which in turn are linked to appropriate learning activities.

Scope and Limits

There has been much debate over the years concerning the relative effective- ness of different methods of teaching. Unfortunately the complexity of evaluating teaching is such that research studies can only offer limited evidence regarding relative effectiveness. First, the vast majority of teachers use a variety of teaching methods, even during a single lesson and even more so over a programme of study. Second, the intended aims of a lesson involve a complex mix of intended learning outcomes in terms of the knowledge, understanding, skills and attitudes being fostered. Third, the effectiveness of teaching depends on both the features of the lesson on the one hand, and the characteristics of pupils on the other. Moreover, these may interact in different ways. Fourth, each teaching method can be used either well or badly. No teaching method is teacher-proof or pupil-proof!

Direct teaching is undoubtedly one of the most important approaches adopted by teachers. It is generally claimed to be effective and efficient, and there is certainly much research evidence to support this (e.g. L. W. Anderson, 1991; Cruickshank, 1990). The largest proportion of such studies has focused on the primary school years and on the learning of basic skills concerned with reading, language and mathematics. As a result, it is now widely accepted that, in terms of fostering basic skills in the primary school years, direct teaching is particularly effective (Slavin, 1991), and it is interesting to note in this respect its widespread advocacy and adoption as part of programmes designed to improve educational achievement in disadvantaged pupils (typically pupils from low-income families living in areas of economic deprivation) in the early years of schooling (e.g. Brent and DiObilda, 1993).

However, a number of authors reviewing the research evidence supporting the effectiveness of direct teaching have expressed some caution regarding its effectiveness when applied to older children and the teaching of other subjects (Slavin, 1991). In this respect, the research evidence is less consistent, although a review of research by Montague and Knirk (1993) does point to the effectiveness of direct teaching with older pupils and in the education and training of adults. However, they argue that contemporary research indicates that things are easier to learn if they are learnt in a context of use and when they make sense to the student, and they feel there is a danger inherent in the use of direct teaching that it may focus overmuch on the teaching of knowledge and basic skills without sufficient reference to the context of use that makes the learning meaningful.

Indeed, one of the major limitations of direct teaching, is that it very much tends to place the teacher's role and authority as the provider of learning at the centre of the lesson (so-called 'teacher-centred learning'). This can relegate the pupil's role to that of being a somewhat passive receiver of learning, and can convey an impression to pupils that, as far as learning is concerned, what needs to be learnt comes from and is directed by the teacher. Used to excess, this can make pupils feel that learning involves the passive absorption of facts and acquisition of skills. This may provide little opportunity for pupils to 'discover' actively what is to be learnt and for such learning to become meaningful to them by allowing them to 'construct' their understanding through their own efforts. This more active approach (so-called 'active learning' or 'pupil-centred learning') is important in providing motivation for pupils by linking the more open-ended and problem-solving approach to the pupils' natural sense of curiosity and exploration.

Whilst the direct-teaching approach is often contrasted with active learning, the distinction between the two can sometimes be far from clear-cut within a single lesson. A lesson based on direct teaching may incorporate some of the features more commonly associated with active learning, such as the elements of discovery and problem solving, and some degree of pupil pacing and control. Nevertheless, the essence of direct teaching does lie in a combination of clear learning objectives, a tightly controlled lesson structure and an explicit delivery of the appropriate content and practice necessary to achieve the intended learning outcomes. There is a fair degree of consensus that direct teaching is most effective when the learning outcomes are clearly identifiable and achievable through exposition or demonstration (such as factual information or the use of a procedure), and less effective where learning outcomes are less tightly prescribed or more experience-based, such as the development of empathy, more open-ended problem-solving skills, or a more personalized sense of understanding.

Editor's Commentary

Direct instruction is best used for knowledge transmission, for showing, telling, modelling and demonstrating. It is never, on its own, sufficient to ensure deeper understanding, problem solving, creativity or group work capacities.

The key phases of direct instruction are to

- provide pupils with clear and explicit goals
- demonstrate/describe/show/tell briefly and clearly
- provide lots of pupil practice with feedback
- provide for the diversity of pupil attainment
- provide longer-term review.

Teachers do some of these things all of the time and all of these things some of the time. Direct teaching loses its effectiveness to the degree that any of the above activities is omitted or carried out poorly. Since direct teaching is the most commonly used instructional technique, it is very important to get it right and to use it only when it is appropriate.

The advice in this chapter can be followed up in the following school-based activities:

- Draw up your own checklist of (1) when to use direct teaching and (2) the requirements of good direct teaching. Plan, conduct and video-record small episodes of direct teaching. Use your checklist to evaluate your performance. Do not forget to evaluate the pupils' experience and learning. Use the evaluation to discuss with experienced teachers how to improve your performance.
- For a range of topics, discuss with teachers your intended teaching technique. Consider especially where it is important to use direct teaching and where it is to be avoided.
- Discuss with teachers particular facets of direct teaching, including especially
  - provision for diversity
  - provision for pupil practice
  - provision for feedback.
  - Ask experienced teachers, using your checklist, to evaluate your attempts at direct teaching. Remember, it is important to make sure that all the phases take place to maximum quality.

Direct instruction is not an all-purpose tool – although some teachers seem to think it is. Children can learn a great deal from listening, watching and practising. But there is also a great deal they will never learn from these activities. The ideas in this chapter should be linked to those in other chapters as follows.

- the range of learning processes discussed in chapter 1;
- other teaching techniques discussed in chapters 7, 8, and 11;
- preparing for the diversity of pupils' styles and attainments is crucial to direct teaching (this matter is discussed in chapter 12).

FURTHER READING

There are surprisingly few books written in the UK which provide a good overview of direct teaching. The best overviews are to be found in American textbooks dealing with teaching methods in general but written by authors well known for writings and research on direct-teaching methods. My recommended texts for further reading are those listed below. All these books also incorporate a good treatment of psychological considerations.

Gage, N. L. & Berliner, D. C. (1992). *Educational psychology* (5th ed.) Boston: Houghton Mifflin.
> Written by two world-famous authors, this book contains an especially good treatment of lecturing and explaining. There is also a good treatment of the effective planning which needs to underpin the successful use of direct-teaching methods.

Good, T. L. & Brophy, J. E. (1991). *Looking in classrooms* (5th ed.) New York: HarperCollins.
> Good and Brophy's writings on teaching methods are of international renown. This book provides an excellent overview of direct-teaching methods, and is particularly useful in summarizing key research findings. Good and Brophy give prominence to direct teaching in their consideration of effective teaching, and in their treatment they consider the key structural features of the direct-teaching approach and provide good research support for their observations.

Kyriacou, C. (1991). *Essential teaching skills*. Hemel Hempstead, England: Simon & Schuster.
> In this book I focus on the key skills involved in effective classroom teaching. These key skills are considered under the following seven headings: planning and preparation; lesson presentation; lesson management; classroom climate; discipline; assessing pupils' progress; and reflection and evaluation. In discussing teaching skills, reference is made to the use of different learning activities, including those characteristic of the direct-teaching approach.

Ornstein, A. C. (1990). *Strategies for effective teaching*. New York: Harper & Row.
> This book presents an excellent overview of teaching methods, with a detailed treatment of direct teaching. It contains particularly useful chapters on instructional objectives, and on instructional technology.

Slavin, R. E. (1991). *Educational psychology* (3rd ed.) Boston: Allyn & Bacon.
> This book presents an excellent overview of direct teaching, and is particularly strong in its consideration of research studies, in its comparison of the work of different authors and in its treatment of the psychological features which underpin direct teaching.

7

Teaching through Discussion

Richard Fox

Unfortunately he shows that classroom conversations do not live up to this specification. These conversations are often routine, predictable and undemanding. Some explanation is given for these shortcomings and some advice is offered on how classroom talk can be made more productive for learning. The advice covers

- rules for conversations
- use of group work.

Richard Fox does not argue that all conversation is useful for learning. Classrooms are the stages for a massive amount of talk, very little of which has learning potential. The good teacher must learn how to promote fruitful talk and how to diminish less useful forms.

Teaching through discussion is a skill all teachers need in their repertoire because it is critical to the promotion of understanding. The chapter provides a structure for professional development in this area.

Introduction

Teaching proceeds mostly in the form of language, a web of words both spoken and written, with which teachers try to communicate with their pupils. Teaching through discussion involves interaction between the teacher and the pupils which may vary from whole-class discussion, in which anyone present is at least in principle invited to take part, to a conversation between the teacher and an individual pupil. The underlying point of using this mode of interactive teaching relates to a particular view of learning and also to a view of the learner. At its best, teaching via discussion is probably the most flexible and powerful form of teaching that there is. More than any other method, it is sensitive to the students' needs and interests. It is not the only effective way to teach, however, and needs to be fitted into the teacher's repertoire, along with direct teaching and co-operative group work.

The Socratic Tradition: Then and Now

Teaching through some form of dialogue, whether it is a dialogue between two people or an interchange involving more than two, is a very ancient tradition in European culture. One of the first examples of systematic teaching to be recorded, over 2,000 years ago, was Plato's account of his own teacher, Socrates, who taught by engaging in a particular kind of dialogue with his students. First Socrates would feign ignorance and set out to get his student to give a clear account of his beliefs on some subject. Typically Socrates would then demonstrate, through a series of questions, that the student didn't really know as much as he initially thought he did. He would trap the pupil in a contradiction or a seemingly obvious absurdity. Once doubt had been thoroughly aroused in the student's mind in this manner, Socrates would then proceed to persuade the student of the truth of his own (Socrates') point of view, again by asking the student to agree or disagree with a series of claims, examples and general proposals about the topic under discussion.

To a modern reader, the Socratic dialogues (Saunders, 1987) may often seem somewhat staged and dramatically unconvincing. In writing about Socrates, Plato's underlying aim was to set out a particular philosophical position; for his didactic purposes, he generally represents the pupil as something of a stooge, with Socrates always emerging as the winner. Nevertheless these ancient simulations enshrine a number of key ideas about teaching which have survived to our own day. In the first place, Socrates and the pupil are presented to the reader as collaborators, partners in an investigation into the nature of things, from which they both may learn. This contrasts with another model of teacher and pupil in which the teacher is the authority on some subject, and chooses to enlighten the essentially ignorant pupil. Socrates always claimed that he possessed only one kind of wisdom: the wisdom of knowing how little he really knew. He aimed to persuade others that they, too, needed to discover the extent of their own ignorance before really starting to construct a more durable and consistent view of the world. Thus Socrates, in Plato's account, is a democratic figure, in so far as he is prepared to learn as well as to teach, and ready to deal with his pupil on an equal footing, whether he is talking to a rich nobleman or a slave boy. Socrates is not equal to the pupil, however, in terms of his knowledge, and his pupils do not often ask questions.

A second key idea which emerges from the Socratic dialogues is that in discussion we can test out our ideas critically, finding out their weaknesses and errors. In European thought this use of discussion has sometimes taken the form of an adversarial debate, or dispute, in which contrasting points of view are compared and judged for their soundness. The underlying theme is that disagreement and conflict can be resolved through talk rather than through fighting. We can allow our ideas to be killed off, rather than ourselves. The ancient tradition of discussion thus includes both a democratic ideal of collaboration in the construction of a common understanding and also a critical ideal of discussion as an impersonal testing ground for ideas.

Socrates described himself in one place as a 'midwife of truth'. In this metaphor he sought to explain how his subtle form of question and answer could help a pupil to realize his own errors and 'give birth' to a new appreciation of a problem. Socrates also believed that he was essentially 'reawakening' ideas which were innate, but dormant, in the student's mind. This view of learning would rarely be defended today, and it would be more common now to argue that the Socratic method uses leading questions to guide the pupil towards the construction of a new point of view or understanding. In any case, there is an underlying view of the learner as an active participant, as having to share in the process of articulating a problem or its solution.

This general view of learning has many variants but they share the idea that knowledge cannot simply be given to the learner. The learner has to make sense of new ideas by connecting them up with previous knowledge, and he or she does this by using the ideas, in talk, writing or action. As the Bullock Report on language in education put it: 'the learner has to make a journey in thought for himself' (DES, 1975, p. 141).

If one takes this point seriously, it is clear that teachers cannot simply tell things to pupils, and expect to be understood. They must get in touch with their pupils' existing ideas about a problem or issue. But though mutual respect between teacher and learner may be an ideal we pursue, the typical imbalance in knowledge between teacher and learner hardly suggests that their roles in a discussion will be identical. Sometimes, of course, a learner turns out to know more about some aspect of a problem than the teacher does. But even when this is not the case, the teacher has to try to attune his or her teaching to the learner's understanding. In this sense, a discussion is a collaborative venture, aimed primarily at furthering the learner's understanding.

In practice, the journey in thought which is undertaken in a primary classroom is not simply an individual affair. At different levels, and to different degrees, there is a common curriculum and there is teaching which is shared amongst many. This makes the idea of a 'dialogue' problematic, for it is extremely difficult to give equal attention to every learner. We shall return to this problem, after looking for some of the roots of dialogue and discussion in the child's early forms of learning.

Early Conversations

Not all teaching need involve language; perhaps the simplest form of teaching is the deliberate demonstration of some activity which is then imitated by the learner. The simplest form of teaching involving language, however, is perhaps a child's questions and an adult's answers. Thus, in the following example, Elizabeth, aged 4, is watching her mother shovel wood ash from the grate into a bucket:

Elizabeth: What are you doing that for?
Mother: I'm gathering it up and putting it outside so that Daddy can put it on the garden.
Elizabeth: Why does he have to put it on the garden?
Mother: To make the compost right.
Elizabeth: Does that make the grass grow?

Mother: Yes.
Elizabeth: Why does it?
Mother: You know how I tell you that you need to eat different things like
             eggs and cabbage and rice pudding to make you grow into a big
             girl?
Elizabeth: Yes.
Mother: Well, plants need different foods, too. Ash is one of the things
             that's good for them.

                                                                (Wells, 1987, p. 59)

It is worth noting some features of this interchange. First, the dialogue is
initiated by the child, who wants to understand something she can see going
on. Second, the mother takes trouble in trying to find genuine answers, which
are pitched at a level of language and imagery which she thinks Elizabeth
will understand. In addition, Elizabeth has plenty of time to ask supplementary questions and to check her own understanding ('Does that make the
grass grow?'). She thus brings her existing knowledge to bear on the situation
and extends it. The mother's knowledge is placed at the service of the child,
as the child asks for it. We can at least feel that Elizabeth has a good chance
here of assimilating some of the new information and thus of enriching her
understanding of how plants can be helped to grow.

These features – initiation of the dialogue by the interested child, matching
of answers to the child's level of understanding and time in which to explore
and elaborate that understanding – seem generally helpful and yet are
difficult to reproduce in a classroom setting. Wells (1987) found, when he
studied the experience of language of a group of thirty-two 4- to 5-year-olds,
both at home and at school, that the children initiated 64 per cent of the
conversation at home but only 23 per cent of conversations at school. In the
classroom, with one teacher to about thirty children, the teacher's language
was far more dominant than the parent's at home. Teachers asked more
questions, made more requests, and generally not only talked more but
controlled the topic of the talk for the most part. The children, not
surprisingly, were left with less to say. Their talk in the classroom was
impoverished compared with their talk at home: it was more fragmented,
less grammatically complex and expressed a narrower range of meanings.
This was true not only for some but for all of the group.

Even before they start asking questions, children participate in interchanges
of meaning with the adults around them, which seem to set the stage for
learning to talk. In infancy, parents share simple activities with their babies
such as holding and clapping together the baby's hands, repeatedly tickling
or kissing his or her face or tummy, hiding and revealing their faces or
repeatedly giving the baby an object which is then thrown or dropped.
Typically, the parent organizes and times the activity so that the baby can
play his or her limited part in the 'dialogue' in spite of not being very skilled.
By clapping the baby's hands together, for example, the parent both does

something to the baby and simultaneously demonstrates what the baby might do. As the infant takes on more and more of an active role, the parent relinquishes control and simply becomes a partner in the enterprise.

Sensitive parents time their actions and communications to fit in with the signs the infant gives of being alert, interested and amused. They offer help when it is needed and they provide praise and feedback on progress. Adults also implicitly pose demands, which seem to anticipate questions. For instance, by setting a rattle near the baby's hand, the adult seems to imply the question: 'What can you do with this?' The baby's response, say of sweeping the rattle off the table, demonstrates a form of comprehension, or of interpretation: 'This is what I can do!' It seems that these repeated playful exchanges mimic features of dialogue, such as turn-taking and joint attention by two people to the same topic, or context. The child's first understanding, and first production, of words fit into just such frameworks of familiar social interaction.

Often in such interchanges, the adult uses language to direct the child's attention to particular features of the situation. In learning to participate in such conversations, children both learn how to talk and learn about a particular culture's view of the world. The words comment in different ways on what is worth noticing. The context of objects and activities provides an immediate reference for possible meanings of the words. If the adult matches what she says and what she does to what the child is currently interested in, she has a good chance of making contact with the child's ongoing train of thought and of extending it.

Summary

- Knowledge cannot simply be given to the learner: the learner must work to make sense of what is offered.
- Dialogue creates the opportunity for a teacher to be most responsive to the learner's sense-making.
- In dialogue teachers and learners are collaborators in making meaning.
- Key features of natural learning dialogues (e.g. between mothers and their infants) include:
  - child initiates the talk;
  - adult responses are paced and matched to the child;
  - time is allowed for supplementary questions.
- These features prove very difficult to reproduce in classrooms.

Vygotsky and the Functions of Discussion

The Russian psychologist Vygotsky (whose work dates from the 1930s but was not published in the West until the 1960s and 1970s) came to believe that human thought was transformed by the child's participation in such conversations. Language originates in such dialogues, Vygotsky argued, with the adult demonstrating how to make meanings with words and how to relate words to things. Adults also listen and provide feedback on how far the child's early utterances are comprehensible. Then, in a crucial developmental move, the child begins to talk as an accompaniment to her own practical activities.

Vygotsky (1978) describes an informal experiment in which children of 4 to 5 years were set the challenge of using a stool and a stick to reach a sweet which had been placed out of reach in a cupboard. The children talked as they tried to solve this problem, initially simply providing a running commentary on parts of what they were doing. Older children talked also about what they were about to do, what they might do and what they had already done. Language gradually took on the functions of planning actions, monitoring progress and evaluating outcomes. What had started as social speech, learned and used in conversations with others, had become 'speech for oneself' which shaped practical activity into an organized structure.

Vygotsky felt that this developing system of control, in which speech increasingly organized the child's own intentions, perceptions and actions, helped to free the child from impulsive acts and from being dominated by the immediate sights and sounds of the concrete perceptual world. He argued that 'the ability or inability to direct one's own attention is an essential determinant of the success or failure of any practical operation.' And again: 'There is reason to believe that voluntary activity, more than highly developed intellect, distinguishes humans from the animals which stand closest to them.' (1978, pp. 35, 37). Nor was this all. Sharing the language of the community led firstly to speech for oneself and then, in another crucial development, to inner speech. Gradually the child learns to carry on a soundless, internal dialogue, which draws on the forms of social speech, but becomes a kind of 'shorthand' system of meaning, operated privately.

In the following example, again from Wells (1987), Simon, aged 4 years and 9 months, has just eaten an apple and talks about the pips, partly to his mother and partly to himself. It seems possible to hear at one and the same time the patterns of dialogue which Simon has practised repeatedly with his parents in the past and the pattern of inner speech which he is in the process of learning, as he examines the apple pips:

> Simon: A pip is a seed. So he can grow. And we might be able to grow some now. Got some apple seeds – apple pip seeds – and if I put even more, Daddy and me might go out one day, which isn't a rainy day, and we might be able to plant the seeds. Or I could plant them tomorrow. (Wells, 1987, p. 65)

This process of internalizing the forms of dialogue provides one clue to the importance of teaching through discussion. It suggests that at least one central type of thinking for oneself is carried on in a silent interior conversation, which feeds off actual conversations and discussions in which one has taken part. Thus it may be that discussion plays three roles in our learning:

- It supports our efforts to construct new meanings, or new understandings, as we explore them in words.
- It allows us to test out and criticize claims and different points of view as we speak to and listen to others.
- It provides raw material for our own, later, private reflective thought.

An Example of Classroom Discussion

The following passage forms part of a long discussion held by a group of four 10-year-olds who had been asked by their teacher to explore comparisons between life in contemporary and in Tudor England. In this excerpt they are led by their own collective talk into a discussion about church attendance;

Teacher: Try comparing the two, what sort of comparisons do you make between the two?

Michael: Well today people aren't that religious; in Tudor times you had to go to church.

Peter: Yes but, don't have to go to church now and that's all right isn't it?

Simone: Yes, but we're not made to go to church, we get the choice but we're not made to go . . .

Michael: Some people's families just go.

Simone: Don't get the choice even if they don't want to, they just say you're going, but now, nowadays they say go and try it out and if you don't like it you don't have to go there.

Adam: Yes that's what my Dad did to me.

Michael: The Roman Catholics, there are still a few around, yes they still have to go.

Peter: Yes but Helen, she doesn't get ordered to go, does she, goes . . .

Adam: She is.

Peter: She goes, but there isn't anyone to tell Simone, she's dedicated to it . . .

Adam: Yes . . .

Michael: She's committed to it, so she does it.

(Burgess and Gulliver, 1989)

In this discussion we can observe many of the different ways in which meaning can be explored, elaborated and tested out during discussion. Thus, the children make explicit various beliefs that they hold, making bids, as it were, for what is worth saying in answer to the original question. They sometimes pick up one another's thoughts and extend them, as when Michael says: 'Some people's families just go', and Simone continues: 'Don't get the choice, even if they want to.' They also support one another by assenting to judgements (e.g. Adam's 'Yes') or by rephrasing an idea in different words (e.g. Michael's 'She's committed to it'). They show an unusual degree of supportiveness and, in the relaxed atmosphere which prevails, they seem ready to offer tentative ideas as well as quite personal accounts, without feeling threatened. They use their own experience in making some possible links with the original question about history, and in this way perhaps build a foundation for further understanding about the social rules and habits of Tudor times. Occasionally they challenge one another's ideas, as when Peter says: 'Yes but Helen, she doesn't get ordered to go . . .'

Perhaps significantly, the teacher is rather reticent, addressing the occasional remark to the whole group, and once to an individual, to ask for elaboration. She refrains from evaluating the children's ideas, on the whole, and allows the children to wander far from the original point at issue. She does not, therefore, get quite the historical discussion she planned for, but she learns a good deal about the level of the children's understanding about religion and about their abilities in speaking and listening.

Some Problems with Discussion in Classrooms

The sort of confident discussion illustrated in the previous section was no doubt the result of extended efforts by this teacher to promote learning through talk in her classroom. It is far removed from a pattern of classroom interaction which has been shown to be very common and which is typified by the following:

Teacher: What kind of evidence would it be?
(Pause. Silence.)
Teacher: What's the special name for it?
(Several hands go up.)
Pupil: Primary.
Teacher: Primary, good lad . . .

Here the teacher checks the pupils' understanding of the concept (of primary evidence, in history) by asking a question. Not getting an immediate response, he rephrases the question, providing a clue as he does so. A pupil then responds with a one-word answer and the teacher evaluates this approvingly. Such cycles are extremely common in classrooms and have been described as 'IRE' patterns, the letters standing for Initiation, Response and Evaluation. The teacher initiates, the pupil responds and the teacher evaluates the response. Whilst such interactions have a perfectly proper place, for example in direct teaching, they do not allow the same kind of meaning-making and testing activities which we have looked at above.

The danger is, then, that teachers may never move far from this kind of tightly controlled communication, in which the pupils have to compete to provide one-word answers to a sequence of 'display' questions (that is, questions which ask pupils to display their knowledge; the teacher, of course, already knows the answer). Such interactions also sometimes degenerate into a sort of guessing game in which the teacher searches in vain for the pupils to come up with a particular word, which she is thinking of herself:

Teacher: What kind of a seashore?
Pupil: Sandy.
Teacher: What else?
         (Silence.)
Pupil: Lonely.
Teacher: and bare ... Let's have a look at the man ... what kind of figure
         is it?
Pupil: It's an old man.
Teacher: I'm thinking about him being alone – another word beginning with
         's' ...

'Solitary' was the word the teacher had in mind (Hull, 1985, p. 165) but it seems pointless to press the children to guess this. Such exchanges provide one example of a number of ways in which teachers may sometimes dominate classroom talk without actually contributing much to the learning which they hoped to encourage (see also Wragg and Brown, 1993b).

A general finding from educational research into classroom talk (Edwards and Westgate, 1987) is that teachers tend to control tightly the pattern of communication, in terms of who is allowed to talk, what is talked about and what kind of language should be used to talk about it. This domination of the discourse by teachers has sometimes seemed depressing to observers, particularly those who are convinced of the possible benefits of learning through discussion, but it probably follows from certain peculiarities of typical classrooms, as places for discussion.

In the first place, teachers have a responsibility to keep order so that learning can occur, and this entails being able to communicate clearly to everyone in the room. Robertson (1981) has argued persuasively that teachers need at least to be *able* to control the pattern of communication if they are to keep order. The simple fact is that if the teacher fails to act to control communication the children rapidly 'fill the vacuum' and take over the control for themselves. If this happens repeatedly the teacher will find it very hard to regain the control which has been lost. Children also find it difficult to take turns in a discussion when they have something significant to say, and they are often much more interested in their own contribution than in listening to others (something which perhaps applies equally to most adults). This makes it difficult to conduct a discussion with some thirty children who may all want to take part at once.

In the second place, teachers have a responsibility to teach a particular curriculum and the business of directing the children's attention towards that curriculum and away from entertaining distractions is a necessary part of teaching. Time is limited, and teachers feel extremely pressed to 'cover the ground' expected of them.

Third, teachers are in general more knowledgeable than the children they teach, at least in respect of the curriculum, and this uneven distribution of knowledge makes their contribution crucial in judging what is 'relevant' and 'correct' in any discussion. Children expect teachers to know more, and they thus find it somewhat disturbing when teachers step down from this position of power and attempt to hand over control to them, the pupils. They also rapidly grow bored if they are required to listen to long rambling anecdotes from a whole sequence of others in the class.

A 'conversation' may be thought of as a particular form of civilized discussion in which the talkers are more or less equal in status, few enough in number, and knowledgeable enough about the topic, for all to participate on equal terms. Conversations are unpredictable precisely because no one has the right to control what is said or a monopoly on what is worth saying. In a good conversation the speakers will neither accept contributions uncritically nor compete too sharply, but will listen and take part, helping to build the overall quality and interest of what is said. None of these conditions is typical of a primary classroom, and therefore it has to be admitted that classroom discussions seems unlikely often to reach the status of genuine conversations. It is no coincidence, for instance, that the extended discussion about churchgoing, quoted above, took place between a group of only four children and a teacher, all of whom knew each other well.

Promoting conversation

Although many difficulties thus seem to beset the enterprise of promoting discussion in classrooms, it should not be thought that good discussion is an impossible goal for the teacher to aim at. Matthew Lipman, for example, who has pioneered an approach to teaching philosophy to children, based on discussion of specially written stories, has shown that if the normal rules of the classroom are redefined, in what he calls a 'Community of Inquiry', classes can be absorbed in orderly and productive discussion for an hour or more (Lipman, 1988; Lipman, Sharp and Oscanyan, 1980).

A Community of Inquiry models a system of democratic discussion, based on ground rules of listening, mutual respect, giving reasons and tolerance of diverse views (Splitter and Sharp, 1994). The teacher still has responsibility, in terms of ensuring that these democratic and reasonable procedures are adhered to. The content and direction of the discussion, however, is largely under the control of the participants. Lipman's (1993) 'Philosophy for Children', which has been used with children aged from 4 years old upwards, and is now being taught in more than thirty different countries, offers one fascinating model of how children can learn through critical and creative discussion in a supportive and self-regulating group.

An alternative approach to free-ranging talk involves splitting the class up into small groups. Here, again, it has to be realized that in handing over greater control to the children we are making them responsible to a far greater extent for the judgements made about what is relevant and what is correct. Choosing when to do this is then part of the teacher's role (see also chapter 8). There is also the case of discussion between the teacher and either an individual or a small group, and it is to this that we now turn.

Conferences with Individuals

Individal attention offers the possibility of teaching which approaches the conditions which obtained in the original Socratic dialogues. Primary teachers often stress the importance they attach to one-to-one teaching, in which the individual child's current state of knowledge and difficulties can be addressed in a detailed discussion. The desire to individualize teaching is largely impract-ical, however, with class sizes of around thirty. Galton, Simon and Croll (1980), in a study of over fifty primary classrooms, found that the average pupil could actually expect to receive on average one minute and twenty-three seconds of individual attention from the teacher in each hour, and a further fifty-four seconds as a part of a small group. Although teachers spent much of their time talking to individuals, the bulk of an individual pupil's interaction with the teacher was actually as a member of the whole class.

The same research showed that even when teachers did talk to individuals, the interchanges tended to focus on making sure that the child knew what to do and was getting on with his or her work. If a teacher tries to break out of this pattern by spending longer in conversation with one child, the typical result is that a queue of children seeking help or direction quickly starts to form. This not only means that the queuing children are wasting time but often leads to minor disputes and to the distraction of children who are trying to work. As with whole-class discussion, only by instituting a different set of priorities and rules can these problems be overcome. The rules should help children over a period of time to understand that they must help themselves, or seek help from each other, before interrupting the teacher. They need to be able to set themselves to some alternative work until the teacher can deal with their query and generally become less dependent on the teacher for reassurance. Only such changes in classroom organization can allow greater time for individual and small-group discussion (see also chapters 8 and 11).

In one area of the primary curriculum, the teaching of reading, teachers have always devoted time to individuals. Contemporary advice on good practice in listening to children read (Wray and Medwell, 1991) suggests that fewer, lengthier individual reading sessions are more useful in the long run than very short daily ones. The main justification for this advice is to allow for longer conversations about the meaning of what the child is reading. Similarly, in the area of teaching children to write, a powerful case has been made for ensuring that children have the opportunity to talk quite extensively to the teacher about their writing during a 'writing conference' (Graves, 1983). Graves offers a wealth of practical advice on organizing the class so that conferences of various kinds, lasting between two and ten minutes, can regularly take place.

Graves also offers three main justifications for teaching via conferences. The first is that children teach us, the teachers, about their own state of knowledge when they explain what they are doing and what they are finding difficult. In other words, the conference functions as a means of ongoing assessment, allowing the diagnosis of problems. Second, by talking about their own writing, children actually learn about it. This is because children, like the rest of us, don't know they know until they start to investigate their own understanding. One way to do this is through talk, which allows us to explore the extent of our understanding and equally our lack of understanding. The third justification is that conferences allow the teacher to provide help, shaped to fit the problems which the child has outlined. In short, the conference, and indeed any other form of one-to-one conversation with a pupil, allows the possibility of

- diagnostic assessment
- self-initiated learning
- teaching at appropriate pace and level.

Graves emphasizes in particular the need to let children lead the way in a conference. The teacher's main tasks are to listen sympathetically and to learn as much as possible about the child's view of the work in hand. Teachers who are used to dominating the discussion in a classroom find this shift towards listening particularly difficult. Only when the teacher is clear about the child's view of the problem does she offer some advice, or ask a question. Such advice is likely to follow one of a number of possible routes, or functions, which the teacher already has in mind. The principal functions can be listed as follows:

- Understanding: the teacher checks that she has understood the sense of what the child is saying.

- Orienting: the teacher draws attention to something she feels is relevant to the problem or its solution.
- Sustaining: the teacher responds so as to encourage the child to say more, to go on with the train of thought.
- Elaborating: the teacher extends the sense of what the child has said, adding to the information or rephrasing it.
- Checking: the teacher has noticed a possible error or problem which the child has overlooked and prompts the child to look again.
- Informing: the teacher gives the child some relevant information.
- Explaining: the teacher offers an explanation for something the child is confused by.
- Challenging: the teacher judges that the child can cope with a challenge or a criticism, to stimulate further thought, or an alternative solution.
- Directing: the teacher suggests what the child needs to do next.
- Encouraging: the teacher offers reassurance, praise or other encouragement, either to celebrate what has been achieved or to motivate the child to persevere.

Several of these functions may be carried out by asking the child a question, and indeed most teachers seem to proceed on the assumption that the first thing to do with children is to question them. Paradoxically, however, this may not be the most effective way of finding out what one wants to know (Dillon, 1990). Questions tend to be 'controlling' moves in conversation, steering the topic in one direction or another. The response of children, and indeed others, is often to be wary of saying too much when answering questions. If the teacher asks, 'Did you enjoy that story?' and the child replies, 'It was okay', the conversation stalls until, as likely as not, the teacher asks another question. Strings of such questions may lead to less and less informative answers.

As Wood (1986) and others have established, it is often a more effective move in conversation not to ask a question at all, but to offer information, or an opinion, and to wait for the child to respond. Exactly the same finding has been made in written dialogues between teachers and pupils (Hall, 1989). If teachers try to initiate a correspondence by asking a written question: e.g. 'How many pets have you got at home?' the child as often as not writes back a one-word answer: e.g. '2' or simply ignores the question altogether. Teachers who instead offer some information about themselves ('I have a friend called Judy') may stimulate first a question in return: 'wot dose she luk like, dose she luk nis', and then some information offered in return: 'I like blond hair My dols got blond hair . . .'

Summary

- Classroom teacher–pupil dialogue is mainly controlled by teachers. It is frequently routine and predictable.

- Vygotsky's theory holds that dialogue promotes internalization of ideas, empowers thoughtfulness and acts as a model for private thought.
- In this theory, thought is internal dialogue.
- The limitations of classroom dialogue are, in this light, a great cause for concern.
- Attempts at child-initiated dialogue seem to threaten the teacher's control, slow down the speed of curriculum coverage and bore the children not involved.
- Classroom dialogue can be successful, however, if certain rules are taught and adhered to.
- Lipman has suggested that rules for dialogue should require
  - listening
  - respect for others
  - speakers to give reasons
  - diversity to be tolerated.
- Classroom conferences between teacher and pupil should focus on specific work. Conferences allow opportunities for
  - assessment
  - children to learn from reflection
  - teacher to offer well-matched help.

Teaching in the 'Zone of Proximal Development'

Vygotsky suggested that our assessments of children should extend beyond estimates of what they are capable of achieving by themselves independently. We should provide prompts, clues and guidance to discover how much further a child can progress when given support. The area of work in which the child cannot manage alone but can progress if given assistance, Vygotsky called the 'zone of proximal development'. In his most succinct formulation of the importance of the 'zone' Vygotsky (1978, p. 87) wrote: 'what a child can do with assistance today she will be able to do by herself tomorrow.' This has proved to be a fruitful way of thinking about teaching as well as assessment, since the teacher's most general role can be formulated so as to assist the child through the zone of proximal development. Wood (1986) provides two very simple rules to use in undertaking this kind of assistance, which he calls 'contingent teaching': if the child fails with an attempt at a problem, immediately increase the degree of help offered, or take over control of some of the problem; if the child succeeds, immediately start to offer less help, or relinquish some control to the child. Though simple in theory, these rules are actually very hard to follow consistently in practice, especially when interacting with several children, one after another.

Tharp and Gallimore (1988) describe four stages of progression through and beyond the zone of proximal development. In the first stage, corresponding to Wood's contingent teaching, a more knowledgeable adult, such as a teacher, selects and organizes activities and resources for a child and provides the 'scaffolding' or help to support the child through to completion of the task. The child may not understand the goal of the activity initially, or at least not in the same way that the adult does. The child might simply want to play with the coloured plastic cubes to make interesting patterns, for example, whilst the teacher intends that she learn about the way tens and units operate, and are written, in our number system. As they interact, the teacher invents sub-goals such as asking the child to make 'thirty-six' in blocks of tens and some units. The child may also shift to another sub-goal, when she wonders if three lengths of ten cubes always makes thirty, so she can simplify the process of counting. As the interaction continues, the teacher estimates how much new information, and what challenges, the child can manage. She helps if the child gets stuck, but tries to allow the child to solve each problem as independently as possible. Language and physical activities with objects or symbols support one another, each contributing to the child's and the teacher's understanding of what is going on. The role of language in the interchange is chiefly to guide both teacher and child towards an estimate of what is known and what remains unknown about both child and task.

The first stage ends when the child can effectively manage a particular task independently. In the second, the child tries out a series of similar problems on her own, without any assistance from the teacher. The child will then use self-directed speech, whether out loud or internally, to give assistance to herself. Regulation by the other has developed into regulation by the self. The third and fourth stages deal with developing routines and with relearning. This is, of course, an idealized description of learning, and in reality the learner may shift backwards and forwards many times between the various stages of dependence and independence. A single activity, such as writing a story, will include different aspects of knowledge and skill each with its own 'ZPD'.

Some Conditions for Effective Discussion

The extent to which teachers can use discussion and conversation in this detailed way to teach is constrained by obvious factors, including class sizes, the broad range of the prescribed curriculum and the many individual differences in understanding and motivation amongst the children in any one class. A completely individualized curriculum, with individualized teaching, is not a viable option in the conditions of the typical primary class. None the less, some individual and small-group teaching can be accomplished, and it is probably best directed towards tasks which are at the end of stage 1 and the beginning of stage 2 of Tharp and Gallimore's extended schema of the ZPD. Some initial understanding of the task should exist, perhaps following direct teaching and demonstration, and the child is moving towards independent performance, or else is trying out self-regulation.

When conducting discussions, the teacher needs not only a sensitivity towards the child and the clues which observation affords about his or her current level of understanding, but also a thorough knowledge of the subject or task being attempted. This is necessary so that prompts, slight changes in sub-goals, helpful simplifications and linking metaphors can all be fluently provided during discussion, without removing control completely from the learner. In this way, teaching via discussion has the potential to get closer to the learner's difficulties and achievements than any other form of teaching. In discussion we think out loud and try to make contact with both our own and others' view of the world. In doing so, we continuously create the possibility for development in thinking, and at the same time practise one of the key functions of language itself.

Whereas during the 1970s and early 1980s there was a significant shift towards valuing talk in the primary school as 'a good thing' which was a powerful means of learning, the trend since then has been towards a more careful and qualified approval of talk, with a closer attention to the quality of talk in different contexts. Talk in the classroom can even be destructive of thought. Constant chatter distracts from attempts an individual child may make to think about a problem in a sustained way over a period of time. It is surely significant that as adults we regularly seek out peace and quiet if we want to write, or compose, or work on a difficult problem. We are coming to appreciate once again the importance of periods of silence in classrooms, in order to allow individuals to conduct the inner dialogue of sustained thinking for themselves. Having said this, examples such as 'Philosophy for Children' (Lipman, 1993) and the work of the National Oracy Project (Norman, 1992) provide powerful examples of the ways in which discussion can breathe life into the process of learning in classrooms.

Summary

- The 'zone of proximal development' is the area in which the child cannot manage alone but can manage with assistance.
- The ZPD is an ever-changing area where teaching for understanding can have its biggest return on effort.
- Teachers' subject-matter knowledge and their ability to conduct conversations are crucial if high-quality teaching sensitive to the learner's needs is to be given.

Editor's Commentary

In this chapter another essential teaching skill – that of teaching through discussion – has been introduced and its importance for promoting understanding explained. Talk is easy; thought-provoking professional discussion which enhances children's understanding is much more difficult. The ideas in this chapter can be followed into practice in the following aspects of school-based work:

- With permission, observe and record (or otherwise make notes on) classroom dialogues intended to promote learning and understanding. Analyse these records with colleagues and experienced teachers. Did the conversations promote learning? How do you know? What evidence have you got?
- Using the materials in this chapter, draw up a checklist for the conduct of good learning conversations. Use the checklist to prepare yourself for such teaching. Use the checklist afterwards to evaluate your efforts. (Of course, appropriate records would have to be kept.) Discuss your efforts with experienced teachers. How can you improve?
- Note how different forms of classroom management can help or hinder learning conversations. Observe a range of organization strategies. What forms of management create the best possibilities for learning conversations?
- Good conversations can be had without a teacher, but they do not happen naturally and certainly not without planning and effort. Work with a group of children to improve their learning conversations. Share your aims and ideas with them from the outset.

The ideas in this chapter are closely linked to those in other chapters in the book. Closely related matters are classroom management and pupil autonomy:

- Classroom management is covered in chapters 4 and 10.
- Pupil autonomy is covered in chapter 11.

FURTHER READING

An excellent collection of work from the National Oracy Project can be found in:

Norman, K. (Ed.). (1992). *Thinking voices*. London: Hodder.

One of a number of practical guides to teaching is provided by:

Laar, B., Laycock, L. & Watkins, L. (1990). *Practical guides, English: Teaching within the National Curriculum*. Leamington Spa, England: Scholastic.

8

Managing Learning through Group Work

Neville Bennett

Editor's Overview

There are some educational goals which can only be attained through group work. These include learning to co-operate and learning to work in a team. But Neville Bennett shows in this chapter that well-planned and managed group work can also increase levels of academic attainment and pupils' self-esteem. This should not be surprising because, as Richard Fox explained in chapter 7 and Neville Bennett emphasizes here, learning for understanding is essentially a social process. Group work creates the conditions for intellectual exchanges which enhance comprehension.

There are problems, however. Group work is widely provided for in classrooms, but it frequently fails to meet its potential. Reviewing available research, Bennett shows that teachers group children by ability. But the tasks given to the groups do not really require co-operation or collaboration, and in consequence children sit in a group but rarely work as a group. They mostly work as individuals. Much of the conversation which takes place has nothing to do with academic work.

Managing group work clearly stands in need of improvement. In this chapter the problems and dangers of group work are carefully analysed and directions are given on how to manage groups more profitably.

Typical Classroom Practice

Walk into almost any primary classroom and you are likely to see the class organized into groups of some four to six children, at least for some aspects of the curriculum. The composition of these groups may be stable, or they may change. This will depend on the philosophy of the teacher. Some teachers believe that groups are more effective if composed of children who are of similar ability or attainment, whereas other teachers deliberately set up mixed-ability groups. Similarly some teachers ensure that there is a mix of boys and girls in each group, whereas others do not. There is, in other words, a rich variety of practice.

But why do teachers organize their classes into groups at all? What are the supposed advantages? And are they effective?

In considering the management of children for learning, the Plowden Report (1967), although avowedly supporting and indeed prescribing, individualization, recognized a practical difficulty. If all teaching were on an individual basis, only seven or eight minutes a day would be available for each child. The report therefore advised teachers to economize by 'teaching together a small group of children who are roughly at the same stage'. Further, these groups should change in accordance with children's needs, the implications being that the class would be organized flexibly, with groups forming and re-forming according to needs and activities. Various advantages were perceived for group work. It would help children learn to get along together in a context where peers could help one another and realize their own strengths and weaknessness as well as those of others. It could make children's understanding clearer to themselves by having to explain something to others, and they could gain some opportunity to teach as well as to learn. It was hoped that apathetic children would be infected by the enthusiasm of the group, while able children would benefit by being caught up in the thrust and counterthrust of conversation in a small group of children similar to themselves.

Unfortunately, research on classroom grouping has provided little support for this rosy picture. In arguing that children in the group should be roughly at the same stage, the Plowden Report, was in effect, calling for ability grouping – and that is what tends to happen. Her Majesty's Inspectorate (HMI, 1978), for example, reported that some three-quarters of classes were grouped according to ability for maths, and that for reading, two-thirds of 7-year-olds and over one-half of 9-year-olds were grouped in this way. In our national survey of open-plan schools we found a similar picture. Sixty per cent of teachers of 6-year-olds and 40 per cent of teachers of 10-year-olds reported using ability groups (Bennett, Andreae, Hegarty and Wade, 1980),

Research which has focused on the observation of group activities in classrooms has also reported sobering findings on contemporary practice, particularly in junior classes. Here most children sit in groups, but for the great majority of the time they work as individuals on their own individual tasks. In other words, pupils work *in* groups, not *as* groups. Further, whilst they are working in groups, the amount of task-related talk is low, interactions tend to be short and the opportunity to co-operate is slim. Finally there appears to be a clear sex effect in interaction. The great majority of talk is between pupils of the same sex, even in mixed-sex groups (Galton, Simon & Croll, 1980). The small amount of research carried out at infant level indicates that there too children work in, not as, groups, but that the sex effect is far less noticeable. Levels of task-related talk are higher, but little of it is task-enhancing, that is, aids the children in understanding their work (Bennet, Desforges, Cockburn & Wilkinson, 1984).

Although similar large-scale studies have not been carried out recently, accounts of HMI and others indicated that little change has taken place (Bennett and Dunne, 1992; Cato, Fernandez, Gorman and Kispal, 1992; Galton and Williamson, 1992; Pollard, Broadfoot, Croll, Osborn and Abbott, 1994).

Typical practice is shown schematically in figures 8.1 and 8.2. Figure 8.1 represents a table at which four children (*) sit, each working on their own individual tasks (a, b, c, d) for their own individual outcomes. An example of this widespread practice is in mathematics, where children often work on published schemes but are at different stages within them.

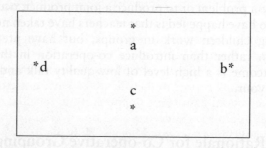

Figure 8.1 Children working individually on individual tasks for individual outcomes.

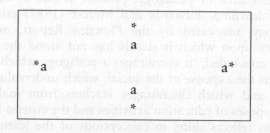

Figure 8.2 Children working individually on identical tasks for individual outcomes.

A second example is shown in figure 8.2. In this case all the children are engaged on the same task (a), but again there is no collaboration, as each is completing the task individually. This arrangement is common in creative writing, where often the whole class is set the same task – writing a story – but each child writes his or her own story.

The major weakness in these grouping arrangements is that there is no specific demand for children to work together, and rarely is a group given the opportunity to work on a group task. Thus Galton et al. (1980) concluded, 'While in most classrooms the pupils are organized in one or more seated groups for the various activities undertaken, with few exceptions they then work largely alone, as individuals. The setting is socialised in this sense but the work is individualised.' This criticism was recently reiterated by Alexander, Rose and Woodhead (1992) who argued that the fact that the children were seated in groups does not necessarily mean that they are working as a group. All too often there may be a mismatch between the collaborative setting of a group and the individual learning tasks which are given to pupils. The result is that the setting may distract pupils from their work. The dearth of co-operative endeavour is also reported by HMI. Their survey of middle schools, for example, showed that 'not many opportunities are provided for extended discussion, for collaborative work in groups, or for the exercise of choice, responsibility and initiative within the curriculum' (HMI, 1983). And at infant level, Tizard, Blatchford, Burke, Farquhar and Plewis (1988) reported that 'Groupwork, where children worked cooperatively on a task or activity, for example to solve a problem or to produce a joint product, occurred rarely.'

What seems to have happened is that teachers have taken note of Plowden's views in having children work in groups, but have preferred to retain individualization rather than introduce co-operation in that context. The unfortunate outcome is a high level of low-quality talk and a dearth of co-operative endeavour.

Rationale for Co-operative Grouping

In this important area of pedagogy, practice is out of step with current conceptions of learning. Edwards and Mercer (1987) criticized the educational ideology advocated by the Plowden Report, arguing that the Piagetian theory upon which it stands has not stood the test of time or research. They concluded, 'it encourages a pedagogy which overemphasises the individual at the expense of the social, which undervalues talk as a tool for discovery, and which discourages teachers from making explicit to children the purposes of education activities and the criteria for success.'

Such criticism reflects shifts in conceptions of the learner over the last decade. Current conceptions stress far more the social nature of learning: 'we have come once more to appreciate that through such social life the child acquires a framework for interpreting experience, and learning how to negotiate meaning in a manner congruent with the requirements of other cultures. "Making sense" is a social process' (Bruner and Haste, 1987). Bruner stresses the importance of the social setting in learning, which leads him to emphasize the role of negotiating and sharing in classroom learning. In this he has been influenced by the work of Vygotsky (1962, 1978), who assigns social interaction a central role in facilitating learning. Vygotsky (1978) argued that 'Learning awakens a variety of internal developmental processes that are able to operate only when the child is interacting with people in his environment and in cooperation with his peers.' Thus the foundation of learning and development is co-operatively achieved success.

A cornerstone of Vygotsky's perspective on learning, therefore, is a stress on opportunities for collaboration and on the quality of social interaction. This belief that talk is central to learning is not new. The Bullock Report (1975) devoted itself entirely to language, and welcomed the growth of interest in oral language, 'for we cannot emphasise too strongly our conviction of its importance in the education of the child'. It was argued that all schools ought to have, as a priority objective, a commitment to the speech needs of their pupils.

More recently, the authors of the English National Curriculum recommended a separate language component for speaking and listening: 'Our inclusion of speaking and listening as a separate profile component in our recommendations is a reflection of our conviction that these skills are of central importance to children's development' (National Curriculum Council, 1989).

Methods of Co-operative Grouping

It is clear from the foregoing that teachers need to set up classroom organizations where social interaction is encouraged, and where co-operatively achieved success is a major aim. There is, in fact, a wide variety of co-operative groups available (see Kagan, 1985, for descriptions), but most are American in origin and tend not to be suitable for use in the British context without modification. In our work on the implementation of co-operative groups in classrooms we have adapted two different types (Bennett and Dunne, 1992; Dunne and Bennett, 1990). The first is called Jigsaw (Aronson, 1978) and is shown schematically below. Figure 8.3 shows the same four children (*), around the same table, as in figures 8.1 and 8.2.

Here, the task is divided into as many parts as there are group members – in this case, four (a1, a2, a3, a4). Each child works on one part of the task, which is divided in such a way that the group outcome cannot be achieved until every group member has successful completed his or her piece of work. At this point the 'jigsaw' can be fitted together. Co-operation is thus built into the task itself, as indeed is individual accountability, that is, it is difficult in this type of group for a child to sit back and let others do the work,

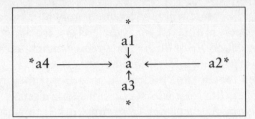

Figure 8.3 Children working individually on 'jigsaw' elements for a joint outcome.

especially since group members are likely to ensure that all pull their weight. Examples of such tasks would be the production of a group story or newspaper, or the making of a 'set' of objects in a practical maths activity.

The second kind of co-operative group, sometimes known as Group Investigation (Johnson and Johnson, 1975), is shown in figure 8.4.

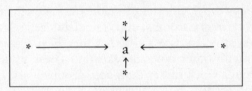

Figure 8.4 Children working jointly on one task for a joint outcome (or discussion).

In this type of group the task is not formally divided as in 'jigsaw'. Children have to work together to produce one product or outcome. Their actitivies therefore must be co-ordinated in some way. Teachers may thus choose to allocate roles to each child – chairperson, secretary, supervisor, reporter etc., or, with more experienced children, allow roles to emerge naturally in the group. Examples of tasks for this kind of group include problem solving in technology, construction activities or discussion tasks. Although collaborative endeavour is necessary for this kind of group to succeed, it is less easy to ascertain exactly what each pupil has contributed, and individual accountability is therefore lower.

These approaches demonstrate that co-operative group work is not a single, specific form of classroom organization but encompasses different approaches, different types of task and different demands for co-operation.

Summary

- There are two main reasons for organizing group work.
- First, making sense and developing understanding are essentially social activities; therefore teachers should create opportunities for social interaction.

- Second, teachers cannot teach each child individually, and diversity in attainment creates problems for whole-class teaching: groups create possibilities for economy of effort and greater matching.
- Most teachers organize children into ability groups.
- Research shows that while children sit in groups, they rarely work as a group, mainly because the tasks set do not require this.
- The prime advantage to learning of group work is thus lost.
- Two ideas of promoting co-operation and interaction are 'jigsaw' and 'group investigation'.

Studies in Co-operative Grouping

There are three kinds of research studies which throw light on the important question: Do groups work? One set of studies has implemented a particular model of group work in classrooms, and tested children's attainments before and after implementation to assess whether they have attained better in the group setting than with other types of teaching. These studies are conceived to investigate *if* groups work rather than *how* groups work.

A second set of studies has concentrated on the *how* by identifying children's behaviour and types of talk in groups and relating these to outcomes such as achievement or self-esteem. A third, and related, set of studies has also focused on the processes occurring in the group, but in this instance their purpose has been to relate these processes to such mediating factors as group composition, types of task and extent of pupil training in social and co-operative skills.

Input–Output studies

The first set of studies are largely American and present a consistent story. Reviewers such as Johnson and Johnson (1985) and Slavin (1987) agree that there is considerable evidence to show that the use of co-operative learning methods increases pupil achievement more than traditional instructional practices. The evidence also indicates that this finding is true of a range of different subject areas and of pupils of different age, sex and socio-economic background.

These same reviewers also point to improvements in the social domain. There is, they claim, considerable evidence that co-operative learning promotes greater interpersonal attraction, enhanced self-esteem and more positive relationships among pupils, particularly between ethnic groups, and the acceptance of mainstreamed children.

Studies of group processes

There is, then, substantial evidence that groups work. But how do they work?

Few studies have addressed the processes within the group that relate to enhanced cognitive and social outcomes. The most frequent aspect to be studied so far has been helping behaviour. These studies have distinguished between receiving and giving help. For receiving help to be effective for learning there must be an explanation rather than a straight answer, it must be provided in response to the receiving pupil's needs, and be understandable. It has been suggested that the effectiveness of help received may constitute a continuum – receiving explanations is sometimes helpful, receiving information has mixed effects, and receiving the answer may be actually harmful (Webb, 1989). For example, receiving an explanation which has been requested is only useful for learning if the explanation provided is relevant, understood and applied by the receiver. Receiving information, on the other hand, is more likely to be helpful more often since it is easier for the helper to frame an adequate response, and for the receiver to understand it. However, receiving only the answer is unlikely to enhance the receiver's understanding.

But what does the giver gain from this helping interaction? When the first peer tutoring system was set up, some 200 years ago, it was argued that the benefit was to the tutor. We learn by teaching. Most modern studies affirm this – giving explanations is positively related to achievement. In explaining to someone, the giver must clarify, organize, indeed reorganize, the material conceptually. Further, if the initial explanation is not understood, reformulation is necessary, utilizing perhaps different language, examples, analogies or representations. All of these, it is claimed, will consolidate or expand the giver's understanding (Webb, 1989).

Another factor studied has been the amount of time spent on task, or the amount of group talk which is task-related. When comparisons have been made between time on task in groups and in whole-class activity, it has been substantially less in whole classes (see Hertz-Lazorowitz, 1990). Similarly, when comparisons have been made between co-operative groups and normal classroom groups, pupil involvement in the former has been substantially higher. Table 8.1 shows the average amount of task-related talk in typical non-co-operative groups, taken from a study by Bennett et al. (1984), and compares these levels with those found in similar co-operative classroom groups (Bennett and Dunne, 1992). These findings indicate that children in co-operative settings demonstrate much greater involvement in their work – the average difference being 22 per cent.

Table 8.1 Percentage of task-related talk in co-operative and non-co-operative groups

Curriculum	Non-co-operative	Co-operative
Language	70	83
Maths	63	88
Technology		93
Computer tasks		99
Average	66	88

Mediating Factors in Group Processes

The third group of studies has considered the effect on group processes of teacher decisions on such issues as group size and composition, the nature of the tasks assigned, and whether the children have been given any training in social and co-operative skills.

Group size and composition

The first question teachers have to ask themselves when setting up groups is how they should be arranged. In practice teachers tend to use groups of between four and six children. Although there is no universally appropriate size of group, the most usual recommendation is for a group of four. Kagan (1985) argues this in terms of patterns of interaction and lines of communication. 'A team of three is often a dyad [i.e. a 'two'] and an outsider. In a team of three there are three possible lines of communication; in a team of four there are six. Doubling the lines of communication increases learning potential . . . teams of five often leave an odd one out, and leave less time for individual participation.' Questions of group composition have always loomed large in teachers' minds. Should they be arranged by ability or be mixed ability? Does it matter if they contain different numbers of boys and girls?

Studies which have compared ability and mixed-ability co-operative groups are few and far between, but they have raised substantial doubts about some aspects of ability grouping. Of particular concern are low-ability groups. When compared to high-ability groups, these devote substantially less of their time to interactions concerning academic content, fewer of their requests concerning academic and procedural issues are responded to appropriately, and few explanations are offered, presumably because they have insufficient skills or knowledge of the subject-matter to offer effective explanations. Not surprisingly, children in these groups show poor understanding of the task on its completion (cf. Wilkinson and Calculator, 1982; Bennett and Cass, 1988).

High-ability children on the other hand appear to perform well irrespective of the type of group they are placed in. They tend to talk more, and more of that talk is academic in content. They are the main sources of help in groups, and provide most of the explanations. These findings support Webb's (1989) contention, referred to earlier, that high-attaining children gain, both academically and socially, from the opportunity to tutor lower-achieving colleagues. It is on these bases that most advocates of co-operative learning prescribe groups of mixed ability. Cohen's (1986) views, based on her research in California, are typical 'heterogeneous groups can represent a solution to one of the most persistent problems of classroom teaching. If students are able to use each other as resources, everyone can be exposed to grade level curriculum and even more challenging material. Lack of skills in reading, writing and computation need not bar students from exposure to lessons requiring conceptualisation. At the same time, these students can develop their basic skills with assistance from their classmates.'

Differential experiences have been reported for boys and girls in whole-class and group situations. The National Oracy Project (1990), for example, argued that 'in general, boys in whole class situations tend to talk more, interrupt more and be more aggressive while girls defer to others' ideas and are more tentative.' It suggested that work in smaller groups had the potential for counteracting some of these trends. However, the research evidence would argue that it depends on the ratio of boys and girls in the group. Webb and Kenderski (1985) and Bennett and Dunne (1992) found that where there were equal numbers of boys and girls, or where girls outnumbered boys, both had similar learning experiences. Where boys outnumbered girls, the girls were disadvantaged. They spoke less, at a lower level of reasoning, and were often ignored by the boys. In such groups boys are much more successful in obtaining help. Webb concluded that the interaction in such groups was detrimental to the girls' achievement – 'they did not learn as much as the males in these group compositions.'

Task design

We have, over several years, been working co-operatively with teachers in order to understand better the issues involved in successful implementation of co-operative grouping. Choosing appropriate tasks for co-operative working has proved to be the most difficult aspect for teachers. As one teacher wrote, 'designing and presenting tasks is one of the biggest problems of co-operative group work.'

There are two facets in the planning process – the cognitive demand of the task, and the social demand. These are shown in figure 8.5. How these are interrelated is best shown with a real example. Imagine that a teacher has

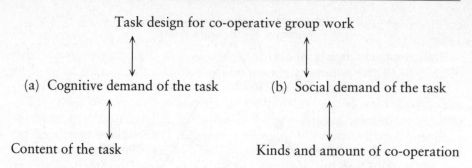

Figure 8.5 Cognitive and social demands for co-operative tasks.

chosen the statement of attainment from the English 'Speaking and Listening' targets: 'Plan and participate in a presentation e.g. of the outcome of a group activity, a poem, story, dramatize scene or play', and that this statement was interpreted by the teacher in terms of children participating in a presentation of a radio news programme.

One way of fulfilling this demand in terms of a group activity is to set up a 'jigsaw' task; that is, children work at individual items for the news programme, but must plan together and must fit the individual items together to make a coherent whole.

In this case, the teacher chose a cognitive demand in terms of a statement of attainment, and then decided on a type of group embodying the social demand she desired, opting for a 'jigsaw' method. It would, however, be possible to decide on a method of working in groups first, (say 'jigsaw'), and then plan the cognitive demand to fit this social demand. Either way, the two are closely linked.

The next step for the teacher is to enable the children to fulfil her plan. At the implementation stage, the pupils will have to make decisions, for example about the new material to be used and the style of presentation, and they will have to write items or reports. Since this is set up as a 'jigsaw' task, it is important that some work is undertaken as a group and some is individual. Pupils will, therefore, have to decide on who does what within the group, who writes which report, check that individual work reaches the desired standard, that they pay attention to each other's ideas, and organize the actual presentation together. Once again, the cognitive demand and the social demand are closely linked; both dictate the way in which children will be expected to operate. Figure 8.6 represents these steps in task design and demonstrates the links between them.

Co-operative grouping is most successful when children are required to share understandings, knowledge and skills to a common end, through some form of problem solving or open task. Barnes and Todd (1977), in their study of lower secondary children, noticed that the co-operating teachers distinguished between 'loose' and 'tight' tasks for group work. Their distinction reflects the difference between those activities that have 'correct'

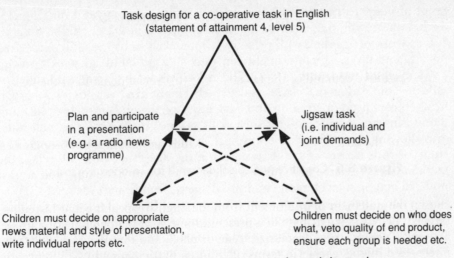

Figure 8.6 Planning for cognitive and social demands.

solutions and those that do not; tight tasks are likely to need responses that are highly focused; loose tasks are unlikely to need 'right' answers, and responses can be more wide-ranging. It became clear that the extent to which tasks were 'tight' or 'loose' had a marked impact on ways of working, and many problems emerged when teachers misjudged this impact. Similar findings have been reported by Cowie and Rudduck (1988).

More recently we have been considering the distinction between tasks demanding action talk and abstract talk. The distinction, derived from Piaget's (1959) ideas on the development of children's conversations, distinguishes tasks which demand no more than talk related to the ongoing action of the moment, from those which demand explanations or reconstruction. Here we found, for example, that tasks demanding abstract talk were rarely found in mathematics and technology, but were more frequent in language tasks (Bennett and Dunne, 1992).

Training

There appears to be an assumption among teachers that pupils do not need any training in social and co-operative skills for group work to be effective. Yet research has shown that when such skills are practised the quality and effectiveness improves. Much of this research is American, although some British resources and techniques for training, focusing particularly at secondary level, are provided by Cowie and Rudduck (1988) and Jenkin (1989).

Kagan (1988) has carried out most of the studies on training primary-age children. He argues that for pupils to benefit from group work 'requires a degree of tolerance and mutual understanding, the ability to articulate a point of view, to engage in discussion, reasoning, probing and questioning. Such skills are not in themselves innate, they have to be learnt, and so taught.'

Our work on training with primary school teachers has been in part based on Kagan's tasks, suitably anglicized into a 'team-building' pack (Austin, 1991; Bennett and Dunne, 1992). The tasks included brainstorming rules for talk, a 'completing the circle' task which emphasized sensitivity to group needs through co-operation, practical tasks on helping through talk, and monitoring group processes for such skills as conciseness, listening, reflecting, and allowing all members to contribute. Initial results are encouraging. In a study of four classes of children covering the age range 5 to 11 years, the amount of task-related talk increased in every class after training, and almost doubled among the youngest children (Bennett, Dunne and Austin, 1991).

This and other research studies lead to the conclusion that teachers should, ideally, set up training or awareness-raising activities through tasks of the type described above. Children should also be given tasks which enable them to monitor and evaluate their own behaviour in groups and become responsible for their own group's performance. In this way both teachers and pupils are participating in the development, monitoring and evaluation of group activities.

Managing teachers' time

The final aspect of teachers' management decision-making considered here is the use of teacher time, since this is crucial in relation to the opportunities for teachers to monitor, observe and evaluate group processes and outcomes.

Pupils make many demands on their teachers all day and every day. It has been our observation that many, if not most, of these demands are either not necessary, or could be dealt with in alternative ways, thus freeing invaluable teacher time. An appropriate alternative was, we felt, the devolution of some teacher authority to the group such that children would not be allowed to make any demand on the teacher until all possibilities of finding an answer from the group had been exhausted.

This was tested out with fifteen teachers, who monitored the demands of their pupils prior to and after devolution of this responsibility (Bennett and Dunne, 1992). Briefly, the average number of demands fell dramatically, from an average of over thirty-eight per lesson to less than five. The type of demand also changed. Before devolution almost two-thirds of the requests concerned checking work and transitions (e.g. 'What shall I do next?'). After devolution these comprised only one-quarter of all requests. The remainder were higher-level requests concerning knowledge or misunderstandings of specific content or concepts. It would thus seem that the group can handle the majority of typical pupil demands on teachers, thereby freeing the teacher to concentrate on enhancing group functioning.

Summary

- Typical group practices in primary classrooms are not based on any identifiable theory of teaching or learning. Rather they are a pragmatic response to the difficulties of individualizing learning.
- In reality they serve well neither the aims of individualization nor co-operation. All the evidence indicates that children working in groups rather than *as* groups results in poor task involvement, poor-quality interaction, a lack of co-operative activity and often unequal learning opportunities for boys and girls.
- Here classroom practice is at odds with current conceptions of children's learning, which stress the important of the social context, the quality of social interaction and opportunities for co-operative endeavours.
- A major implication for teachers is thus for structuring classroom organizations which encourage talk and collaborative activities. Incidentally, this is not to argue for the abandonment of individual or whole-class work, but for a shift in balance towards more co-operative work, notably with tasks demanding problem solving.
- Research on co-operative grouping indicates enhanced gains in both cognitive and effective domains, and research on classroom implementation has demonstrated that the quality of group processes is mediated by group composition, task design, training in social and co-operative skills and in the organization of teacher time.

Editor's Commentary

This is another chapter about the development of teaching skills in pursuit of learning. In it was explained the unique value of group work, and solid advice was given on how to capitalize on the potential of groups.

If you have grasped the points made about learning in earlier chapters you will now appreciate how to make the most of this advice. You could, of course, organize your own version of how to avoid the pitfalls and how to make the most of group work. You should debate your view with other learner teachers with a view to refining it. You should attempt to practise your knowledge and arrange to get feedback on your performance. You should not expect miracles. Experienced teachers find the management of group work for learning difficult. Note: managing group work to keep children busy is a lot easier.

The material in this chapter, then, should be followed up in the following school-based work:

- Carefully observe children in groups in classrooms. Do they work as a group? Do they help each other to understand the content of the work? If not, why not?
- Using the material in this chapter, draw up a comprehensive checklist for managing learning through group work. Discuss and revise your checklist in collaboration with other learner teachers (who may be very experienced teachers).
- Use your checklist to plan and implement group activities to promote learning. Arrange to get detailed evaluation of your plans and actions.

Like all teaching skills, managing learning through group work takes a lot of practice.

The ideas in this chapter may be related to other chapters in the book as follows:

- Revise the account of the social nature of learning in chapter 7.
- Relate the problems of group work to the wider issues of classroom management discussed in chapter 4.
- Consider how group work might be especially effective in learning the personal and social skills described in chapter 14.

Further Reading

The three most recent books on co-operative learning and groups each report research on group processes in classrooms, and provide practical advice on effective implementation.

Bennett N., & Dunne, E. (1992). *Managing classroom groups*. London: Simon & Schuster.

Biott, C. & Nias, J. (Eds.). (1992). *Working and learning together for a change*. Milton Keynes, England: Open University Press.

Galton, M. & Williamson, J. (1992). *Group work in the primary classroom*. London: Routledge.

Finally a text devised for teacher workshops on effective use of groups is:

Dunne, E. & Bennett, N. (1994). *Learning and talking in groups* (2nd ed.). London: Routledge.

9

Organizing Learning Experience

Sarah Tann

Editor's Overview

Whoever decides on the official curriculum content, it is the class teacher who converts it into a programme of activities in the classroom. Children never meet the official curriculum: they only meet what their teacher provides. In organizing classroom learning, experienced teachers make a range of decisions which fundamentally influence how and what children learn. As a teacher, these will be your decisions.

  In this chapter Sarah Tann explores and examines some of the decisions which teachers make and shows how closely they are related to teachers' assumptions about subject content, children's learning, motivation and autonomy. The development of quality teaching requires that your decisions about the organization of learning should be made with great care and understanding of the impact they have on your pupils' learning. This chapter will help you link your views on learning and curriculum to practical decisions about planning and organizing the following:

- work
- resources
- timing of activities
- communication and interaction.

Teachers face a daunting task. A primary teacher usually has the same class of thirty pupils for a whole year. What will pupils learn during this time? How might a teacher organize the class, the room and the curriculum to help that learning? Answers to these questions are never easy. They depend on so many imponderables. Two factors make answers particularly difficult.

First, answers to these questions depend on beliefs and personal values concerning what education is about and what schools are for. Whilst some teachers might believe education is for individual personal development, others might subscribe to the view that education is an instrument to change society, or to conserve and sustain existing traditions or to fit individuals for future jobs. Such differences in beliefs and perceptions will lead to very different answers regarding what pupils should learn and on what basis the curriculum should be constructed. Second, there is little firm evidence for how the curriculum should be experienced. There are plenty of descriptive anecdotes about curriculum experiments but it is hard to assess the outcomes and to distinguish between the effects of children's abilities, the teacher's abilities, or the curriculum content. This is especially so if we consider learning to be more than the accumulation of factual knowledge (which is easy to assess) and to include skills, such as research and communication, and attitudes, such as tolerance and self-discipline (which are difficult to assess).

In this chapter I shall examine some principles for the organization of learning experience, and then consider frameworks for planning how pupils might learn from experience.

Principles of Organizing Learning Experience

Since the 1960s English primary education has evinced three main features relevant to the organization of learning. All of these were reflected in the highly influential Plowden Report (1967) and can be thought of as the basis for what came to be known as the 'Plowden model' of primary classroom practice.

The first of these principles was the view that the division of knowledge into subjects was unnatural and artificial to the way young children think and experience the world around them. Instead, knowledge and understandings were viewed in a holistic fashion, as an integrated 'seamless web' of sensory perceptions which gradually became refined, clarified and categorized as the child's intellectual appreciation developed (Blenkin and Kelly, 1983; Sellack, 1972).

Second, it was assumed that children are naturally curious and learn best through active inquiry modes of learning, such as doing, making and practical problem solving. Allowing children to learn naturally by these means was believed to harness their motivation, making learning effective and enjoyable. This, it was believed, facilitated the combination of two aspects of learning which should be integral – the cognitive, intellectual aspect and the affective, emotional aspect (Donaldson, 1978; Woods, 1988). The learning process was assumed to need both aspects in order to be effective. Hence children were believed to learn best by following their interests and by doing, by 'discovery', inquiry and experimentation. Nevertheless it was also conceded that significant adults could provide a 'scaffolded' structure within an atmosphere of trust and support which also promoted the child's learning.

Third, it was assumed that children of primary school age naturally associate in groups, and that this context allows for social interaction which is vital to facilitating children's learning and confidence. It was believed that talking things through helped learning: the opportunity to articulate learning in progress was thought to consolidate as well as expose the nature of that learning. Further, the group context also facilitated a co-operative rather than a competitive climate, which was itself valued. Co-operation was believed to enhance cognitive development and extend learning beyond facts, to include social skills and attitudes (Johnson and Johnson, 1975; Peterson et al., 1984).

These three concepts – the holistic curriculum, an inquiry approach and a social (group) context – have operated as key features in organizing learning experiences in the primary classroom. They represent beliefs about how children learn. They also lead on to the corollary of what children should learn.

Options for Organizing Curriculum Content

Most of us are familiar with the notion of two main disciplines: arts and sciences. Within these we speak of the subjects of philosophy, religion/ethics, literature, fine arts and also the human and environmental studies such as history and geography. Within sciences we include pure sciences such as physics and chemistry, also biology and the applied sciences such as technology. Such divisions are typical in secondary schools and essentially view the curriculum as a collection of knowledge organized in subject disciplines. However, the curriculum can also be viewed as a learning process, or as problem-solving experiences. Different views of the curriculum offer fundamentally different ways in which the curriculum might be organized.

Teachers wanting to follow the 'Plowden model' often preferred to adopt the process and problem-solving alternatives. In such cases the curriculum was related to how children were believed to learn naturally, i.e. in a more holistic way and through active engagement. This was associated with a 'topic approach', which usually involved a combination of class topics which the teacher chose and initiated, as well as individual topics which the children chose for themselves. Teacher topics were more likely to be concept-based, such as 'Water', 'Change' or, more concretely, 'Our town'. Such topics were usually highly interdisciplinary and aimed to include linked activities on different aspects of the chosen topic. These activities were intended to incorporate the whole arts–science spectrum. Pupil topics were more likely to be interest-based, and might focus on individual hobbies such as 'Football', 'Cats', 'My holiday in Holland'. Such topics were also interdisciplinary, but less so.

The principles underpinning such an approach derived from a recognition of the psychological importance of intrinsic motivation (which relied on the natural curiosity of the pupil) as opposed to extrinsic motivation (which relied on the manipulation of rewards and penalties such as 'stars' and 'lines'). The chance to choose their own topic was also believed to enhance pupil desire for learning, as it encouraged pupil responsibility and initiative and also enhanced self-esteem. It created possibilities for individualizing the curriculum to meet every child's personal needs in terms of level and interest. Topic work was also believed to provide an opportunity for inquiry learning, which further increased motivation and harnessed the pupils' presumed inherent curiosity and predisposition for active modes of learning. Such topic work required pupils to discover information for themselves, which provided a means of developing self-discipline and autonomy.

Teachers were also aware of the opportunity to develop a wide range of research and communication skills through an inter-media approach. This was in keeping with theories put forward by Bruner (1966) which demonstrated the different modes of representation favoured by different learners. This was related to different stages of familiarity with the subject matter or learning experience. For example, at first some practical experimentation (enactive representation) might be preferable, e.g. using beads to assist in addition. Then beads could be replaced by illustrations (iconic representation). Later, addition can be performed in the head from 'symbolic' notation, i.e. numbers and '+' signs. Hence topic work on farming, for instance, might include making a hands-on visit (enactive), using posters and brochures (iconic and symbolic). The work produced as a result of the research could include a model, a diagram and some writing – usually a report in transactional prose, though some schools encouraged the inclusion of narrative stories and poems.

The inclusion of these different modes of representation was believed to be in harmony with the pupil's range of learning predispositions. The approach was therefore likely to lead to feelings of success and achievement in the pupil. Such success would in turn breed confidence and lead to greater willingness for further active learning, increased risk-taking and adventurous experimentation, which itself was believed to be an important part of the skills and attitudes contributing to creative 'good thinking' (Fisher, 1987).

However, topic work was not always successfully carried out along these lines (Tann, 1988). Pupil research sometimes resulted in a reliance on secondary book-based resources (which in unfortunate instances resulted in large amounts of copying) rather than an active problem-solving practical-inquiry approach. The attempt at covering all areas of the curriculum sometimes led to some very spurious thematic links (e.g. when a topic on

'Water' includes floating and sinking activities with boats (science and technology), the story of Noah and the Ark (RE), the riverine civilization of the Egyptians (history), Bangladeshi floods (geography), marbling (art). In addition, the practice of topic work in some primary schools was criticized as often resulting in a very fragmentary learning experience for children, which was highly idiosyncratic as it depended on individual teacher and pupil choices. Therefore, on moving to the secondary school, there was no consistency of experience amongst the new intake. A series of HMI reports (1978, 1984) beginning in the late 1970s on each sector of the education system raised many questions concerning curriculum provision. They highlighted not only the issue of topic work but the whole question of the nature of the curriculum.

The debate focused on differences between the 'subject' approach (with content defined by experts) and 'topic' approach (defined by teacher and pupils' interests, which emphasized processes psychologically suited to the pupils' learning). This raised two key sets of questions. The first concerned selection and sequencing for learning. Was there a definable body of basic knowledge which all pupils should experience by a particular age? What balance of time and priority should be allocated to the components? The second concerned the processes and procedures of learning. Should learning be restricted to memorization of facts? Should it include the development of skills and attitudes? What should be the balance between these?

In the midst of the renewed debates surrounding the curriculum during the 1980s the Government opted for a statutory National Curriculum to which every child in England and Wales was entitled. This was partly in the interests of encouraging a greater standardization of common learning experiences for primary pupils. It was also believed that the increased clarification which this would bring would help to raise the overall standard of learning. The documents which emerged emphasized a traditional 'subject' approach which was believed would be best understood by the majority of people concerned with education – particularly parents and governors as well as teachers and pupils.

This established a 'core' curriculum of English, maths and science (and Welsh for schools in Wales), with a 'foundation' curriculum consisting of technology, geography, history, art, music, physical education and the 'basic' subject of religious education.

Summary

- Through the recent history of primary education there has been a debate about the basic main building blocks of the curriculum. Should it be the academic subjects or should it be interdisciplinary topics?
- The Plowden ethos favoured topics as most likely to capitalize on children's natural ways of making sense of experience. The National

Curriculum emphasizes subjects as most likely to provide a clear planning basis for progression in learning.

- Teachers have always tended to mix their choices in teaching some elements as subjects and some as topics.
- The National Curriculum leaves teachers with the choice on this matter so long as the manner of subject cover is clear.

Planning for Learning Experience

The Plowden ideology prioritized flexibility, responsiveness to individual children's needs and the importance of relating to children's interests for both motivational reasons and in order to harness what was believed to be the natural way children learnt. Whilst this did not preclude planning it certainly did not give it the high priority which planning has achieved in the National Curriculum era.

The notion of a National Curriculum breaks away from much of the child-centred approach which dominated the previous era. Hence the emphasis in planning is now influenced by what is believed to be the logical structure of the subject rather than the response to the psychological needs of the child. In considering planning it is important to recognize the different forms it might take in terms of scope (whole school, year group, individual class), and in terms of time span (long-term (more than one year), medium-term (one year), and short-term (termly, weekly, daily)). It is also important to recognize the thinking behind the National Curriculum and to accommodate this in curriculum planning. This included four key concerns:

- the need for breadth of input to cover the whole range of subjects and balance between the subjects;
- continuity and progression within each subject (from 5 to 16) so that coherent development is assured;
- relevance of the subject-matter to pupils to make the curriculum interesting and worthwhile;
- differentiation of the subject-matter to be taught so that it meets the varied needs of pupils at different levels of ability.

Many more schools are now asking for a far more explicit form of class planning. Some require teachers to submit yearly, termly and weekly planning sheets, indicating what is intended and then what is achieved. This is a far cry from the 'mental jottings' upon which teachers relied in the days when systematic planning was rare (Calderhead, 1984). The need for planning has been seen in terms of clarifying goals, so that the purpose of classroom acitivities is communicated more effectively to pupils and parents (which in itself is believed to enhance motivation and allows home and school to work

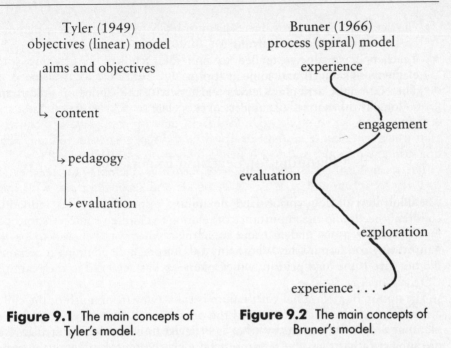

Tyler (1949)
objectives (linear) model

aims and objectives

↳ content

↳ pedagogy

↳ evaluation

Bruner (1966)
process (spiral) model

experience

engagement

evaluation

exploration

experience . . .

Figure 9.1 The main concepts of Tyler's model.

Figure 9.2 The main concepts of Bruner's model.

together). It also makes explicit the content covered and makes the teaching–learning process more accountable.

Alternative models of planning have long existed and can be related to different perceptions of teaching and learning, their purposes and processes. These models include Tyler (1949) (figure 9.1) and Bruner (1966) (figure 9.2). Each of these models makes different assumptions about how pupils learn and also about the nature of academic subjects.

Tyler's objectives model assumes that pupils learn in a linear step-by-step fashion, and that this is best served by teachers selecting, sequencing and structuring activities. This is in keeping with the assumed logical structure of the knowledge-base of the subject which can be dissected into simple and complex concepts, into aspects which can be introduced in a concrete then abstract fashion. This also assumes that, as professionals, we know enough about the logical structure of subject knowledge to be able to achieve such a sequencing: even the best schemes fail to live up to this claim.

The process model assumes that pupils learn in a more holistic manner, and that their understandings are gradually refined through revisiting key concepts and skills which they continually develop through actively using them. This relies less on any hierarchical notion of subject structure, and more on the belief that any concept can be introduced to a child of any age in an intellectually honest manner. In this situation the role of the teacher is to select or negotiate learning experiences and to join with the learners in exploring them to develop and extend the learning possibilities in accordance with the pupil's capabilities.

Criteria for planning

Some psychological theories of learning underline the central need to diagnose, evaluate and meet the child's needs and abilities; utilize and generate motivation in children; offer appropriate rewards and penalties; cast learning in an active mode; give feedback; develop a positive self-concept; plan using a moderate amount of novelty; and recognize the (limited) place of automatic response and rote learning (Morrison and Ridley, 1988, p. 17).

The recent changes have highlighted particular dilemmas for teachers as they try to accommodate the new demands and reconcile these with their existing beliefs and principles. These relate to

- the clash between planning and spontaneity
- the question of pupil negotiation and choice
- the need for differentiation and progression.

Planning for spontaneity

The increased attention to planning has required a heightened consciousness of the specific criteria which need to be included in any planning process. This is particularly important when trying to strike a balance between those who believe that a statutory curriculum poses a dichotomy between planning and the spontaneity to be able to respond to individual needs. However, it is perhaps possible to 'plan for spontaneity'. Such a plan could provide a framework of teachers' goals and intentions which is clear enough to help to guide a teacher's decision about flexible adaptations: for example, which spontaneous initiatives it would be advantageous to take into account. After all, a plan is not a blueprint: it merely serves as a guide. Other initiatives from either pupils or teacher, if found to fit in with the overall plan, could therefore be accepted. Initiatives could improve on the original plan and therefore be welcomed. In this way the existence of a plan, the making of which clarifies the teacher's thoughts, allows a teacher to make on-the-spot changes as they reflect-in-action, and it frees them to be spontaneous with confidence.

Planning for negotiated curriculum content

The teacher is responsible for the 'delivery' of a standard curriculum for all pupils. This leads to an increasing emphasis on teacher control of the planning process and outcomes. Nevertheless this does not preclude another feature of the Plowden classroom – the opportunity for pupils to participate in planning their own learning. This was encouraged in many classrooms as it was believed that it gave ownership of learning to the pupils, and thence responsibility for learning. This in turn enhanced motivation and self-esteem as it increased the likelihood of pupils understanding what they were doing and why, and thus make greater sense of the learning undertaken. The National Curriculum also actively encourages the idea of developing responsibility and learner autonomy by suggesting that pupils share in the critical analysis of their own work and, for example, learn to appraise and improve their technology designs or their story writing. Despite the fact that the National Curriculum has reduced the likelihood of allowing pupils freedom to negotiate the content of their work, it still allows pupils some freedom to negotiate their own preferences and exercise autonomy within prescribed bounds. Hence the need to 'plan for negotiation' should also be a feature of teacher planning.

Planning for negotiated routines

Instead of negotiating content, there are also opportunities for pupils to make decisions regarding 'routines' relating to the ordering and duration of tasks. For example, pupils can be set tasks for the day or week, and they decide in which order tasks will be completed. Having made their choices, the teacher may only remind them when to move on to the next task. This may be at a given 'all change' signal (which can alleviate pressure on any resource area and ensure that pupils are distributed safely around the classroom). Some teachers allow pupils to decide whether to do a little of each subject daily or in large blocks of concentrated time. The pupils are therefore free to choose when they change. Such a system is often combined with the additional responsibility for the pupils to mark their own work using the 'Teacher's answer book', for example for regular computational exercises in maths, cloze exercises in English or multiple choice checks in other subjects.

Planning for differentiation

Although the curriculum entitles all children to common, standardized content it is also necessary to match the curriculum to meet individual needs in terms of levels of achievement. This requires a considerable amount of differentiation. This is typically achieved in a number of ways. Teachers can plan the same task for every pupil and expect differentiation in terms of the quality and quantity of output. Or differentiation can occur through varied input achieved by the teacher's adaptation of the task to suit different pupils' abilities. Or differentiation can be directed at the support stage: after giving the same task to all pupils, the teacher can plan more help to particular groups or individuals as is appropriate in order to help them to understand and complete the task and thereby experience success. Hence 'planning for differentiation' is also an important component of teacher planning.

Planning for progression

This can include moving from simple to complex concepts, basic primary to derived secondary ones, from concrete to abstract ones. Tasks and materials, too, are important: from closed (right/wrong) to open (interpretative/imaginative) tasks, from first-hand to secondary resources, artefacts to information books. The demands of the social context should also be considered.

In addition to these concerns, which derive from beliefs about motivation, needs and learning, a teacher's planning role covers two main areas of operation: that of practical learning organization and that of pedagogical learning interaction. The first addresses aspects of classroom management, which include organizing the curriculum, organizing the pupils, organizing the resources (time, materials), and the second, different forms and functions of communication between teacher and pupil, and between pupil and pupil.

Practical learning organization

Such planning needs to focus on the range and balance of learning experiences which the pupils will encounter. Components might include balancing:

- subjects (amount of time spent on each per day/week/month; whether presented separately or integrated)
- media of learning (observing, listening, discussing, reading, writing, drawing, constructing/investigating, performing)
- task type (open, semi-structured, closed)
- task familiarity (introduction, practice, extension, application)
- resources (primary materials, television, secondary book-based)
- social contexts (class, group, individual)
- assessment (individual across several subjects, several individuals in one subject, group process in an integrated topic)

Balancing these components will not only address the questions of what knowledge and skills the pupils will experience, but also how they will learn, with what, with whom. Underpinning each of these decisions the teacher will have in mind 'why' and 'which' areas of knowledge and elements of learning are expected. Finally teachers need to decide what evidence they will need to ascertain how well the pupil has succeeded, and how these data will be collected and monitored.

The clarity of such objectives in the teacher's mind, together with the grasp that the pupils have of the what, why and how of their own learning, should provide a positive backdrop for the teacher to be able to adapt the plan confidently to accommodate new ideas or even temporarily suspend the plan in the face of new initiatives or changed circumstances.

Teachers' planning in England and Wales is now dominated by the content demands of the National Curriculum. Nevertheless, how an individual teacher organizes the learning experiences of individual pupils remains dependent on the professional expertise of that teacher. This expertise will include detailed knowledge of the nature of the learner and the nature of the learning process as it applies to each of the individual pupils in that class.

Pedagogical learning interaction

The decision regarding how to organize learning for any pupil and how much freedom for choice should be given is fundamental to the planning process. Such decisions will depend on the teacher's assessment of the learners, their characteristics and needs, their learning styles and dispositions. It also depends on the teacher's understanding of the nature of the subject-matter required to be taught and how this subject-matter should be experienced (holistic/spiral/linear form). This leads the teacher to make important plans regarding the learner – teacher interaction process. Such processes also need to be balanced so that the pupils learn to extend their repertoire of learning strategies. The balance of teaching strategies will depend on the teacher's beliefs relating to the role of the learner (active/passive), the role of the teacher (transmitter/facilitator), the availability of resources, and the ecological constraints and possibilities of individual classrooms.

Another very important area of decision-making for the teacher concerns how the individual lesson will be organized so that the timing and rhythm flow as naturally as possible. Three important principles which underpin these decisions include how to orientate pupils at the beginning (through questioning, telling, instructing), how to activate pupils (through supporting, extending, refining their ideas), and how to encourage reflection and analysis (through checking, praising, constructive criticism).

Organizing the classroom

The learning environments within the classroom will normally reflect the beliefs which the teacher holds regarding what and how pupils learn, and will therefore be seen to correspond to many of the above-mentioned criteria (organization of subjects, resources, social contexts). The two major distinctions are:

- mixed-focus (flexiday) integrated day: a system whereby a number of different curriculum activities are simultaneously 'on the go' in classrooms. Pupils may be working as individuals or as groups. Pupils may be free to move from one activity to another when they are ready. This allows pupils the opportunity to take some responsibility for their own activity patterns. It can also be a practical way of overcoming resource shortage by directing only one group to use equipment while others engage in different tasks. Such a system can be used with an 'integrated' curriculum, where the topic tasks cut across subject boundaries, or with a 'subject-specific' curriculum, where each task will be subject-based and not necessarily linked by cross-curricular themes.

● single-focus, discrete subjects: based on a subject-specific approach which can be used in conjunction with whole-class teaching, though it can also be used with group or individual work in the same subject area. This approach allows the teacher greater control over the timing and duration of tasks and the rhythm of work in the classroom. It is sometimes therefore seen as easier to manage and control.

A further aspect of the learning environment with which teachers need to be concerned is the visual impact of the classroom. In this respect display is an important feature. It can relate to the way in which the learning materials are stored: if this is highly visible and accessible to the pupils, it can encourage them to fetch items for themselves, with the responsibility of replacing them appropriately. This would reflect a teacher who believed in the importance of developing pupil autonomy and delegating control.

Organizing the learning environment

Apart from the general materials, many teachers also try to make their classroom inviting, welcoming and stimulating. This in itself helps pupils to feel respected and valued. Display can serve many different functions with obviously different outcomes. For example, a teacher may create:

● An initial 'stimulus' display to introduce a new topic and to catch pupils' interests and motivate them. This could be a static display for pupils to look at, or even to bring things from home to add to the teacher's items. Or the display could be interactive and invite the pupils to touch, try, taste, solve puzzles or quizzes or look up and find out.

● A 'process' display which shows the thinking and development stages of the work in progress. This kind of display shows the parents how pupils tackle an assignment and what they learn from the way in which they set about solving it. It also reminds the pupils of how they started and how their ideas changed, so that they can compare and evaluate their own working methods.

● The 'celebratory' one which shows off the final outcomes of the assignments where they can be exhibited and admired.

Each of these kinds of display can add a valuable dimension to the learning achieved within the class, and it can also be shared with parents and other classes in the school. They can help to excite learning, improve awareness of techniques of learning or add to the self-esteem of the learners, and can thus enhance the overall quantity and quality of learning.

Summary

- Class teachers have a great deal of choice in planning how the pupil meets the curriculum.
- Teachers' plans reflect their assumptions about learning, pupil autonomy and curriculum content.
- In planning, teachers must take into account
  - available resources
  - spontaneity
  - differentiation
  - progression
  - motivation
  - communication
  - organization
  - interaction.
- Children know very little about curriculum theory. They meet the curriculum in the form of classroom activities. The nature of these activities, their resourcing and organization, and the pupils' role in designing and enacting them critically influence the quality of their learning experience.

Editor's Commentary

Sarah Tann has shown that primary teachers have, in general, shared three guiding principles in organizing learning. These are that

- learning is holistic: subject divisions are unnatural;
- children learn best through inquiry;
- learning is a social activity.

Although widely espoused, these principles are less widely practised.

She has also noted that whilst the Government has recently imposed a subject-based model for describing the curriculum, teachers still have choice in how to organize the curriculum as it is experienced in their classrooms. Teachers' choices are fundamental in their impact on children's learning.

In exercising their choice, Tann argues that teachers should have, in their planning, a regard for

- spontaneity
- pupil choice
- differentiation according to pupil attainment
- pupil progress in learning.

Planning must also take into account

- the practicalities of schooling
- the organization of resources
- modes of interaction and communication
- the quality of the environment.

In short, Sarah Tann's chapter is about classroom management as it influences learning.

Classroom management is at the heart of teaching. In following up the ideas in this chapter, it would be better to link them first to ideas in closely related chapters as follows:

- Children are insightful interpreters of teachers' classroom management. What teachers intend is not always what they get. This theme can be pursued in chapter 4.
- Classroom management influences order, control and learning. This is explained in chapter 10.
- Classroom management influences the quality of pupils' intellectual life. This matter is considered in chapters 7 and 8, and more fully in chapter 11, where the idea of pupil autonomy is examined.

Classroom management is a very practical business but it is very powerfully influenced by ideas. Often these ideas are merely pragmatic. Management in some classrooms is dominated by practical considerations, such as where to put the tables so that people can physically get into the room. This is an obvious and important consideration but, make no mistake, its resolution will send a signal to the pupils and will be interpreted by them as saying something about their teacher's priorities.

The organization of learning experience and its impact on pupils' learning should be carefully studied in school-based work. The following projects should prove profitable:

- Use this and related chapters to devise a planning framework for learning. This should set out all the main factors to be considered when organizing learning experience. Discuss this framework with other learner teachers and make appropriate revisions.

- Using the framework as a guide, discuss the organization of learning experience with experienced teachers. The key question is: How does their planning assure pupil learning?
- Share your plans for the organization of learning experience with other learner teachers. Are they comprehensive? How do they assure pupil learning?
- A key question in regard to teachers' provision for learning is: How do pupils interpret and respond to it? What teachers want and what they get do not always correspond. Examine pupils' responses to and interpretations of some of your provision. Display is an easy place to start. Set down what you intend to achieve from a particular display. Observe what children do with it. Ask them what they make of it. Evaluate their responses and reactions, and consider whether your provision should be revised if it is to attain its goal.
- The above exercise can and should be repeated for all aspects of your provision. Remember that the fundamental question is not whether children like the provision or not; it is whether or not it promotes their learning and understanding.

FURTHER READING

Campbell, R. J. (Ed.). (1993). *Breadth and balance in the primary curriculum*. Basingstoke, England: Falmer Press.

A new book that brings together articles of the key current issues surrounding the curriculum. A useful analysis in these confusing and constantly changing times.

Dean, J. (1991). *Organizing learning in the primary classroom* (2nd ed.). London: Routledge.

This new edition of a valuable and very practical book will continue to be useful for another generation of students.

Laslett, R. and Smith, C. (1992). *Effective classroom management*. London: Routledge.

Another updated edition of a long-standing book with sections on organization, teaching methods and feelings as well as mediating and modifying behaviour of individual pupils.

Moyles, J. (1992). *Organizing for learning in the primary classroom*. Milton Keynes, England: Open University Press.

A book which explores the influences of why and what teachers do in their classroom, in terms of values and perceptions of teaching and learning.

Waterhouse, P. (1983). *Managing the learning process*. London: McGraw-Hill.

This focuses strongly and effectively on managing individual and group work, and on the techniques of learning applicable to these particular contexts.

In terms of subject-specific books relating to planning and managing learning there are many books coming out in a number of different series produced by a range of publishers too plentiful to list. However, the non-statutory guidelines associated with each subject folder of the National Curriculum also contain many useful and practical examples of ways of organizing learning.

10

Teaching for Order and Control

Charles Desforges

Editor's Overview

Pupils and teachers intensely dislike classroom disorder. Without good order, little serious academic work takes place, and even less learning. A central concern for all teachers, and a particular concern for beginning teachers, is how to establish and maintain a well-ordered learning environment.

In this chapter I identify the nature of order conducive to learning and describe what effective teachers do to achieve it. The lessons from research are simple in principle, but they take a great deal of thoughtful hard work if they are to succeed in practice.

Effective teachers use a programme of whole-class work as a vehicle to teach directly a set of rules and procedures for good classroom management.

Effective teachers do not establish order for order's sake. They establish it as a foundation from which they strive to work for pupil autonomy in learning. If disorder is a threat to learning, order itself does not guarantee quality learning. Effective teachers go beyond order in ways I describe here.

However well teachers establish order, they will always meet misbehaviour of varying degrees of severity. I explain some of the causes of misbehaviour and what teachers might best do about them.

Establishing order is a crucial aspect of classroom management. Successful techniques are worthy of careful study and practice.

Order and control are two of the most pressing anxieties for young teachers. As pupils, most of us have had direct experience of teachers who lost control of their classes. Images of riotous behaviour, even mob rule, can easily be brought to mind. As active participants in, or callous spectators of, classroom mayhem, it is easy to recall the noise, the chaos, the cheap fun and games of teacher and student teacher persecution. The idea of being on the receiving end of this is indeed frightening. 'Will I be able to control them?' is a question young teachers often ask and even more often worry about. They are right to do so.

It is an extremely important question, and not only to the teacher. Teachers, of course, have their personalities, egos and status to consider. Classroom chaos is humiliating. Teachers have little respect for colleagues who cannot control a class. But from the pupils' point of view there is a lot more at stake than status and peer regard. If pupils are to learn anything worthwhile in school they need a consistently ordered working environment. They need to be able to operate in a sustained and purposeful manner. They need to know what they are doing and why. Their activities need to be reliably resourced. Any threats to good order are very direct threats to learning.

Most teachers understand this simple idea and work very hard to secure and sustain an ordered working environment. Most pupils also understand this principle. There have been many studies of what pupils regard as a good teacher. Very high on the list of most pupils' criteria of good teaching is the ability to exert strong control over lesson content and classroom behaviour (Kutnick and Jules, 1993). Pupils do not generally like disorder. In principle at least, teachers, pupils and school managers all agree that good order and control are highly to be desired and infinitely to be preferred to disorder and loss of control. With so much agreement, you might expect there would be no problem with classroom order. Little could be further from the truth.

Anyone with any experience of schools recognizes that disorder, in various degrees, can be commonly observed. It ranges from the outright riotous (which is thankfully very rare) through the chaotic to the inefficient. In the riotous cases, all control has been lost and lessons have become a bear garden in which the hapless teacher plays the role of the bear to be taunted and humiliated. In the chaotic cases, the teacher has some general control of gross behaviour in that pupils will sit in their places and on occasion go through the motions of classroom work. But little purposeful learning takes place. In the inefficient cases, there may be high levels of activity and a noisy bustle. But closer inspection shows that much of the activity and almost none of the noise has anything to do with work, let alone learning. Clearly, productive order and control are not always easy to establish in classrooms. Surveys have shown that inexperienced teachers have particular difficulty in classroom management (HMI, 1992).

In this chapter I intend to discuss some of the problems associated with order and control and to suggest some ways in which they may be established and sustained in order to promote efficient learning. I should emphasize at the outset that there is no shortage of advice on these matters. Any teacher and almost every person in the street has plenty to say on this issue. Poor classroom order has frequently been blamed on incompetent parents who, it seems, have failed to bring their children up properly. Such parents ought, it seems, to be fined. Alternatively, Government is frequently blamed for not providing sufficient resources for classroom work, or sufficient teachers to keep class sizes to a manageable level, or for not laying the foundation for a peaceful and just society and thereby creating the frustrations which, in some children, lead to aggressive or even criminal classroom behaviour.

It is possible that these theories of classroom disorder have some merit. Certainly order is more difficult to establish in some neighbourhoods and some schools and some classrooms than in others. And some children appear to be more co-operative in pursuit of learning than others. These differences are worthy of exploration and explanation. I do not, however, intend to pursue these matters here. Nor do I intend to list the advice on how to obtain classroom order that is readily available in any staff room. One reason for this is that, in my own experience, it is vague advice. 'When you get a new class, look as if you mean business' is well intended but what does it mean? A second reason for standing off such advice is that again, in my experience, it does not work. I can recall being told not to be 'friendly' with a new class, and certainly 'never smile until Christmas'. Being friendly and smiley by nature, this was not going to work for me short of a personality transplant. The most important reason for turning away from commonly available advice, however, is that it has never been tested. We have to take it on trust that it works. Maybe at one point in time, for one teacher with one class, good order was established through the innoculation of the facial muscles to achieve a smileless first term. And that with a particular class in a particular place in a particular year. Whether advice actually works or not in general is a very important and a very different matter.

What I offer in this chapter is advice on how to secure order, which has been generated from research which has examined and tested the practices of effective teachers. It is advice, therefore, with a good track record, and it is advice about what can be attempted in the classroom. It says nothing about parents and Governments. This is not because parents and governments do not have some responsibility in regard to classroom order. Parental practices and Government provision can obviously have considerable effect on the conditions of classrooms. The problem is that it is difficult to influence parents and Governments in a reasonable time scale. And teachers have much more effect than either of these agencies. In short, teachers make a difference to classroom life, and they get a much bigger return on effort if they look at what they can do directly rather than what others might be persuaded to do indirectly.

Order and Learning

The question of establishing and sustaining order is often raised in some anxiety. In such a state it is easy to assume that order is an end in itself. It is not. It is a means to an end. Order is essential in classrooms as a necessary condition for learning to take place. It is absolutely necessary to keep this idea in mind. Only particular kinds of order and control are conducive to learning. Order does not simply mean tidiness or quietness or neatness. Graveyards often show all these characteristics, but they are not noteworthy for promoting learning. Control and its cousin, discipline, are not necessarily associated with learning either. Parade grounds are often associated with firm discipline, clear control and immaculate performances. But military discipline in the form of rasping sergeant-majors and well-drilled platoons is unlikely to encourage higher levels of intellectual life.

It cannot be emphasized too strongly that, in democratic countries at least, the purpose of education is to prepare for a mature and autonomous participation in society. In school, therefore, pupils must, in the end, learn self-control and self-discipline. Certainly, pupils need to learn a lot of basic skills, facts and procedures. But they must also learn to think for themselves, to solve problems and to manage their time and their work. Anything a teacher does in the name of order and control must meet these longer-term objectives. Some inadequate teachers never set up a system of order and control. Some teachers set up systems of order which meet short-term purposes. Pupils do as they are told. They are well behaved and quiet. But they are not required to take responsibility for anything other than doing the teacher's bidding. This form of order falls well short of educational acceptability.

The most effective teachers set up a system of order and control which establishes the conditions for disciplined learning and requires that pupils take responsibility for their work and develop enhanced levels of autonomy. What is it that effective teachers do? In the rest of this chapter I shall discuss what research has revealed about order and control as practised by effective teachers. First, I will deal with what might be called normal circumstances in which teachers are dealing with average children in average classes. This constitutes the vast bulk of teaching experience. It should be emphasized that ordinary children in ordinary classrooms can, if not taught with expertise, become the source of very grave problems for teachers. There is nothing natural about classrooms. It is not natural to compel thirty-five youngsters to spend their time indoors in cramped conditions. Special skills are needed to make these circumstances productive, and it is these skills I shall discuss first.

Following that I shall consider more unusual circumstances and particular problems exposed when normal processes do not appear to work well.

Summary

- Classroom order is essential for learning.
- Pupils respect order and teachers who keep it.
- Order and control can work against learning.
- Effective teachers manage order in pursuit of learning.

Effective Teachers

Most of the research I shall draw on in the following sections will be found in Wittrock (1986). In these studies a distinction has been made between more effective and less effective teachers. Three criteria have generally been used to make this distinction. Effective teachers are defined in this research as those whose pupils, all other things being equal:

1 achieve greater than average gains in learning (Rosenshine and Stevens, 1986);
2 show longer than average times of engagement on the work set them (Good, 1983; Kounin, 1983);
3 show greater initiative and spontaneous participation in their own learning (Doyle, 1986).

Such teachers may be identified in many different ways. One approach has been to study a broad range of teachers and then pick out the effective ones on the above criteria. Another method has been to examine pupils' test gains and then identify the teachers who, for pupils of a given social area, are associated with the most success (Rosenshine and Stevens, 1986).

Once effective teachers, defined in these ways, have been identified, their methods of establishing order have been carefully studied. Clear patterns in their teaching have emerged. In some cases these patterns of behaviour have been taught to less effective teachers to see if indeed they could be used to secure a good, educationally useful form of order. Such studies have been generally successful. What works for some teachers can work for other teachers (Borg and Ascione, 1982).

What Works with a New Class?

Effective teachers recognize that the early stages of life with a new class are critical to the establishment of good, long-term working relationships (Ball, 1980). These teachers have a clear strategy with short- and long-term goals.

They have clear and specific plans. And they have a sharp focus on which they spend a great deal of effort.

The general strategy used by effective teachers has the crucial long-term aim of encouraging and developing individual attainment and autonomy, with pupils taking increasing responsibility for their work and progress, and for setting themselves challenging targets for learning progress. The short-term aim is to teach a whole range of rules and procedures for the conduct of classroom work as a foundation on which later ambitions can be built. The strategy involves a gradual transition from the whole-class teaching of routines to the development of individual autonomy.

The focus for this teaching is work. Effective teaching here has little to do with personality or appearance. It has everything to do with the detailed preparation and planning of work appropriate to the short- and long-term goals of the strategy. The stages of the strategy are shown in figure 10.1. It should be said that many teachers achieve the early stage in teaching routines and procedures but do not advance to the later stage. Such teachers do not show up as effective as defined earlier.

Use lots of straightforward work as a setting to teach rules and procedures

Use a whole-class focus and didactic teaching

↓ gradual transition

Intermediate stage

Use more differentiated work
Use more challenging work
Use greater variety of group and teaching methods
Teach, demand and promote greater pupil autonomy

Figure 10.1 Work and the establishment of classroom order.

How is this general strategy put into practice? The blunt answer is that it takes a great deal of thinking, time, hard work, planning and preparation. It also takes determination if the longer-term aim of pupil autonomy is not to be lost.

Effective teachers, as identified in these studies, take the view that order means a working system. For such a system they determine that the class will need sets of rules and procedures. The teachers anticipate that, with large numbers of people, a busy curriculum and limited resources of time, space and materials, problems are bound to occur. Their rules and procedures are ways of dealing with such problems. Rules regulate conduct likely to disrupt working conditions or to cause injury or damage. Teachers design rules for regulating lateness, talking or the bringing of materials to school. Young children, for example, like to bring their toys to school because they find it comforting to have some treasured or favourite item with them. Unfortunately this can also cause congestion, envy and fighting over disputed ownership, as well as creating the conditions for rivalry and theft.

Some teachers take the view that these problems create valuable learning opportunities for pupils and that, should disputes happen, these should be use for object lessons and for opportunities in which children can exercise autonomy and develop their own rules.

This is not the view taken by the effective teachers in the studies cited. Rather, these teachers keep their focus on learning in the curriculum. They judge that it is too early in the life of the class to be constantly distracted by events and happenings needing object lessons in social learning. With their focus on academic learning, effective teachers anticipate such problems and make up their own rules.

These teachers also anticipate needing a set of working procedures. Procedures are ways of conducting work, duties and privileges. They include procedures for getting out and putting away materials, for handing in work, for getting a drink, for getting changed, for moving from one room to another, and for changing activities, from maths to science for example. It is important to these teachers to anticipate as many problems and procedures as possible. Of course this is easier to do after direct experience of many situations. But lacking experience, a novice teacher, by careful attention to detail and by thinking through the real activities of early sessions, should be able to spot the most pressing causes of disruptions. Accidents (with paint pots, for example) and transitions from one activity to another have great potential for disruption. They can readily be anticipated, and plans may be laid to minimize disorder.

Armed with a set of carefully thought-through rules and procedures, effective teachers resist the temptation to bury their pupils under this load of legislation. Instead, they plan a large amount of straightforward work which can be done using a whole-class organization (Evertson and Emmer, 1982). They then use this work to explain, teach and practise their rules and procedures in the meaningful context of the curriculum. The key word here is 'teach'. Very often children fail to use a procedure for the same sort of reason that they fail to learn a concept in science or mathematics. They did not understand it or they have forgotten it or they have not had an opportunity to practise it.

Procedures are explicitly taught by effective teachers using all the skills and processes relevant to direct instruction. The thinking behind the procedure should be explained and be clearly justifiable: it should be practised. Feedback should be given with lots of praise for good performance. And revision or even reteaching will be necessary from time to time.

The general processes for establishing order are shown in figure 10.2. The whole system can be illustrated by an example of a procedure for moving around the classroom. Primary school teachers frequently collect their class together first thing in the morning to call the register, discuss news and introduce the morning's activities. Behind the pupils will be their tables all laid out with the materials necessary for work. The less effective teacher might simply dismiss the class from the circle to get on with their work. The teacher might be lucky and get away with this.

---

1   anticipate problems and threats to order

2   design rules and procedures for handling these threats

3   plan a whole-class work schedule

4   use the work schedule to teach the rules and procedures

5   teaching involves explaining
                    describing
                    modelling
                    practising

6   monitor and insist on the use of procedures

7   remind, revise and reteach the procedures where necessary

---

Figure 10.2 Processes in establishing order.

However, the conditions have been created for loitering or rushing, for barging or damaging materials. These problems can be anticipated, and a procedure designed in which the class leaves the teacher and moves to their tables group by group in an agreed order. The procedure would need to be explained, shown, practised and monitored. Very soon, if it is properly taught and insisted on, all the teacher would need to say is 'Get on', and there would be a slick movement to work. The children have not been drilled or conditioned. They have been taught and have engaged in effective practice. Pupils respect teachers who seek and establish such order because, generally, they actually prefer work to chaos.

The Transition to Autonomy

There are threats to the effectiveness of this approach to order in classrooms. The first threat is a lack of attention to detailed planning and preparation. A recent study of six effective British primary school teachers (HMI, 1991) has shown just how important detailed planning is to classroom management. The more difficult the children, the more important is detailed planning. Some children are more forgiving than others.

The second threat is a lack of consistency and persistence in teaching and monitoring procedures. Children may appear to be resistant to following procedures, and this may be interpreted as their disobedience or wilfulness. And so it might be. But it is more likely that they have forgotten or were distracted. Persistence is as necessary to teaching procedures as it is to teaching anything else (Evertson and Emmer, 1982).

This persistence is necessary with every new class a teacher takes. It might be thought reasonable to expect that where children are experienced pupils, that is, where they have been in school many years, they would know all about classroom order and come ready and prepared to use the procedures of earlier years. This simply does not happen. The same class of children will behave very differently with different teachers. The system of order set up one year does not appear to transfer to another. Knowledge of classroom rules and procedures cannot be taken for granted. The system has to be rebuilt at the start of each year. By setting rules, 'a teacher communicates his or her awareness of what can happen in a classroom and demonstrates a degree of commitment to work' (Doyle, 1986, p. 413).

Paradoxically, perhaps, other threats to order include overloading children with procedures and rules and nagging. These, of course, are the reverse problems of lack of planning and lack of persistence. Sensible judgements, a sense of proportion and a sense of humour all help in getting a good balance. Teachers do not have to nag about procedures any more than they need nag about teaching reading. And procedures only need introducing as and when they become necessary (Shultz and Florio, 1979).

But certainly the biggest threat to this approach to classroom order is that, having laid the basis for a good, productive, progressive learning environment, too many teachers stop there and do not make the transition to pupil autonomy. Their system for using whole-class teaching and straightforward work ossifies and becomes their sole means of engaging their pupils with the curriculum. In these classrooms there is order of a kind, but it is order to no very great purpose, since the most crucial objectives of education cannot be met in such a system. In other words, there is a real tension between using classroom work to achieve order and assigning classroom work to achieve high-level intellectual objectives.

In attempting to move away from the management functions of work, teachers have to set tasks requiring higher-level intellectual processes (including, for example, understanding, reasoning and problem solving). Cockburn (chapter 4 in this volume) has discussed pupils' resistance to this sort of challenge. Students' reactions to these sorts of task create problems for teachers and they commonly find it easier to fall back on routine tasks to which pupils react more positively (Doyle, 1983). Cockburn's analysis shows that pupils are by no means passive in response to teachers' work management. Order is negotiated, albeit not explicitly, between pupils and teachers. Co-operation is a key matter as a balance is struck between the requirements of good order and the requirements of higher levels of intellectual work. In some cases, higher-level tasks never or very rarely appear in classrooms in the first place (Bennett et al., 1984; Stodolsky, 1981).

The problem posed by the threat to management of higher-level tasks is particularly acute with low-attaining pupils. Teachers seem to perceive such pupils as a particular threat to good order and, as a consequence, tend to stick with tasks which are high on management power (i.e. routine tasks) and low on learning potential (Good, 1981). This problem is extremely difficult. It requires extensive examination and treatment. This is provided in chapter 11 by Susan Nolen.

Summary

- With effective teachers, pupils
  - attain greater than average learning progress
  - spend more time on-task
  - show greater levels of initiative and spontaneity.
- Effective teachers invest a lot of time and planning in establishing order.
- They pay particular attention to this with new classes.
- Effective teachers use a whole-class programme of work to teach a set of rules and procedures conducive to good order.
- Good order provides the foundation for progress to the exercise of pupil autonomy.
- Twin threats to learning are
  - failure to establish order
  - failure to make progress to autonomy.

Misbehaviour

Misbehaviour is an enduring fact of classroom life. At its extreme it takes the form of crime in the legal sense and may be manifest as violence, robbery or vandalism, for example. In fact such extreme behaviour is rare. More common forms of out-of-order behaviour include lateness, tantrums, calling out, inattentiveness, refusals, insolence, swearing and failure to bring appropriate equipment or materials. Each of these activities threatens the working pattern of the classroom. Each is more or less prevalent in any classroom. There are several theories as to why this might be. Doyle (1986) has listed the most common accounts including the views that:

1 school work is trivial and boring, so disruption is more interesting than the work;
2 children quite naturally rebel against the authoritarian, adult regimes imposed in schools;
3 teachers are 'weak and muddle-headed' and therefore do not assert themselves;
4 pupils enjoy the attention created by disruption.

Each of these accounts has some attraction and is worth thinking about seriously as a basis for planning sensible action to minimize misbehaviour. You will recall from personal experience that some teachers are exceedingly pompous and/or boring. Some parts of the curriculum are seen by pupils as particularly esoteric. A great deal of the material taught in schools is never justified to the pupils in terms that they can make sense of. If pupils find themselves in, to them, a boring and meaningless situation, almost anything serves to break up the tedium and add a little interest and diversion. The simple (and it *is* simple) implication of this observation is that teachers should work hard to relate the curriculum to sensible purposes, to explain the point of it to pupils. Additionally, it is necessary to plan a variety of activities which use a rich diversity of media and materials. This is not to pander to children. It is to see the work through their eyes.

For older adolescents there is a considerable tension between the culture of the school and the culture of pupils (Harris and Rudduck, 1993). Pupils, it seems are much more interested in socializing with their friends and in minimizing the effort needed to get work done than they are in meeting the academic demands of teachers. Such accounts, however, are less convincing for younger children, who appear to enjoy school work (Bennett et al., 1984) but who still evince extensive, albeit generally less violent, misbehaviour.

Another source of tension lies between the culture of the school and the culture of various sub-groups of pupils. Acceptable behaviour in some homes or on some streets is not necessarily acceptable in school. Some of the problems created by cultural differences are discussed in detail by Weiner in chapter 13.

The operation of these factors can be exceedingly subtle. The story is told of the child who joined a reception class from a strict, no-nonsense family. The pupil was given an extensive choice of activities and relished this freedom. At break time the teacher went round the classroom saying to individuals, 'Would you like to tidy up?' The new pupil was even more pleased to be given choice in this matter. But when the teacher turned to see the pupil still playing, she was concerned. Was this child going to be disobedient? She decided to nip this problem in the bud. Going back to the child she hissed, 'I thought I told you to tidy up!' The child now was most unhappy. What bad luck to end up with a schizoid teacher with aggressive tendencies. Although no doubt apocryphal, the sorts of misunderstandings illustrated here can have long-term consequences for the relationships and communications which obtain between teachers and pupils.

These problems can be much more serious than implied in this illustration. Gregory (1993) has shown how young children starting school from different cultural backgrounds bring with them powerful ideas, based on their home experience, of what it means to learn to read. Some of these meanings do not coincide with school meanings and, consequentially, the pupils' participation in class is unexpected and unproductive. This can easily be seen as misbehaviour. More fundamentally, it leads to learning failure, which can promote frustration and aggressiveness.

The implication of this line of argument is that it is essential for teachers to understand the cultural backgrounds of their pupils both in general and in the detailed particularities of culturally determined approaches to learning, communication and relationships.

Intervening in Misbehaviour

Whatever the tensions and their origins, the teacher confronted with misbehaviour in the classroom has to do something about it if the system of order is to be maintained. Misbehaviour is, by its nature, public in that the rest of the class is a potential audience. Teachers also generally see misbehaviour as contagious in that there is the possibility that it will spread rapidly to other class members. Teachers have to decide how, if at all, to intervene.

There are no easy guidelines here. Young teachers are often advised to be consistent in their response to misbehaviour, but in fact experienced teachers tend to see particular actions in particular contexts, or to consider the possible ramifications of particular acts. In this sense a rule infringement might be misbehaviour in one context but not in another (Hargreaves, Hester and Mellor, 1975).

For example, with regard to calling out, teachers tend to make allowances for the age of the pupils, the time of day (calling out at the end of the day is a lot less serious than at the start of the day). Teachers also react very differently to different children on the realistic calculation that a call-out from one child may be a unique act of excitement, whereas, from another, it is a routine challenge to order or call to arms. In deciding whether or not to intervene in misbehaviour, teachers take the likely consequences into account as well as the act itself.

If a teacher decides that intervention is called for, the question arises as to the scale and form of the intervention. If the teacher's main purpose is to sustain a steady work programme, some forms of intervention (e.g. shouting, prolonged public dressing down) create more of an interruption to the work flow than the misbehaviour itself. If, on the other hand, the teacher does nothing, the pupils may learn important lessons about the seriousness of his or her commitment to work.

Decisions have to be made quickly and, as I have indicated, many factors have to be taken into account. Of course, experience helps a great deal in informing the rapid judgements necessary, but experience is precisely lacking in the new teacher. Fortunately research can give a useful framework for responding to misbehaviour. Interestingly, the research shows that pupils and teachers disagree on what methods are most effective in dealing with misbehaviour (Merrett and Tang, 1994). Merrett and Tang showed that teachers spend a great deal of their time, 'nagging, scolding and grumbling at their pupils. The fact that they are doing this day in and day out ... demonstrates clearly that the device is having no effect except to produce stress, anxiety and confrontation' (p. 92). In Merrett and Tang's survey of the opinions of primary school children it was found that pupils felt that a letter home praising them for good work or reprimanding them for misbehaving would be the most effective form of sustaining good behaviour. Immediate praise and reprimand were also considered to be effective providing they were offered privately. There is evidence that a combination of private praise and private reprimand actually works well in classrooms. Houghton, Wheldall, Jukes and Sharpe (1990) monitored the effect of these actions on the amount of time pupils spent on-task. The effects are shown in figure 10.3. Initially the pupils in this study showed only modest levels of application to their work. Private praise produced a clear improvement, and the combination of private praise and private reprimand brought application to significantly better levels, although these were by no means perfect.

Private praise and reprimand have some considerable advantages over many other methods of dealing with misbehaviour. First, they are not in themselves disruptive. Second, they avoid confrontation. Third, pupils appreciate these methods: they are neither humiliated nor embarrassed by them. Finally, and gratifyingly, they actually work in practice.

Persistent and Serious Misbehaviour

If teachers take the trouble to establish an ordered working system in their classrooms and continue to prepare interesting work in detail and in the light of their understanding of their pupils' cultural backgrounds and general interests, most misbehaviour will constitute only a slight threat to the work system. The threat will normally be temporary if teachers act quickly, determinedly, persistently and privately, using a balance of praise and reprimand. Unfortunately such diligence will not see the end of misbehaviour. Some children persist in serious misbehaviour. And serious and enduring threats to the work system are common in some schools.

Sometimes it is clearly the teacher who is implicated in the generation of

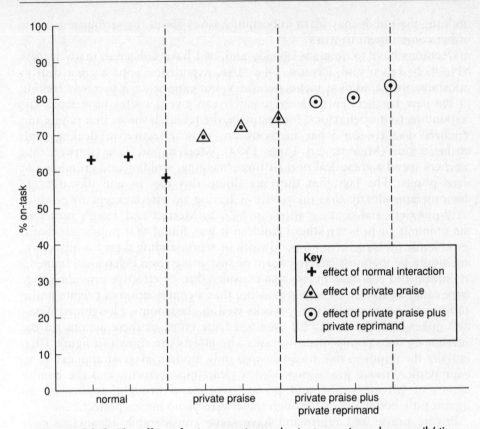

Figure 10.3 The effect of private praise and private reprimand on pupils' time on-task.

Source: After S. Houghton, K. Wheldall, R. Jukes and A. Sharpe. (1990). The effects of limited private reprimands and increased private praise on classroom behaviour in four British secondary school classes. *British Journal of Educational Psychology, 63*(3), 255–265.

bad classroom behaviour. This is obvious in the not uncommon cases in which a class is like a flock of lambs with one teacher and a pack of wolves with another.

Equally, the most industrious and sensitive of teachers may be confronted with enduring classroom behaviour problems or, at the least, the persistent challenge to authority. This is more frequently the case in some neighbourhoods than others. Enduringly bad behaviour in classrooms is commonly associated with poor social and material conditions. Noting this, it is tempting to assume that poverty causes or exacerbates bad behaviour. Unfortunately for this theory, there exist schools in areas of material deprivation with good records of classroom conduct and with reputations for establishing a work ethic. In these cases it is clear that a whole-school policy is actively in place to sustain a persistent approach to good working conduct.

In challenging situations, individual teachers cannot successfully work in isolation in the pursuit of orderly working relationships. A system involving the whole school staff and co-operation of parents and the local community is necessary to achieve a consistency of approach. Developing and managing such a system is well beyond the remit of a beginning teacher.

This systematic approach does not detract from anything I have said earlier. Indeed it builds on it. Even here, however, there are individual children who stress the system. In such cases it is very tempting to describe children as criminal, seriously disturbed, delinquent and so on. The fact is that whilst there may be technical merit in these labels (a youngster over a certain age convicted of physical assault is a criminal), they are not in the least bit helpful in determining what to do in these circumstances.

A number of specialized methods have been developed for dealing with such pupils, where 'dealing with' means attempting to inculcate more productive forms of classroom behaviour. Various therapeutic or behaviour modification techniques have been designed and given extensive trials in classrooms. Each has its devotees and critics. The reader interested in behaviour modification might consult, for example, Wheldall and Merrett (1985). This is not the place to review these approaches. Fundamentally they are techniques for when all else has failed. They require considerable investment in the development of specialized skills and techniques, and necessarily require considerable curriculum expertise if the teacher is to capitalize on any pro-social behaviours culminating from such regimes.

Summary

- Order and control are best seen in terms of the establishment of a productive working system.
- The system, taking the form of rules and procedures for work and conduct, has to be established anew with each class a teacher takes.
- The early stages of interaction with a new class are critical in building an ordered working environment.
- It requires detailed planning and preparation on the part of the teacher, together with high-quality direct teaching of rules and procedures within a curriculum context.
- However well such a system is built, it will be challenged through the misbehaviour of normal children. Misbehaviour is a threat to the good working order of the classroom.
- The better the working system is laid down in the first place, the more robust it will be to the threat of misbehaviour.
- Even so, teachers must consider and be prepared to deal with misbehaviour. First, they need to be sure that particular behaviours are misbehaviours and not merely exuberances or genuine upsets. Second, it helps if teachers can be sure that they are not the cause of the misbehaviour

through inadequate planning, boring presentations or culturally insensitive actions. Here it is essential for the teacher to understand pupils and their culture.

- Once identified, teachers must respond to misbehaviour. Pupils see teachers as the custodians of classroom order.
- The most effective means of responding involve the use of private praise and private reprimand. Least effective are nagging and confrontation.
- Some misbehaviour is persistent in the face of a teacher's best efforts. In some settings the individual teacher can only be effective where a whole system of good order is in place and actively managed.
- In exceptional circumstances, special methods have been developed to work with pupils who confuse or confound the system.

Editor's Commentary

I have not attempted to deal with all aspects of disorder in this chapter. I have not, for example, dealt with the wide range of cases of disturbed children. I have dealt with 95 per cent of the causes of disorder. Other causes and problems certainly exist, but they are likely to be unique and will need particular, case-specific, knowledge and reactions.

The approaches I have described provide for a context in which threats to order are minimized and special cases can be identified for what they are, whereupon special advice can be taken.

In common with the authors of some earlier chapters, I have described some specific techniques by which teachers might achieve an important goal. As in other instances, the techniques require careful planning and plenty of persistence and practice if they are to work. The suggestions here might be pursued in the following school-based activities:

- Conduct careful classroom observations of the working practices in classrooms available to you. Describe instances where smooth procedures are in place for the conduct of work.
- Discuss with teachers the circumstances where they feel procedures to be essential, and establish what the teachers do to achieve them.
- Discuss with a sample of children what they perceive the classroom rules to be. Do they feel cramped or liberated by them?
- In discussion with supervising teachers, identify instances where you might teach a working procedure (for transition between activities, or for putting away apparatus, for example). Plan and carry out a teaching programme for this procedure.

It is essential that the ideas in this chapter be linked to those in other chapters as follows:

- Rules and procedures need to be carefully taught. Re-read chapter 6 on 'direct teaching' in planning your approach to teaching for order.
- Order can be as big a threat to quality learning as disorder. If order becomes regimentation for control, pupils will learn not to use their initiative. Relate the ideas in this chapter to those in chapter 11, where pupil autonomy is discussed.

FURTHER READING

Rogers, B. (1994). *Behaviour recovery: A whole school programme for mainstream schools*. Melbourne, Australia: Australian Council for Educational Research.
    This book humanizes behaviourism. In it, Bill Rogers explains in a step-by-step way, using lots of clear practical illustrations, how to deal with behaviour disorder in the classroom.
Fontana, D. (1985). *Classroom Control*. London: Methuen.
    This is a justifiably celebrated book analysing common classroom behaviour problems and offering good advice based on psychological theory and wise experience.
McNeil, L. M. (1988). *Contradictions of control*. New York: Routledge.
    This book explains how control so frequently works against learning. The author shows that this is not inevitable. Control can create the conditions for pupil autonomy and understanding – but only if schools and teachers work for these goals.

11

Teaching for Autonomous Learning

Susan Bobbitt Nolen

Editor's Overview

One of the central purposes of schooling is to develop children's capacities to take a full part in a democratic society. In order to participate, pupils need to know their own mind, to judge things for themselves, to know right from wrong and to act accordingly within the law. These capabilities are known collectively as moral and intellectual autonomy.

In this chapter Susan Nolen explains why she sees the achievement of student autonomy as the highest goal of schooling. She describes what teachers have to do if, sharing this aspiration, they plan to promote pupil autonomy. She also analyses the threats to autonomy which come from school or district administrations or from the teacher's own limitations. Understanding these threats helps us to know how to overcome them.

The ideas in this chapter are fundamental to primary education. Most differences in classroom practices have, at their heart, different views about what schooling is for and what teachers think young children are capable of. Susan Nolen challenges you to make up your own mind.

Peter, aged 8, on learning science: 'We should really do it in life. Scientists aren't inside doing worksheets. They are in the world finding things.'

Nicholls and Hazzard, 1993, p. 94.

Why are you reading this chapter?

Did you choose to read it? If yes, did you choose *freely*, or was your choice constrained in some way? If the chapter was assigned or included in a course syllabus, how might your instructor have structured the course or assignment so that you would feel more autonomous? And what would that mean, exactly? Why is autonomy important? Is it? Can a teacher set goals for student learning and yet foster intellectual and moral autonomy? How?

Take time to consider each of these questions seriously. If possible, get together with one or more classmates and discuss the questions – you may find some interesting differences in your answers. These differences, or their lack, give rise to another question: Where do the answers come from? Assuming your answers represent your beliefs about autonomy and learning and education, how did you arrive at your particular beliefs? What experiences influenced their development? These are not purely academic questions, but are at the heart of an understanding of autonomous learning.

Why should we promote autonomy in schools? Many claims have been made by proponents of increased pupil autonomy. Much research has suggested that learning done for its own sake, rather than to fulfil some external requirement or to gain a reward, is more likely to be retained, and retained longer, and more likely to have involved deeper levels of understanding and more useful learning strategies (Nolen, 1988; Nolen and Haladyna, 1990; Pintrich and DeGroot, 1990). Others have credited increased autonomy with sustained motivation to learn, feelings of academic competence and more sophisticated reasoning skills (Kohn, 1993). Beyond the view of autonomy as a means to an end, however, is the intrinsic value of student self-determination. As Kohn (1993) suggests, 'allowing people to make decisions about what happens to them is inherently preferable to controlling them' (p. 12). This principle is at the foundation of a democratic society. Such a society should provide for development, in its schoolchildren, of the values and skills necessary for citizenship.

What Counts as Autonomous Learning?

Many people have written about autonomy, but different writers have used the word to mean different things. At one extreme, A. S. Neill felt that pupils' autonomy should be complete, including choosing whether or not to attend any classes at all, and constrained only to the extent that it infringed upon the rights of others. At the other extreme is what Alfie Kohn (1993) calls 'pseudochoice', where the child is told that she may choose between what the teacher wants her to do and some punishment. As Kohn states, 'This gimmick uses the word *choice* as a bludgeon rather than giving children what they need, which is the opportunity to participate in making real decisions about what happens to them' (p. 6).

Deciding how to promote autonomy depends upon what one means by the word. In this chapter I will describe different types of autonomy, from a narrow 'autonomy of means' – control over the strategies they use to learn –

to a much broader 'intellectual autonomy', where students have a say in what they study, how, why, and to what end. Along the way I will consider the implications for teachers and students of promoting each sort.

Autonomy of Means

Why *are* you reading this chapter? You may have had it assigned as required or optional reading. It is also possible that you have independently decided to read the chapter for some personal reason. If you are reading this chapter entirely of your own volition, one could say that you are learning autonomously. But what if the chapter was assigned? Does that automatically preclude autonomous learning?

Not if your definition of autonomy is what I call *autonomy of means*, or control over the strategies used to carry out a task without the guidance of a teacher (cf. Shuell, 1988). In that sense, you are probably learning autonomously right now, even if this chapter is required, and even if your main reason for reading is that you will be tested on the material it contains. In this view, the teacher promotes autonomous learning by teaching pupils strategies for learning independently. For example, a teacher might train her students in the use of various note-taking or outlining strategies. The pupils would then be autonomous, in the sense that they can choose which (if any) of these strategies to use when studying assigned readings (and others) independently (Mayer, 1987; Palincsar and Brown, 1984).

Though important, control over one's own learning strategies is a limited sort of self-determination, one unlikely to lead to the benefits claimed by proponents of autonomy in schools. Other forms of choice can be considered autonomy of means: choosing which of a set of assigned tasks one will do first, deciding whether to do an oral or written book report (but not whether to do a book report at all), even choosing whether to do the odd or even maths problems on an assigned page. All have been recommended as ways to increase a sense of self-determination, but none results in a meaningful increase in real pupil autonomy. A broader definition would include control over the reasons for your own learning: what I call *autonomy of purpose*.

Autonomy of Purpose

'There is, I think, no point in the philosophy of progressive education which is sounder than its emphasis upon the importance of the participation of the learner in the formation of the purposes which direct his activities in the learning process' (Dewey, 1938, p. 67). There is little evidence that most schools actively foster autonomy of purpose, despite the exhortations of

Dewey, Neill, and other progressives. For the most part, adults set the curriculum; adults are the ones expected to answer the question: 'Why do we have to learn this?' Teachers themselves often feel constrained to teach what is mandated by others (Haladyna, Nolen, and Haas, 1991; Smith, 1992). Given these conditions, can autonomy of purpose exist in real schools? Though teachers (and administrators) can help or hinder the development of this kind of autonomy, the learner also plays a critical role.

Consider two situations: a time when you were studying required material primarily to prepare for an examination, and a time when you were studying such material *and* you saw it as interesting and valuable in its own right. In the second case, you created additional goals for your own learning, beyond those set by your instructor. How were these two experiences different? Students surveyed in my own and others' research used somewhat different strategies in these two situations. They experienced the passage of time differently, dragging in the externally motivated situation, and passing quickly when they were interested or engaged. They were able to recall the interesting or useful information more easily, and were more likely to see how it related to other things that they knew. These more positive-feeling learning experiences are similar to those reported by those engaged in freely chosen activities, who by definition have autonomy of purpose (Deci and Ryan, 1985; Grolnick and Ryan, 1987; Rigby, Deci, Patrick and Ryan, 1992).

Chapters are not uniform, however, and one which starts out interesting may deteriorate as topics shift, writing style irritates or material becomes incomprehensible (Schiefele, 1991). Your use of various learning strategies may change as these conditions influence your purposes for learning. External pressures to learn certain bits of information may also constrain your use of such elaboration strategies as you attempt to memorize what will be required in an examination (Nolen and Haladyna, 1990). Even if this chapter was assigned, you are, in fact, likely to have multiple reasons for learning, reasons which may change as you read and respond to the material, which are likely to differ from student to student, and which are partially determined by the context of the course and its instructor (Nolen and Haladyna, 1990). Autonomy of purpose, then, may be a relative thing.

Perceptions of Autonomy

How might your instructor have structured this assignment (or the entire course) so that you and your peers perceive yourselves to have autonomy of purpose? Perceptions of autonomy, according to Deci and Ryan's (1985) theory of self-determination, are a function of both personality and the environment. Deci and Ryan suggest that different dimensions of social contexts influence learners' perceived autonomy. Informational aspects of a context are those that provide feedback to individuals about their progress or growth, without emphasizing social comparison or attempting to coerce or control the individual. Controlling aspects emphasize external reasons for performance or learning, such as doing better than others, avoiding embarrassment or gaining a reward. Their work, as well as other related research, suggests that contexts where the controlling aspect is most salient undermine a sense of autonomy (Rigby et al. 1992).

Schools are mixed environments, where there is plenty of information available about student progress, but often a pervading atmosphere of control. But students do not all perceive their educational environment the same; indeed, they actively interpret classroom events in unique ways. Although a teacher may give primarily informational or mostly controlling feedback, students may not interpret the feedback as intended. Some persons, who have what Deci and Ryan (1985) call a strong autonomy orientation, tend to focus on the informational aspects of a setting, and to seek settings where they can be autonomous. Those who tend to have a strong controlling orientation may focus on the controlling aspects, or interpret informational settings as controlling, despite the good intentions of the teacher.

In my own teacher education courses, I allow students to resubmit work that does not meet standards (mine or the individual's). Some students interpret this as allowing them the freedom to take risks and to get additional feedback on their ideas, without the pressure of 'getting it right' the first time. Other students in the class see this as 'jumping through hoops': they didn't figure out how to please me the first time and now I'm 'making them' redo the assignment. Students preoccupied with teacher-pleasing see high marks as the ultimate goal; therefore, by withholding high marks I force them to resubmit their work.

How do pupils come to these orientations? There is undoubtedly a complex relationship involving long-term and short-term goals for learning, interest in the material, pupils' perceptions of the purpose and value of the work and the learning, the amount of effort required, as well as feelings of progress and their perceptions of the teacher's goals. Pupils develop theories about life in a particular classroom, making sense of social and work norms, their interactions with the teacher and fellow pupils (Thorkildsen and Nicholls, 1991). Using these theories, they retain the ability individually to accept or reject teachers' purposes for learning, or add their own. Teachers can promote autonomy of purpose by inviting them to construct socially the purposes for learning in school, and helping them develop the skills necessary to become autonomous learners. Ways in which this might be done are described later in the chapter. But first we must explore a third sort of autonomy.

Intellectual Autonomy

We have discussed two possible meanings of 'autonomy': control over the means of learning, and the opportunity to set the purposes for learning. A third possible meaning is found in the work of Piaget and other constructivists. Even if you have autonomy of purpose in reading this chapter, you may still rely on the instructor to judge your level of understanding. Or you may find yourself struggling with information that conflicts with what you have learned elsewhere, and long for someone to tell you the 'right' theory, the one that will lead unerringly to greater understanding of your pupils and more effective teaching. Your pupils may find themselves in a similar position in studying mathematics. Much traditional instruction leads students to the belief that mathematics knowledge is handed down from above, having been figured out by geniuses. Mathematics learning then becomes memorizing the 'right' algorithms for solving various problems (Kamii, 1985; Schoenfeld, 1989). Such instruction, says Constance Kamii, leads to what Piaget and others have called intellectual heteronomy, depending upon others to tell you what is true and what false, or whether you have learned or not.

But as Bikson (1978) states, if inquiry is autonomous, 'it is self-responsible, or conscious and critical of itself as inquiry' (p. 70). Intellectual autonomy is the ability to judge things for oneself, after taking into account a variety of evidence and the views of others. It requires that students participate in the evaluation of their own work as well as in setting the standards of their performance (Wolf, 1993). Similarly, moral autonomy is the ability to judge right from wrong, independent of any rewards or punishments, considering but not slavishly adhering to the views of others in the social group.

Piaget considered the development of intellectual and moral autonomy to be the most important aim of education (Kamii, 1985; Piaget, 1973). One could argue for its importance by citing the research demonstrating that perceptions of autonomy are associated with various positive outcomes, greater conceptual learning, more effective strategy use, increased motivation to continue learning and so forth. But one can also argue that, in order to thrive in a democracy, individuals within the democracy must have this sort of autonomy (Levin, 1993). Ethically, then, the development of intellectual and moral autonomy should be our highest goals. This belief is echoed in the work of many progressive educators (e.g. Dewey, 1938; Neill, 1960; Nicholls, 1989).

Summary

- Intellectual autonomy is the ability to judge things for oneself, after taking evidence and various views into account.

- Moral autonomy is the ability to judge right from wrong and to act accordingly.
- Autonomy is essential for the proper working of a participant democracy.
- Pupil autonomy is associated with deeper levels of understanding and longer retention of learning.
- Pupils may be given 'autonomy of means', i.e. control over learning processes, and/or 'autonomy of goals', i.e. control over learning objectives.

Structure and Freedom: Teaching for Autonomy

Intellectual autonomy is a cornerstone of constructivist teaching. Based on the premise that students construct their own understanding, constructivist teachers design tasks and activities that allow students to explore and experiment, developing understanding and skills, and testing them against both physical evidence and others' understandings. The teacher in such a classroom is not the sole judge of the adequacy of a problem solution or of a piece of writing. 'Answers' to intellectual problems become symbols of understanding, not ends in themselves. In the example below, we will see how the way in which one arrives at an answer, and the understanding or skill that the process represents, take on primary importance.

Paul Cobb, Terry Wood and Erna Yackel (1989, 1991) worked with elementary school teachers in the Purdue Mathematics Project to develop a constructivist approach to early mathematics instruction. In a typical 'lesson', the pupils would work in pairs to solve a set of related problems, without direct instruction or algorithms provided by the teacher. After about twenty minutes, the class would reconvene as a large group and pairs would explain their solutions. Lively discussions of divergent solutions followed, as the group debated whether various solutions made mathematical sense.

Cobb et al. (1989) stress the emotional as well as cognitive changes in the 7- and 8-year-olds learning mathematics in these contexts as they discovered they could 'figure it out' on their own. At the beginning of the year, many students were embarrassed to make mistakes in their problem solutions, and anxious to get the right answer, regardless of its source. Later, heated exchanges would develop if another student tried to take away their right to find their own solution. The following excerpt illustrates how important it was to the children:

Connie: (To Rodney) The answer is 21.
Rodney: (Angrily) No it isn't. This is – look! I'm going to figure it out my *own* way!
Connie: I already told you.

Rodney: I don't want to copy. (At this point, the teacher comes by to
          observe the group working.)
Rodney: (To the teacher) I don't want them to tell me the answer!
Teacher: They want to – I know you're trying to work –
Rodney: (Interrupting her) I want to try to work it out myself, but they're
          over here telling me the answer and everything. I think it should be
          18 because . . . (Rodney explains his thinking to the teacher.) (p.
          136)

Others' problem solutions were not acceptable until pupils were sure that
they made sense mathematically. I have a video tape of one such discussion,
a spirited fifteen-minute debate over whether the problem 6x3 might be
written 3x6. The reversibility of the expression had to be *proved* to young
sceptics by their peers, a second-grade version of the formal proof necessary
to convince a community of mathematicians. The teacher's role in this
process is to design the activities and facilitate these episodes, rather than to
teach directly the mathematical concepts. In addition to the mathematics, she
must help set classroom norms for doing and discussing mathematics. It is a
critical and difficult role that depends on an understanding of both the
subject matter and how children's understandings in that subject develop.

Students in this classroom learn much more than the commutative property
of multiplication through such discussions, and they probably *believe* in this
property more than students learning it 'because the teacher says so'. These
students also learn about the structure of the discipline of mathematics, how
mathematical knowledge is created and communicated, and that such knowledge can be trusted because they have proved it to themselves. This is Piaget's
intellectual autonomy.

Approaches to teaching what Schwab (1978) has called the 'syntactic
structure' of a discipline (see chapter 2) tend to foster intellectual autonomy.
When students see the development and evaluation of new knowledge as
something they can do, when they gain control over the canons of evidence in
a discipline, they are becoming autonomous. They are not idiosyncratic, not
irrational, they are coming to their own decisions through careful consideration of relevant factors. Rather than learn a set of 'facts' from a textbook,
history pupils might learn to use documentary evidence to construct arguments
for a particular interpretation of historical events (Wineburg and Wilson,
1991). Young scientists might design experiments to test hypotheses of their
own development, and then debate their findings with their classmates (Watson
and Konicek, 1990). Lessons learned about how history and science are
conducted will serve pupils well as participating citizens of a democracy.

Current 'workshop' approaches to teaching composition (see Nancie
Atwell's excellent description of one such approach (1987)) focus on the
writer's communicative goals, audience response, and purposeful use of the
writer's craft to create new literature. Student writers work through the
various stages of the writing process (planning, drafting, revising, editing),

within a community of fellow writers. Teachers emphasize developing the writer's control of the work, again promoting intellectual autonomy. Reading and analysing published literature in various styles and genres, developing writers can then experiment with the use of various techniques and conventions in their own writing. Because their writing is read by other members of the class (including the teacher), who provide valuable feedback, young writers receive a wealth of information to use in evaluating their progress towards their communicative goals. Portfolio assessment (Valencia and Calfee, 1990; Wolf, 1993) provides a vehicle for self-evaluation of both product and process. As in the Purdue Mathematics Project, the teacher's role in a 'writers' workshop' is a facilitative one, neither as sole dispenser of knowledge nor as sole judge of competence, but rather as a guide to the syntactic structure of the discipline and a supporter of students' developing autonomy.

Classroom environments that foster intellectual autonomy seem to share some general features. We have already mentioned how the role of the teacher differs from that of a more traditional classroom. As Grossman, Wilson and Shulman (1989) point out, such methods require more, not less, knowledge of a content area. The teacher must be ready to deal with a variety of student questions, concerns and theories that may coincide only partially with the concepts or theories or events under discussion. An adept teacher can see the connections between the students' understanding and what she is trying to teach, and help students make and extend those connections themselves. When knowledge is tightly controlled through lecture and other teacher-directed techniques, such flexibility is not as critical. Questions and potentially interesting, though controversial, 'tangents' can always be shunted off with 'that's too complex to go into at this time' (McNeil, 1986).

Establishing a Social Context for Autonomy

Beyond subject-matter knowledge, teachers must know how to establish social norms that will allow students to become autonomous learners. Fostering intellectual autonomy requires mutual respect. Teachers must respect students if they are truly to listen to their ideas, and if students are to respect the teacher's. The question of mutual respect is delicately bound up with the power relations in the school. In the realm of interpersonal relations, Dreikurs, Grunwald and Pepper (1983) stress *social* equality in a democratic classroom, where teachers and students follow the same code of conduct. For example, if the class decides it is unacceptable to carry on a casual conversation while others are working quietly, it should be unacceptable for the teachers to do so as well as the students. This does not mean that students and teachers have the same responsibilities or authority in the classroom; teachers still have the responsibility to help students establish reasonable norms and sanctions. (See Cobb et al. 1989; Dreikurs et al. 1983; Nicholls and Hazzard, 1993 for examples of establishing classroom norms that foster mutual respect.)

Perhaps most importantly, students' ideas must be seriously considered by the classroom community. Ball (1991a) describes an elementary school teacher who encourages her students to come up with divergent solutions to mathematical problems by giving them equal weight to her own suggestions. This entails spending similar amounts of time and effort exploring the mathematical reasoning involved, writing or drawing representations of the solution on the board, and so forth. The message is clearly, 'I respect your ability to reason.' Contrast this with the often heard, 'Yes, that's another way it could be solved. Let's move on to the next problem . . .'

Respect for students' abilities to reason also means that teachers do not 'rescue' their students who are struggling, by showing them a solution to a problem. For many teachers this is very difficult to do. My colleague Sam Wineburg showed teachers a video tape of a teacher letting her students struggle in an intellectual 'blind alley' while trying to interpret a time–distance graph. After thirty minutes or more, the students suddenly see why their approach is unworkable, and go on to solve the problem themselves. Teachers watching this tape had mixed reactions, but most were quite uncomfortable with the amount of time the teacher 'wasted' letting her students struggle. 'She should have stepped in when it was clear they were on the wrong track', was a common suggestion. But then students would have learned yet another lesson in dependency on a higher authority, not the lesson they clearly did learn: that they can depend on their own intelligence to solve scientific problems. Recall the response of the pupil in the Purdue Mathematics Project, indignantly rejecting peers' attempts to usurp his right to 'figure it out'.

Part of teachers' attitudes towards student autonomy may stem from their beliefs about the role of errors in student learning. I have often asked my own classes of both novice and experienced teachers what they would do if a pupil made a mistake working a maths problem in front of the whole class. The vast majority of responses centre on minimizing the pupil's embarrassment, often quickly asking a second pupil to 'help' his or her classmate to 'get the right answer'. When I suggest that the student be left at the board to figure out the problem on his or her own, most of my students are aghast. The same teachers who will tell students 'mistakes are a part of learning' often behave in ways that send the opposite message. For example, a new mathematics concept is introduced and homework assigned. Though pupils are expected to learn through practising the concept (a process bound to include many mistakes) this homework is often marked and entered into the course grade. In this and other ways, students learn that they should strive for 'errorless' learning. This emphasis on correct answers over understanding promotes not intellectual autonomy, but the kind of mindless answer-grabbing decried by John Holt (1982) and other critics of education.

How does intellectual autonomy relate to the autonomy of purpose or of means? In the Purdue Mathematics Project classes, children clearly developed autonomy of means by creating and evaluating their own solutions to mathematical problems. Although they may, at first, have participated because the teacher expected them to, there is also considerable evidence that doing maths became intrinsically motivating, perhaps as an extension of children's natural tendency to learn and explore. Cobb et al. (1989) report frequent exhibitions of excitement and glee when new problems were solved and new concepts learned, interest in the variety of possible solutions, and irritation when other students tried to co-opt their right to find solutions that made sense to them. So, although clearly one can have autonomy of means and even autonomy of purpose without being intellectually autonomous, classrooms that foster intellectual autonomy also foster the other two. Intellectual autonomy provides a reason for developing means and purposes.

Promoting Autonomy in School: Risks and Constraints

So, if autonomy is so wonderful, why isn't everybody promoting it? In fact, why is it relatively rare in schools today to see classroom environments that foster intellectual and moral autonomy? There are a variety of possible constraints on developing this kind of environment, various combinations of which may be present in any educational situation.

Foremost, perhaps, in the mind of many learner teachers, is fear of losing control of the classroom. One is aware that one rules by consent of the governed, and that physically one has no way completely to control thirty to thirty-five students if they decide to rebel. For many novice teachers, unfamiliarity with the characteristics of the age group makes pupil behaviour difficult to predict. This makes it difficult to trust students to be able to deal with autonomy without overstepping their bounds. Teachers in such a situation typically strive to maintain at least the illusion of control at all costs. Interestingly, one of the benefits often mentioned by teachers who foster autonomy is that it frees *them* of having to maintain classroom order, as students will share the responsibility when they are included in the rule-making (and rule-adjusting) process (Dreikurs et al. 1983).

If students are autonomous, they will probably be working on different tasks in different ways. This results in a more complex and less predictable environment than one in which the teacher retains tight control. Novices (at anything) have yet to develop routines for many of the tasks they face. This means that they must think consciously about the hundreds of routine decisions that more experienced teachers make almost automatically (what to do if pupils forget materials, how to deal with a noisy disagreement among students across the room while working with a small group, etc.) This increase in their cognitive load makes it hard to keep track of everything in a classroom; the load is further increased if there are a variety of learning activities happening simultaneously.

Even experienced teachers may doubt that children can be allowed the kind of autonomy we have been considering. Beliefs about certain age groups may influence teachers' willingness to relinquish even a modicum of control. Early adolescents increasingly feel the need for greater autonomy and are increasingly capable of complex reasoning. At the same time, many teachers trust this age group the least in matters of self-control and ability to learn independently (Eccles et al. 1993). This 'mismatch' between teachers and students has been associated with increased teacher control over classroom activities, and decreased autonomy, learning and motivation in junior high schools.

Factors beyond the expertise or personal beliefs of teachers may also play a significant role in the amount of self-determination allowed students. McNeill (1986) describes how the administrative structure in four US high schools interacted with teachers' beliefs about students, resulting in teachers maintaining almost complete control over all aspects of classroom life. The desire to maintain order led to the control of knowledge through fragmentation of content into easily memorized groups of facts, reduction of complex phenomena in history to lists of events, and the mystification of complex concepts ('That's a very complex topic that would take more time than we have . . .'), effectively shutting down potentially controversial and emotional discussions. The teachers themselves saw this control of knowledge to be necessary, given pressures or lack of support from administrators. Goodlad's (1984) study suggested that this situation is the norm in the large majority of schools in the US. On the other hand, deCharms (1976) found that systematically working to increase the perceived autonomy of teachers increased the autonomy they allowed their students, which in turn led to greater student learning and motivation.

Pressures originating outside the school can also limit teachers' willingness to relinquish some of their control. In the US, for example, the use of state-mandated, nationally normed standardized tests to compare teachers, schools, districts and entire states can result in intense perceived pressure on teachers. In our study of several hundred teachers and administrators in one such state (Haladyna, Nolen and Haas, 1991), we found many felt that they were obligated to 'teach to the test'. When they perceived their own autonomy to be curtailed, they were understandably less willing to allow students any latitude to explore ideas on their own. More general societal pressures contribute to the lack of student autonomy as well, including issues of future employment, political structure and class structure (Bowles and Gintis, 1976; Willis, 1977).

By restricting autonomous learning to its most narrow definition, control over the means or strategies of learning, teachers can retain control over curriculum, mode of instruction and information. Broadening our conception of autonomous learning to include autonomy of purpose or intellectual and moral autonomy requires taking risks, trusting students to be able to learn under such conditions. As Judy Siekerk (1988), an elementary school teacher in Phoenix, Arizona states, 'Taking time to discuss behaviors with a class or an individual or to prolong lessons so that a student becomes actively involved until he "gets" it, can be a risk for teachers. There is often the prevailing opinion that there is not enough time for this. I do not believe . . . that we are aiming to prepare students for a life without risks. Should we ask less of ourselves?' (p. 6).

Teachers can retain control over their own goals and objectives for student learning while promoting autonomous learning. In a constructivist approach to history, for example, one could decide upon a set of essential learnings, including, say, understanding the role of context and source in evaluating documentary evidence, and yet foster the kind of intellectual autonomy I have described.

Summary

- Teaching for autonomy makes special demands on teachers.
- Conditions necessary for developing pupil autonomy include:
  - teachers confident in their knowledge
  - teachers responsive to students
  - teachers with respect for students
  - discussion approaches to learning
  - good use of errors as sites for learning.
- Factors which make the development of autonomy difficult include:
  - fear of loss of control
  - limited beliefs about what children can cope with
  - school administration demanding uniformity
  - limited subject knowledge of teachers
  - effect of some assessment regimes.

Broadening the Definition of Autonomous Learning

An even broader sense of autonomy would include students helping to decide what knowledge is of most worth, and how it should be studied. This could take the form developed at Summerhill by A. S. Neill (1960), in which students choose whether or not to attend classes, and which they will attend. No pressure is applied to shepherd the reluctant student into formal study, yet most students, after a period of weeks or months, choose to attend and participate actively. This individualism is in contrast to the school community's creation and enforcement of its social code. At weekly all-school meetings, where each staff member and student has a single vote, anyone can propose and argue for (or against) modifying the rules of conduct. The debate engendered by this approach to social discipline (an approach echoed in other democratic approaches to education) promotes moral reasoning by asking pupils to reason morally.

Much rarer than this kind of moral discussion is debate about what knowledge is most valuable and how it should be studied. Although there is a growing call for considering students as rational critics of education, and even as curriculum theorists, this form of debate is not common, even in democratic schools (Nicholls and Hazzard, 1993). Of all aspects of schooling, this is one the adults believe they, by definition, know best, and therefore they should make the decisions. Even in Summerhill, where freedom is the watchword, teachers set the schedule; students merely choose from a menu of classes, rather than negotiating what might be offered.

Yet there is evidence that even young students have much to offer in debates about content and method (Sozniak and Perlman, 1990; Stodolsky, 1988; Thorkildsen and Nicholls, 1991; Thorkildsen, Nolen and Fournier, 1994). Many striking examples can be found in a recent ethnographic study, a collaboration between a university researcher and a second-grade teacher (Nicholls and Hazzard, 1993). A major focus of the research was to elicit the views of Hazzard's 7- and 8-year-old pupils on matters of educational practice, especially on what was worth learning about and how subjects would best be studied. The following excerpt is from a discussion about how the class might learn science, and shows how a skilful teacher can encourage and challenge students' thinking without shutting down the debate.

[February 22] 'What's the best way to learn about science?' asks Sue.
  'Have a scientist instructor.'
  'Science projects.'
  'I like to see pictures,' declares Dan. 'Not just people telling. And it is neat how people can share ideas. Like, some of my friends have weird ideas. Ulp! I don't mean they're stupid. I think they are silly, but then I think about it, and it makes sense.'
  'We could have an hour or 30 minutes and *do* things about science. Then we can write about it and tell it,' says Peter, developing Dan's ideas.
  'I think we should have experiments in the room,' says Dan.
  'How would you do it?' asks Sue.
  'Use measuring things.'
  'Make time bombs and see what would happen,' says James.
  'How would you do experiments?' Sue repeats. 'Would you want me to do them?'
  'I want us to do it. Like on our desks,' says Dan. 'We could have a center and probably make a book about it.'
  'We could get paper and everyone can make a picture of what happens.'
  'Science is what you're thinking about and what you discover,' says Peter.
He seems to know, as William James (1907) put it, that scientists have not

'deciphered authentically the eternal thoughts of the Almighty' (p. 56), that their theories are only 'a man-made language' (p. 57), that 'no theory is absolutely a transcript of reality' (p. 57). Peter's thought resonates.

. . . 'Should I teach science like reading?' asks Sue, to provoke clarification. A chorus of 'no's indicates the inappropriateness of the idea, not a dislike of reading.

Peter leaps to rule out workbook-type tasks. 'We should really do it in life. We get tired of answering lots of questions. Scientists aren't inside doing worksheets. They are in the world finding things.'

'Peter, do scientists write things?'

'They write after their experiments,' says Peter.

'So you want to write afterward?'

'We could write lists of what we want to do and then do them and then write it or maybe type it and then tell it,' suggests Dan, who a couple of weeks earlier had been resisting any form of writing.

. . . Sue asks, 'Do you think you will know enough to teach each other?'

'That's not what I mean,' says Dan, groping for the conception of experiment and dialogue he articulated earlier. 'We could tell each other stuff, what we did learn.'

'So, you just want to be reporters,' says Sue, pushing harder.

'No, no,' says Wole. He has said little so far, but senses that Dan and Peter have a more complex case that deserves consideration. 'If we're right, we can tell people.'

'Don't you need a grown-up to tell you if you're right?' Sue challenges.

'If you read a book and you're sure it's true, you could tell.'

'Mrs. Hazzard, you don't get what I'm saying. We can give them information.' Dan appears to imply that others can evaluate the information themselves.

'How can *I* tell you got it right?'

'We can prove to you by doing something – like making a light or something. We could do it by attaching wires and showing you.'

. . . 'You have my mind swimming with ideas,' says Sue. 'You want to be explorers, and what will I do?'

'Help us.'

'Sit around and wait.'

'What for?'

'For us to finish.'

As Nicholls and Hazzard point out, such discussions 'about the nature of knowledge, about what knowledge is useful, and whether a topic should be studied in a manner consistent with the principles that governed its choice' are rare. 'Yet these questions are central to any community committed to democratic life' (p. 102). One can clearly see the beginnings of what Schwab calls the syntactic structure of the sciences in the discussion above. Along with a sense of intellectual autonomy, these students are developing a shared sense of what it means to do science, how one creates new knowledge and convinces others of its worth, and how the structure of subjects like science and reading differ from each other.

To lead these discussions, teachers must be willing to take seriously students' thoughts, questions and suggestions. This does not mean they must be the *only* guide to curriculum and instruction, but that they can and should be considered and discussed. To do this adequately requires teachers who have thought about these issues themselves, who have their own real answers to the question: 'Why do we have to learn this?' But it also requires teachers who can listen respectfully and thoughtfully to students' answers to this question, and who can and will take those views into account in their planning.

Taking the Risk

Earlier in this chapter I suggested that the strategies you use to promote autonomous learning will depend on your definition of autonomy. The way you define autonomy, in turn, will depend in part on your own feelings of autonomy as a teacher.

Even using the narrowest definition, however, autonomy requires allowing students sufficient freedom to try and fail, to experiment and adjust. Children learn to walk only if adults let them try, fall and try again on their own. Teachers who provide too many supports, who plan and strategize *for* their students, cannot hope to develop autonomous learners, even in the sense of autonomy of means. As one broadens the definition of autonomy, the teacher must relinquish more and more direct control – a prospect that many teachers find uncomfortable or even frightening.

Though schools and teachers can help students develop this sense of autonomy, it may require a radical restructuring of the social and academic context of the classroom (Montessori, 1965). But in these settings more students might develop the 'autonomy orientation' that Deci and Ryan (1985) suggest leads people to see themselves as self-determining even in controlling contexts. Theresa Thorkildsen tells of one graduate of a public Montessori school where teachers work to foster intellectual autonomy: 'Charles, an 18-year-old African American student and graduate of Mac-Dowell Elementary School ... told me, "I've encountered a lot of racism among teachers since I left that school. But that doesn't scare me or keep me down because I know how to decide if I know something without the help of any teacher. My teachers at MacDowell Elementary School taught me that lesson"' (Thorkildsen, 1992).

As teacher Judy Siekerk says, we are not preparing students for life without risks. Risks involve taking a stance where there is no certainty. By retaining control over the content and direction of curriculum, the modes and pace of teaching, and the evaluation of learning, we teach pupils to look for the right answers, for non-controversial knowledge (McNeill, 1986). We teach them that there is certain knowledge, already known to teachers and other experts, and that their role is to learn what we already know. But the great questions, the important ideas are not certain – if our pupils are to become creators of knowledge and judges of the claims of others, we must help them to develop intellectual autonomy in the broadest sense. We must be willing to take risks ourselves, to let our students get the most out of any learning situation by exploring it to the fullest, blind alleys and all. Rather than wait until we have 'prepared' our pupils for autonomy by teaching them all of the skills and knowledge they will need to make the 'right' decisions, we must be willing to provide an environment in which they can learn to be autonomous by being autonomous. For as Dewey (1938) claimed, 'The ideal of using the present simply to get ready for the future contradicts itself. It omits, and even shuts out, the very conditions by which a person can be prepared for his future' (p. 49).

ACKNOWLEDGEMENTS

Thanks to John Nicholls, Terri Thorkildsen, and Charles Desforges for their helpful comments on an earlier draft of this chapter. Correspondence concerning this chapter may be sent to Susan B. Nolen, 322 Miller Hall DQ-12, University of Washington, Seattle WA, USA 98195.

Editor's Commentary

The main theme of several of the previous chapters has been how to help children acquire usable knowledge. Pupils' academic progress, it has been emphasized, is a major concern of schooling.

In this chapter, Susan Nolen has raised a more fundamental issue. The issue is: To what end should we use our knowledge? Her answer is that the purpose of having knowledge is to help us to play a full part in a democratic society. To play this part, it is necessary for citizens to be able to know right from wrong, and to be able to make up their own minds on private and public issues. Of course their subsequent actions must remain within the law. Autonomous people do not do just as they please. They think what they like but behave within democratically agreed procedures.

How can teachers help children to know their own minds? In other words, how can teachers help children to be autonomous learners? This is a difficult task. Many of the ways in which we administer schools and classrooms defeat autonomy and make pupils dependent and submissive. Susan Nolen has analysed these problems and suggested ways in which they can be avoided.

The ideas here should be linked to those in other chapters as follows:

- Chapter 14 focuses on personal, social and moral education. Personal growth is a prerequisite for autonomy.
- Order and control can be achieved through careful classroom management either as ends in themselves or as a foundation for pupil autonomy. This issue is discussed in chapter 10.
- Discussion methods of teaching are essential to the promotion of autonomy. These are discussed in chapter 7.

In relating your thinking on the matter of pupil autonomy to classroom practice you need to be able to recognize autonomy and its converse when you see it. Autonomous learners set themselves clear and significant learning goals: their learning activity is important to them personally, and not just because a teacher says so. Autonomous learners make productive use of their learning environment. They are willing to take risks and they attempt to learn from their mistakes.

Classrooms which promote autonomy show evidence of

- pupil choice of methods and objectives
- pupils who know where their learning is going and how to develop it
- opportunities for discussion and feedback about risks and mistakes
- pupil willingness to take risks and show initiative
- a wide range of learning materials readily accessible to pupils.

The matter of pupil autonomy can be considered in the following school-based projects:

- Draw up a checklist of indicators for classrooms which promote autonomy. Discuss the list with other learner teachers.
- Use your checklist as a guide to classroom observation and discussions with children. Is autonomy being developed? If so how? If not, why not?
- Recall that skills basic to autonomy have to be taught. Draw up a list (using this chapter and chapter 7) and plan and enact a scheme of teaching with a small group of children to promote their autonomy. This is a large, longer-term project which you should monitor carefully in conjunction with a supervising teacher.

FURTHER READING

Dewey, J. (1938). *Experience and education*. New York: Collier Books,
  A seminal work, this small volume gives a clear description of progressive education and Dewey's views on autonomy and democracy.
Dreikurs, R., Grunwald, B. B. and Pepper, F. C. (1983). *Maintaining sanity in the classroom*. New York: Harper & Row.

A handbook for teachers who want to establish democratic classrooms. Clearly written, very practical, excellent resource for beginning and experienced teachers.

Nicholls, J. G. and Hazzard, S. P. (1993). *Education as adventure: Lessons from the second grade*. New York: Teachers College Press.

A collaboration between a respected educational psychologist and a veteran elementary teacher, this is a fascinating look into children's thinking about educational practices, curriculum and learning. Implications for teaching and research are both thought-provoking and true to the concerns of teachers.

Wolf, D. P. (1993). Assessment as an episode of instruction. In R. Bennett & W. Ward (Eds.), *Construction versus choice in cognitive measurement*. Hillsdale, NJ: Erlbaum.

An excellent treatise on the role of students in assessment and evaluation, as well as the role of assessment in instruction. Focuses on portfolio assessment in a variety of subject-matter areas.

12

Teaching for Diversity

Phil Bayliss

Editor's Overview

The range of attainments and capabilities in a class of children is staggering. Teachers must learn to cope with this diversity. In this chapter, Phil Bayliss describes ways of thinking about and planning for diversity.

Diversity is most evident at its extremes, where children are often described as having special needs. Principles for helping these children may be applied to all children. But special needs children also prosper better when their teachers have knowledge and skills specific to their needs. Phil Bayliss introduces a set of models and principles which have general teaching application, but he also illustrates how important it is that teachers acquire specific information in support of specific cases.

I was recently invited to visit a primary school to observe a student teacher during her school experience. 'Have you any pupils with special needs?' I asked. 'No,' she replied, 'all the children with problems go to see the special needs support teacher for this session; it's just the normal group.'

We went to the class and I watched her teach a lesson focused on maths to a lively group of six pupils. It immediately became apparent that one pupil, David, had a left-side hemiplegia (a condition associated with cerebral palsy, where one brain hemisphere, in this case the right, is underdeveloped or damaged, resulting in underdevelopment, or in extreme cases, atrophy of one side of the body.) For David, the weaker left arm was 'carried' throughout the lesson, but, because he wrote with his right hand, he copied from the board and completed some of the tasks associated in tessellation (the main area of work of the lesson). Towards the second half of the lesson, pupils were asked to draw shapes, cut them out and experiment to see if they would tessellate. Blank paper and scissors were provided, and this part of the lesson plan was to allow the ideas presented in the first part to be explored by the pupils. This was a good development of the work.

As soon as David finished the formal part, he found the paper and scissors, but instead of exploring ideas, he fidgeted, pushed the articles around the table in front of him, talked to his immediate peers, sighed deeply and fidgeted some more. After a short while he was out of his chair, talking to peers the other side of the room. When the student asked why he was moving around, David gave a range of plausible explanations: 'I need a pencil'; 'Louise is lending me her rubber'; 'I'm looking at Robert's work to give me some ideas'. By the end of the lesson, David had completed nothing of the extension work.

When I asked the student at the end about David and his particular difficulties, she replied that he worked hard, but 'sometimes he was lazy and had to be pushed'. When I pointed out his cerebral palsy, she looked blank, and told me that her supervising teacher had not passed on any recommendations about how to deal with David's needs.

David, as we found out later, was receiving assistance through the school's special needs provision and that he needed help with 'visuo-motor co-ordination' because the impairment to his right hemisphere was likely to cause 'difficulties in spatial perception'. The task the student had organized for the extension work, the tessellation of shapes, required pupils to use 'visuo-motor co-ordination' and 'spatial perception', that is, David needed to recognize and manipulate shapes in the tessellation task. Given David's difficulties in this area, it was highly likely that his observed behaviour during the second part of the lesson did not stem from 'laziness', but occurred because his particular physical impairment caused difficulties for him. The 'easiest' way to overcome these difficulties was to avoid the task.

For the student (and possibly for the class teacher) the term 'pupils with special educational needs' was synonymous with 'intellectual inferiority', and the responsibility for meeting such needs lay with the 'special needs support teacher', whose main role was to 'help them with their reading and writing'. David was not seen as 'special needs' because he was not 'stupid and he can read', although 'he could be difficult'.

For David, an understanding of 'cerebral palsy' and the effect such an impairment has on his learning will provide directions for teaching styles and choice of tasks: if right-hemisphere cerebral palsy affects visual perception, tasks which require articulated perceptual skills will lead to a learning difficulty; the learning difficulty can be ameliorated by directed teaching or by changing the task or the way the pupil is expected to complete it. Here an understanding of psychology will help to direct principled approaches to meeting needs, and it is the intention of this chapter to explore some of these matters.

Diversity and Education for All

> At the heart of the work of every school and every class lies a cycle of planning,
> teaching and assessing. These general arrangements in a school take account of
> the wide range of abilities, aptitudes and interests that children bring to school.
> The majority of children will learn and progress within these arrangements.
> Those who have difficulty in doing so may have special educational needs.
> (DFE, 1993, p. 4)

The Education Reform Act, 1988, guarantees a 'broad and balanced
curriculum for all', and the recent Draft Code of Practice on the Identification
and Assessment of Special Educational Needs (DFE, 1993, p. 1) states as
fundamental principles:

> the needs of all pupils who may have special educational needs either through-
> out, or at any time during their school careers must be addressed. The Code
> recognizes that there is a continuum of needs and a continuum of provision,
> which may be made in a wide variety of forms ... children with special
> educational needs require special educational provision to ensure the greatest
> possible degree of access to a broad and balanced education, including
> maximum access to the National Curriculum. (p. 1)

Following the spirit of the Education Act, 1981, the Code of Practice states
that the needs of most pupils with special educational needs in England and
Wales will be met in mainstream schools. For some children who traditionally
may have been educated in segregated special schools, it is now possible that
they may also be educated in mainstream schools, if their parents request it
and such placements are deemed 'appropriate'.

The pattern of primary school populations is changing to reflect this spirit
of integration (Booth, Swann, Masterton and Potts, 1992; Wolfendale,
1992), and the focus is shifting to the role of the 'effective school' (Ramasut
and Reynolds, 1993) in meeting the needs of *all* their pupils, not just those
who experience 'special educational needs.' Here it is appropriate to talk of
'diversity'. The Code of Practice talks of a 'continuum of need' which may,
if we discuss intellectual needs, range from 'giftedness' to 'severe learning difficulties' with a range of values of learning needs in between. If we
take this view and broaden it to consider educational needs (however they
may be defined), then *all* pupils have educational needs and we have to
consider those issues which make some educational needs 'special', that is,
why some pupils experience difficulties with the 'normal' arrangements of
schools.

As we can see with David, 'special needs' are not just about general
learning problems, 'being slow' or reading difficulties. David's cerebral palsy
is part of the particular characteristics he brings to the learning environment
which may impede his learning in certain areas. The teaching style adopted

by the teacher may support, or, in this case, ignore, his physical difficulties in that she did not attempt to support his cutting out or manipulation of the shapes, while the choice of the tasks David is required to undertake will affect David's learning as well. Where there is equilibrium between these three aspects of learning, seen from the child's point of view, the child will not have a problem, and learning will proceed. Where a mismatch exists between David's particular abilities or disabilities, teaching style or choice of task, a 'special educational need' (that is, David's learning will not be supported) will arise out of the interaction between these variables. For David, an understanding of the psychology of his needs, how the particular condition of cerebral palsy will affect learning, will help to point the way to more efficient teaching to meet those needs, either by changing teaching style (working one-to-one) for brief periods and physically helping him to cut out and arrange shapes) or by changing to a task which David can succeed in doing, for example by using jigsaws or 3D shapes placed within outlines. If we can understand the 'special educational needs' of particular children in this way it is possible to develop teaching styles and school environments to support education for all because 'It should (not) be overlooked that among the most disadvantaged children in our schools are those in ordinary schools who have special educational needs about which little is being done' (Brennan, 1987, p. 141).

What is Diversity? Impairment, Disability and Handicap

The Code of Practice describes a 'continuum of need'. 'Need' is not a unitary concept but contains a variety of dimensions, each of which implies a lack of something. For example, 'needs' seen from a biological point of view, are concerned with survival: the need for food, warmth or shelter. 'Social needs' arise from human requirements of affiliation, and to have friends and acquaintances. Where these needs are met, satisfying the self-esteem needs of being competent and recognized as such become important (Hayes, 1984). In this way, 'needs' may be seen in a variety of ways: physical, emotional, social, aesthetic, spiritual, intellectual (Maslow, 1970).

In an educational sense, 'special needs' arise when the child is prevented from learning those things his or her peers are capable of learning (Warnock Report, 1978, para. 3.1:36). Those factors which prevent him or her learning may be due either to characteristics of the child or characteristics of the environment, or due, as has become more accepted (Gulliford and Upton, 1992; Norwich, 1990), to the interaction of the child and his or her environment. Here, it is useful to distinguish between impairment, disability and handicap.

Impairments may be seen as problems or difficulties which an individual experiences at the physical or organic level. Thus, hearing or visual impairment, physical impairment, intellectual impairment may arise from congenital (inborn) or traumatic (accidental) factors.

If an impairment contributes to difficulties experienced by individuals which interrupts their functioning *as* individuals, this may be termed a *disability*; if such a disability results in disadvantage relating to their social role, this would be termed a handicap (Oliver, 1993, Sugden, 1992; Wood, 1981). For example, people who experience a physical impairment (lower spine injuries) may be confined to wheelchairs, which interrupts their functioning as individuals (described in mobility terms); if the world they live in makes no allowance for wheelchairs, they experience disadvantage, that is, they are handicapped by their disability. If access is provided, the handicapping effects of their disability arising out of their impairment may be diminished or largely removed.

As a further example, I experience short sight (i.e. I have a visual impairment) and I wear glasses. Wearing glasses allows me to function as an individual and I cannot be said to be disabled. If I wished, however, to be a pilot, I would be barred from such a profession, because of my imperfect vision. I would therefore, with respect to flying, be handicapped.

However, handicap may exist without any underlying causal relationship to a disability of impairment. Aspects of handicap which arise from social or cultural differences do not imply a *deficit* (i.e. a within-child impairment) but, instead, such disadvantages may arise from *difference*. The Code of Practice, for instance, is careful to differentiate between those children with a learning difficulty, that is, a significantly greater difficulty in learning than the majority of children at the same age, and those children disadvantaged solely because 'the language or form of language of the home is different from the language in which he or she is or will be taught' (DFE, 1993, p. 4). We may extend this view to other cultural norms as possible handicapping conditions, for example ethnicity, class or gender. This view may provide explanations for the view expressed by the Warnock Report that, at any one time, up to 20 per cent of the school population may experience a 'special educational need' (1978). For those children whose class, ethnicity or gender result in disadvantage due to inappropriate curricula, underachievement will be seen as a 'special educational need.'

Given the distinctions between impairment, disability and handicap, it is reasonable to assume that, for any given child, a clear understanding of how these aspects of his or her development arise, and the relationships between them, may offer directions for intervention. Thus, providing glasses may reduce (or remove) the disabling effects of a visual impairment; changing the rules relating to flying may remove the handicapping effects of wearing glasses, Further, in the past, where women were barred from various employment activities like flying because of their gender, a policy of equal opportunities removes the handicapping conditions of a cultural norm, as it relates to flying.

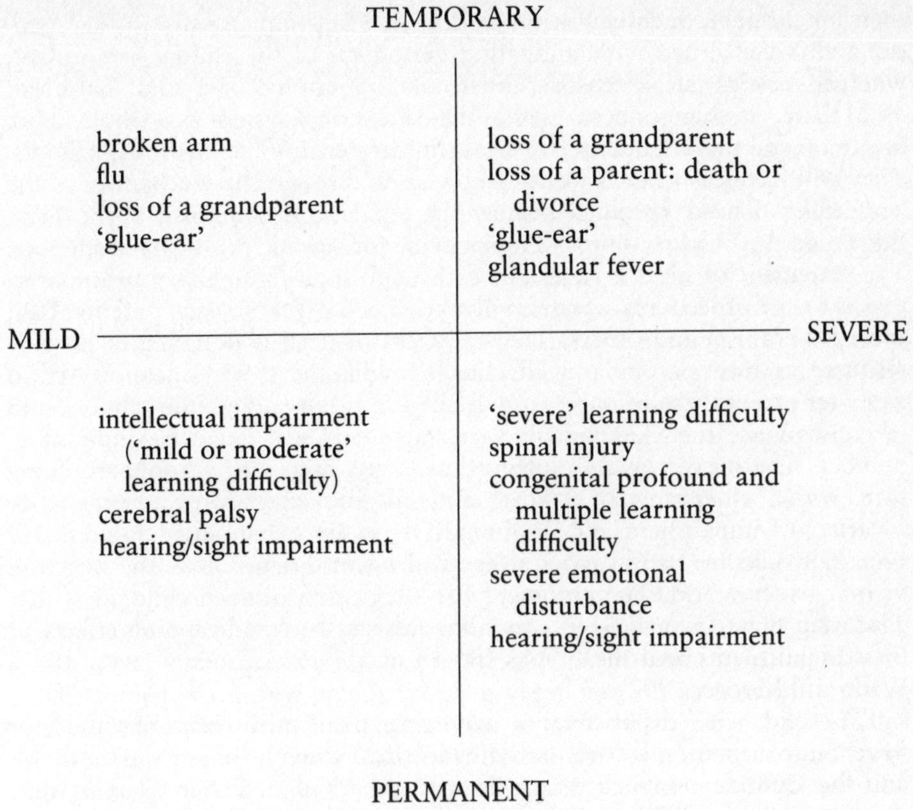

TEMPORARY

broken arm	loss of a grandparent
flu	loss of a parent: death or
loss of a grandparent	divorce
'glue-ear'	'glue-ear'
	glandular fever

MILD ——————————————————————————— SEVERE

intellectual impairment	'severe' learning difficulty
('mild or moderate'	spinal injury
learning difficulty)	congenital profound and
cerebral palsy	multiple learning
hearing/sight impairment	difficulty
	severe emotional
	disturbance
	hearing/sight impairment

PERMANENT

Figure 12.1 Dimension of 'need'.

A further consideration must be taken into account. 'Special educational needs' are not fixed, 'once-and-for-all' attributes of children. Even for children with severe disabilities, their needs and requirements change over time. Figure 12.1 sketches two dimensions relevant to a description of changes in special educational needs over time and over severity. Given this view, the concept of 'special educational needs' become dynamic, relative and complex. Needs change over time (the needs of a 5-year-old are different for the child at 15, which are different again for the adult at 35 years) and they can fluctuate in severity or duration. Thus, the condition of Down's syndrome is a permanent condition, but its effects may be mild or severe in any given individual, while 'glue-ear', an infection of the middle ear which affects a child's hearing, may be of short or long duration, with mild or severe hearing loss.

Children with permanent severe impairment may have their special needs recognized before compulsory school age, and may require extra help from the local education authority or the health service (DFE, 1993, p. 1). For the majority of such children, their schooling is concentrated in special education, where the aim is to support development to lessen the disabling effects of their impairment. Such education is described as compensatory or therapeutic, and is concerned with mitigating the effects of the child's impairment, whether it be physical, sensory, intellectual, emotional or a combination of all of these. As changes occur within the educational system as a whole, more and more of these children are being integrated into mainstream schools. They will have their needs identified by LEAs through the mechanism of the 'statement of need' (produced under the regulations contained in the 1981 Education Act) and recommendations made for specific professional support. The statement of need is determined through multidisciplinary procedures, that is to say procedures which involve teachers, psychologists, parents, GPs, speech therapists and others. The statement of need is designed to provide resources to meet particular needs, but following the 1993 Education Act, to a greater extent these resources are deemed to be already within schools, and in consequence the likelihood is that statements will begin to diminish in number. The move towards integration is growing, and schools are being faced with a wider range of children in mainstream education who experience a variety of impairment and disabilities. To what extent such children will eventually become handicapped in the wider world depends on the structure of that wider world. The argument for integration of such children is that educating them in integrated situations lessens the handicapping effects of their impairments and disabilities (Booth et al., 1992; Soder, 1981, 1992; Wade and Moore, 1992).

The child who experiences a mild/permanent, (or temporary/mild or /severe impairment) may only become identified when he or she starts school, and the identification process starts with the child's teacher ('The 5 stage assessment process, DFE, 1993) who will notice that the child is experiencing some kind of learning difficulty. Under the Code of Practice, each school has a special needs co-ordinator and a governor with responsibility for supervising the school's arrangements for meeting special educational needs within the school. A 'whole-school' approach will establish policy for meeting special needs and define processes of supporting them. However, within the classroom, while help is available, the immediate responsibility for meeting the range of complex, dynamic and relative needs of children at present rests with the class teacher.

If we are to move away from seeing the problems of special educational needs as being solely rooted in the child (and therefore the responsibility of the special needs co-ordinator), classrooms must become more conducive to meeting the needs of *all* children. The issues this raises go beyond the classroom; it moves meeting needs in the wider sense towards whole-school approaches and partnership models of support teaching, team teaching and co-operation between special needs teachers and class teachers (Best, 1991). The whole-school approach to meeting special educational needs requires that the changes necessary to meet a range of children's needs are rooted in the school, not in the requirement of a separate, specialist provision (Ramasut and Reynolds, 1993). The changes necessary to accomplish this will take place at the management and policy levels of school organization, as well as involving classroom change for the individual practitioner.

Further, the changes required raise issues about the nature of the curriculum. Before the introduction of the National Curriculum, meeting the special educational needs of learners focused on two processes (Bradley and Hegarty, 1981): providing access to the curriculum enjoyed by the majority of learners, or modifying that curriculum to meet particular needs. Since the 1988 Education Reform Act, the second option is no longer available: all children in England and Wales must be given supported access to the National Curriculum, particularly in those areas of the curriculum which were formerly considered by some to be inappropriate. Here, a whole-curriculum approach (National Curriculum Council, 1990), encompassing the key principles of breadth, balance, relevance and differentiation (Carpenter, 1992) must be the central focus of meeting pupils' special educational needs.

This is a a straightforward statement, but, given the constraints of the classroom, how can intervention be organized to meet the wide variation in children's needs?

Summary

- Pupils in any one class vary enormously in characteristics relevant to learning, including intellectual and physical characteristics.
- Teachers attempt to plan for the needs of all their pupils, but at the extremes of certain characteristics children may be considered to have special needs and therefore to merit special attention.
- Difference is not the same as deficit.
- Important distinctions may be made between impairment, disability and handicap.
- Handicaps may be mild to severe, temporary or permanent: each needs carefully appraising, and a system of minimizing its effects and capitalizing on pupil strengths must be designed.

Learner–Teacher–Task Relationships and Diagnostic Teaching

I considered above the interrelationships of the characteristics of the learner, the teaching processes and the tasks which learners have to complete (Bennett and Desforges, 1985; Montgomery, 1990; Norwich, 1990). To support learning, there has to be a match between learner, teaching processes and tasks (Tomlinson, 1985), and the teacher's role is to ensure this match.

The role of the teacher, and of the school, is crucial (Bennett & Desforges, 1985; Doyle, 1980). Mortimore, Sammons, Ecob and Stoll (1988) and

Mortimore, Sammons, Lewis, Ecob and Stoll, 1989), in a large-scale study of school effectiveness, found that schools do affect the way children develop, and that changes in children's learning and development, which may be ascribed to schooling, are substantial. The study described twelve key factors as underpinning the 'effective school'. For our purposes here the following are relevant.

The study found that teachers who organized a structured framework within which students could work, and yet allowed them freedom within this structure, were likely to be successful. Further, teaching which was intellectually stimulating and challenging, which had a limited focus within sessions, and which made use of higher-order questions and statements to encourage children to use creative imagination and problem solving, resulted in greater progress.

The study found positive effects where the teacher geared the level of work to a student's needs and where there was the maximum communication between teachers and pupils in class-based or small groups.

Behaviour difficulties were seen to be closely linked to attainment, 'especially amongst younger children. In particular, [there was evidence] that students with a higher rating in learning difficulties in one year tended to make less progress in reading in the next year. Similarly those with lower reading scores in a given year tended to show an increase in behaviour difficulties (especially those concerned with learning difficulties) in the following year' (Mortimore, et al., 1989, p. 760). The results of the study show that the relationship between behaviour and progress in learning is complex; each influences the other.

The cultural characteristics of pupils were also recognized as relevant: children of semi-skilled, unskilled manual workers, whose fathers were absent, were significantly more likely to exhibit behaviour difficulties in school, and boys generally were more likely to be assessed as having behaviour difficulties in all years. For children of different ethnic backgrounds, the study reported that if the complex relationship between behaviour and achievement is taken into account, there was no further specific association between ethnic background and behaviour.

However, the study also concluded that 'the school made a far larger contribution to the explanation of progress than there was made by background characteristics, sex and age' (p. 762).

The study makes links between attainment and behaviour. Weinert, Schrader and Helmke (1989, p. 901) lists some further variables relevant for student achievement:

1 opportunity and pacing of instruction;
2 whole class vs. small group vs. individualized instruction;
3 giving information (including structuring, clarity, pacing and enthusiasm);
4 questioning students (including the difficulty and cognitive level of questions);

5   reacting to student responses;
6   classroom management (individual or group work, and homework).

Here, it can be seen that meeting educational needs it is not simply providing learners with 'opportunities to learn'. Instead, the teaching process must be interactive, structured, and have purpose and relevance for learners in general. For those pupils whose educational needs are 'special', the general framework must be extended to allow teaching to be directed and to support specific interventions to meet individual needs.

This goes beyond the view that differentiation is synonymous with good teaching (Moore, 1992) and that meeting the needs of learners with special educational needs will be embedded in a framework of good practice (Carpenter, 1992). Good practice must also include strategies for meeting the needs of pupils with permanent severe impairments: the child with severe dyslexia or severe hearing impairment, or the child whose attainment levels are disrupted to such an extent that he or she becomes a behaviour problem and is excluded from school (Parffrey, 1993). Unless such strategies become commonplace, such learners will be excluded from the mainstream of educational practice.

Directed Intervention

Directed intervention as a teaching process must be principled, in the sense that it must be goal-directed. Learners' needs must be specified, and arrangements made to meet those needs with reference to the development of knowledge, skills, attitudes and values within a curricular framework (National Curriculum Council, 1991). This in turn requires that classrooms be organized, children's learning assessed and programmes evaluated. This process is not static; it is dynamic or iterative, in the sense that feedback loops within the process of directed intervention 'recycle' the process in order to develop flexibility and response to change in order to meet the dynamic, relative and complex nature of classroom interactions (Doyle, 1980) (see figure 12.2). If we view the classroom as an 'ecology', we must use 'ecological' methods (Cohen, 1980; Cooper and Upton, 1991) to manage the learning of children within it, particularly for those children who fail within the normal 'ecology'. For such children, 'if [they] cannot learn through the way we teach, can we teach the way children learn?' (Chasty, 1993, p. 27).

The model presented is an attempt to provide an interactive approach to meeting children's needs in general. In this respect it resembles action-research and reflective-practitioner models (Vulliamy and Webb, 1993), which require teachers to adopt the role of researcher and to develop problem-solving skills based on observation, review and evaluation to develop flexible teaching approaches. 'Teachers should develop skills of

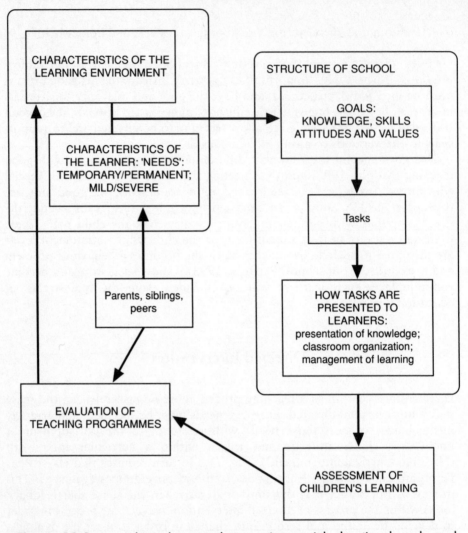

Figure 12.2 An ecological approach to meeting special educational needs: goal setting.

perceiving relevant features of the pupil as well as those of flexibly adapting their approach to suit such features' (Tomlinson, 1985, p. 107). Such adaptive teaching requires teachers to start from the learner. Further, 'an interactive awareness points up the need for adequate theories of human learning to inform the acquisition of what are thereby seen to be complex skills of flexible intelligent teaching' (ibid., p. 111).

This holds good for all children, but for those children, who through impairment, disability or handicap, fail to learn within 'ordinary environments', the teaching process must not only adapt to the child's particular needs; it must be predictive of the next step to take, especially where, for some children, what constitutes the 'next step' is problematical. In this sense, teaching must not only be adaptive; it must first be diagnostic.

Diagnostic teaching requires that the teacher possess a knowledge of developmental processes, and teaching must be congruent with the learner's developmental requirements (Hunt, 1971; Snow, 1989), that is, teaching must match learner to task, and tasks to learners. This will affect *planning*: what tasks to select will require qualitative information as to levels of the child's expected competence or abilities (gained from a variety of sources; e.g., special needs co-ordinators, educational psychologists, parents, colleagues and other ancillary professionals, speech therapists, physiotherapists, etc.); the characteristics of the learners will determine how *knowledge is presented;* the nature of the tasks chosen will determine the form of *classroom management; monitoring of pupil behaviour* will provide feedback for the teacher and pupil and presupposes an interactive *relationship* between teacher and pupil (see figure 12.3).

If teaching within the primary classroom comprises predominantly 'housekeeping' or 'domestic chores' with little (or intermittent) rich qualitative interaction between teacher and learner (Meadows and Cashdan, 1988), teaching will be based on outcomes (i.e. what pupils produce) rather than processes (how they come to achieve outcomes and the strategies they use to that end). For children who fail, an outcomes-led approach will compound failure, whereas a process approach will allow for interpretative feedback, which will further inform the planning process within the iterative cycle (Wood and Shears, 1986). Knowing *why* children fail, as opposed to knowing simply that they failed, is crucial to supporting learning (Sharron, 1987). For example, miscue analysis or the use of cloze analysis in diagnosing reading difficulties (Beard, 1992; see also Clay, 1992) within a mild/severe reading difficulty will provide clear information relating to a child's difficulties, which will inform the development of a teaching programme.

Matching Tasks to Learners

I have argued that a diagnostic teaching approach is rooted in an understanding of children's development, whether this be linguistic, intellectual, emotional, social, moral, physical, aesthetic or spiritual (Bloom, 1956). The particular 'stage' or 'developmental level' the child has reached will determine the starting point for an intervention programme. Knowing where to start will require some form of assessment. This process of initial assessment may be done formally, in the sense of using norm-referenced, standardized tests, to compare the individual with the standard group, or it may be criterion-referenced, i.e. task-based, where the learner's level may be described with reference to a set of tasks.

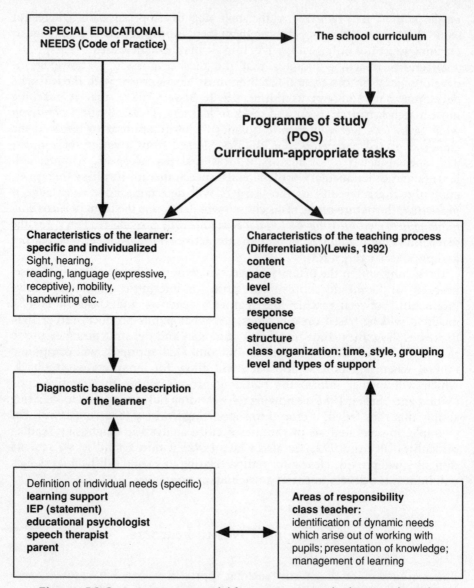

Figure 12.3 An interactive model for meeting special educational needs.

Standardized testing, normally the purview of the educational psychologist, will allow the description of 'developmental profiles'. This form of testing generates a great amount of information and is generally available to special needs specialists, who can also provide advice relating to specific children. The difficulty facing the class teacher is to translate the information, as part of the planning cycle, into effective teaching practice.

Thus, for David, whom we met earlier, specific information relating to visuo-motor co-ordination, or general physical development (or even general intellectual development) will not help the teacher, unless she or he can develop specific teaching strategies to meet his specific needs. The specific information received from specialists will provide a baseline description of David's skills and insight into specific areas of difficulty in gaining access to the National Curriculum, that is, it provides a 'snapshot' of where David is developmentally, with regard to language or reading, handwriting or problem solving, etc. This skills-based information will enable the teacher to plan what Helmke (1989) describes as the 'entry level'. In order to plan the next step, the teacher must have an understanding of processes of developement.

Feuerstein (Sharron, 1987) criticizes the 'traditional view' of intelligence testing as not being process-orientated and offers a 'test–teach–retest' design to examine learning potential in children in order to gain a dynamic view of progress in learning. This test–teach–retest approach helps teachers to avoid the view that aptitudes (in the sense of aspects of intelligence) are fixed in the individual. Some earlier views of child development (see, for example, Burt, 1955; Gould, 1992) saw aptitudes as genetically determined and fixed at birth. Some later views (Snow, 1989) take into account the effects of the interaction between genetic and environmental influences of experience, and the possibility of intervening at critical periods in the child's development. From an educational view, the idea that aptitudes are not fixed, but are amenable to change through intervention, allows for the possibility of change. If parents, teachers and pupils themselves do not see change as possible, 'it promotes beliefs about school learning that can degrade motivation and eventually lead to learned helplessness' (Snow, 1989), where the child (and parent) sees the inability to succeed as inevitable.

Given the possibility of change, how can baseline knowledge of a particular learner be developed into a coherent programme?

Snow (1989, p. 973) states that 'no optimum method of adapting instruction to individual differences has yet been invented', and Claxton (1984, pp. 214ff.) notes that while educationalists are busy devising diagnostic tests of 'cognitive levels' and are devising curricula structured according to 'cognitive difficulty',

> this method is expensive, crude and generally ineffective. The alternative is to have a rough, intuitive shot at what the next thing to teach might be, and modify it according to the learner's response. Let [the learners] tell you whether it feels right or not . . . If you are sensitive to how your teaching is going down, you will very quickly find the right level. A learner's readiness to learn from what you are presenting is indicated clearly by his interest. If he feels challenged, then he's ready. This in turn makes teaching challenging and fun.

This pragmatic view may reflect the greater likelihood that teachers may, in practice, be sensitive to learners' needs, but are not equipped to modify their teaching appropriately (Bennett and Cass, 1989), especially when they are faced with a learning difficulty which defeats 'intuition'. Here, teachers must be given some guidance. Several strands of research present themselves as a way of supporting teachers' 'intuitive' processes.

Summary

- Two general models for making special needs provision have been described, namely
  - an ecological approach
  - an interactive approach.
- Special needs teaching includes but goes beyond good general teaching.
- Special needs provision requires
  - specialized knowledge
  - specific diagnosis
  - particular materials.

Models of Learning and Teaching Processes

Learning difficulties which focus on difficulties of language, reading and number have been described as essentially *cognitive* difficulties (Dockrell and McShane, 1992). As has been argued above, teachers need a clear idea of the processes involved in cognitive development (see chapter 3).

Developmental principles are exemplified by Feuerstein (Sharron, 1987), whose work with refugees emigrating to Israel rested on the premise that children of disadvantaged groups who presented severe learning problems when faced with assimilation into a foreign culture were not intellectually impaired, but rather lacked the constituent skills which supported their problem-solving capabilities. The programmes designed by Feuerstein were based on the fundamental premise that all learning is mediated by a caregiver (parent, grandparent, teacher), and the role of mediation is to 'modify selected aspects of the environment to optimize the child's acquisition of cognitive functions' (Notari, Cole and Mills, 1992, p. 170). Although Feuerstein's original work was with disadvantaged adolescents, the procedures developed have been used within many special education settings and for pre-school and infant children (Klein and Feuerstein, 1985). The educational programmes developed from Feuerstein's original approaches are concerned with learning experiences, mediated by a teacher (a mediated learning experience, MLE) which comprises three essential components:

- Intentionality: Introduce and guide the children to the situation by means of materials, other children or events and explain what you expect them to learn from it. Organize the learning experience for the children so that the concepts and skills they will be working on will be clear to them.

- Meaning and purpose: Offer the children reasons for the classroom experiences and life events you organize. Explain academic tasks, school rules and problems as they arise. Include reasons why adults behave the way they do.
- Transcendence: Relate the children's experiences, their immediate needs and their concerns beyond the here and now in space and time. Have the children reflect on what they are doing and understand how it relates to other experiences. (Notari et al., 1992, p. 172)

Feuerstein also included the mediation of a sense of competence, the need for challenge, controlling and sharing behaviour, and goal setting: 'encouraging children to set goals and then making them explicitly state the means for their achievement is a very enriching form of mediation – the elaboration of the process of some task being as important as its accomplishment' (Sharron, 1987, p. 48).

The Mediated Learning Programme has been used to effect with 'developmentally delayed' children and 'children with medical diagnoses' (e.g. Down's syndrome) (Notari et al. 1992, p. 172), who showed improvement within information-processing ability, and whose general representation and language abilities were enhanced: 'improvement in general representational abilities and in language may have positively influenced the more specific academic skills . . . on which the children made unexpected gains' (Notari et al., 1992, p. 176).

The approach has also been used to support literacy development (Englert, Raphael and Andersen, 1992; Kriegler and Kaplan, 1990); thinking skills in adolescents with sensory (hearing) impairment (Thickpenny and Howie, 1990); and it has formed the basis of a programme of instruction, 'The Somerset thinking skills course' (Blagg, Ballinger and Gardner, 1988), which has been used with a variety of children in mainstream and special schools.

The mediation approach is concerned with development of cognitive processes, and as such may be described as 'content-free' – indeed, the approach favoured by Feuerstein makes great use of abstract materials which focus directly on processes.

In contrast, a specific skills-training programme adopts an approach using itemized lists of hierarchical learning objectives (Coupe and Porter, 1986; Ainscow and Tweddle, 1979) and favours what might be termed the 'small-steps approach'. This teaching methodology has been used extensively within special educational practice and has supported remedial education within a 'basic skills' framework. For example, a child with spelling or handwriting difficulties may have a 'small-steps' programme designed for him or her, which breaks down larger tasks into smaller components.

The 'small-steps' method makes extensive use of behavioural learning theory. Stimuli are controlled and presented to the learner, who produces the required response, which is then rewarded. Mistakes are ignored, and the stimulus is repeated until the learner can consistently produce the required response. When he or she has mastered the particular item, the programme moves on to the next 'small step'. This form of teaching has been very successful for teaching children and adults with severe learning difficulties, and programmes developed from the methodology include DI (Direct Instruction), the DISTAR Programme (Gersten, Woodward and Darch, 1986), Precision Learning (Raybould & Solity, 1980) and ARROW (Lane, 1990), all of which may be used to support reading development.

Understanding Tasks

I have discussed the processes of learning and matching tasks to learners. A further aspect of teaching children with special educational needs is to understand what demands a particular task or activity makes on a learner. Tasks are seldom unitary or simple, in the sense that they require a simple response. Even specific tasks related to Direct Instructional methods (which on the surface only require a direct response to a specific stimulus) make demands on the learner in terms of understanding what response is required (i.e. what is expected by the teacher); what information to process and what responses to make. For instances, within mathematics programmes, the carrier language (i.e. the language of instruction) sometimes requires greater understanding than the mathematical task itself, and if a child has a reading difficulty, changing the form of the instructions will help the child to complete a mathematical task successfully. Here the linguistic nature of the task, rather than the intellectual understanding required, results in greater difficulties for the child.

Where we require differentiated responses to complex tasks, it is important for the teacher to know what aspects of the task may provide difficulties for learners (Bricker and Woods Cripe, 1992). Some further examples may be provided if we think of specific areas of difficulty. If David has a physical difficulty, a task which requires a physical response will provide a problem; for a child with a hearing impairment, understanding the task might provide a problem if it is set up by the teacher using speech. A task which requires problem-solving will provide difficulties for a child with a learning difficulty; a reliance on written instructions will provide difficulties for a child with a reading problem, and so on.

Task analysis is a formal approach to task description which helps identify pupil problems. A formal approach to task description is one which uses task analysis. The teacher details (as a series of teaching objectives) the specific requirements of a task and leads the pupils through the steps (using a direct instruction approach). Task analysis has led to a criterion-referenced approach to setting teaching objectives, the 'checklist approach'.

A different view is for the teacher to have an understanding of task requirements, which through mediation can provide an understanding of why a particular pupil is having difficulty. For example, with David and the tessellation exercise, knowing that the task requires physical skills (cutting and physical manipulation of shapes) will help the teacher to 'spot' that David is having difficulty and will allow the teacher to intervene in an effective way, in this case by helping David to cut out the shapes, cutting the shapes out for him, or getting a peer to work with David – here a range of strategies present themselves, some of which arise out of the nature of the activity itself.

If tasks are seen in this complex way, for any given task there will be a series of inherent aspects or components (see figure 12.4), and any one or

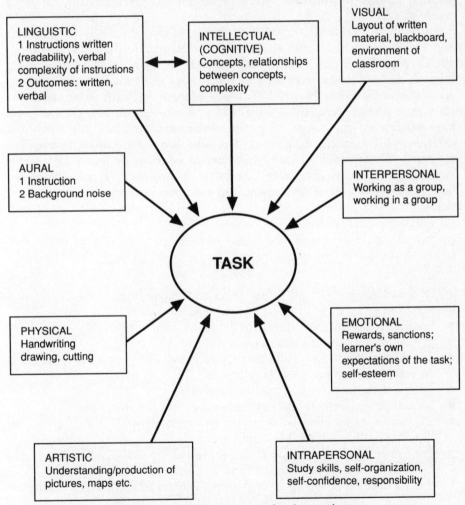

Figure 12.4 Components of task complexity.

Source: After H. Gardner. (1983). *Frames of mind: The theory of multiple intelligences.*
New York: Basic Books.

more of these aspects may provide difficulties for the child. For David, for example, it might be important that the extension work on tessellation be the focus (intellectual aspect), in which case, the physical aspects of the task (which cause him difficulties) may be a secondary consideration. It is therefore legitimate for the teacher to provide support for those physical problems (helping with the cutting out, or giving physical support with manipulating shapes). If the physical difficulties are the focus (i.e. supporting David to develop his cutting, drawing, colouring skills), he will be encouraged to complete the task (at this level) himself.

The prioritization ought not to be static; rather than establishing a single priority, a range of priorities should be set for any given child or group of children.

All children, irrespective of whether they have special educational needs or not, will have strengths and weaknesses in the range of domains: linguistic, visual, physical, interpersonal etc., as well as intellectual, and shifting focus to address these strengths and weaknesses in flexible and imaginative ways (Gardner, 1983; Hoerr, 1992) will address the learning needs of the class as a whole. Here, the identification of the composition of tasks will have effects for the *range* of pupils within a class, not only for those children with learning difficulties, but also for those children described as gifted. These children may show enhanced learning potential in, for example, intellectual (cognitive) domains (Young and Tyre, 1992), but may require support in developing, for example, interpersonal or physical skills.

Summary

- A broad range of pupil attainments and capabilities is evident in any classroom.
- Special needs children are at the limits of their range: they might have general or very specific characteristics.
- Teaching special needs children requires specialized knowledge and skills on top of normal good teaching practice.
- Special material provision may be necessary.
- Special programmes might have general or specific objectives.
- Classroom tasks must be subjected to especially careful analysis in the light of specific children's learning needs.
- Fundamentally, teachers need to believe that special needs children can learn with the help of ingenious and well-informed teachers.
- Special needs children make evident the general principles of teaching for diversity.

Editor's Commentary

In chapter 4, Anne Cockburn showed that pupil diversity is a major challenge for teachers and one which they frequently fail to meet. About 50 per cent of the work in primary classrooms is not well matched to pupils' attainments, and therefore it makes little contribution to their learning progress. The problem of mismatching may be exacerbated for children at the extreme ranges of diversity, or for those with specific learning problems.

Phil Bayliss has offered a range of ways of looking at this problem which is profitable for all pupils. He has focused on

- teachers' attitudes
- general models of the problem
- specific knowledge, skills and materials.

Development of the ideas in this chapter may be pursued in the following school-based work projects:

- Observe a whole-class lesson. Discuss the lesson afterwards with the highest attainers and the lowest attainers in the class. Identify what understandings they developed in the lesson. Discuss with experienced teachers how the lesson might be followed up to meet different pupils' needs.
- Take a piece of work from a class work book. Using the scheme in this chapter, carefully analyse the demands it makes on pupils. Redesign the task so that it would promote learning for the highest and lowest attainers in the class. Discuss your designs with other learner teachers.
- Working with a supervising teacher, discuss children with a range of special needs in the school. For each child consider
  - how diagnosis of the need was made,
  - what provision is made for learning,
  - what records are kept of progress,
  - how provision is reviewed.
- Begin to build a file on aspects of special needs, and evaluate the factors in the above project in the light of the schemes and concepts described in this chapter.

The ideas in this chapter relate to those in several other chapters as follows:

- Many special needs refer to the personal rather than the academic growth of the child. This aspect is considered in chapter 14.

- Special needs may be hidden in the hurly-burly of classroom life. Re-read chapter 4 to alert you as to how this comes about.
- Special needs require particularly careful approaches to assessment. These matters are raised in chapters 16 and 17.
- Diversity refers to all children. Consider how diversity is provided for in direct teaching as described in chapter 6.
- Gender and race are particularly important dimensions of diversity. They are considered in chapter 13. Here a key point is revisited. How teachers treat children is heavily determined by what the teachers believe about children — especially by teachers' expectations of what children can achieve.

FURTHER READING

Booth, T., Swann, W., Masterton, M. & Potts, P. (Eds.). (1992). *Learning for all: Curricula for diversity in education*. London: Routledge.

Dockrell, J. & McShane, J. (1992). *Children's learning difficulties: A cognitive approach*. Oxford, England: Blackwell.

Gulliford, R. & Upton, G. (1992). *Special educational needs*. London: Routledge.

Jones, K. & Charlton, T. (1993). *Learning difficulties in primary classrooms: Delivering the curriculum*. London: Routledge.

Leadbetter, J. & Leadbetter, P. (1993). *Special children: Meeting the challange in primary schools*. London: Cassell.

Montgomery, D. (1990). *Children with learning difficulties*. London: Cassell.

Wolfendale, S. (1992). *Special needs in the primary school*. London: Cassell.

13

Ethnic and Gender Differences

Gaby Weiner

Editor's Overview

Gender and racial characteristics are strikingly visible examples of differences between pupils. Are they differences of any significance to schooling? They certainly have been assumed to matter in contrast to other visible differences (e.g. eye colour), which are assumed not to matter.

Many teachers and administrators believe that gender and race are associated with strengths or weaknesses which must be taken into account in teaching. We have seen in many previous chapters that how teachers treat children is strongly influenced by the teachers' beliefs.

Because many beliefs about gender and race are negative in their potential effects (e.g. 'you cannot expect girls to be good at maths'), they are particularly dangerous to pupils' learning progress and to their self-esteem.

These problems and the ways of talking about them are extremely sensitive. They are known to provoke heated reactions. They cannot be avoided, however, if pupils are to be afforded equality of educational opportunity regardless of race or gender.

In this chapter, Gaby Weiner analyses some of the ways of talking about gender and race in schooling. She shows that the common conceptions are

- complex
- ever-changing
- contentious.

She analyses the conceptions as they refer to

- language
- self-concept
- socialization
- teacher expectations
- curriculum
- achievement
- classroom processes.

Finally, she offers some alternative ways of looking at conceptions of gender and race, suggesting that conceptions can be created in situations to reflect the way power relations are expressed.

Introduction

A great deal has been written about equal opportunities and equality issues in education over the last few years, generating many questions about how and why differences between pupils occur and how these relate to pupils' educational experiences and eventual achievements. Do working-class and/or black pupils face prejudice and discrimination from their teachers? Are boys, indeed, better at mathematics than girls? Which groups of children are most likely to cause discipline problems in the classroom? Is it true that there is an over-representation of African-Caribbean boys in special schools, and so on? You may or may not be familiar with the statements implied by these questions, and I am sure you can think of many more taken-for-granted or 'common-sense' perceptions about why pupils perform differently at school. Which of these statements are true? Which are not?

The exploration of such common-sense perceptions (which may also be viewed as stereotyping or labelling of certain groups as 'bad') forms the basis of this chapter. The principal questions for teachers about such notions are whether they actually encourage and perpetuate the differences that their pupils exhibit, or whether the causes of these differences lie outside their control. Most importantly, teachers need to know how their professional practice can contribute to greater equality of educational outcome for their pupils.

This chapter will discuss some of these very complex questions and should thus be seen as a starting point or introduction to gender and racial issues in education. Since much of the research in these areas is conceived in terms of *differences* between individuals and groups, the first section seeks to explore the difficulty in applying the concept of educational difference to gender and 'race' and the problems in exploring what may be seen as contentious, emotive and 'political' issues in education. Inverted commas are used here to denote the problematic nature of 'race' as a concept. They are used to indicate the broad area of racial division/difference rather than alluding to distinct races or genetic combinations. I have also, for the most part, avoided using the term 'ethnicity' because, rather than focus on what minority ethnic groups have in common, its use may implicitly emphasize differences between them. As Sarup (1986, p. 98) puts it, the problem lies with rascism rather than cultural difference and using the concept of 'ethnicity . . . masks the problem of racism and weakens the struggle against it.'

The second section identifies the main research themes relating to how gender and racial difference in classrooms have been conceptualized and understood, particularly as they affect pupils. These themes include language, pupil self-concept, socialization, teacher perspectives, curriculum, pupil performance and achievement, classroom context and relationships between pupils. One of the aims of knowing about such work is that it can raise consciousness about current inequalities in the schooling system and thus make change possible. However, caution is needed in our expectation of what can be achieved by the teacher or schools alone, without any fundamental change to the present economic and social structure within which schooling is located.

The third section suggests an alternative way of looking at equality and difference in education, which takes us beyond comparing supposedly disadvantaged groups of pupils or defining particular groups of pupils as 'problems' for the system.

Conceptualizing Difference and Researching Inequality

At the outset, it is important to understand that the concept of difference(s) itself is problematic and needs to be explored to see how it has been applied to research studies and school practices. It is problematic for a number of reasons. First, the notion of difference has been used in a variety of ways for differing purposes. It has been used, among other things, to celebrate diversity (viz. differences between religious or cultural groups), to denote injustice (viz. differences in the way students may be experiencing their schooling) and to ascribe inferiority to individuals or groups (in arguments that girls are not naturally high achievers or good at science).

Second, it is a concept used more by educational psychologists than sociologists or teachers. The latter two groups are more likely to conceptualize the problem of educational difference in terms of how educational inequality within the school can be related to how unequal power relations are manifested in schools and society generally. Hence teachers may be more likely to see differences, say, between the sexes in school management hierarchies (where men tend to be grouped in the most senior positions) as an indication of patriarchal relations rather than implying any deficiencies among women teachers.

In contrast, rather than focusing on how a social order maintains itself or how schools may perpetuate existing unequal social relations, educational psychologists have tended to concentrate on identifying patterns of gender difference at psychological and interpersonal levels. Thus psychologists have focused on the gender labelling of babies, sex roles in personality and cognition, sex differences in play, socialization patterns in childhood, adolescence and adulthood, sex roles in relation to work and leisure and so on (all reported in Hargreaves and Colley, 1986; see also Golombok and Fivush, 1994).

Third, exploration of educational differences has a higher profile in studies of gender, compared with those of 'race'; possibly, because racial difference (particularly its political implications) is far more complex than the relatively distinctive male/female dualism. It is inconceivable, for example, that teachers would ever line up pupils according to their specific racial group; though there is no such apprehension in regard to girls and boys.

Fourth, it is important, to see theories of difference as they have emerged historically and culturally. For example, biological attributions of sexual and racial inferiority held in Britain in the nineteenth and early twentieth centuries, thankfully, have lost ground in the second half of the twentieth century as societal and educational factors have emerged as more important, reliable and acceptable. Consequently there is less likelihood of the blame for poor academic performance being attributed to so-called natural differences or inherited traits than previously.

Fifth, there has been some debate about the extent and nature of gender and racial difference. For example, in their early but still relevant comprehensive survey of sex differences, Maccoby and Jacklin (1974) found relatively little overall differences between the performance of females and males, and currently in the UK, girls' overall performance in examination at 16 is at least as good as boys', and better in some subjects (CSO, 1990). So, what, if any, is the problem of gender in our schools? Also, given the educational effects of factors such as low income and the relative diversity of cultural groups in British society, how do we explain and deal with educational differences between cultural groups as they emerge?

Thus we might ask whether it is indeed helpful to identify difference in order to increase educational equality – particularly given the fundamentally unequal society in which we live. Social (and educational) equality cannot be achieved by education alone. Sarup poses the following question: 'If society is differentiated on the basis of power, wealth and education, how can children coming into the educational system from various parts of that differentiated society ever, as it were, line up equally' (1986, p. 3).

Sixth, is there much point in separating out the exploration of gender and racial difference in education, since they are inextricably linked? It could be argued that by treating the two separately (the main identified problems being typically underachieving white girls and hostile black youth), black and minority ethnic girls are likely to be rendered marginal, and thus their specific needs may be ignored.

Seventh, the identification of black and female students as a so-called problem for the system has been challenged in a number of studies (for example, Williams, 1987; Mac an Ghaill, 1988). Mac an Ghaill came to see black students from a new perspective in his 1988 ethnographic study of secondary Asian and Afro-Caribbean students, where initially, he implicitly took up the conventional white norm of classifying back students as a problem. He began to redefine the black youths in his study as operating at several levels to counter racism in a society structured by 'race' and gender. This was marked by their needing to develop in school a different reality from the white majority, which continued to see them in deviant terms and as at odds with the system: 'I shifted the research away from the conventional "race-relations" focus on the youths' culture as the main problem with their schooling and began to investigate the assumed unproblematic nature of the teachers' ideologies and practices. In this way, I "made" the research problem, (Mac an Ghaill, 1993, p. 149).

This leads to a final point concerning the conventional understanding that research should be detached and objective. This has already been much challenged in the social sciences, and such an objectivist stance appears especially difficult to sustain when considering gender and 'race' issues. As Rizvi (1993, p. 2) points out in the case of research on racial issues, the researcher cannot but be involved and affected by the research process, since he or she is also part of a racialized (and gendered) culture.

> The researcher cannot simply stand apart from the social and political relations that constitute the research process . . . In seeking knowledge about racism, the researcher enters into a relation with the object of knowledge. And as these relations change, then so might the way the researcher theorizes racism . . . In this sense the personal cannot be divorced from the research process.

More generally, Said criticizes the conception that there is such a thing as reality or true knowledge from which people (including scholars and scientists) can maintain detachment: 'No one has ever devised a method for detaching the scholar from the circumstances of life, from the fact of his involvement (conscious or unconscious) with a class, a set of beliefs, a social position, or from the mere activity of being a member of society' (Said, 1978, p. 10).

Nevertheless, despite all these challenges to claims by researchers that they have accurately identified differences between the sexes and between racial groups, knowledge of their work and the patterns of educational inequality they have found are important as long as we scrutinize their findings critically and with considerable care. The next section will be devoted to the main themes taken up by researchers exploring gender and racial issues in education.

Research Themes relating to 'Race' and Gender

Language

Language has been identified as one of the main means by which the male, white dominance of power relationships is sustained and re-created. Spender (1980) criticizes the ways in which language in the classroom, and more generally, is used both to subordinate girls and women and to define them sexually. Thus, the dominant male experience is both reflected and constructed through language, so that women are defined principally in sexual or domestic servicing roles. In fact, patterns of girls' non-verbal participation in classes begin to emerge at primary levels (Grugeon, 1993) and are clearly developed by the secondary stage of schooling in a way that parallels the fact that 'women don't talk as much in mixed company [so] girls don't talk as much as boys in mixed classrooms' (Spender and Sarah, 1980, p. 148). In effect, what schools seem to be implicitly communicating to girls is that they should learn to stay silent in the company of men.

Language has also proved problematic for black and minority ethnic students with the emergence of linguistic deficit hypotheses which accorded little respect to dialects. According to such hypotheses, the dialects used by Black American and British African-Caribbean pupils were thought of as simply mispronounced and poorly spoken Standard English. However, in the 1960s this position was challenged by social scientists who began to see Black English as a valid dialect of Standard English. However, problems arising from linguistic differences still continue, as emphasis on Standard English is increasingly being promoted, for example, in the National Curriculum of England and Wales. A strategy to overcome these differences suggested by Cooper and Stewart (1987), is to point out differences without criticizing student speech, thus highlighting linguistic differences rather than linguistic deficit.

Other features of language usage are those of reading choice and writing style. Female pupils are likely to read more widely and gain greater enjoyment from fiction than their male counterparts, who, in contrast, tend to focus their reading on informational, non-fictional texts (Gorman, White, Brooks, Maclure and Kispala, 1988). It is argued that these reading patterns have an effect on writing styles, where girls prefer essay-type narratives in contrast to boys' preference for factual, briefer forms of communication (Stobart, Elwood and Quinlan, 1992).

Pupil self-concept

How pupils feel about themselves has been perceived as crucial to their school performance: thus studies of differences in pupil self-concept have been of much interest. Researchers have explored whether boys have a better self-concept or greater confidence than girls; however, research evidence varies. Findings range from little evidence of differences in self-perception between male and female pupils (Chapman and Boersma, 1983) to males having far better self-images (Connell, Stroobant, Sinclair, Connell and Rogers, 1975). No research study yet, to my knowledge, has found girls to have a better self-concept than boys. A claim that black children come to see themselves as failures and are non-achievers because of their negative self-concept and low esteem has also been challenged. Milner (1983) suggests that black people who are ashamed of their colour feel this way because white society has forced them to accept its own appraisal of them as inferior while Stone (1981) found British research on black self-concept and self-esteem to be inconclusive and contradictory. In her view, there is no basis for the belief that black children have poor self-esteem and negative self-concept; rather, the negative self-concept hypothesis serves to obscure the real issues of pupil underachievement which involved inequalities in power and class, and racial oppression.

Socialization

Socialization into what it means to be a girl or boy pupil and/or a black or white pupil, it has been argued, begins within the family from the moment a child is born. Milner (1983) maintains that the socialization process is the most important determinant of prejudice, and Nash (1979), that children learn to apply stereotypes whether in relation to gender or to racial difference before they start school.

Cultural factors such as language, literature and art also contribute to stereotypical and prejudicial thinking by conventionally using whiteness as a metaphor for all things good and pure, and blackness to denote badness and evil. Schools condone and reflect rather than challenge these stereotypes. Thus, just as parents give more attention to their sons and are more likely to reprimand them and have different expectations of their behaviour – boisterous and cheeky – compared with their daughters, who are given greater praise for their appearance and pleasing manners, the same patterns of expectation are apparent within the school. As Measor and Sikes (1992, p. 66) report: 'Teachers said that they thought boys were more aggressive . . . Different standards of tolerance were applied, and also the same behaviour was characterized differently depending on the sex. Boys were allowed to be noisier and get away with more of this aggression, but "It is not nice to see a young girl fighting"' [quoted from Clarricoates, 1980].

Teacher perspectives

Much has been made of variations in the amount of time and attention given by teachers to girls and boys respectively. For instance, in an early study in the United States, Fagot (1977) reported that teachers are more likely to chastise boys and pay them more attention (Spender, 1980, came to similar conclusions in the British context) though, at the same time, teachers create greater dependency in their treatment of female pupils. Other studies found that male and female teachers tend to encourage in their female pupils stereotyped traits of obedience and passivity, yet prefer their male students to adopt the more male-identified characteristics of aggression and independence. These expectations start early. Delamont reports a North American study by Serbin (1978), who spent five years observing pre-school classrooms in New York schools. 'The staff told Serbin that little girls were boring, and clung too closely to them, while boys were more independent. These teachers did not realize that their own interaction patterns were reinforcing the very behaviour they disliked. Little girls *had* to stay close to the teacher to get any attention, while the boys did not' (Delamont, 1990, p. 31).

Research has also shown that teachers have lower expectations of female pupils (as do parents and pupils themselves), are more intellectually encouraging and demanding of male pupils, yet reward girls for good behaviour and tidy presentation. They are also likely to direct male and female pupils into conventional subjects and careers and believe girls' careers to be less important than boys' (Arnot and Weiner, 1987). Further, they are likely to be sexist in their allocation of tasks within school, for example, at primary level, choosing girls to help keep the classroom clean and tidy, and the often physically smaller boys to move furniture or equipment (Clift, 1978; see also Delamont, 1990).

Similarly, black children and children from minority ethnic communities are perceived as 'problems' rather than potentially enriching to school life, with teachers having lower expectations of their abilities and potential achievements. For example, a study by Proctor (1984) in the United States found that low expectations of pupils are associated with minority group membership, non-conforming personality and non-standard speech. Mac an Ghaill noted similar, apparently unconscious, discriminatory practices in Britain:

> Mr Young was surprised when I showed him how he had responded to a number of incidents involving students who had 'interrupted' the lessons. Although out of a class of 34, there were only five Afro-Caribbeans, they had been identified nearly twice as many times as causing an interruption as the 27 Asian and 2 white students. Most important ... was that his different perceptions of Asian and Afro-Caribbean youths, affected his definitions of what constituted a 'classroom interruption'. (Mac an Ghaill, 1993, p. 150).

There is also a tendency to encourage black pupils' sporting and musical abilities to the detriment of their academic studies. Moreover, teachers tend to be more severe in disciplining black students, and blame so-called bad behaviour on what teachers see as the inadequacies of black family life (Brah & Minhas, 1985; Phoenix, 1987).

Is the sex of the teacher important in terms of interaction with pupils in the classroom? There have been no recent studies on this, but there is little evidence to indicate that male and female teachers differ in their generally 'traditional' and stereotypical treatment of their pupils.

Curriculum

Attention has focused on both the formal and 'hidden' (informal and unwritten) school curriculum. In terms of the formal curriculum, syllabuses and content (including those within the National Curriculum in England and Wales) have tended to exclude the experiences of girls and women, whether black or white. For example, Gill (1990) points out that in the early National Curriculum history documentation, of the named individuals, white European males far outweighed any other representative group, so that National Curriculum history was still to be centred on the historical experiences of white men. Further, textbooks and reading schemes have continued to convey an outmoded view of the typical family as white, middle-class and conventional (Deliyanni-Kouimtzi, 1992). As Delamont points out in her review of school texts and children's books and comics, 'Thus we can see that the world in which British children grow up is a gender-segregated world, in which all facets of their lives at home and in the community are deeply impregnated with stereotypes of masculinity and femininity. Boys are tough, aggressive and creative, girls mild, verbal and domestic' (Delamont, 1990, p. 22).

Where choice is available, not surprisingly, girls tend to opt for the humanities, languages and social science, and boys for mathematical, scientific and technological subjects despite various initiatives to counter this trend (Elkjaer, 1992).

It has also become evident that the implicit, hidden curriculum also exerts enormous pressure on pupils (and teachers) to conform in sex-specific ways, for example through teacher expectation as outlined in the previous section; at institutional level, where there may be gender-specific regulations on clothing (especially in Britain with its increasing adoption of school uniform) and discipline, and at pupil level, where sexual harassment and name-calling have been found to be common features of school life (Lees, 1987).

Similarly, black and ethnic minority experience is underrepresented in the content of school syllabuses and texts, and racist institutional practices continue to inhibit the progress of black pupils in climbing the educational ladder. Thus there is evidence to show that, irrespective of proven ability, black pupils tend to be assigned to lower-ability groups compared with their white counterparts and are, consequently, restricted in the level of school qualifications open to them (Wright, 1987) and future channels into higher education and the labour market (Brennan and McGeevor, 1990).

Pupil performance and achievement

Attempts to establish differences in intelligence and inherent ability between various social groups have been much challenged in recent years, on academic as well as ethical grounds. In fact, Pidgeon (quoted in Goldstein, 1987) argues that differences emerging from tests are necessarily created by the test rather than natural in the individual taking the test. The argument goes that contemporary cultural assumptions and expectations about differential performance have permeated the thinking of test constructors, so that the tests themselves produce the relatively poor performances from lower-status groupings (Gould, 1981). According to Pidgeon, any differences, say, between male and female pupils' test performances are likely to be due to a difference in balance of items favouring one or the other sex. It is therefore notionally possible for fair tests to be constructed where appropriate selection of items will yield tests without gender or cultural bias.

Styles of assessment are also likely to affect the relative performance of male and female pupils, in such a way that boys achieve better with multiple-choice examinations and girls with essay-type questions (Stobart et al., 1992). There is little research on the different test responses of minority ethnic groups. It seems, then, that test constructors are confronted with ethical decisions as to whether it continues to be legitimate, as is currently the case, to formulate a theoretical description of achievement which is sexually and culturally biased; that is, which explicitly includes a sex difference or a difference between social groupings (Goldstein, 1987). Instead, should test constructors now be working towards a more gender and culturally fair mode of assessment as Stobart et al. (1992) suggest?

The appearance of differences between social groups in subject areas has proved less controversial. As Measor and Sikes point out, boys and girls tend to achieve differentially in various areas of the curriculum: 'As a general rule, girls tend to do well at language-based skills and boys do better on the mathematical and science side of the curriculum. We know that boys seem to have more difficulty learning to read than girls, and we know that girls have more problems with mathematics' (Measor and Sikes, 1992, p. 53).

Further, girls tend to be more academically ahead in the earlier years of schooling. One perceived reason for this is that the primary school atmosphere is more feminine and thus more comfortable for girls. Another perceived reason is that girls are relatively more mature than boys, though the concept of maturity in relation to academic achievement (rather than physical size) is heavily criticized by Goldstein (1987).

As young women progress up the school, however, their achievement levels slip relative to those of boys, particularly in mathematics and science (Isaacson, 1988). A variety of reasons have been given for this. For example, Scott-Hodgetts (1986) argues that girls favour *serialistic* learning (proceeding from certainty to certainty, learning, remembering, recapitulating), whereas boys are likely to take a *holistic* approach (more exploratory, working towards an explanatory framework). Following this, Scott-Hodgetts suggests that male pupils are likely to be more successful learners, say in mathematics, as their holistic approach enables them to be more versatile, and thus more capable of switching learning strategies where necessary.

Other studies have found that female pupils are more likely than their male counterparts to display what has been termed by Licht and Dweck (1987) 'learned helplessness'. Thus, boys are likely to attribute success to ability and failure to lack of effort, whilst girls relate success to effort and failure to lack of ability. Likewise girls show a stronger tendency to view their successes as due to factors such as luck, which also implies some uncertainty about their ability to succeed in the future (Nicholls, 1979).

Whilst such research studies may provide a useful background for teachers, care needs to be taken in how such findings are understood. It is all too easy to blame the sex of the pupils for such differences in attitude rather than the social (and school) situations in which such perceptions are encouraged to flourish.

Classroom context

Mixed-classroom studies have repeatedly found that male pupils receive more teacher attention than female pupils (e.g. Galton, Simon and Croll, 1980), and, as we have seen, a factor in this is teachers' tendency to place more importance on male learning and give boys more teacher time. Yet, it is often boys themselves who demand attention, for example by asking questions or by making heavier demands on the teacher in other ways. But teacher attention need not necessarily be thought of as positive, as we saw in Mac an Ghaill's study earlier. In her ethnographic study of a comprehensive school in Birmingham (England), Wright (1987) similarly found that African-Caribbean pupils, both male and female, received more attention than their white counterparts, but that this attention was often demoralizing and prejudicial in achievement terms.

Other studies have found that the greater number of contacts that male pupils have with teachers relate not only to misbehaviour (viz. negative attention) but to academic contexts, which are both teacher- and pupil-initiated (viz. positive attention); and also that boys receive a higher percentage of abstract (rather than factual) questions, showing a greater willingness to guess when unsure of the answer. On the other hand, girls have a higher percentage of positive contacts with their teachers but are more likely to remain silent in classroom discussion (Delamont, 1984; Sikes, 1971; Stanley, 1993).

These patterns of classroom interaction may be found at all levels of education. However, there are some specific age-related factors.

Primary classrooms

An early review of British primary schools by Brophy and Good (1974) found that although boys are criticized more often than girls, they are praised as often, and sometimes more often. Teachers not only check on boys' work more but also tend to question them more during the lesson. Further, boys are more likely to call out answers, and thus proactively make greater demands on the teacher. A study by French and French (1984) similarly revealed that boys are far more able to make their comments heard and to be dealt with by the teacher; and that certain boys in the class develop 'strategies' which increase their chances of being asked a question by their teachers, and which ensure, during the lesson, that they become the focus of attention for the whole class.

On average, primary school boys appear to misbehave much more often and more intensively than girls, thus eliciting more frequent criticism and punishment for misbehaviour. However, this praise and criticism of boys is not distributed equally among all boys in the classroom. Brophy and Good (1974) found that a large proportion, sometimes even the majority of the criticism, may be directed to a small group of boys who are perceived as likely to misbehave and who are often low achievers. In Britain, this group typically includes an overrepresentation of black and minority ethnic students. Meanwhile a high proportion of praise (for academic accomplishment) goes to another small group of generally white boys, this time those who are high achievers.

Overall, then, research suggests that differences between primary boys and girls in patterns of interactions with their teachers are as likely to be due to differences in the behaviour of the students themselves as to the tendency of teachers to treat the two sexes differently.

Secondary classrooms

However, as we have seen, the advantage in achievement by girls at the primary level is often not sustained as they move up the school, though in England and Wales girls' performance in examinations improved in the 1990s. Thus whilst the first set of figures for GCSE (1987–8) showed a higher proportion of girls (62 per cent) than boys (54 per cent) leaving school with one pass in A to C grades, boys still did better in mathematics, physics, geography and chemistry (CSO, 1990).

As male pupils grow older and move towards college, university and employment, the conflict that once seemed to have existed between the good pupil role and the male, sex role seems to disappear. The converse happens to young women as their perceived future domestic role as wife and mother narrows their career aspirations. Patterns of vocational choice become more sharply differentiated at this stage, since achievement in school is perceived as a stepping stone towards later performance as the family breadwinner or carer, and concern about future occupation therefore becomes urgent. At the same time, familiar patterns of classroom interaction continue. Stanworth (1983) found that secondary schoolgirls found it more difficult than boys to engage in conversation successfully with the teachers and that they were less memorable. Many of the teachers in Stanworth's study found difficulty in recalling girls' names and admitted to the fact that they could not, in some cases, distinguish one girl from another.

Relationships between pupils

Many pupil experiences in school are shaped by the informal curriculum relating to how they are perceived by their peer group. Evidence is now emerging that indicates that students are profoundly affected by these experiences. Two studies illustrate this concern; the first regarding the subjective world of adolescent girls (Lees, 1987), and the second on the impact of racism on primary children's lives (Troyna and Hatcher, 1992).

Lees's study aimed to explore the system of social relations in the school – how boys treat girls and how girls respond in the classroom. What emerged was that, regardless of social class or ethnic group, adolescent girls' school experiences are profoundly affected by their sexual reputation – that is, whether they are 'slags' (girls who sleep around) or 'drags' (girls who do not and who are considered by boys as marriageable rather than 'easy lays'). Lees's comments on the sheer volume of denigratory terms for women, interpreting this as evidence of society's attempt to control girls' behaviour, with the specific aim of protecting their sexual reputation.

Offensive labelling also plays a significant part in the lives of black children. In their study of predominantly white primary schools, Troyna and Hatcher found, first, that 'race' and racism are typical features of school life and, second, that racist name-calling is by far the most common expression of racism.

> There is a wide variation in black children's experiences of racist name-calling. For some it may almost be an everyday happening. For others it is less frequent, with occurrences remembered as significant events whose reoccurence remains a possibility in every new social situation. For all, it is in general the most hurtful form of verbal aggression from other children. (p. 195)

Significantly, the study also showed that any differences between the experiences of children in different schools were accounted for in terms of the effectiveness of the stance of staff and particularly the head teacher in dealing with racist incidents. Again, as in the Lees study, name-calling was found to induce fear and construct systems of control over black students.

What is notable and welcome about Troyna and Hatcher's study is their finding about the positive impact of school policy on children's (and teachers') behaviour. Throughout the 1980s, increased attention was devoted to equal opportunities policy-making at school and local authority level (though 1980s government administrations have been no more than luke-warm to equality issues – see Arnot, 1987), and this has undoubtedly brought benefits to some black pupils and also to some girls. Thus, since the earlier studies quoted in this article, gains have been made by girls in terms of their overall examination performance at 16-plus and in some previously 'male' subjects such as physics and mathematics. However, questions still need to be asked about which girls have benefited most, in which subject areas and with what consequences in adult life and at work.

Alternative Perspectives on Educational Differences

Another way of exploring educational difference is to consider how individuals or groups operate in particular settings. This perspective can yield different understandings compared to the work of researchers such as those mentioned above, who tend to look for broader patterns and causal relationships. Rather than use what it sees as existing static dualisms such as girl/boy or black/white as categories of analysis which may mask other inter-relating categories such as socio-economic group or ethnicity, this new perspective suggests that it might also be fruitful to focus at individual school or local level; at what Ball (1987) calls the micropolitical level of the school.

Ball sees the micropolitics of schools as operating in relation to three interrelated areas of activity: the interests of the actors (i.e. pupils and teachers); the maintenance of organizational control; and conflict over policy. Every school struggles to reconcile these differing interests, and all those involved in the school, whether boy or girl, teacher or pupil, nursery nurse or head teacher, pupil or teacher from a specific racial group, are affected and involved within these struggles. Thus, the position of each individual may be seen at various times as powerful or powerless, good or bad, feminine or masculine, worker, helper or mother etc., depending on the particular situation in which he or she is positioned. Women teachers might be powerful in the classroom, but less powerful in the staff room or at home in the family. The working-class boy might be relatively powerless in the classroom but more powerful in the playground, among his friends or within the family. In this view, no one can be seen as always in authority or always oppressed or only representing one category of difference.

Moreover, each context (or discourse) in which we operate (i.e. the school, family, among our friends) has a particular code of practice with particular rules as to how we should behave. These rules are seen as normal behaviour, and social relations between the sexes are created and embedded within these codes of behaviour. Girls and boys are expected to behave in appropriately feminine and masculine ways, and these change according to the context in which they find themselves.

From this point of view, normality is socially created. Theories or bodies of knowledge emerge at specific historical moments and consolidate what we think of as real, natural and normal in, say, pupils' learning. An example suggested by Walkerdine (1988) of a specific body of knowledge with normalizing features is child development, a core element of all initial teacher education courses for much of the twentieth century. In child development, identification of the normal pupil, the well-socialized girl or boy, or the normal sequence of learning, implies a set of social practices which necessarily also provides room for a pathology of those whose behaviour defies such practices. If a child does not follow a locally perceived normal pattern in development or behaviour, he or she can only be categorized as abnormal. Thus these normalizing practices, outside which no child or teacher can remain (they can only be normal or abnormal) provide systems of classification, regulation and normalization whereby the position of each child is understood or read: 'I . . . use the concept of *positioning* to examine further what happens when such readings are produced and how children become *normal* and *pathological*, fast and slow, rote-learning and displaying real understanding and so on . . . These produce systematic differences which are then used as classifications of the children in the class' (Walkerdine, 1988, p. 204).

In this view, what we consider appropriate behaviour for children might appear commonsensical and normal but, in fact, is manufactured and infused with power connotations. To understand each set of power relations we need to understand who sets the rules and what space is available for action. Drawing on the French philosopher Foucault, the concept of power used here does not rely on physical threat or overt ambition to dominate, but rather it produces the willing subject: it tells us how to behave in a way that we can understand and accept willingly.

In another study drawing on some of these ideas, Walkerdine (1990) explores the ideology of progressive pedagogy, which, although conceived in terms of the liberation of children, she sees as simultaneously oppressive to the female teacher. She argues that the progressive primary classroom can only operate properly with the active, male-as-norm child and the passive, female-as-norm teacher. Here the independence and autonomy of the teacher are sacrificed, through her role as quasi-mother, to observing and facilitating the so-called naturally developing activity of the child. The progressive classroom is thus organized *for* the middle-class boy and the female teacher. The working-class, female and/or black child (and the male primary teacher) are all seen as somewhat of a problem, since they cannot correspond to this specific progressive idealization of child and teacher.

Thus, according to Walkerdine, in what she calls the fiction of the progressive classroom – of freedom, democracy, safety and nature – there is a denial of power and of the possibility of inequality. The discourse simply does not allow for power and inequality to be considered – and this blindness to inequality has been one of her main criticisms of child-centred practices.

What is important about these studies is that they point to a way that takes us beyond 'deficient' or 'victim' models of difference, for example in the case of gender by: 'provid[ing] new possibilities for understanding girls' socialization or the "production of girls", which go beyond seeing girls primarily as "disadvantaged" and socialized within oppressive patriarchal structures' (Jones, 1993, p. 157).

According to Jones, discussions about classroom inequality and difference need to be informed by greater understanding about how pupils and students themselves help create a classroom climate in which they may be dominant or subordinated, as well as how they might experience inequality within the education system. She suggests that complexity rather than normalizing patterns should prevail, in which 'girls [and other classroom actors] are seen as multiply located, and not unambiguously powerless . . . [and] classroom research must shift away from the "disadvantage" focus. An interest in the *unevenness* of power means that . . . studies might focus on the ways in which girls are *variously* positioned in the classroom' (Jones, 1993, pp. 160–161).

One point of action for change, drawing on this perspective, is to promote in pupils (and college students) a critical awareness of their positioning within educational discourses, so that they 'get smart', as Lather (1991) puts it, in circumventing the system that tries to constrain them.

Concluding Comments

In seeking to provide an overview of the debates and research findings which concern gender and 'race' issues in education, this chapter should be seen as an introduction to the wealth and richness of debates within this area, and only, as it were, representing the tip of the iceberg. The intention has been to provide a critique of notions of difference, to survey the main themes emerging from a very broad literature and to offer an alternative way of viewing difference and inequality.

The aim has been to strengthen possibilities of challenging educational inequality, by raising awareness of current themes, controversies and debates that have arisen from previous attempts to identify and confront inequality.

Editor's Commentary

We have seen in several chapters how teachers' thinking and beliefs influence their planning and their teaching interactions. Areas of belief important to teaching are teachers' conceptions of

- academic subjects
- learning and teaching processes
- pupils' abilities
- pupil anatomy
- gender and race.

In this chapter, careful attention has been paid to gender and race. Gaby Weiner has shown how conceptions of these two aspects of pupils permeate teachers' thinking about curriculum, achievement and classroom processes. These are areas where mistaken belief can be extremely prejudicial to pupils' learning and to their self-concept.

Of course prejudice has to be received as well as offered. Someone might think you are stupid, but if you do not rate them as important you do not take their opinion seriously. Teachers might have poor expectations of pupils; but if the pupils do not regard this opinion as serious or worthy of serious consideration, it need not affect them. It is in this sense that psychologists describe labelling processes as interactive. It takes two to make a 'dumb blonde', for example: one to think and say it, and the blonde to believe and act upon it.

But in some interactions one party is so much more powerful than the other. Interactions may be constrained. If teachers believe that female pupils are not good at maths they are likely to give only simple work. There is not a lot the pupils can do about this. Lacking any challenging experience in maths, they will appear weak in the subject. The teachers' opinions thus appear to be verified.

Because of your power, it is absolutely crucial to be clear about your beliefs as a teacher and to test and upgrade them continuously in the best interests of pupils' learning and self-esteem.

The ideas in this chapter should be linked to others in the book as follows:

- Teachers' beliefs about academic subjects are discussed in chapter 2.
- Teachers' beliefs about self-esteem are raised in chapter 14.
- Beliefs about learning and classroom processes are considered in chapters 1, 7, 8 and 9.
- Beliefs about the pupil's role in learning are considered in chapters 7 and 11.

Issues of gender and race are extremely sensitive but enormously important. The best way to link the ideas in this chapter to school-based work is through discussions with head teachers on their schools' policies for equal opportunities. Useful projects to consider with the head are:

- Use the chapter (and related chapters) to draw up a checklist for a good equal opportunities policy. Discuss the list with supportive head teachers.
- With the support of the head teacher, use the school's equal opportunities policy to evaluate curriculum and material provision for learning. Discuss your evaluation with supporting teachers.
- Using your own checklist, examine your own lesson planning for a range of lessons and evaluate your provision. Discuss your evaluation with other learner teachers.

FURTHER READING

Arnot, M. & Weiner, G. (Eds.). (1992) *Gender and education: Special issue – Women's education in Europe*, Oxford, England: Carfax.
> Research accounts from Portugal, Denmark, Holland, Greece, Denmark, Malta, and Poland and concerning Europe in general, offer an overview of recent European concerns regarding gender issues.

Delamont, S. (1990). *Sex roles and the school* (2nd ed.). London: Routledge.
> An examination of research findings relating to gender and strategies for change, based on the argument that both sexes lose out from sexist schooling.

Gipps, C. & Murphy, P. (1994). *A fair test: Assessment, achievement and equity.* Buckingham, England: Open University Press.
> An examination of research from a wide variety of countries on differences relating to gender and ethnicity, in performance on various forms of assessment, offers an up-to-date perspective on assessment issues in schools.

Klein, G. (1993). *Education towards race equality.* London: Cassell.
> An examination and clarification of 'race' issues for teachers, with helpful information on recent legislation and on the developmental materials and resources.

Mac an Ghaill, M. (1988). *Young, gifted and black: Student–teacher relations in the schooling of black youth.* Milton Keynes, England: Open University Press.
> A behind-the-scenes account of inner-city school life based on a five-year study of the schooling of female and male youth of Afro-Caribbean and Asian parentage in two schools: a boys' secondary school and a sixth form college.

Measor, L. & Sikes, P. (1992). *Gender and schooling.* London: Cassell.
> Different approaches to the study of gender in schools are reviewed, including those relating to socialization, achievement and inequality.

Mirza, H. (1992). *Young, female and black.* London: Routledge.
> Drawing on studies in America, Britain and the Caribbean and, in particular, on a study of black female students in two secondary schools in south London, current notions of underachievement, the black family and black womanhood are challenged and reconceptualized.

Weiner, G. (1994). *Feminisms in education: An introduction.* Buckingham, England: Open University Press.
An overview of developments in feminist thinking on education over the past two decades, which includes curriculum and practitioner concerns and developments.

14

Personal, Social and Moral Education

John Thacker

Editor's Overview

This chapter re-emphasizes the view met earlier, in chapter 11, that education must go beyond subject knowledge if it is to maintain civilized values. All individuals, John Thacker argues, must attain a productive understanding of themselves as persons in a society. They must develop a self-concept which promotes personal growth and socialized living. This aspect of education is referred to as 'personal and social'. It is the essential bedrock of values on which knowledge might be founded.

What should we teach and how should we teach it to provide such a foundation of values? John Thacker argues that content for this aspect of the curriculum can be found in the everyday concerns and issues which are met by individuals or groups in a school.

Methods of teaching include discussion and debate. The school ethos can also be an ever-present model of values in action.

Of course, if issues are taken as they come, or if values are expected to be 'caught' from the school or class ethos, a great deal is left to chance and the experience of a particular pupil might be rather *ad hoc*. This problem is clearly recognized in this chapter, and a whole-school policy and principles are recommended as ways of bringing coherence and management to this aspect of education.

Introduction

Why should we bother to spend time teaching personal and social education? When resources for education are scarce, not least in terms of space on the timetable, it can be seen as tempting to trim back to the 'basics'. Where there is also a stress on the testing of 'core subjects' this temptation can become overwhelming. I want to argue that this is an unhelpful view of education if we are to keep a focus on learning and achievement and to develop effective schools. 'Effective schools are demanding places, where teachers expect and ensure high standards of work and behaviour; at the same time they are responsive to pupils, for the teachers are approachable and, since they value pupils, seek to involve them in the life and work of the schools' (Hargreaves, 1990).

An important part of ensuring that schools are responsive to pupils' needs and involve them in the life of the schools is the provision for personal and social education. This is not a frill or add-on extra. The National Curriculum Council in England emphasized that 'Personal and social education (PSE) is arguably the most important of the cross-curricular dimensions' (National Curriculum Council, 1989c) and 'Personal and social development through the curriculum cannot be left to chance but needs to be co-ordinated as an explicit part of a school's whole curriculum policy, both inside and outside the formal timetable' (ibid. para. 10). A central purpose of this chapter is to provide some help in thinking about how personal and social education (PSE) can be co-ordinated as part of a school's whole-curriculum policy. Taking the personal dimension of education seriously in school does lead to better academic achievement. Aspy and Roebuck (1977) summarize work over seventeen years in forty-two states and seven countries outside the USA. In all, they state that they have worked with 2,000 teachers and 20,000 students. Their overall finding is: 'Students learn more and behave better when they receive high levels of understanding, caring and genuineness, than when they are given low levels of them.'

Let us look in more detail at the 'understanding, caring and genuineness' referred to above. They are based on the lifetime work of the distinguished American psychologist, Carl Rogers. In his inspiring book on education, *Freedom to learn* (Rogers, 1983), he summarizes these three key qualities in effective helping and teaching as follows:

> Those attitudes that appear effective in promoting learning can be described. First of all a transparent realness in the facilitator, a willingness to be a person, to be and to live the feelings and thoughts of the moment. When this realness includes a prizing, a trust and a respect for the learner, the climate for learning is enhanced. When it includes a sensitive and accurate empathic listening, then indeed a freeing climate, stimulative of self-initiated learning and growth, exists. The student is trusted to develop. (p. 133)

Let us look at these in a little more detail.

Realness/genuineness

It is suggested that the teacher can be a real person in her relationships with her students. She can be enthusiastic, can be bored, can be interested in students, can be angry, can be sensitive and sympathetic. Because she accepts these feelings as her own, she has no need to impose them on her students. She can like or dislike a student product without implying that it is objectively good or bad or that the student is good or bad. She is simply expressing a feeling for the product, a feeling that exists within herself. Thus she is a person to her students not a faceless embodiment of a curricular requirement nor a sterile tube through which knowledge is passed from one generation to the next. It is obvious that this attitudinal set . . . is sharply in contrast with the tendency of most teachers to show themselves to their pupils simply as roles. (p. 122)

Prizing, acceptance, non-possessive warmth

It is a caring for the learner but a non-possessive caring. It is an acceptance of this other individual as a separate person having worth in her own right. It is a basic trust − a belief that this other person is somehow fundamentally trustworthy . . . it shows up in a variety of observable ways . . . can be fully acceptant of the fear and hesitation of the student as she approaches a new problem as well as acceptant of the pupil's satisfaction in achievement. Such a teacher can accept the student's occasional apathy . . . personal feelings that both disturb and promote learning − rivalry with a sibling, hatred of authority, concern about personal adequacy. What we are describing is a prizing of the learner as an imperfect human being with many feelings, many potentialities. (p. 124)

Empathic understanding

When the teacher has the ability to understand the student's responses from the inside, has the sensitive awareness of the way the process of education and learning seem to the student, then again the likelihood of significant learning is increased. This kind of understanding is sharply different from the usual evaluative understanding, which follows the pattern of 'I understand what is wrong with you.' When there is a sensitive empathy, however, the reaction in the learner follows something of this pattern 'At last someone understands how it feels and seems to be *me*, without wanting to analyse me or judge me. Now I can . . . grow and learn.' (p. 125)

I have quoted Rogers's own words at some length to illustrate these core qualities which he sees as rare and not fully achieved. It may sound like a counsel of perfection, but realistically, developing a little more of these qualities will produce important benefits as shown in the studies by Aspy referred to earlier (Aspy, 1977).

In addition to its contribution to effective learning and achievement, a concern for the well-being of the whole child is a long-standing part of education in Britain. PSE and pastoral care have a direct contribution to make to the pupils' personal and social development at school and in preparation for adult life.

An important underlying value here is that of respect for pupils as persons. This is the principle adopted by Richard Pring (1984), which he suggests should underlie a personal and social education programme. For him this principle leads to a series of questions to

> ask of the curriculum and the other experiences pupils are receiving in schools: does the curriculum, for example.
>
> (i) respect pupils as people who can think, that is, have their own ideas and points of view, capable of contributing to the various explorations, enquiries, or activities that children and adults engage in?
> (ii) assist pupils to see others as persons whatever their colour, creed or appearance?
>
> [A common psychological mechanism which allows one group to oppress another is to see the oppressed group as somehow different or inferior. An example would be in the treatment of the Jews in the Second World War.]
>
> (iii) enable pupils to see themselves as persons, able not only to think and reflect and to develop a point of view, but also able to accept responsibility for their own behaviour and future?
> (iv) foster that attitude of respect for oneself and others as persons, that is, as people who have legitimate points of view and that can and should be held responsible for what is done? (p. 31)

If this value can be successfully represented in the real life of the school it is helpful for the development of the child. According to Piaget: 'Young people need to find themselves in the presence not only of a system of commands requiring ritualistic and external obedience, but a system of social relations such that everyone does his best to obey the same obligations, and does so out of mutual respect' (1932, p. 134). The hope is that the lessons will also serve to prepare the pupils for their adult role in the wider democratic society. Kohlberg tried to construct such a system in his 'just community' schools: 'the current demand for moral education is a demand that our society becomes more of a just community. If our society is to become a more just community, it needs democratic schools. This was the demand and dream of Dewey' (Kohlberg, 1982, p. 24).

Cultivating the psychological qualities outlined by Rogers and holding the principle of respect for pupils as persons form a useful base for the teacher preparing him- or herself for work in personal and social education. We will now turn to the question of how to design a suitable educational content for a personal and social education programme.

Summary

- Personal and social education supports academic learning.
- Pupils learn more and understand more if they work in settings characterized by
  - warmth
  - understanding
  - respect.
- Personal and social education is a central goal in its own right.
- Academic work has meaning only if it is used to acceptable moral ends.

Where does the Content of PSE Come from?

As we have already argued, personal and social education is a whole-school business, running across the entire curriculum and inside and outside the formal timetable. A useful starting definition is given by Chris Watkins: 'Personal and Social Education is the intentional promotion of the personal and social development of pupils through the whole curriculum and the whole school experience' (Watkins, 1992). The content is drawn from three major areas shown in figure 14.1.

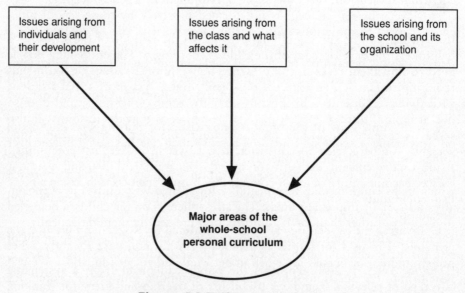

Figure 14.1 The content of PSE.

Content arising from individuals

A useful way of deriving the content from the perspective of the individual is by looking at the notion of self. This is used to highlight the person and the social context of his or her relationships. It is not meant to encourage sloppy or individualistic thinking (such as can be heard in 'Oh well, he's got a poor self-image'). Self cannot occur in isolation. In a very fundamental sense, the self is a product of a person's interaction with others. Therefore examination of the self in action demands examination of the social, cultural and political context, including considerations of race and gender.

The central idea is that a person's self develops in relation to the reactions of other people to that person, and that he/she tends to react to himself/ herself as he/she perceives other people reacting to him/her (Mead, 1934). The self is a social product, and thus the influence of the people at school on a child of primary school age is of crucial importance. Children receive many opportunities in school to evaluate their skills and abilities, and this evaluative information contributes to the formation and modification of their self-concepts. Note the use of 'self-concepts' in the plural, since recent evidence suggests that the self-concept is hierarchically organized (Marsh and Shavelson, 1985; Shavelson and Bolus, 1982), with a general self-concept located at the top of the hierarchy and specific sub-area self-concepts towards its base. Self-perceptions in specific areas such as English and mathematics combine to form the academic self-concept, which in turn combines with those in social, emotional and physical domains. Once again there is a cross-curricular dimension, this time in the development of a self-concept.

However, the self-concept is not formed passively by these school influences. Recent formulations (e.g. Markus and Wurf, 1987) stress that it is a dynamic structure – active, forceful, and capable of change. It does not just reflect ongoing behaviour, but instead mediates and regulates this behaviour. Such a view fits in well with current accounts of learning, which view pupils as active seekers and processors of information (Pintrich, Cross, Kozma and McKechnie, 1986).

This dynamic view of the pupil is one reason for putting stress in school on developing a sense of control – a sense that one has some power over things within and outside oneself. In a later section of this chapter (PSE lessons) we will examine the role of group work as a teaching approach which helps children take responsibility for their own inquiries into personally and socially important areas. The stress there is on the children being led to discovery rather than having information pressed on them didactically.

There is also an important contribution to be made to the development of self through what is often called 'self-understanding' or 'self-knowledge' (Damon, 1983, p. 248). For this the pupils can profit from a systematic coverage of relevant themes. A useful list of overlapping areas for thinking about the issues which affect all individuals is given below:

- bodily self: heightened awareness of bodily changes, comparisons, affecting self-image
- sexual self: developing sexuality and finding its place in relationships
- social self: awareness of communication, self-presentation, understanding others
- vocational self: thinking ahead to what sort of contributing adult to be: work, family, non-work
- moral/political self: developing ideas about what is right/wrong, and how to take action about it.

This has been developed from Wall (1947), and an expanded version of the list, with additional content in these areas, is contained in Watkins and Thacker (1993).

Content arising from the class

Each class develops a life of its own over the course of the year with the class teacher, and over several years in the case of family or vertically grouped classes. This is affected by both external and internal events. Pupils can learn from what happens to them, and from how events are handled. Some of these elements can be predicted and planned for, whereas others might become part of what we term the 'responsive curriculum'. Some illustrative examples are given in table 14.1.

Table 14.1

	Could be planned	*Responsive*
Triggered from outside	Beginnings, endings (of years, etc.)	Bereavement, loss
		New members arriving
	Special occasions, celebrations, rituals	Group members leaving
		Property
		Changing friendships
Triggered from inside	Transitions	Group conflicts
	Bullying	Changing group loyalties

Content arising from the school

There is an important set of themes which arises from

- making sense of school
- getting the most out of school as an organization

- getting the most out of learning
- progressing through school.

They are grouped together here under this heading, because they arise from the way that schools are organized and run (in contrast to the other headings about individual development and group issues).

The important point about these themes is that to address them we address personal and social processes. Again there is no simple set of fixed knowledge or strategies which teachers can recommend to different pupils.

- **self as a learner**
  - to reflect on present study strategies
  - using others as resources in learning
  - developing skills of self-assessment
  - to engage in group activities for learning
  - coping with anxiety
  - managing time
  - organizing independent work
  - developing a greater range of learning strategies
- **self in the organization**
  - to use organizations in constructive ways
  - to be an active participant in organizations
  - to access help in an organization
  - to handle transitions between organizations
  - to make best use of available choices

(This section has drawn extensively on ideas which are more fully developed in Watkins and Thacker, 1993).

Deciding on Where this Content should Go

These headings provide a basis for talking about the contribution of **all** the aspects of the whole school. It may, however, be helpful to think of there being two major dimensions to be considered: a general dimension and a specific dimension. The main items considered under each heading are outlined below.

- **The general dimension**
  - School ethos and organizational culture
  - Classroom ethos and organization
  - Individual tutoring role

- **The specific dimension**
  - PSE lessons
  - National Curriculum lessons

The general dimension is important but insufficient on its own; the specific is isolated and trivialized without the support of the general. For example, the general might contain a stated policy on fighting, but without some work on conflict resolution in the PSE programme, the pupils may not be able to develop alternative ways of sorting out interpersonal problems. Again, in the specific dimension there might be a module on the importance of consultation in a democratic society in a PSE lesson, with no opportunities provided for consulting the pupils about the life of the school, which would be in the general dimension.

The General Dimension

School ethos and organizational culture

In the general aspect we have that dimension of the school often referred to as the 'ethos', 'climate' or the 'atmosphere'. It is important to look closely at this area since it is this 'hidden curriculum' or 'the way we do things around here' which is traditionally the main way of teaching personal and social behaviour in English primary schools. There is very little tradition of direct teaching of PSE, other than through the use of assemblies (Alexander, 1984). Appropriate attitudes and behaviour are often thought to be 'caught' rather than 'taught'. In many ways this attitude has a lot to commend it. It could be argued that much of traditional schooling is too remote from everyday life and that the gap between lessons and real situations is too large for children, especially young children of primary age, to bridge without help. If the PSE 'lesson' is embodied in the relationships between people, and especially in the way the children are treated, this will have a real impact on children's personal and social development. However desirable this emphasis on the whole experience of school as a vehicle for learning, a problem in explicit planning is that PSE is often seen as a largely intangible area. It is difficult for teachers who are interested in creating a positive atmosphere for personal and social development to know just what aspects of their schools make a difference in this regard.

A number of different approaches have been used in an attempt to pin down and specify what constitutes an ethos, and, more importantly, how it can be changed. Rutter and others (Rutter, Maughan, Mortimore and Ouston, 1979) have tried to construct some idea of a school's ethos and what influence it might have by looking at a number of schools and trying to tease out what are the important factors which are seen in successful schools. This and similar work has resulted in long lists of features of schools which have been linked to climate and outcomes. Some of the most consistent findings of this school effectiveness research, largely carried out in secondary schools, indicate that the following factors are particularly important for personal and social development (summarized in Galloway, 1985; Reynolds, 1982; Reynolds and Sullivan, 1987):

1 Encouraging the active participation of pupils in lessons, and allowing them to use their own initiative to carry out their own lines of inquiry.
2 Giving pupils responsibility for the wider aspects of school life. For example, responsibility for their own well-being in terms of helping to plan how to make the lunch times peaceful and productive. This should include children from right across the spectrum of ability.
3 Creating a pattern of relatively relaxed and informal relationships in the classroom, where confrontations are avoided, and with a warm quality in teacher–pupil relationships.
4 Keeping the number of school rules to a minimum and, in accord with the principle in (2) above, giving the pupils some say in what they should be.
5 Emphasizing a positive approach through praise and recognition of good work and behaviour rather than a negative approach of punishment for stepping out of line and for poor achievement.

While these general guidelines are useful, it is helpful to have some way of relating them to each other in real school contexts. In looking at how these factors link together in the life and work of a school community, a number of researchers have adopted a more holistic strategy using the concept of 'culture'. Culture is the pattern of basic assumptions generated by any group as they develop the outside work of an organization as well as learn to work together to achieve their ends. One of the problems about studying this aspect of organizational life is that these shared values and expectations become less visible and more taken for granted over time, and become 'the way we do things round here'. They are then 'taught' to new members as the correct way to perceive, think and feel about what happens in the organization. There have only been a few studies based specifically in education. This is surprising, since it is a way of looking at organizations which seems particularly applicable to schools, since they are run by people, for people and with the development of people as their aim.

One book aimed specifically at the primary school is based on a recent study by Nias and her colleagues (Nias, Southworth, and Yeomans, 1989). This looks at the usefulness of the concept of culture in a number of different primary schools. They found that some schools embodied what they called a 'collaborative culture'. These schools valued individuals as people and their contributions to each other, but within a framework of interdependence and belonging to a group with a commitment to a common task.

The present writer has looked at a primary school which, in Nias's terms, would be called a 'collaborative culture'. A novel feature of this study is that it is a collaborative inquiry (Reason, 1988), with the whole school staff acting as co-researchers rather than outside researchers coming in, observing and writing up what they see. In the first year of this project we clarified the nature of the organizational culture as perceived by the staff, and the role played by the head in fostering this culture. This was written up as an interim report for the staff (Thacker, 1993) before embarking on a second year of the inquiry, where we looked at how the individual teachers came to be at the school. We looked at this in terms of our own educational life histories and how our own values match those of this corporate culture. Further, we examined how our histories are intertwined in both producing and being affected by this culture. Finally, and perhaps most importantly, we looked at how the culture affects the teaching of the children in the day-to-day work of the classrooms and in the general life of the school, and what view the children have of all this.

Findings from this in-depth study, conducted over time with the active collaboration of a school staff, will be used in this present chapter to complement the insights obtained by Nias as well as from more large-scale studies, such as Rutter's, of important variables.

The importance of the ways the staff relate to each other in these 'collaborative cultures' is seen by the teachers concerned both as important in its own right but also as having an impact on the children. It does this in at least three ways. In the first place, if the teachers feel good about themselves and their own relationships, they will be able to give of their best to the children. Second, these good adult relationships will serve as a living example to the children of civilized and considerate interactions between people. And third, the teachers will be able to create a similar collaborative atmosphere with the children, both within their classrooms and throughout the school. In combination, these three effects make a major contribution to the general PSE provision in the school through the relationships between members of staff inside and outside the classrooms, the relationships between pupils, and those between pupils and teachers. In all cases, a fundamental value displayed is a respect for staff and pupils as persons. We have seen a similar value earlier, in the work of Pring (1984).

Leadership is crucial in creating and maintaining this sort of culture. In our study, the head is seen as expressing this respect by trusting the staff to do the best job they are capable of. This investment of trust is seen by the staff to be a liberating experience. This was spoken about by one of the teachers in our inquiry when she said:

> I think I don't have to keep up appearances here – I can really be myself whereas in other schools I have worked, I've been acting I suppose. You don't want to show any chink in your armour in many schools because it doesn't seem safe to do that and because of that you carry on living a lie. When I came here I could really be myself . . . and because of that my life did change because

I could look at it and see what was not true and do something about it. So it empowers you because you are allowed to acknowledge . . . the dark side and the problems you have which you may have been pushing away. (Thacker, 1993)

This fits in with the quality of realness or genuiness we have already seen in the work of Rogers (1983). This stress on the person of the teacher rather than the role is generally true of English primary schools (e.g. Nias, 1989), but here there seems a deeper level of honesty than exists in many schools. This is made possible by an acceptance of the need to voice doubts, uncertainties and even mistakes without judgement being passed, but rather with support and understanding being offered. This is similar to the quality of empathic understanding outlined by Rogers (1983), and it has enabled a high level of trust to grow between staff members, which contributes to a feeling of safety.

In its turn, this allows people to be creative and to take risks. This is made possible by the trust and support, but also by the space and time given by the head for all class teachers to develop their own ideas and to contribute their creativity to the whole school. As another teacher said in our inquiry, 'we are allowed to have space and freedom and be professional and use our own intelligence and ideas and express ourselves.' This is seen as an exciting challenge by the staff, who see themselves as setting their own high standards and challenging themselves. In this culture there is a co-operative rather than a competitive ethic underlying all this, and it is seen as releasing creative energy for high achievement. A common phrase heard around the school is 'anything is possible.'

These values are a conscious part of the personal and social education in this school. They also contribute right across the educational provision through the teachers being able to provide trust, support and space for their pupils, since they, the teachers, have created such conditions for themselves. Thus these effects are seen to cascade throughout the whole school, and the good relationships at every level are seen to be connected through this shared culture of collaboration. In the words of one of the classroom assistants in our inquiry, 'He [the head] gives you that space the same as you do to the children. You can explore something, make a mistake and learn from it. He's not going to say "you can't do that" and "it won't work" because he is open to anything. You can try it out and the children are allowed to do that.'

This description is based on a school with such a collaborative culture. Another school might stress different attributes such as obedience, conformity and competition. This would result in a different ethos and organizational culture, and thus provide a different personal and social educational experience. Whatever the values held by the staff of a school, they will inevitably have an effect on the culture, whether we choose to recognize this or not, which in its turn will provide a lesson for the pupils. It may be that, in bigger or more divided schools, it is more useful to talk about cultures in the plural.

This view of a number of subcultures, often existing in a state of tension or even conflict, is possibly an even more common state than the more uniform 'collaborative culture' discussed earlier. This means that the pupils in these schools may receive a number of conflicting messages which will affect their personal and social learning. Whether such learning is useful in pointing out how inconsistently organizations work in real life, or whether it is unnecessarily confusing to young children, is a moot point.

In the present state of education the values portrayed in these relationships will have not only educational but also political implications, and the values expressed in a school are also in their turn affected by the wider society. For example, a comprehensive school committed to the concept of providing an integrated education for all the children in a neighbourhood will find itself in some conflict with an approach to education which espouses the values of the marketplace. This is currently the case in England, where successive Education Acts since 1980 have deliberately placed schools in such a marketplace, where their survival depends on their ability to attract the parents of prospective pupils.

Whether or not this is generally desirable is a matter of debate, but it will undoubtedly influence the climate in the school, and thus part of its personal and social provision. As a very concrete example of this let us consider the way that the marketplace-value position outlined above might affect the level of understanding and provision for pupils with special needs.

A pessimistic view is that it will increase the tendency to blame pupils for their own problems rather than to understand the problem as reflecting an interaction between the child and the provision made for him or her within the school. This may lead schools to seek to remove such children, or at least to gain exemption for them from the National Curriculum requirements. Whether or not these moves are in the interests of any particular child, it is certainly in the interests of a school, at least in the short term, to ensure that its scores on the simple 'league table' results are as high as possible. The outcome of these decisions will show in a very clear way how individual differences are understood and treated. This in its turn will influence how the children see themselves. As Hargreaves (1982) points out, children's sense of personal identity develops in a social context. Outside the family, the principal influence is that of school. If the school has regard for the dignity and worth of each individual and for the development of the whole person, there will have to be real care taken with this social context. In the special needs example given above, how this is resolved in practice is a personal and social lesson of the first importance, especially if you are the pupil who has special needs. This concern for children will need to be reflected in all school policies and not just those with a PSE label.

Summary

- In defining the content for a curriculum in personal and social education, issues may be found in
    - the concerns of individual pupils
    - matters raised by classes of children
    - school-wide matters.
- Settings for teaching a personal and social curriculum include
    - individual interactions
    - class discussions
    - the hidden curriculum of the school ethos.
- Appropriate teaching methods include
    - discussion
    - living values.
- Direct instruction is rarely conducive to personal growth.

Classroom ethos and organization

In this section we shall look at how learning in an ordinary class can contribute to personal and social education. Again we need to start from values, and if our goal is to promote a co-operative learning atmosphere, then conscious attention needs to be paid to creating a suitable climate. One of the main classroom strategies here is to encourage co-operative activities, especially in small groups where there is more opportunity for interaction. This can provide valuable skills and experiences of personal and social benefit, such as opportunities for pupils to learn how to co-operate; how to respect the views of others; how to question and challenge; and how to listen. Again, simply putting the children into small groups and hoping that they will work together is not enough. Following the suggestion in the Plowden Report (1967) about the social benefits of groups, it became fashionable for teachers to group children around tables, but often with work which was essentially individual. To remedy this there have been at least two main approaches.

One is to concentrate on the nature of the task and the outcomes of learning. This is represented in the work of Bennett (see chapter 8). The other broad approach to co-operative learning is represented by the work of the present writer (Thacker, Stoate, and Feest, 1992) at the primary level and Button (1981, 1982) at the secondary level. Here the approach is based on the use of a variety of groupings and activities to encourage a supportive social atmosphere in the classroom, in which children can explore and value similarities and differences between themselves and find ways of resolving conflicts in a creative way. The stress is upon raising the level of understanding of how groups can be helped to work well and to provide the opportunities for children to become more skilled in fostering good working relationships between themselves. While these principles can be drawn on by children in any curriculum area, some of this work can be usefully done as part of work in tutorial groups at secondary schools, and during reflective times for personal and social themes in the primary school. This will be discussed in more detail in the section on the specific dimension of PSE.

Such group approaches also have the advantage of helping hard-pressed teachers see methods of working with classes of thirty children in realistic ways. Much recent legislation has concentrated on the identification and meeting of individual needs, and teachers can feel daunted by implementing individual programmes for each child. Group work can help in this as well as providing a realistic social context to foster children's social development. Perhaps somewhat surprisingly, group work is also a way to foster autonomy or pupil self-direction. This cannot arise from purely individualized instruction, since this is most likely to lead to dependence on the teacher. It seems best thought of as a social product, developed through varied relationships with adults and peers. With effective peer interaction, the child has an alternative to counterbalance teacher dependence and control. Overall, pupils working effectively with each other and thus developing better relationships with each other may simultaneously relieve the pressure from teacher dependence while at the same time gaining a firm basis for autonomy from this co-operative working experience.

Individual tutoring role

In this section I want first to introduce the idea of being a teacher as consisting of two main roles: that of a subject tutor and that of a personal tutor. This distinction has been found helpful in relation to secondary schools (Watkins and Thacker, 1993) and, with the increasing stress on subject specialisms, is increasingly relevant to primary schools. Recognizing that a teacher works in these two roles with both individuals and classes, this gives the idea of what we have called the four faces of tutoring. Some illustrative examples are given in table 14.2.

These are not hard and fast distinctions, but they point to the fact that at different times in the daily life of a teacher one or other of these roles will predominate. In this section I want to point to the personal tutoring role, especially as it concerns individuals. At first glance this may seem to be that part of the teacher's role which is furthest from the 'main' function as some see it – that of running classrooms. It is the part of the job which some teachers feel least at home with, and for which their initial training has least prepared them. Developing the skills of active listening and empathic responding necessary to help a pupil to explore difficulties and to find a way forward is beyond the scope of this chapter, but a number of books have been produced in recent years to help teachers achieve these good communi-

Table 14.2 The four faces of tutoring

	With individuals	*With a group or class*
Personal tutoring	helping pupils to improve their relationship in a group talking to pupils about their feelings of being under pressure from their parents	looking at the skills of working together effectively
Subject tutoring	helping a pupil plan a piece of writing helping pupils assess how well they have met their goals in a piece of work	helping a class tackle a new sort of task (like field mapping in geography, or pond dredging in science)

cation skills (e.g. Hall and Hall, 1988; Watkins and Thacker, 1993). They do not aim to turn teachers into counsellors, psychologists or social workers. Rather, they aim to use good psychological principles, common to helping and counselling, to enable teachers to develop this personal tutoring side of their central role.

The Specific Dimension

PSE lessons

This is where more personal areas of content might be located, such as a consideration of friendship or those requiring some specialist information, such as drugs education. However, there is a danger that such sessions might seem unrelated and rather incoherent. Also, the style of learning adopted in these sessions is as important as the content. If pupils are to be able to incorporate the information, attitudes and skills which make up the specific content of PSE, then they must learn in a way which engages them actively, and in which they have a large part to play.

This is where many schools have adopted an approach such as that outlined in *Group work skills* (Thacker et al., 1992), which aims to give a coherent account of a suitable approach to teaching and classroom interaction, and which is particularly suited to work in this area. 'Group work' encompasses knowledge, attitudes and skills which, when put into effect, allow a group of whatever age to work together constructively, achieving their tasks in a way with which everyone is happy. Just as with tool skills such as writing, group work can be learned in a conscious, thoughtful and systematic way.

For such a systematic approach, it has been found to be useful to set aside a special time for this purpose. This gives a clear signal that it is important and worthwhile. Making a conscious space for pupils to explore the process focuses attention on its importance and allows time to look systematically at the knowledge, skills and attitudes involved. By giving group work a time of its own, it can be focused on in a way which is not confused by other subject matter; the picture can be made clear.

This time can be used for developing issues related to personal and social education which benefit from a group work approach. Thus we would see the 'special time' as an opportunity for personal and social issues to be raised into full consciousness, issues of trust and care focused upon and nurtured and the skills of social relationships reflected on and practised. These issues and skills, which are important in themselves, also make a vital contribution to the way in which children tackle other curriculum areas and actively encouraging them to develop contributes to the general ethos of the school. Group work . . . has a contribution to make across the whole life and work of the primary school. (Thacker et al., 1992, p. 7)

National Curriculum lessons

This active, group-work approach is also well suited to delivering the National Curriculum, with its emphasis on working in groups. The skills of co-operative work learned in group-work time can be drawn upon in this area. Further, the content of the National Curriculum can be examined to see what areas of content derived from our earlier analysis can be taught through the programmes of study of the core and other subject areas.

Putting it All Together: Whole-School Policy

We have seen that choosing a content for a personal and social education programme means looking at the needs of developing children and the social conditions which surround and offer challenges and support to them at home and at school. All aspects of the school provide potential locations for this content, and there are contributions to be made at a whole-school level by a consideration of ethos and organizational culture; at a classroom level through the teaching approach adopted, the classroom atmosphere and relationships engendered; and at an individual level by the interactions between a teacher and an individual pupil. The specific dimension can be addressed through the formal timetable. Planning for the general and specific dimensions across the whole school would ensure that PSE is genuinely 'a cross-curricular dimension'.

Editor's Commentary

What is the purpose of a personal and social education (PSE)? What should the PSE curriculum contain? How should PSE be taught? These are the three big questions raised in this chapter. In brief, the answers offered here are:

- PSE should establish, for each pupil, a constructive self-concept as a basis for productive social living.
- The content of a PSE curriculum comprises a selection from the issues, challenges and problems of everyday living as met by the pupils in and out of school.
- Methods of teaching include modelling and discussion.
- Coherence can be achieved in a PSE programme through carefully managed provision and a set of agreed principles of procedure — in short, through a whole-school policy showing clearly designated roles for class teachers and tutors.

The ideas in this chapter bear some resemblance to those in chapter 11 on autonomous learning. They should also be related, for a consideration of appropriate teaching methods to

- chapter 7 on discussion
- chapter 8 on group work.

The discussion here on PSE can be related to classroom practice through the following school-based projects:

- Obtain a copy of the school's policy on PSE. Discuss with supervising tutors and teachers how the policy is put into practice.
- Attempt to describe the ethos created by you in your classroom. In what ways is it conducive to good PSE as described in this chapter? In what ways might you profitably develop your classroom ethos?
- Tape-record a discussion you have with a small group of children about a matter which they raise as of concern to them. In conjunction with other learner teachers, evaluate the contribution the discussion might have made to the pupils' PSE. Consider, with the wisdom of hindsight, how the discussion might have been improved.

FURTHER READING

Lang, P. (Ed.). (1988). *Thinking about . . . personal and social education in the primary school*. Oxford, England: Blackwell.

This is one of the few books aimed specifically at a primary audience and is based on a wide range of papers presented at a conference held under the auspices of the National Association of Pastoral Care in Education.

Pring, R. (1984). *Personal and social education in the curriculum*. London. Hodder & Stoughton.

This is a short overview of the topic aimed at teachers and students. A good general introduction.

Thacker, J., Pring, R. & Evans, D. (Eds.) (1987). *Personal, social and moral education in a changing world. London: NFER-Nelson.*

A collection of essays covering a wide range of topics in this field.

Thacker, J., Stoate P. & Feest, G. (1992).*Group work skills: Using group work in the primary classroom.* Crediton, England: Southgate.

This is a very practical book, aimed at the classroom teacher, which shows how classroom groups can be used effectively as part of a personal and social education programme.

15

Managing Time

Neville Bennett

Editor's Overview

In this chapter, Neville Bennett discusses the management of time in schooling. Time is a key resource in education. Governments allocate time to schooling by determining the length of the school year. Head teachers allot time to different subject areas, and class teachers designate time for particular activities. The amount of time spent working on a topic is an important determinant of pupil progress in that topic. Your skills in the management of time are, in this light, important to the management of learning.

Neville Bennett shows that because different teachers and head teachers make different decisions about time allocations, different pupils receive hugely different experiences of the curriculum. He also shows that pupils are not passive in regard to the length of time they pay attention to their teachers' activities. Even within the same class there are large variations between pupils and between subjects in the duration of pupils' time on-task.

The important concept of evaporated time is introduced. This is the time allocated to schooling but not used for learning. It refers to the time pupils stand about waiting, or spend moving about the school, or use for getting changed for activities such as PE. Evaporated time is a major loss in some classrooms. Teachers differ in their effectiveness at managing time.

Neville Bennett discusses ways in which time can be better managed, paying special attention to

- monitoring how time is used
- minimizing evaporated time

- increasing pupil time on-task by the use of appropriate activities and group organizations
- using homework to extend available time.

Time spent, says Neville Bennett, is never a sufficient condition to assure learning, but it is, he argues, a necessary condition for assuring equitable and well-balanced engagement with the curriculum, and it provides the context for assuring quality.

Time management is clearly an important topic for a teacher's attention.

Introduction

'It cannot be seen, heard or touched, and is almost impossible to define. Yet it can be described, measured, structured and managed ... it cannot be compressed or expanded. It cannot be transferred or stored and has to be spent. Yet it is inexhaustible. And all financial resources in schools have to be converted into units of it before they can be used' (Knight, 1989). What is it? – time!

Teachers are well aware of the time constraints that impinge on their classroom practice, particularly where demands for accountability to state or national curricula are high. These time factors also impinge at the level of the school. Knight (1989) recognizes this by organizing time into three categories, which he calls macro-structures, micro-structures and individual patterns. The first concerns the school year, week and day, determined often by external forces, for example Government policy. The second concerns the timetable, lessons, extra-curricular activities and the like. The third relates to teachers, pupils and ancillary staff who have their own patterns of time use determined partly by need and habit, but also by the macro- and micro-structures. Campbell and his team (Campbell and Neill, 1992), in a series of recent studies of teacher time, see time as the basic component in the structuring of teachers' work. In their studies they have used the following framework:

- total time spent on work or work-related activities, including out-of-school time;
- time during the school day spent with other adults, with children or alone, teaching, administering, parents' evenings etc.;
- time spent with children, time spent teaching and supervising children's activities, including assembly, registration, supervision etc.;
- time spent on curriculum, time spent teaching and assessing.

These schemes for categorizing time use in schools are perfectly acceptable for the purposes for which they devised, e.g. to study how teachers typically

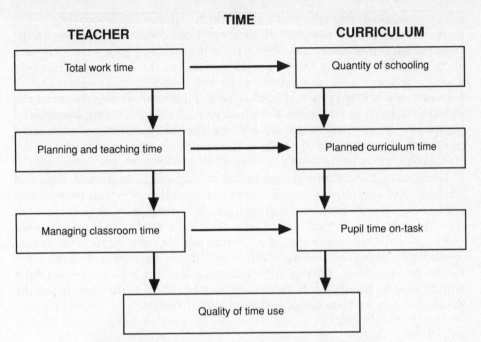

Figure 15.1 A model of teacher and curriculum time.

spend their time, but they are too limited to show the impact of time on both teachers and pupils. Figure 15.1 presents an elaboration of these schemes by considering two parallel aspects of time – relating to teachers on the one hand, and to curriculum on the other.

Figure 15.1 draws on the scheme utilized by Campbell and his colleagues, and on models of teaching and learning which link pupil achievement to aspects of time use (Bennett, 1978, 1982). In this model, quantity of schooling is the total amount of time that the school is open for its statutory purpose, and is defined by the length of school day and school year. This amount of time for schooling can be amended by, for example, pupil absences from school, or by such teaching actions as setting homework. Teachers' total work time is not, however, bounded by the amount of time the school is open, since they fulfil professional obligations, such as planning and recording at home as well as undertaking in-service training, home visiting and the like. Thus a proportion of this total work time is devoted to planning and teaching the curriculum. In this planning phase, the time available for teaching is allocated to various curriculum areas. This is identified in the model as planned curriculum time. This planning, whether done individually by the teacher, or more likely these days, at school level, results in curricula which vary considerably in emphasis and balance from class to class and school to school. In other words, there is no such thing as *the* primary curriculum, even when dictated by national mandate, as we shall see later.

The amount of time allocated to a particular curriculum area or activity is unlikely to match the actual amount of time pupils will spend on it. Disruptions, distractions, lack of interest in the task and poor persistence are all factors likely to reduce the use a pupil makes of the opportunity to study a given activity. This is represented in the model as time on-task. The teacher's task in managing and optimizing pupil time on-task is shown in the model as managing classroom time, and is a deciding factor in determining the quality of time use. In this sense the teacher can be seen as the manager of the attention and time of pupils in relation to the educational ends of the classroom.

The presentation of time factors in this way allows us to see how time and teachers' activities impact on such issues as curriculum planning, balance and entitlement. But its limitations should also be noted. Increasing curriculum time, or pupil time on-task, are of little avail if the quality of the curriculum tasks or activities are poor, not worthwhile or not related to pupils' capabilities. Necessity and sufficiency should not be confused here. Time factors are necessary, but not sufficient, conditions for high-quality teaching and learning processes in classrooms. With that in mind, the elements of the model in figure 15.1 are now considered in more detail.

Quantity of Schooling

The length of the school year in England and Wales is fixed, for reasons lost in the mists of time, at 190 days. However, there are no legal requirements about the length of the school day, or on the minimum number of hours per week that schools should be open. The informal guidance is that children aged 5–7 should be taught for a minimum of twenty-one hours per week, and those aged 8–11 years for a minimum of 23.5 hours (NCC, 1993).

However, evidence gathered over the last twenty years has shown consistent, and wide, variations across schools in the amounts of time that they are open. A study in the early 1970s found that the amount of time schools were open varied from twenty-two to twenty-seven hours per week, and when lunch times, breaks, assemblies and administration were deducted the amount of time left for teaching varied from nineteen to twenty-four hours per week (Hilsum and Cane, 1971). More recent evidence, from the Department of Education, shows a similar pattern. Nearly half the schools teaching 8- to 11-year-olds failed to teach the recommended 23.5 hours. One school in twelve fell short of this target by between three and four hours per week (NCC, 1993).

So both studies, although twenty years apart, found that children have differential opportunity with regard to the length of time they spend in school, which at the extreme, amounts to almost one day a week. The knock-on effects of such differences in terms of the opportunity teachers and pupils have to cover the curriculum adequately are obvious, and these probably underlie the positive relationships between length of school day and pupil achievement (Stallings, 1975).

Quantity of schooling can be increased or decreased depending on school and/or teacher decisions, and individual pupil circumstances. One approach to increasing time is to set homework, a practice which is not widespread at primary school level. Mortimore et al. (1988), for example, reported that less than a quarter of the schools they studied had a policy for setting homework, whereas one in six positively frowned on the idea. In the rest of the schools there was no policy at all. It was left to individual teachers to decide if, and when, to give it.

There appears to be no clear reason for this pattern. The Plowden Report (1967), for example, did not discourage it. It argued that 'Homework should be a matter for discussion and agreement between home and school and the schools should give thought to the form of homework most suitable to children's varying circumstances.' Although there is little research in this area, the evidence indicates that homework enhances pupil achievement. The most recent study to report on this concluded that 'homework showed the strongest relation to learning even though the amount of time spent on homework was relatively small' (Alton-Lee and Nuthall, 1990). Campbell, Emery and Stone (1993) argue that the potential of more systematic approaches to homework as a way of increasing curriculum time ought to be considered, including extending parental involvement and partnership schemes.

Loss of school time can come about by pupil absences, whether adventitiously through such events as illness, or deliberately in the form of truancy. Studies which have related absences to achievement have reported that the former adversely affect the latter. The largest of these used data from the National Child Development Study to examine relationships between attendance at ages 7 and 15, and reading and maths achievement at age 16. It concluded, 'Children with high attendance levels obtain on average higher scores on tests of reading, comprehension and mathematics' (Fogelman, 1978). This finding held true irrespective of social class membership. There was also a low positive relationship in attendance at age 7 and achievement at age 16, which could suggest that the effect of early absence could persist into later schooling.

Teacher Time

Quantity of schooling has so far been considered in terms of overall time available for teaching. However, a focus on how teachers organize their time presents a wider brief, since much of this takes place outside normal school hours. A series of studies on this issue undertaken by Campbell and his colleagues (Campbell, Evans, Neall and Packwood, 1991; Campbell and Neill, 1992) among teachers of 5- to 7-year-old children found that these teachers worked on average 52.4 hours per week, with one in three working over 55 hours. This represents a substantial increase of approximately 15–20 per cent when compared to similar surveys in the 1970s (Hilsum and Cane, 1971). Of these 52.4 hours, forty were spent on school premises and a further twelve hours at home. When this time was broken down into categories of work, it was found that just one-third, about eighteen hours, was actually spent teaching. Teachers spent nearly as long, 14.5 hours, on preparation, including lesson planning, marking and recording, and organizing learning materials, thirteen hours on administration (registration, assembly, supervision of children) and seven hours on in-service activities.

Primary teachers, then, appear to be working under pressure, which is not helped by the lack of non-contact time. The House of Commons Education, Science and Arts Committee (1986) argued that primary schools could not be expected to make further improvements in standards unless they were staffed in ways that provided class teachers with some time in the school day away from their classes. However, this has not been achieved. Mortimer et al. (1988) reported that, among junior schools, 44 per cent either had no non-teaching time or less than one period per week (presumably thirty to forty minutes), and about one-third had one period per week. Campbell and Neill studied infant school teachers, and here over a third of their sample had no non-contact time at all, and one-half had less than one hour per week. These figures are very similar to the OFSTED report (1993a) which reported that non-contact time varied considerably from school to school, and that one-quarter of schools had no non-contact time at all. In the remainder, the maximum was half a day per week, and in the majority of schools the use of that time was left to the total discretion of the teacher.

Curriculum Allocation

The time available for schooling is allocated to the different areas of the curriculum. The responsibility for this allocation varies. It could be the individual teacher, as it was in Britain prior to the implementation of the National Curriculum; it could be the school, or, more likely these days, be decided upon in the light of state or national mandates or guidance. Irrespective of where the responsibility lies, these decisions dictate pupils' curriculum entitlement and the breadth and balance of the curriculum they will experience. Not surprisingly, therefore, this aspect of primary practice has attracted considerable research. More surprisingly, perhaps, has been the consistency of findings, despite differences in method, definition of curriculum areas and date of study. Thus questionnaire surveys by Bennett (1976) and Bassey (1977), observational surveys by HMI (1978), Galton, Simon and

Croll (1980), Bennett, Andreae, Hegarty and Wade (1980), Tizard, Blatchford, Burke, Farquhar and Plewis (1988), Alexander (1992) and Pollard, Broadfoot, Croll, Osborne and Abbott (1994), and analyses of teacher diaries and reports by Campbell and Neill (1992), all indicate that about half of the available time is, and has been since about the mid-1970s, allocated to English and mathematics. This, as Campbell, Emery and Stone (1993) argue, leaves, at the most, fifteen minutes per day for the remaining subjects in the National Curriculum, which hardly seems adequate for worthwhile treatment.

These studies also point to large variations in the allocation of time between schools, and also between classes in the same school. Typical findings are presented in figure 15.2, based on one continuous week's observations in a national sample of infant and junior school classrooms (Bennett et al., 1980).

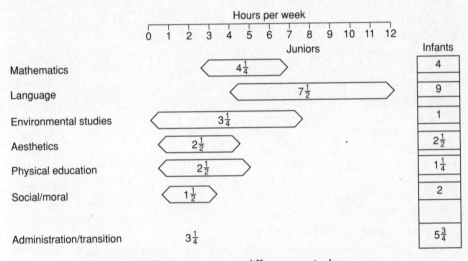

Figure 15.2 Time spent on different curriculum areas.

Figure 15.2 shows, for example, that although the average amount of time spent on maths in junior schools was four and one-quarter hours per week, the time varied from two hours a week in some classrooms to seven hours a week in others. Similarly, the average amount of time spent on language work was 7.5 hours a week, but varied from four to twelve hours a week. The number of subjects composing the curriculum also varied from five to ten, and the pattern of time allocations also varied across the days of the week. Some teachers felt that maths, for example, should be taught daily, others were more flexible, whilst a minority felt that no regular commitment was necessary.

Slightly more time is devoted to maths and language activities in infant classes, as might be expected. But the most significant difference between infant and junior time use was time spent on transition activities, that is, time between activities including cleaning up, waiting, moving to a new location, getting dressed after PE, etc. Nearly six hours per week was consumed by these activities in this study – about 20 per cent of the total available time. More recently Campbell and Neill (1992) have also reported on the extent of what they call 'evaporated' time and the implications of its loss to teaching time.

The picture presented in figure 15.2, although reported in 1980, is not dissimilar to that portrayed ten years later, after the implementation of the National Curriculum. Her Majesty's Inspectorate (1989b) in reporting on this implementation, observed that of the twenty-one hours' teaching time in infants' schools, about 70 per cent was devoted to the core subjects. This was made up of approximately seven hours for English, i.e. 33 per cent of teaching time, five hours for mathematics (23 per cent of teaching time) and three hours for science (14 per cent of teaching time). There was a wide range of time allocations, which were largely explained by the different views held by the schools as to what constituted the subject and how much time was attributed to it across the curriculum. Variations in English were from two hours to twelve hours, in mathematics from one to ten hours, and in science from one to eight hours. However, they accepted that the younger the children, the more likely they were to be involved in activities which are not easily described in single-subject terms, making for great inconsistencies in the way the use of teaching time is analysed and reported.

In their later survey, they expressed concern that few schools had planned the amount of time spent on each subject in the National Curriculum with any degree of accuracy. Time allocations were generally left to the class teacher, and this had led to wide disparities: for example, PE ranged from 5 to 15 per cent, and maths, from 14 to 25 per cent of curriculum time. They also argued that the amount of time devoted to the core subjects was not always well used (OFSTED, 1993b).

Clearly there is no such thing as *the* primary school curriculum, even with a nationally or state-mandated scheme. Each classroom achieves it own unique balance of curriculum activities. There is no suggestion here that a best balance exists, only to caution that a different curriculum is likely to result in different patterns of knowledge acquisition.

These patterns of time use in British classrooms are not much different from those elsewhere. In a recent international comparison of primary curricula in seventy countries, it was shown that about one-third of time is spent on the national language, and about one-sixth on mathematics. Science, social studies, art, PE and RE get about a tenth of the time each. It was concluded that 'the stylised character of the overall outline of the curriculum is striking. Put simply, curricular categories, and even allocations of time to these categories, conform to a standard world outline' (Meyer, Kamens and Benavot, 1992; cf. Burns, 1984).

Another perspective on curriculum allocation is to consider what children actually spend their time on within and across the subject areas. Good and

Beckerman (1978) identified fourteen pupil activities and found that 50 per cent of their time was spent on just three of them – writing (22 per cent), listening (16 per cent), and reading (12 per cent). Interacting with an adult accounted for only 7 per cent of the time. Non-academic activities, such as chatting, sitting, walking and waiting occurred about a quarter of the time. Alexander (1992) observed that the curriculum as experienced by primary pupils was largely constituted of ten generic activities. These activities are not mutually exclusive, so direct comparison with earlier studies is not possible. Nevertheless writing and reading occupied over half of the available time. This study also considered the pattern of generic activities in subject areas and found, for example, that English was dominated by reading and writing, science was a mix of working with apparatus, collaboration, writing and drawing, but little reading, and topic work was mainly writing, drawing, painting and reading. In raising questions about curriculum content and balance, therefore, the balance and disposition of these generic activities must be considered. Indeed, argues Alexander, it is very clear that to define curriculum balance solely in terms of subject time allocation is both superficial and misplaced.

Pupil Involvement

If we conceive curriculum allocation as the opportunity that is afforded pupils to study a given curriculum area, then pupil involvement is the use that pupils make of that opportunity. It has numerous synonyms in the research literature – attention, time on-task, task engagement, active learning time, to name but a few. However, all are concerned with what pupils actually do with the work they are assigned.

The importance of pupil involvement for achievement has been recognized for a long time. William James, for example, wrote in 1899, 'whether the attention comes by grace of genius, or by dint of will, the longer one does attend to a topic the more mastery of it one has.' In other words, attention, or task engagement, is a necessary condition for learning. A string of studies has reported positive relationships between involvement and learning. The latest concluded, 'The relationship between time and learning was strong and consistent' (Alton-Lee and Nuthall, 1990). Student involvement may not secure learning, but it is a necessary step (Stodolsky, 1988), and this view has consistently been supported by research evidence, albeit with variations relating to subject area, type of task and classroom context.

Here, as with curriculum allocation, the research findings are remarkably consistent despite differences in methodology and definition. On average, pupils are involved in their work between 60 and 66 per cent of their time (Boydell, 1975; Galton et al., 1980; Bennett et al., 1980; Alexander, 1992; Pollard et al., 1994.) However, huge variations are apparent from subject to subject, class to class and pupil to pupil in the same classroom. In some classrooms average involvement is over 80 per cent, whereas in others it is less than 50 per cent. This range of variation is also true of different subject areas. Studies typically report that involvement is lowest in English and maths, that is, those subject areas allocated most time (Bennett et al., 1980; Alexander, 1992, Pollard et al., 1994). Alexander also considered differences in task-related behaviour in the ten generic activities he identified, and found that the activities which kept children on-task were those like structured talk with the teacher, the class or other children in the group, planned collaborative work, looking and listening, and making things. He concluded: 'in general, the most work and least distraction occurred in the rarest activities. The striking feature of the activities at which children worked for a high proportion of the time was involvement with other people. Conversely, most of the activities at which children worked for lowest proportions of time – writing, reading, drawing, painting – involved no other people and could have effectively been carried out in isolation.'

Stodolsky (1988) reported differences in pupil involvement in maths and social studies tasks in relation to the cognitive level of the task and its pacing and context. She concluded that the cognitive complexity of the task and co-operation hold the keys to student responsiveness: 'A clear pattern of increasing student involvement as a function of cognitive complexity occurs in both subjects. Children's average involvement was highest when they were working co-operatively. The responsive student in our classrooms . . . lives up to the expectations of theorists who view students as efficient, curious, seeking challenge and benefiting from co-operation and collaboration.'

It is interesting in the light of these findings that HMI (1989a) criticized work in English and maths for concentrating on tasks of low complexity, that is, practice rather than problem solving, and for neglecting oral work in English in favour of an overabundance of writing. They thus argued that adjustments need to be made to the balance of individual, group and whole-class teaching to make more effective use of time. However, four years later they were still arguing that in most schools the balance in relationships between whole-class teaching, group work and individual work were not as productive as they should have been, resulting in the ineffective use of valuable teaching time.

It should be said, however, that although high time on-task is often found in co-operative group work contexts (Bennett and Dunne, 1992), this is not universally so. Many research studies have reported enhanced pupil involvement in what have been variously called structured or teacher-directed classrooms where the predominant mode is whole-class activities. The latest study reports that 'classrooms where high levels of class work were recorded are also likely to have been coded with relatively high levels of pupil task engagement, low levels of pupil task management and fairly low levels of pupil distraction. Classrooms with high levels of individual work are likely to have relatively low levels of task engagement . . . Groupwork falls between these two patterns' (Pollard et al., 1994).

Managing Classroom Time

There are several aspects of managing classroom time, one already mentioned above being the appropriate use and balance of whole-class, group and individual teaching in relation to the purpose of the activity or task set. HMI have constantly criticized this balance, arguing, for example, that adjustments needed to be made to make more effective use of time (HMI, 1989b).

Delay is one of the unpublicized features of school life according to Jackson (1968), and observation studies bear this out. Queuing or waiting for the teacher have been shown to constitute up to 10 per cent of observations (Bennett et al., 1980; Pollard et al. 1994), with obvious impact on the time available for learning. The problem, according to Bennett et al. (1984), is that teachers often appear to adopt a crisis management style, whereby they try, with the best intentions, to be all things to all pupils at all times. But the consequences of such a style have been shown to include constant interruptions, divided teacher attention, inadequate supervision of the class as a whole and lack of teacher opportunity to assess pupils' work adequately – in short a recipe for teacher frustration.

Much of the teachers' time in this study was taken up by their willingness to react to pupils' requests, many of which were of a low order. In language work, for example, they were constantly harassed for spellings. Bennett and Dunne (1992) thus attempted to amend teachers' management style by helping teachers, within co-operative group work settings, to devolve some of their authority to the group. In this experiment, children were not allowed to make any request to the teacher until all possibilities of finding an answer had been exhausted in the group. The evaluation of this simple modification showed that the average number of demands fell dramatically, from an average of over thirty-eight per lesson to less than five. The type of demand also changed. Before the change, almost two-thirds of requests concerned checking work or transitions between activities. After the change, this type of request dropped to one-quarter. Most of the requests that remained were of a higher level, relating to issues of instruction and understanding. The experiment was so successful, in fact, that it made some teachers feel guilty. One said, 'I found it very satisfying teaching in this way because the children were so involved in their work. It gave me a lot of free time . . . at times this made me feel that I was not doing my job.'

The crisis-management style no doubt also relates to the amount of transition and evaporated time referred to earlier. The amount of transition time has been regarded by some theorists as a reflection of teacher management competency, and the answer lies in improved classroom management systems. As Lemlech (1988) argues, good organization creates time.

There are other solutions to effective classroom time management, such as the use of non-teaching assistants or parents. When used well, these do indeed improve the teachers' lot, but caution too is needed. Unless well organized, teachers' time devoted to managing non-teaching assistants and parents could exceed their usefulness. On these grounds NCC (1993) concluded that a more realistic, and ultimately more effective, solution to time management lies in the use of better classroom organization and planning.

Editor's Commentary

It has been argued in this chapter that pupil time on-task is an important determinant of learning progress. It has been shown that there are significant variations from school to school, class to class and pupil to pupil in the way time is allocated and used in schooling. Some of these variations seem to be caused by differences in management effectiveness.

In improving the management and use of time, particular attention should be paid to the following questions:

- How can planned curriculum time be extended?
- How can evaporated time be minimized?
- How can the quality of time use be enhanced?
- How can time be allocated to ensure a balanced treatment of the curriculum?

In considering these questions the following factors might be kept in mind:

- the role of homework in extending the school day
- the role of good classroom order in minimizing lost or evaporated time
- the role of complex tasks and well-managed group work in increasing pupils' levels of attention.

The ideas in this chapter can be pursued in school-based work as follows:

- Observe a range of children working on the same task. Do they allocate the same attention to it? What factors influence the amount of time they spend on-task?
- Focusing on two or three children, observe a class for a whole day. Keep records of how much time is lost from learning, i.e. evaporated time. How might that time have been minimized?

- Discuss with head teachers and class teachers their rationale for making time allocations to different curriculum areas, and their systems for assuring that allocations happen in practice.
- In regard to your own work, set a group of children a range of tasks of different complexity and observe the effect this has on their levels of attention. Evaluate, with other learner teachers, what lessons can be learned from this.
- Tape-record your own classroom talk through a day. Analyse the tape to ascertain how much of your time is spent on lower-order management decisions. How could these responsibilities be devolved to children?
- Keep records of your pupils' behaviour at points of transition from activity to activity or place to place. Is there time lost here? How could any time loss be minimized?

The management of time is closely related to other aspects of classroom management. It perhaps goes without saying that the management of time does not involve regimentation. Procedures should not be used which threaten pupil autonomy. Quite the reverse.

Time management can usefully be seen in the context of ideas in other chapters as follows:

- Good time management is made more possible by good order. Order is discussed in chapter 10.
- Time management can be devolved to promote pupil autonomy. The principles of pupil autonomy are discussed in chapter 11.
- Higher-level, demanding tasks and well-managed group work enhance time on task. These factors are discussed in chapter 8.

FURTHER READING

Three new studies of time and the nature of teachers' work are:

Evans, L., Packwood, A., Neill, S. R. St J. & Campbell, R. J. (1994). *The meaning of infant teachers' work*. London: Routledge.

Campbell, R. J. & Neill, S. R. St J. (1994). *Primary teachers at work*. London: Routledge.

Campbell, R. J. & Neill, S. R. St J. (1994). *Secondary teachers at work*. London: Routledge.

Each book provides a detailed picture of how teachers spend their time on work, both on and off school premises.

Part IV

Assessment and Evaluation

16

Approaches to Educational Assessment

Bryan Dockrell

Editor's Overview

This is the first of two chapters on assessment. The extensive treatment of this topic is in recognition of its importance in schooling. Whether formally or informally, a large amount of time is spent on assessment in schools. Over and above examinations and tests, pupils experience teachers' own quizzes. Pupils' work is continuously monitored and commented on. Most interactions between pupils and teachers involve some assessment component even if it is only a whispered 'well done'.

Assessment is known to have a very large effect on teaching and learning. For this reason teachers need to develop a powerful understanding of assessment, of its purposes and techniques, and of how it can be used to promote quality learning. Bryan Dockrell's objective in these two chapters is to get you well started on a path to such understanding.

There are important distinctions to be made between the various purposes of assessment. A technical language helps in understanding these distinctions, and some of the terms of this language are introduced here. This is not jargon. Teachers cannot afford to be amateur about assessment.

In the first of his chapters, Bryan Dockrell describes the different purposes of assessment and observes that different purposes require different assessment tools or techniques. In this chapter he focuses on the forms of assessment carried out at the end of a programme or course. This form is called summative assessment.

Summative assessment is used to

- make selection decisions
- allocate resources
- make awards
- monitor standards.

There are many problems in assessing achievement at a particular point in time. These include

- agreement on standards
- design of tests
- variability in performance
- variability in marking.

These problems are particularly acute if non-academic factors are being assessed (e.g. effort).

Methods for minimizing these problems and for making most sense of the outcomes of summative assessment are described.

Primary teachers often design their own tests or buy commercial tests for assessing and allocating pupils to groups or classes. The lessons in this chapter can be applied to these purposes.

Introduction

Exasperated teachers can sometimes be heard to complain that there is too much testing and not enough teaching, particularly in response to the demands of assessment for the National Curriculum. Are they right? All too often they are, but they should not be. Much assessment is a waste of time because it has no clear purpose. Any assessment should be an attempt to find the answer to a question. Usually, that question is: 'What should I do next?'

If assessment is used properly, it is a powerful tool contributing to learning. Of course it matters what teachers teach and how they teach it, but research indicates that regular assessment and feedback are high on the list of the procedures which teachers can use to improve learning. There is a technique called meta-analysis which is used in many fields, including medicine and the social sciences, to combine the findings from a number of studies which are not conclusive individually but are when they are taken together. Meta-analyses indicate that assessment and feedback provide a highly effective way of improving learning at all stages from primary school through to higher education (Kulik, Kulik, Bangert-Drowns and Morgan, 1991). Further evidence is provided by a study of the teaching of reading around the world (Postlethwaite and Ross, 1992), which found that a general emphasis on assessment was a significant factor in improving reading but, more important, so was the assessment of a range of specific skills like decoding, the use of background knowledge and sentence understanding. The proper use of assessment can make a substantial contribution to teaching and learning.

Assessments make many contributions to education, and, like any other tool, they must be fit for their purpose. The kind of assessments that we make and the way that we make them should be determined by the use to which they are to be put. This chapter will look at the various purposes of assessment and how these different purposes affect the assessments which are made. The British programme of assessment of the National Curriculum has been criticized on the grounds that it is being used for too many different and conflicting purposes (Broadfoot, Dockrell, Gipps, Harlen and Nuttall, 1993). As teachers we have not gained as much as we could from testing, examining and assessing because our assessments have not been suitable for the purposes for which they have been used.

The Uses of Assessment

Assessments can be made before a programme of learning is begun, in the course of the programme or after it. They can be used to guide learning, to improve teaching or to provide a basis for making decisions about individuals or about policy issues. Table 16.1 shows the variety of ways in which assessment can contribute to education.

Table 16.1 The uses of assessment

	Before learning	*During learning*	*After learning*
For learning	classifying learners placing	assessing progress diagnosing difficulties	motivating guiding
For teaching	setting expectations planning	appraising instruction modifying curricula	accountability assessing effectiveness
For decision-making	directing resources	continuous assessment recording development	certifying/selecting monitoring standards

Certifying and Selecting

The most familiar use of assessment is the one in the bottom right-hand corner of table 16.1, for certifying and selecting. Most people, when they think about assessments, think of the examinations they took for GCSE or of their concern to get the necessary A level grades for admission to higher education. Indeed, in the past, thinking about assessment has been dominated by the use of assessments for decision-making, particularly for selection. Assessment at the end of a course or programme which sums up the outcomes is often called 'summative' by contrast with assessment which is meant to inform practice and is called 'formative'. This more familiar summative use of assessment will be considered here, and the more formative use of assessment, to improve teaching and learning, will be addressed in more detail in the next chapter.

The initial interest in examinations in the nineteenth century arose from the first public examinations for admission to the Civil Service. These examinations had to be effective: that is, they had to select the right candidates; they had to be seen to be fair; and, equally important, they had to be relatively easy to administer so that they would not cost too much. These three concerns are still the crucial considerations in public examinations. The one most often discussed is effectiveness for purpose, which is often referred to as 'validity'. A valid assessment is one which effectively fulfils its purpose. In practice, it is not the assessment which has been used but the purpose to which it has been put and the perceived fairness of the whole selection process that can be crucial, as, of course, can be cost.

The familiar examinations for schools, set up by the universities at about the same time as examinations were introduced into the admission procedures of the Civil Service, were the precursors of GCSE and A levels. Their initial purpose was to improve learning in schools, but they rapidly came to be used in much the same way as the Civil Service examinations, for selection, not only for admission to the universities themselves but for a range of occupations. What is ostensibly a certificate of attainment is often in practice a covert means of selection and rejection.

Selection tests, whether for educational or occupational selection, rarely incorporate a fixed level of attainment above which all candidates will succeed and below which all will fail. Usually they place candidates in a rank order or in groups, best, next best and so on. There are almost always some limitations in the system which result in error in these placings. The error arises from a number of causes which are often collectively called 'reliability'. Though the term 'reliability' is still frequently used, its various meanings are now subsumed under generalizability theory. At its simplest the question is: Would any particular candidate get the same score from a similar test or indeed from the same test on a different occasion? Does performance in the assessment generalize to performance on another test, on another occasion, in other circumstances? The failure to generalize may stem from the assessment procedure itself, the performance of the candidate or the criterion, the measure of success.

The Content of the Assessment

The problem of generalizability may lie with the content of the assessment. Any form of assessment procedure can usually include only a sample of the relevant activites, whether the assessment is a fairly straightforward examination like GCSE or a more elaborate work-based procedure for employment. The items are chosen to be as representative as possible of the full range of the relevant knowledge, skills or behaviours. In educational assessment the area to be assessed is often called a 'domain'. One candidate may be lucky and find that a high proportion of the items actually chosen to represent the domain happen to include knowledge or skills that he or she had learned. Another candidate may be unlucky and find the reverse: only a small part of the assessment happens to consist of material that has been learned. In neither of these extreme cases does the test give an accurate picture of that candidate's knowledge of the domain. The same is true for all assessments to a greater or lesser extent. They do not fully represent the knowledge, or lack of it, of any particular individual. There is therefore some degree of error in the score which virtually every candidate actually obtains. One essential characteristic of all forms of assessments is that they must adequately represent the domain. What any individual person does know of the whole domain and would score on a perfect test covering the whole of that domain adequately, is often referred to as that individual's 'true score', as contrasted with the score obtained on a particular test on one occasion.

The Contribution of the Assessor

When there is an element of judgement in the appraisal, additional issues arise. Judgement comes into play not only with portfolios and projects but with most written work, like essays or essay-type examinations. One appraiser or examiner may rate a particular performance more highly than do others and thus give it a higher score than they would. We are familiar with the different points awarded to the same performance in international ice skating competitions by different judges, and the different points awarded to the same song in the Eurovision Song Contest. There are comparable differences in the grades awarded to the same performance by different assessors of academic assessments, as we have been aware for many years. Indeed one appraiser may judge the same performance differently on a different occasion. Inconsistency of individual assessors, as well as differences among assessors, is a frequent problem where there is subjective marking.

Even when they agree on the relative merits of performances, different assessors may give them quite different marks. The disparity in the mark awarded need not indicate a difference in the assessors' judgement of the performances but their different uses of the scale. One may regard 60 per cent as a high mark and grade accordingly, while another regard 70 per cent as a low mark. The disparity between the marks actually awarded may arise, then, from the standards of the assessors. One is a hard marker, another an easy one.

Yet a third issue arises when there is more than one assessor involved. Assessments are often marked out of 100, in theory at least. In practice, assessments are rarely given 1 or 100. The effective scale is usually very much less than the apparent scale. What is more, assessors differ in the extent to which they spread their marks over the full range available to them. If the mark is a percentage, two assessors may give the same average, say 60, but one may regard 70 as the appropriate mark for a very good piece of work, but another, while agreeing about the relative merit of the performance, may give a mark of 80. It is not that the markers disagree about the work, it is that they differ in their use of the scale. The first uses a restricted scale, the second a much fuller one. This is not a problem uniquely true of educational assessments but is found in other fields. A wine columnist in a weekend magazine apparently awards marks out of twenty, yet never gives less than a 9 or more than 16. He chooses to limit the discrimination among the wines he tastes to seven categories.

These are the three crucial issues which face all systems of assessments when more than one assessor is involved. They arise not only where several assessors are assessing the same work, but with particular force when, as with GCSE and A levels, different assessors are marking the work of different candidates. They are differences in rank order, differences in the mark awarded for an average performance and the extent to which marks are spread across the scale.

In education we have developed techniques for tackling these problems. First, standards are specified so that all examiners are briefed on what is expected. Second, they apply these criteria to sample scripts and discuss the basis for their marks. Examination Boards have systems where scripts are marked by several examiners. This makes it possible to compare standards of different markers and, if necessary, to adjust the marks awarded by the use of 'moderation', where assessors meet and explain their assessments to each other and try to arrive at a consensus.

All the issues that arise with assessments used for certification and selection tests apply also to the criterion measures. Even if a university entrance examination like A levels had no error at all, it would not predict success perfectly because the criterion itself, success at the end of the university course, has a large error component.

Candidates too give different performances on different occasions. Like sportsmen, they may not be on form because of nerves or illness, and thus the score they obtain may not accurately represent their real level of achievement.

Choosing the Best

The better the selection test or certificate, the more accurately it represents a candidate's real level of attainment and the closer it is to the true score. However, there is some error in virtually all certifying or selection procedures. Consequently, the group with the highest score on the selection test will include some people who will fail to meet the criterion as well as those who will meet it. Each successive group will have a higher proportion who will pass the selection test but will fail to meet the criterion. Conversely, those successive groups will exclude fewer who could meet the criterion. Those who pass the selection procedure but fail to meet the criterion are usually called 'false positives', those who fail the selection but could meet the criterion are called 'false negatives'. The smaller the proportion of false negatives and false positives, the better the selection process.

The level at which the pass mark is set is important. In the top group of a good selection test there will be very few false positives. Nearly all will be true positives. The lower the passing level is set, the more will pass who should fail, but the fewer will fail who should pass. Setting this level is a matter of judgement. If the decision is irreversible, as for instance with murder in a country which still retains the death penalty, the jury might want to be very certain indeed before finding the accused guilty. However, were the sentence life imprisonment, not death, they might be less rigorous because they believed that there was the possibility of reversing their decision at some future point should they prove to be mistaken. It is an argument sometimes used against the death penalty. Juries may be reluctant to convict. The distinction is between reversible and irreversible decisions. There are now few educational assessments that result in irreversible decisions, but there are some. Obtaining the number of points needed for admission to a medical degree is one of them. Very few people indeed have the opportunity to apply again or to apply elsewhere.

It is important to distinguish between the effectiveness of the assessment and its use. A particular use of a technically valid assessment process can have unacceptable social consequences if it is thought to be unfair. The examination that was formerly used for selection for secondary education, the eleven plus, is a case in point. The problem did not lie with the examination; it was indeed remarkably effective. In those authorities where few were admitted to the selective schools, relatively few passed the eleven plus who did not succeed in the School Certificate (the equivalent of GCSE). There were few false positives. However, in these authorities many children who could have succeeded in the School Certificate were rejected. There were many false negatives. On the other hand, in those authorities where many were selected there were fewer potentially successful candidates who were not admitted (few false negative), but many were admitted who later failed (false positive). It was the size of the quota that caused the problem. There were many examples of false negatives, so parents whose children failed the eleven plus were critical of the examination. It was argued by the proponents of selection, on the other hand, that too big a quota resulted in a large number of pupils who found themselves allocated to a programme where they could not succeed and which they did not find congenial.

The examination itself did not say what outcomes were desirable; it merely told who were and who were not likely to succeed and how many false negatives there were likely to be with different sizes of quota. Assessment techniques cannot solve the complex educational or social problems that they are sometimes called on to address. However, specialists in assessment are now emphasizing that the concept of validity should not only include the technical effectiveness of the assessment but should take into account the uses to which it is likely to be put.

The decision about the size of the quota, how many to admit and how many to exclude, was a political one. In the end the procedure was thought not to be fair, and the general decision was to move to the now familiar comprehensive schools. Not having the examination did not solve the problem of differences in programme in the secondary school. It merely deferred and blurred the decision-making. Ending the examination did, however, defuse the argument. The eleven plus examination was a good example of where the messenger, the examination, was blamed for the message, admission to grammar school, which was a political decision.

The political nature of the decision about the size of the quota has been made quite overt in Britain in the case of higher education. The government has made quite explicit its decisions about the number of students it is prepared to pay for at tertiary institutions, no matter how many qualified candidates there may be.

Selection is one sensible use of assessment. It is necessary in education, where there is a limited supply of physical facilities or suitably qualified teachers, as there is still at secondary level in many countries, and at tertiary level in all but a very few. In many circumstances we need to know not only who can succeed but also to answer the harder question, how many we can afford to provide for and consequently which of the qualified applicants is likely to do best. The same is true of jobs. If there are more candidates than jobs, then we may want to be able to pick out the one with the greatest likelihood of success in order to make the most effective use of limited resources. There may well be a conflict between the persepective of the institution where a rigorous selection process may be most economical and that of the individual who might prefer a chance to try even at the risk of failure. For example, in some countries the school-leaving certificate is a qualification entitling all who pass to proceed to higher education. the consequence is that many, in the American phrase, 'flunk out'. Many European systems have a large failure rate. The institution in this case is the state, which has paid for the university education. From that perspective, the failures may be regarded as a waste of resources. The individuals, though, may welcome the opportunity to try.

The Influence of Selection Tests on Assessment

These obvious and important uses of assessment have influenced the way teachers assess. Through much of secondary schooling teachers' assessments have been seen as a preparation for the external examinations which will largely determine a young person's future. So much so that in Britain examination reform has almost come to be synonymous with curriculum reform. Much of the research about assessment has been devoted to certification and selection. So has the professional effort devoted to the construction of examinations. The technical terms used, like validity, generalizability, true score and norm, are derived from the research on certificates and assessments used for selection. Selection has come to dominate thinking about what assessment is for and how assessments should be designed. However, what you want to know after a programme of learning is completed may be very different from what you want to know during the course of learning. A good assessment procedure for the typical external examination is one that discriminates, that is, put students in a rank order, and not one that shows how much they have learned of what the teacher was trying to teach. The consequence has been that, until recently, the other uses of assessments, particularly their potential contribution to learning and teaching have been neglected.

Assessing to a Standard

A recent development of assessment for certification is for assessments to be referenced to a criterion. The difference is rather like that between the two kinds of results we get from the Olympic games. We know the rank order, who was first and got the gold medal, who was second and got the silver and who got the bronze and what was the position of the British participant. However, we also know the precise performance of each competitor, how fast they ran or how far they jumped. In educational assessment the first piece of information, rank order, is called 'norm-referencing'. The traditional certificates discussed above have been mainly norm-referenced. They tell us what broad group a person falls into but not what he or she knows. The second kind of information, saying what a person knows or can do, is called 'criterion-referencing'.

Criterion-referenced assessments are more like driving tests. They are certificates of competence for particular activites. This too is a valuable use of assessment. We need tests which assess and certify a minimum level of competence in many areas, from plumbing to brain surgery. The assessments for the National Vocational Qualifications are criterion-referenced and are designed to certify competence at a given level. Assessment of this kind has proved easier in some areas than others. It has, for example, proved relatively easy to define the skills involved in joinery, decorating and other construction crafts; to set standards which can be recognized; and to use these standards to structure teaching. In other areas, like the care of children or the elderly, the quality of the care is more important than the actual actions of the carer. Some lecturers feel that these, perhaps nebulous, qualities are easy to recognize though they are difficult to define. Many of them find it difficult to define these social competences in criterion-referenced terms, though they feel confident about making comparative, more or less, statements.

This distinction between norm-referenced assessments, which place individuals in a rank order, and criterion-referenced assessments, which say what someone knows, is not absolute. Most assessments include both elements but place greater emphasis on the one than the other. As noted above, GCSE and A level grades give primarily rank order information. We know approximately what broad band a candidate falls into, but the certificate does not specify what each candidate knows or doesn't know, nor what he or she can or cannot do. The examination is, however, based on a defined curriculum and is a rough guide to what any individual is likely to know.

Conversely, a criterion can usually be related to its incidence in a defined population and often is, explicitly or implicitly. For example, the police may only recruit women of a particular height, so the requirement is criterion-referenced, but the criterion itself is reached by knowing about the height of the population. There would be no point in restricting recruitment to women over eight feet tall because there aren't any. Nor is it set at four feet because that would include virtually everybody. A criterion is set which is appropriate for a particular purpose, and that nearly always takes account of the realities of a particular situation.

Nor is a criterion-referenced assessment limited to certifying one level of minimum competence. Criterion-referenced assessments can be graded. There may be a separate advanced test, as with driving, or a single assessment may recognize performance by different invididuals at one of a series of defined (criterion-referenced) levels, as with a swimming certificate which certifies the ability to swim 25, 50 or 100 metres. Both are criterion-referenced and both report differing levels of attainment.

It has proved more difficult to apply criterion referencing to academic attainment. The National Curriculum assessments and the General National Vocational Qualifications are examples of the move to more criterion-referenced assessment. The outcomes are defined much more specifically than in the past. For example, at Key Stage one (year two), assessment of spelling includes not only 'produces recognizable (though not necessarily always correct) spellings of a range of common words' but also 'spells correctly, in the course of own writing, simple monosyllabic words they use regularly which observe common patterns' and 'recognizes that spelling has patterns, and begins to apply knowledge of patterns in attempts to spell a wider range of words' and 'shows knowledge of the names and order of the letters of the alphabet'.

Some subjects like modern languages had developed graded tests which approximate the driving test. Some other subjects, however, do not fit easily into this model of linear development. There is no natural sequence, and consequently concepts and skills can be taught effectively in different orders. Unlike swimming, there are no successive levels of skill which can be assessed. The curriculum levels relate to the order in which we choose to teach, and not to any natural progression of learning.,

Licences to practise, like driving licences and plumbers' and brain surgeons' certificates, should be criterion-referenced because we need to be assured of a minimum level of competence. Academic certificates are rarely used in this way. The user may be satisfied to know roughly what holders of a certificate know and can do, but mainly how well they compare with others. A largely norm-referenced assessment is appropriate for these purposes. However, criterion-referenced assessments are essential if they are to be used for teaching and learning. This use is covered in the next chapter.

Assessment by the Teacher or by an External Examination

Certification does not necessarily require external examinations, though that is the British and French pattern at secondary school level. In some countries certification is based largely or exclusively on internal assessment, as with the American High School Diploma or the German Abitur. Increasing use is being made here and elsewhere of teachers' assessments of course work and of folios of students' work. At tertiary level assessment for diplomas and degrees is based largely on internal assessments moderated by external examiners.

Teacher assessment is no soft option. All the issues that have been discussed above with regard to external examinations apply to teachers' own assessments. They too must be valid, must be fair and must not be too expensive of teachers' time and effort. They must give an adequate picture of what each learner knows. They must cover the whole curriculum. The marking must be accurate. Each set of marks must place learners in the right order, must have the same average and spread the marks in the same way as other teachers do or they will be misleading. It matters, for they too will be used for selection and so must predict the success of each student as well as possible.

Assessment for certification is not only made at the end of a course or programme. Assessments of modules, norm- or criterion-referenced, may be combined for the award of a certificate. Continuous assessments which are made during the course of learning may simply be accumulated to provide a final mark.

Assessing the Non-Academic Outcomes of Learning

Teachers, and indeed many others, are called upon to write references which go beyond the acquisition of knowledge and skills. Records of Achievement which result in a final summative statement are now required for each pupil in school. They are not simply another form of school-leaving certification but are an integral part of the educational and assessment process. As a summative statement they, like references and reports for prospective employers, are not merely a cumulative record of academic achievement but also frequently contain statements about general transferable skills and personal qualities. The subject reports included in the record may go beyond knowledge and understanding, and in history, for example, report on 'understanding points of view', in technology 'proposing solutions and choosing the most appropriate', in business studies 'organizing information, making decisions, communicating'. Tutor group reports summarize these assessments of skills and personal qualities to include 'communication, problem solving, organization'. Personal and social education may report on rather different personal qualities like 'co-operation with teacher, ability to work without supervision, ability to lead a small group'.

These skills and qualities too have to be assessed fairly. Yet one researcher commented, 'At the moment we have the disquieting situation in which teachers make their judgements like amateurs in the field of those objectives which are often regarded as the most important and are subject to all those prejudices, stereotypes, distortions, etc. to which all people are exposed when they have only their common sense to rely on' (Ingenkamp, 1977). Like the assessments of knowledge or skill that have been considered so far, assessment of personal qualities must accurately report typical behaviour and must be comparable across pupils. Teachers should have evidence for their assessments and not simply rely on impression. Reports are much more likely to be accurate and fair if they are descriptive and not judgmental.

A technique for assessing these non-academic qualities was developed some years ago. Industrial supervisors were asked to give examples of important activities that distinguished employees who were high in a particular quality from those who were not. This procedure, the 'critical incidents' technique, provided teachers with the basis for making their assessments of personal qualities. The most frequently reported personal quality is 'effort'. But how can it be assessed satisfactorily? A group of teachers using the technique arrived at a set of descriptions of actual behaviours which they agreed fairly and adequately represented what they meant by effort. They were not an exhaustive list but were exemplars which allowed pupils and teachers to rate particular behaviour. They ranged from level one 'as soon as one process/job is completed this pupil is eager to get on with the next one' through intermediate stages 'works well in class when given a job to do' and 'requires constant prodding' to the lowest level 'even when pushed this pupil will look for excuses to stop work'. Teachers knew what they were looking for, and pupils knew what was expected of them.

Assessment to Monitor Standards

So far this chapter has been concerned with the most familiar use of assessment, for certifying and selecting. This is not the only use of assessment that impinges on teaching. Another use of assessment that has become familiar to most people is monitoring standards. The league tables of GCSE and A level performance that appear annually are a means of monitoring the performance of individual schools and local authorities. A school which obtains better examination results is taken to be a good one.

Teachers may object that these comparisons are unfair. Sociological research has long shown that school attainment is determined largely by personal, family and social factors. We can see among our friends that people differ in their aptitude for academic work and in their effort and motivation. Families too differ in the extent to which they value learning. Some families give more encouragement to succeed in school than do others. They provide more books or computers and other facilities. Social factors matter also, variables like the availability of libraries; whether education is valued by a particular community; and whether it is seen as primarily a male or female prerogative. One international study found that around the world the number of books in the home was the best predictor of academic success.

Yet schools do make a difference. Without them most of us would not learn to read or write. Before there was universal schooling in this country most people were illiterate, and in many parts of the world where there are still no schools, at least for the poor, there is general illiteracy. For the most part we learn what we are taught. Individual schools too make a difference. Some are more successful than others with comparable children. Merely comparing raw results is a poor monitoring measure because it does not take account of the level of atttainment of the children on entry and so does not measure progress. What is needed for monitoring is a system that tells us what the school has contributed to the learning of individual students.

Adequate monitoring also requires more detailed information. While school ethos may make a difference, what goes on in the classroom is most important. There are differing levels of success for different subjects in individual secondary schools. Lumping all subjects together provides very limited and possibly misleading information. We do not know in which aspects of the curriculum students in general have done well nor where they have done badly. The tables do not provide information about different approaches to teaching and learning which teachers can use to improve performance. Sophisticated systems of monitoring like the A-Level Information System (Fitzgibbon, 1992) do provide teachers with such formative information.

There are other and arguably much better ways of monitoring performance of an educational system. In England the Assessment of Performance Unit was able to monitor national progress by testing carefully chosen samples of children. This approach made little demand on individual pupils and classes but provided a great deal of valuable, detailed information about many aspects of the curriculum. This use of assessment for monitoring was derived from the surveys of the 1950s and 1960s in Scotland, where similar surveys continue to show their value, and is similar to the National Assessment of Educational Progress in America.

Assessment for Planning

A rather different use made of assessment by teachers is for setting expectations and planning before a programme of instruction begins. These are the uses given in the first column of figure 16.1. Teachers will usually make use of criterion-referenced assessments for these purposes so that they have reasonable expectations of their pupils and can plan their teaching more effectively. They will need assessments of reading, writing, arithmetic or whatever, which tell them not only how an individual's or a group's performance compares with, say, that of other 10-year-olds, but also what they can do already. Teachers often use norm-referenced assessments to give themselves criterion-referenced information. Knowing that a child is average may not give precise information about a learner's knowledge but may give an impression of the general level.

A traditional concern of secondary school teachers has been with the attainment of pupils coming to them from primary schools. In the past, they did not know what to expect of these new pupils because they did not know what had already been taught in the primary schools. Assessments for the National Curriculum should alleviate this problem. In future, teachers should not have to guess what to expect of a new class; they should know what part of the curriculum has been covered, and they should have a precise statement of what each pupil has mastered. They should therefore be able to plan their first-year programmes much better.

Criterion-referenced and norm-referenced assessments are used for rather different purposes in classifying and placing. Either criterion-referenced or norm-referenced assessments permit the grouping of pupils according to a predetermined plan. Norm-referenced assessments which indicate whether a pupil is in the top, middle or bottom third may be a useful basis for planning. The plan may be to group or stream pupils according to their level of achievement, or conversely to ensure that schools or classes have a comparable balance of pupils. On the other hand, when planning provision for children with special educational needs, for example a sensory handicap, criterion-referenced assessments are likely to be more useful. We usually want to know the extent of a visual or hearing loss in deciding whether special help will be needed and what form it should take.

Assessments made for planning almost inevitably result in the allocation of resources, as for example with statements of special educational needs. Many children with special needs are still placed in special schools or classes where there is additional provision of staff and facilities. Even when the decision is for a particular child to be in the regular class, additional support may be provided for the class teacher. Another example of the use of assessments for directing resources is provision for the disadvantaged. Authorities may want to know the level of attainment of pupils who will be enrolled in particualr schools or classes in order to allocate additional resources to those with the greatest need.

Teachers have two interests in this use of assessment. First, their own assessments may be part or all of the basis for identifying need; and second, they may benefit (or suffer) from the allocation of resources.

Conclusion

Some uses of assessment are generally familiar, like school-leaving certificates, Records of Achievement, league tables. Others like National Vocational Qualifications and Standardized Attainment Tasks are becoming so, especially to the students affected by them and to their parents. It is this assessment for summative purposes that has been covered in this chapter. For teachers, however, it is the formative use of assessment for teaching and learning that can be the most important. It is assessment for these purposes which is described in the next chapter.

Editor's Commentary

In this chapter, methods for using summative assessment for

- selection
- allocation
- certification
- monitoring

have been described.

Problems in making sense of the scores from summmative assessment have been raised. This is because a particular score on a particular day is influenced not only by student attainment but also by

- the design of the test
- vagaries of marking
- the state of the pupil.

Ways of designing the tests, conducting the marking and interpreting the results have been described which maximize the sense that can be gleaned from summative assessment.

As well as the above purposes, it has been emphasized that summative assessment, properly designed and interpreted, can provide useful information about starting points for teaching. This is particularly important at points of educational transition where pupils move from school to school or class to class.

School-based work projects and related readings have been held over on this topic until the end of chapter 17.

FURTHER READING

Gipps, C. & Murphy, P. (1994). *A fair test? Assessment, achievement and equity*. Buckingham, England: Open University Press.

> One of the continuing concerns in testing both of ability and attainment has been fairness. Do test scores reflect accurately the abilities and attainments of boys and girls and members of different ethnic groups? This is a thorough and thoughtful analysis of these issues.

Munby, S., Phillips, P. & Collins, R. (1989). *Assessing and recording achievement*. Oxford, England: Blackwell.

> Students or teachers concerned with profiling or records of achievement should consult this book. It covers a number of related topics and includes a section on classroom approaches and ideas for teachers.

Murphy, R. & Torrance, H. (1988). *The changing face of educational assessment* Milton Keynes, England: Open University Press.

> This book consists of a series of chapters by different authors on a range of issues. It explores issues involved in the assessment of modules, graded testing and records of achievement. It is not a manual for teachers but a good first approach to a number of developments in testing.

Wood, R. (1991). *Assessment and testing*. Cambridge, England: Cambridge University Press.

> Students who wish to pursue any of the issues raised in this chapter should refer to Wood's book for more detailed consideration. It provides a thorough and wide-ranging review of the research on many topics.

17

Assessment, Teaching and Learning

Bryan Dockrell

Editor's Overview

In this chapter Bryan Dockrell continues his discussion of assessment, but with a focus on formative assessment, that is to say, assessment which is embedded in the teaching and learning programme and which is intended to help steer that programme towards the teacher's goals.

Formative assessment is intended to provide usable information, usable, that is, by teachers and learners.

Bryan Dockrell describes various techniques for collecting evidence, including

- observation
- teacher–pupil discussion
- questioning
- scrutiny of classwork.

He explains, using examples from a variety of classrooms and subjects, how assessment devices can be designed, administered, interpreted and related to teaching and learning. He also shows that the techniques can be applied to PSE as well as subject teaching, and that good-quality formative assessment can lead to gains in

- pupil learning progress
- pupil attitudes
- teaching efficiency

Introduction

How can assessment be used to improve learning and teaching? Learners need to know whether or not they are doing what is required of them if they are to learn at all, and they need to know what they are doing right and what they are doing wrong if they are to improve. Teachers need to know how effective a particular mode of teaching has been so that they can change it if need be. Teachers have always used their own assessments to provide learners with this kind of information, to recognize success and draw attention to errors and misunderstanding, and to improve their own teaching.

In Britain, more attention has been given to this formative use of assessment to improve teaching and learning since that publication of the report of the Task Group on Assessment and Testing (TGAT, 1987). A crucial recommendation was 'that the basis of the national assessment system be essentially formative . . . [and only] . . . at age sixteen . . . it should incorporate . . . summative functions' (para. 27). Certification was to continue at the upper end of secondary schooling, but assessment for the National Curriculum should be formative. The primary purpose of assessment was to be the provision of usable information about precisely what individual pupils could and could not do, so that pupils, parents and teachers could take appropriate action. In practice, though, much of the emphasis remains on the summative use of assessments.

A major part of this appropriate action involves teachers changing their teaching practices to meet the needs of their students. The importance of the formative use of teachers' assessments as a means of improving teaching is recognized. 'Teacher assessment lies at the heart of the learning progress in that new learning must be matched to what a pupil already knows and can do. It is the teacher in his/her classroom, day in day out, who undertakes this vitally important task of formative assessment' (SCAA, Key Stage 2, 1993, p. 24). The point is spelt out: 'Continuous teacher assessment is part of everyday teaching and learning. Sometimes activities naturally lend themselves to assessment, but at other times teachers will need to plan specific activities for assessment' (ibid., p. 24) It is this formative use of assessment that improves pupil performance.

The improvement comes from differentiation, that is, identifying the different needs of each pupil and not treating the class as an undifferentiated whole. Formative assessments tell teachers about the achievements of individual pupils as a basis for providing different approaches to teaching. Children thus progress at their own rate through the curriculum. Many teachers see differentiation in teaching and allowing children to progress as fast as they can as the key outcomes of formative assessment.

Do we need a structured system to achieve the improvement in learning that results from regular assessments? There is evidence, and it suggests that we do. Gipps and her colleagues (McCallum, McAlister, Brown and Gipps,

1993) studied the assessments made by primary school teachers in response to the demands of an experimental programme of assessment at the end of year two. They found that in classes where the system of teacher assessment required by the programme had been adopted 'children are given work on the basis of previously recorded assessment. The process becomes cyclical. Diagnostic assessment feeds into planning for individual, group and class activities' (ibid., p. 318).

There are similar findings at secondary level. A programme of research covering a substantial part of the secondary curriculum showed that the use of structured diagnostic assessments influenced teachers' teaching and, most important, improved students' learning (Dockrell, 1988). The assessments that teachers make, and the use that they make of those assessments, can improve learning substantially.

A Structured System in the Primary School

What does this mean in practice? The best evidence that we have of the impact of teachers' formative use of assessment is from the study of Gipps and her colleagues referred to above. This team investigated the response of teachers to the requirements of a new system of assessment. They found that one group of teachers, whom they called 'systematic planners', had incorporated the principles of formative assessment into the way they made their assessments and the use they made of those assessments. They set aside time specifically for assessment, some integrating their assessment with their teaching more than others, and 'the planned assessment of groups and individuals informs future task design and classwork' (p. 317). Teaching was what mattered, but they believed that 'continuous diagnostic assessment' made them more effective teachers.

All of these teachers spent a designated part of the week assessing. They recorded their assessments and explicitly used their results to guide their testing. However, they varied in the way they made their assessments. Some put more emphasis on 'specific activities for assessment', others relied more on evidence gathered in a variety of ways. The latter group did, though, record their assessments and used them to plan future work. The report quotes one teacher as saying, 'You're making some assessment of previous work because you have to assess in order to teach . . . whether they are ready to go on to the next stage' (p. 318), and they observed that 'children are given work on the basis of previously recorded assessment. The process becomes cyclical. Diagnostic assessment feeds into planning for individual, group and class activities' (ibid.).

This did not mean that the teachers had an elaborate system of testing which interfered with teaching. They chose what was appropriate in particular circumstances from a range of assessment techniques, some of them formal and some informal. They used the information that they gained both for formative purposes and to provide the evidence that they would need for their summative teacher assessments. The researchers reported that the techniques which were used by these teachers included

- observation
- open-ended questioning (the questions varying from child to child)
- teacher/pupil discussion
- running records
- scrutiny of classwork.

Do we need a formal analysis of what is to be learned to achieve the improvement in learning that results from regular assessments? Do we need to spell out the attainment targets with statements of attainment for each level as is done in Britain for the National Curriculum, or can we rely on a teacher's impressions of the general level of a pupil's attainments? The teachers in the Gipps study were quite clear. They did want to know 'what a pupil already knows and can do' in specific detail. Indeed they broke the prescribed statements of attainments down into smaller steps with 'descriptions of what a child might say or do to demonstrate attainment'. The researchers quote one teacher as saying, 'Even with Statements of Attainment there are still smaller steps. Like, the Statement of Attainment says "knows number facts to 10". But the steps before that in basic addition – there are all sorts of ways of going about that.'

These teachers have in mind the major purposes of assessment, the summative report and the formative feedback into their teaching. 'They see systematic diagnostic assessment as adding to their professionalism . . . stressing that they have teaching in mind but "teaching based on assessment done some time earlier. The greatest thing is to make notes so it informs your teaching"' (p. 320).

Not all teachers involved in the study used their assessments to inform their teaching. As the research team noted, 'the degree to which the groups of teachers used assessment results for formative purposes varied . . . systematic integrators, however, incorporated formative assessment into their weekly forecasts of work, while systematic planners used assessment to feed into individual and class planning on a daily basis' (p. 321).

Formative assessment needs a detailed breakdown of the learning task so that each element can be identified and assessed separately. It requires the specification of what would be adequate evidence of success or failure in that task. Finally, it requires the choice of the appropriate procedure or technique for assessing performance in relation to the defined outcome.

These three processes are illustrated in the work of the primary teachers. Much of the detailed definition had been done for these teachers by the National Curriculum, though they required even more detailed specification on at least some occasions. The teachers had to decide what was a satisfactory performance and what evidence they needed. Much of the early in-service and moderation exercises focused on these two points, what was a satisfactory performance and what evidence was needed.

A Structured System in the Secondary School

One substantial programme of work in the development of formative assessments for secondary schools is described in a series of publications (Black and Dockrell, 1984; Dockrell, 1988). In secondary schools the situation was different from that described by Gipps and her colleagues. Teachers did not have the advantage of an existing curriculum analysis stated in terms of learning outcomes, like that provided for primary teachers by the National Curriculum. For the most part the programmes that they followed contained only general statements of the content to be mastered and guidance about how it might be taught.

The teachers themselves had to make the analysis of the curriculum and had to define the learning outcomes. They decided that it would be impossible to assess all desirable outcomes, and chose instead to divide them into a core and extensions, those aspects of the curriculum which were essential and those which, though desirable, were not essential. They assessed formally only the core outcomes, those which they considered essential.

They had to devise appropriate ways of assessing each outcome. Like the primary school teachers, they used a wide range of techniques both formal and informal as the bases for their assessments. In the secondary schools, though, there was greater reliance on traditional forms of testing. The techniques they used included

- formal tests
- performance measures
- observational schedules
- essay marking scales
- attitude scales.

They also had to specify what level of performance was satisfactory. Since there was no great penalty in having false negatives, that is, requiring pupils who had mastered a concept or skill to do additional work, they generally set stringent standards. In some practical tasks they specified tolerances within which the product must fall. In written tests they usually permitted a maximum of one error in the five or more items that were used to assess a particular outcome.

These formative or diagnostic assessments were the work of groups of teachers supported by a team of researchers. The researchers worked collaboratively with teachers of geography, modern languages, home economics and technical studies to prepare a range of assessments. The researchers not only participated in the various stages of preparation of the assessment procedures and did most of the analyses of results; they also studied the use that the teachers made of them. The researchers observed how the assessments were used, how their use influenced the teaching, how it affected pupils' learning and how both teachers and pupils responded to their introduction.

The geography teachers already thought of their curriculum in terms of core and extensions, so they readily identified the core outcomes. For a unit on the environment they had prepared a test which covered the six core concepts. By breaking down the total score into components which related to each of these concepts, they were able to use the test to analyse the performance of each pupil. Instead of simply giving a total score, as they would have done in the past, and telling some pupils that they had done well, others that they were in the middle and the rest that they had done badly, they reported to each pupil their score for each of the concepts. In this way they were able to say to even the highest-scoring pupil, 'you did well but you seem to have a problem with this concept.' They were able to tell those in the middle where they had been successful and precisely where their problems lay. They were able to tell the pupils who had made the lowest scores that they had mastered some aspects of the curriculum but were having problems with others.

They had detailed information which they proceeded to use formatively. They provided all pupils with remedial help in those areas where they needed it, and with extension work when the remedial activities were completed.

Table 17.1 shows the results for one class. Failure to make a satisfactory score on a section of the test is marked ◯. Even the pupil with the highest score did not meet the criterion on every section and had some remedial work as well as extension activities. On the other hand the lowest achiever did meet the criterion for one section and could experience some success. By using the test formatively to determine exactly what was needed by each pupil, teachers focused their attention on the specific needs of each pupil, so that time and effort were not wasted on going over material which had already been mastered.

Teachers made a major switch to more individualized methods. There was less class teaching and teacher-led questioning, and more group work and individual work. Teachers guided and supervised learning, using materials that they had prepared in advance. The techniques were those of the laboratory or the practical class and less those of a class lecture.

When the test was readministered after the remedial activities twenty-three of the twenty-six pupils had now mastered some concept or concepts which they had not mastered initially. Nearly half of those who failed to acquire a concept first time had acquired it after the remedial instruction. There had been improvement on all sections of the test by at least some pupils, and two of the six concepts had now been mastered by all pupils. In total there had

Table 17.1 Feedback from a diagnostic test on the environment: the section scores of a class on the 'Environment' test

Pupil	Conservation	Vandalism	Dereliction	Man-affected environment	Natural environment	Pollution	Total
A	6	2	3	3	(2)	5	21
B	5	2	(2)*	4	(1)*	4	19
C	(4)*	(1)*	3	3	3	4	17
D	(3)*	(1)*	3	3	(1)*	5	16
E	5	2	3	3	(2)*	4	19
F	5	2	4	(2)	(2)*	4	19
G	(4)*	2	3	(2)	(2)*	5	18
H	6	2	4	3	(2)*	5	22
I	(4)*	3	3	3	(2)	5	20
J	5	2	3	(2)*	3	5	20
K	5	2	3	(2)*	3	5	20
L	(4)*	3	3	(1)	3	5	19
M	5	(1)*	4	4	4	5	23
N	5	2	4	3	(2)*	5	21
O	(4)*	2	4	3	4	5	22
P	(3)*	2	4	(2)	(2)*	(3)*	16
Q	5	2	4	3	(2)*	5	21
R	6	2	4	3	(2)*	5	22
S	5	2	3	(1)*	3	4	18
T	5	2	3	3	(2)	4	19
U	(4)*	3	3	(2)	3	4	19
V	(2)*	3	(2)*	(2)	3	4	16
W	5	2	3	3	(1)*	4	17
X	(0)*	2	(1)*	(2)	(2)*	(3)*	10
Y	(3)*	2	(2)	(1)	(1)*	(2)*	11
Z	(4)*	2	(1)*	(1)	(2)	4	14
Number of items in section	6	3	4	4	4	5	
Pass score	5	2	3	3	3	4	

○ Students failing to attain pass score.   * Fail modified to pass on post-remedial test.

been fifty-four failures to meet the required standard initially but after the remedial work that figure was reduced to twenty-six.

After this initial use in one school the test was reviewed by a group of teachers who had not been involved in its preparation and by the researchers. A number of items were revised and some were added to ensure that all the sections of the test assessed the given concept adequately. The process of testing, remedial activities and retesting was then repeated in a number of schools.

When the revised test and the remedial activities were used in other schools there were similar effects. The results for 500 pupils are given in table 17.2.

The assessments were designed to provide teachers with information which would allow them to identify the problems of individual pupils and decide what remedial work was necessary. However, it became clear that they could also be used to review the curriculum and the ways that it was taught. Some concepts were clearly more difficult than others. After the completion of the remedial work virtually all pupils had mastered the notions of vandalism, dereliction and pollution, but many had still not mastered the other three concepts: conservation, man-affected environment and natural environment. Should the curriculum be revised? Should the standard be one that everyone could reach, as with vandalism and pollution, or should it be higher? If the standard was to be one that everyone could reach, then conservation and the natural environment were too difficult. Formative assessment does not answer this question but does raise it.

The same issues were studied in the analysis of the assessments for another unit in the geography syllabus. The question of teaching was also addressed. The test was administered in a large comprehensive school with 12 year nine geography classes. They were mixed-ability classes, each taught by one of the five geography teachers in the school. This unit was concerned with settlement. A test similar to the one used in the environment unit described above was prepared and administered. Table 17.3 gives the results for the first administration of the test.

It is clear that service field is a relatively easy concept. Virtually all pupils managed to acquire it without remedial help. On the other hand uniformity in cities was difficult. In no class did half of the group master it, and in three classes less than a quarter did so. Spatial differences in cities was of middle difficulty. It was mastered by nearly all pupils in two classes and by over 60 per cent in all the others. These figures again raise the question of the appropriate difficulty level. Should all of the core concepts be within the grasp of all pupils, or should some be pitched at a level that only some could be expected to attain? What should be the level of difficulty?

The second question about teaching is raised most strikingly by the results for the concept of optimum site. In one class no pupil acquired the concept, in four others it was 10 per cent or fewer. Yet in one class three-quarters mastered it, and in two others more than half. The scores on the other part of the test show that it was not a general lack of ability on the part of the

Table 17.2 Percentage of pupils attaining mastery after remedial treatment following a diagnostic test

Test section	Number of pupils who failed pre-test	Number of these pupils who passed post-test	Percentage of pre-test failures showing post-test success
Conservation	130	57	44
Vandalism	29	16	55
Dereliction	55	36	66
Man-affected environment	121	43	36
Natural environment	136	48	35
Pollution	29	19	66
Whole test	500	219	44

pupils. Not did the problem lie with the teaching in general; it lay with the teaching of the specific concept. Classes L and R had been taught by the same teacher. She reflected on her teaching of the two classes and hypothesized a possible source of the problem. As a departmental group, the teachers reviewed their results and revised their lesson plans.

Another example of formative assessment is a test of German. In this test the teachers used the kind of mistakes the pupils made to reveal the nature of the problem. The use of the dative pronoun poses particular problems for British students. The teachers drew on their experience of teaching of this

Table 17.3 Percentage of students attaining given concepts in geography settlement unit

Class	Optimum site	Service field	Spatial differences in cities	Uniformity in cities
A	7	89	64	36
B	7	100	81	40
C	29	95	62	38
D	52	100	85	48
E	59	96	93	41
G	11	100	89	19
H	25	92	71	17
L	0	96	78	44
M	28	100	76	40
N	33	100	63	38
R	77	92	73	23
V	8	92	73	27

concept to hypothesize the nature of the errors that pupils made. When they should be using the dative plural students tended to use the masculine dative singular (error 1), the feminine dative singular (error 2) or the dative second person plural (error 3). The teachers prepared a test which gave a series of sentences with a section underlined. As can be seen from figure 17.1, the students had to select, from the four sentences provided, the one with the correct pronoun. In addition to the correct response, there were examples of each of the three common errors. In this case the teachers decided that more than one error in a particular area indicated a significant problem. Figure 17.1 gives an extract from the test and the key.

The test was administered about two-thirds of the way through the course. The pupils were given their scores but their tests were not returned to them. Some pupils had mastered the concept; others were showing a whole range of errors, but others were making specific errors as their teachers had hypothesized. During the following week, those who needed it were given remedial teaching based on the particular error or set errors revealed by the test. Those with no errors were given extension work. Table 17.4 gives the results of the initial administration of the test and of the repeated adminis-tration after the remedial work.

Most had improved, eliminating all or some of the errors that they had previously made. Some, like pupils B and G, had mastered the concept and now made no errors. Others, like pupils D and T, had eliminated some errors but were still making some. There were still some, like pupils A and E, who had made no improvement. Some of those who had made no errors in the first test, perhaps lulled by a false complacencey, made some errrors second time round. The changes are summarized in table 17.4. There were twenty-three specific errors the first time round. After the remediation no one made more than one type 1 error, so it was assumed that this error had been eliminated. Five pupils still made type 2 errors and four type 3 errors.

These teachers had prepared formative assessments which could be used to identify pupils' weaknesses and had used remedial activities to reduce if not eliminate those problems.

The Assessment of Attitudes

As was noted in the last chapter, education is concerned with knowledge and skills, but also with attitudes. A Scottish Education Department report on the curriculum in the secondary school had asserted that among the aims of schooling were those concerned with attitudes and values. Specifically, the report asserted that schools were, or should be, involved in helping pupils 'to be capable of co-operating with other people and forming relationships with them; to be tolerant and fair' and so on (Munn, 1977). If changing

Class III   Pronouns Test

If you replaced the underlined words by a pronoun, the correct answer would be A, B, C, D. Put a tick in the appropriate box.

1   Ich spiele mit <u>den Kindern</u>

   a   Ich spiele mit ihm
   b   Ich spiele mit ihr
   c   Ich spiele mit ihnen
   d   Ich spiele mit Ihnen

2   Wir gehen mit <u>den Madchen</u> spazieren

   a   Wir gehen mit ihnen spazieren
   b   Wir gehen mit ihm spazieren
   c   Wir gehen mit Ihnen spazieren
   d   Wir gehen mit ihr spazieren

3   Die Klasse sitzt vor <u>der Lehrerin</u>

   a   Die Klasse sitzt ihr
   b   Die Klasse sitzt vor Ihnen
   c   Die Klasse sitzt vor ihm
   d   Die Klasse sitzt vor ihnen

4   Der Junge ist bei <u>seinen Schwestern</u>

   a   Der Junge ist bei ihm
   b   Der Junge ist bei Ihnen
   c   Der Junge ist bei ihr
   d   Der Junge ist bei ihnen

KEY
   I – Error I
   II – Error II
   III – Error III
   * – Correct

5   Der Mann spricht mit <u>den Frauen</u>

   a   Der Mann spricht mit ihr
   b   Der Mann spricht mit ihm
   c   Der Mann spricht mit ihnen
   d   Der Mann spricht mit Ihnen

Figure 17.1 Extract from the test for the use of the dative plural in German and the item rationale for the whole test.

Table 17.4 Summary of pupil responses to a test for use of the dative plural in German

	Test 1				Test 2			
	Correct	Error 1	Error 2	Error 3	Correct	Error 1	Error 2	Error 3
Pupil A	6	0	0	3	7	0	0	2
B	6	0	0	3	9	0	0	0
C	1	3	3	2	5	1	3	0
D	4	2	2	1	6	0	2	1
E	5	0	0	4	5	0	0	4
F	4	3	2	0	6	1	1	1
G	5	0	3	1	9	0	0	0
H	9	0	0	0	8	0	0	1
I	5	1	1	2	6	0	1	2
J	3	0	4	2	5	0	3	1
K	5	0	0	4	8	0	1	0
L	9	0	0	0	7	0	2	0
M	9	0	0	0	8	0	1	0
N	3	0	3	3	7	0	1	1
O	1	4	1	3	8	1	0	0
P	9	0	0	0	9	0	0	0
Q	9	0	0	0	8	1	0	0
R	5	2	2	0	4	1	4	0
S	9	0	0	0	9	0	0	0
T	2	3	4	0	6	0	0	3
U	9	0	0	0	8	1	0	0

Notes 1 Only the nine items requiring a dative plural response are included in this analysis.
   2 Only pupils who took the test twice are included in this analysis.

pupils' attitudes is part of their purpose, teachers need to know whether they have been successful.

Two groups of teachers wanted to know whether or not they had succeeded in changing their pupils' attitudes to third world countries, whether their pupils now were more 'concerned for other people'. They prepared questionnaires designed to assess the attitudes of their classes. These teachers wanted to assess the impact of their teaching, just like those concerned with knowledge and skills discussed above. They therefore gave the questionnaires to their classes before and after the unit was taught, in order to measure change.

The first questionnaires told the pupils to 'imagine that your class has collected £20 to donate to charity. The money is to be given out in £5 units. Using the list of charities below, show how you would distribute your donations by putting one tick under each £5 opposite the charity of your choice.' The charities included cancer research, sports equipment for their own school and Help the Aged, as well as a range of third world charities. The questionnaire was administered to a year group of over 200 pupils. Even before the unit had been taught, third world charities were attracting a great deal of sympathy from the pupils. Seventy-nine per cent of them said that they would wish to contribute to health clinics for the third world. The provision of clean water had attracted the support of 71 per cent. After the unit had been taught, support for these two causes went up to 85 per cent and 84 per cent respectively. The teachers had changed attitudes as they intended. They had also increased their pupils' concern not only with the more obvious provision of medical services but with the more fundamental and perhaps superficially less attractive provision of supplies of clean water.

The questionnaire prepared by the second group of teachers was a little more complex. In this case the pupils were told that 'a world banking organization had set up a world cities improvement fund. Money is to be given to projects aimed at improving the quality of life in the cities of the world.' Two cities were described. One of them was called Slumsville, USA and the other Shanty Town, India. The instructions went on, 'the projects listed below are designed to help the two cities; decide which projects are the most urgent. Put them in order of importance in the boxes below.' The projects included the modernization of old houses in Slumsville, clean water for Shanty Town and restoring the ancient temples in Shanty Town. The three most popular causes before the unit was taught were all from Shanty Town, health clinics, clean water and helping the people to build their own simple houses. Ninety-four per cent of pupils had put at least one of these in their top three. That went up slightly to 96 per cent.

Those teachers now knew that they had influenced their pupils' attitudes in the way that they intended. They also knew that the children were already very sympathetic to the third world. They had to ask themselves whether their attempts to influence attitudes in this way were necessary. Perhaps their time could be spent more effectively in other ways. The crucial point is that attitudes can be assessed, and these assessments can be used to guide teaching.

Knowledge and attitudes should not be bundled into different compartments. They are related. In one study a questionnaire was combined with a test of knowledge to assess the impact of different ways of teaching young people about AIDS. Four schools had made different provision for covering this aspect of their personal and social education programme. Only one of those programmes affected pupils' knowledge and attitudes. When the combined test of knowledge and questionnaire about attitudes was administered before the unit was taught, these 14-year-olds showed that they were already well informed. There were gaps in their knowledge, and there were some widespread misapprehensions. Their attitudes to sexual relationships and their intentions about their future behaviour seemed likely to put them at risk of AIDS. After the unit had been taught there was no increase in knowledge, no correction of their misunderstandings and no change in attitudes or intentions in three of the schools. However, in the fourth school, more of the youngsters had an accurate understanding of AIDS, had more sympathetic attitudes to AIDS sufferers and had intentions about their future behaviour that were less likely to put them at risk. These teachers now knew what were the effects of different teaching programmes.

These are examples of formal assessments and attitude scales. Other groups of teachers used practical tasks, observational schedules, and essay-marking scales which they had devised to give them formative information (see Black and Dockrell, 1984). They too used that information formatively to modify their teaching and to improve pupil performance.

As with the primary schools described at the beginning of this chapter, formative assessment had an impact on secondary pupils and teachers. Pupils who had extended experience of formative assessment had a generally more positive attitude to assessment. Assessment was not seen as a weapon which teachers used against them but as a means of helping them to learn. They particularly appreciated getting feedback on the nature of their own particular problems and the help to overcome them.

The teachers who were involved in the work were virtually unanimous in seeing the benefits of the formative use of assessment. They thought that making pupils aware of their specific problems and their strengths made them more willing to seek help. They believed, too, that they could organize their teaching more effectively because they were aware of their pupils' problems.

Classrooms where teachers were using these formative assessments and a control group of classes where they were not being used were observed using a standard observation schedule. These studies showed substantial differences between classes where formative assessment was being used and those where it was not. In geography the amount of time devoted to teacher exposition reduced from 20 per cent of class time to 8 per cent. Instead they now spent 15 per cent of their time on individual work and more time was spent on pupils working together with other pupils, up from 5 per cent to 11 per cent. Perhaps because work of this kind was new, more time had to be spent receiving instructions from teachers, up from 9 per cent of time to 15 per cent.

Like most good curriculum development, preparation of good formative assessments is time-consuming. It became clear that individual teachers cannot be expected to prepare a set for a whole year's work on their own. Review of the assessment procedures is essential, and it can only be done with the participation of teachers in a number of schools. The teachers working on this project prepared sets of assessments and remedial activities which other teachers can use or adapt to their own needs, and which can be used as models for the preparation of additional assessments for other aspects of the curriculum.

Using Summative Examinations for Formative Purposes

A further formative use of assessment is provided by the A Level Information System (Fitzgibbon, 1992) This system provides teachers with information about their success in teaching for A levels. The pass rate provides crude information about success, but the ALIS system allows them to compare the results of their pupils with those of other students, similar in previous attainment as measured by GCSE, similar in ability as measured by a standardized test and similar in family background. It thus provides a fair comparison.

The system also provides formative information for teachers. Their teaching methods are compared with those of other teachers of their subject. They can compare the approach to learning and teaching in their classrooms with those of the teachers who obtained the best examination results at A level and with those who inspired their students to want to continue their study of the subject in higher education. They can see whether they have more or less class discussion than the most successful teacher, set more or fewer essays, provide more or less examination practice, and so on. Teaching can be a lonely profession, with teachers not knowing what their colleagues' practices are and with no feedback about the likely effectiveness of their own. The ALIS data on classroom processes do not provide a formula for effective teaching but do provide an opportunity for the reflective teacher to consider his or her own practice, not in the light of unsubstantiated impressions but of evidence. This is an example of the successful formative use of the assessments used for a different purpose.

Conclusion

This chapter began with a question. How can assessment be used to improve teaching and learning? The rest of the chapter has looked at three examples of the formative use of assessment. There are others to be observed in many primary and secondary classrooms. It seems clear from the systematic studies that the effort required to prepare and use formative assessment is worthwhile. These assessments can contribute substantially to the improvement of learning. Many more pupils can reach the levels now attained only by a minority. Testing by itself does not achieve these improvements. It is the use that teachers make of this additional information that achieves the results, but it is the assessment that shows what teaching is necessary.

Formative assessment makes new demands on teachers. Not only do they have to assess in new ways and analyse the results of their assessments more closely; many also have to change their existing classroom practice and acquire new skills. Its use raises new issues. For teachers it raises issues about the differentiation of teaching and how to provide for different rates of progression. There are issues for the design of the curriculum and about the level of difficulty of different aspects of the curriculum. Perhaps most important, it provides evidence about the effectiveness of different approaches to teaching.

Editor's Commentary

This commentary refers to chapters 16 and 17.

Like it or not, assessment has a considerable effect on teaching, learning and other processes of classroom interaction. It influences pupils' learning methods, their progress and their attitudes.

In his second chapter on assessment, Bryan Dockrell invites teachers to take control of these processes and use assessment to the good.

The principles of good assessment, whatever the method, remain constant. They include:

- Assessment should be designed with teaching and learning in mind.
- Assessment is a device for gathering evidence: it should be designed with that clear focus.
- The evidence should be carefully moderated and interpreted: its implications for action should be considered by teachers and pupils.
- The principles of assessment apply just as well to PSE as to academic subjects.

The ideas in these chapters should be linked to others in the book as follows:

- Chapter 4 shows how assessment influences learning, whether we like it or not.
- The professional development of teaching skills described in chapters 6, 7 and 8 relies critically on good evidence as to their effectiveness in promoting learning. The collection of appropriate evidence starts with the definition of objectives.
- Attempts to promote PSE and autonomous learning should be subject to assessment. The goals of PSE should be clear. These matters are treated in chapters 11 and 14.
- In chapter 12 the problem of providing for pupil diversity was raised. Assessment evidence is crucial in identifying the range of diversity for which provision should be made.

Teachers use assessment very informally and rarely capitalize on assessment evidence in systematic ways to look for efficiencies in teaching and effectiveness in learning. Working up assessment skills should be a major project for your professional development. You should follow up the ideas here with the following school-based projects:

- Find out what your school's assessment policy is and discuss its practical implementation with supporting teachers.
- From these chapters, draw up guidelines for the design of formative assessment devices. Discuss and revise your guidelines with other learner teachers and with experienced teachers.
- For a small learning programme in (1) an academic subject area and (2) a PSE topic, design an appropriate formative assessment procedure.
- Revise it in the light of discussion and then use it to assess pupils you have taught.
- Discuss with other teachers what lessons can be learned from the evidence collected above, and how they can be used to guide your subsequent teaching.
- In conjunction with your headteacher, discuss the types of summative assessment devices the school uses. Familiarize yourself with their administration and management. Find out about the rationale behind them and consider how far this relates to your teaching objectives.
- Discuss with pupils their reactions to formative and summative asssessment devices you have used.
- The matter of assessment raises the question of how best to keep records of assessment. Through discussion, clarify your views on why records are kept. Consider records made available to you. Do they meet the espoused purposes? How might they be amended to improve their utility?
- The development of autonomous learners requires that pupils play an active role in assessment. Using your checklist for quality-formative assessment, discuss with other teachers how pupils can be more actively involved.

FURTHER READING

Black, H. D., & Dockrell, W. B. (1984). *Criterion referenced assessment in the classroom*. Edinburgh, Scotland: Scottish Council for Research in Education.

> The studies of formative assessment in secondary classrooms referred to in this chapter are covered in more detail in this book. It explains what the various groups of teachers did and documents the effects of this approach on students' achievements and attitudes and on the ways teachers taught.

Black, H. D. & Dockrell, W. B. (Eds.). (1988). *New developments in educational assessment*. Edinburgh, Scotland: Scottish Academic Press.

> A number of the issues raised in this chapter are covered in more detail in this book, as are a number of other specialized issues.

Wolf, A. (1994). *Competence based assessment*. Buckingham, England: Open University Press.

Much of the assessment of vocational and pre-vocational attainments is now couched in terms of competences. In Britain, the US and Australia the emphasis is now on specific competences. This book describes the nature of competences and their assessment, but also reviews the problems involved.

References

Ainscow, M. & Tweddle, D. A. (1979). *Preventing classroom failure: An objectives approach.* Chichester, England: Wiley.

Alexander, R. (1984). *Primary teaching.* London: Cassell.

Alexander, R. (1991). *Primary education in Leeds.* Leeds, England: University of Leeds.

Alexander, R. (1992). *Policy & practice in primary education.* London: Routledge.

Alexander, R., Rose, J. & Woodhead, C. (1992). *Curriculum organisation and classroom practice in primary schools.* London: HMSO.

Alton-Lee, A & Nuthall, G. (1990). Pupil experiences and pupil learning in the elementary classroom: An illustration of a generative methodology. *Teaching & Teacher Education, 6,* 27–46.

Anderson, L. M. (1989). Classroom instruction. In M. C. Reynolds (Ed.), *Knowledge base for the beginning teacher.* Oxford, England: Pergamon Press.

Anderson, L. W. (1991). *Increasing teacher effectiveness.* Paris: UNESCO.

Anderson, L. W. & Block, J. H. (1987). Mastery learning methods. In M. J. Dunkin (Ed.), *International encyclopaedia of teaching and teacher education.* Oxford, England: Pergamon Press.

Arnot, M. (1987). Political lip-service or radical reform? Central Government responses to sex equality as a policy issue. In M. Arnot & G. Weiner (Eds.), *Gender and the politics of schooling.* London: Hutchinson.

Arnot, M. & Weiner G. (Eds.). (1987). *Gender and the politics of schooling.* London: Hutchinson.

Aronson, E. (1978). *The jigsaw classroom.* Beverley Hills, CA: Sage.

Aspy, D. N. & Roebuck, F. N. (1977). *Kids don't learn from people they don't like.* Amherst, MA: Human Resource Development Press.

Atkinson, R. C. & Shiffrin, R. M. (1968). Human memory: A proposed system and its control processes. In K. W. Spence & J. T. Spence (Eds.), *Advances in the psychology of learning and motivation* (Vol. 2). New York: Academic Press.

Atwell, N. (1987). *In the middle: Writing, reading, and learning with adolescents.* Upper Montclair, NJ: Boynton/Cook.

Austin, L. (1991). The impact of training on the quality of social interaction in cooperative groups. Unpublished MEd dissertation, University of Exeter, England.

Ausubel, D. P. (1968). *Educational psychology: A cognitive view.* New York; Holt, Rinehart & Winston.

Ausubel, D. P., Novak, J. D. & Hanesian, H. (1978). *Educational psychology: A cognitive view* (2nd ed.). New York: Rinehart & Winston.

Baddeley, A. D. (1990). *Human memory: Theory and practice.* London: Erlbaum.

Baddeley, A. D. & Hitch, G. (1974). Working memory. In G. A. Bowers (Ed.), *Recent advances in learning and motivation* (Vol. 8). New York: Academic Press.

Ball, D. L. (1990a) With an eye on the mathematical horizon: Dilemmas of teaching elemetary school mathematics. Paper presented at the annual meeting of the American Educational Research Association, Boston.

Ball, D. L. (1990b). The mathematical understandings that prospective teachers bring to teacher education. *The Elementary School Journal, 90*(4), 449–466.

Ball, D. L. (1991a). Research on teaching mathematics: Making subject-matter knowledge part of the equation. In J. Brophy (Ed.), *Advances in research on teaching* (Vol. 2). Greenwich, CT: JAI Press.

Ball, D. L. (1991b). Teaching mathematics for understanding: What do teachers need to know about subject matter? In M. Kennedy (Ed.), *Teaching academic subjects to diverse learners.* New York: Teachers College Press.

Ball, S. J. (1980). Initial encounters in the classroom and the process of establishment. In P. Woods (Ed.), *Pupil strategies: Explorations in the sociology of the school.* London: Croom Helm.

Ball, S. J. (1987). *The micropolitics of the school: Towards a theory of school organisation.* London: Methuen.

Barnes, D. & Todd, F. (1977). *Communication and learning in small groups.* London: Routledge.

Bassey, M. (1977). *Nine hundred primary school teachers.* Nottingham, England: Trent Polytechnic.

Beard, R. (1992). *Developing reading, 3–13.* London: Hodder & Stoughton.

Bennett, N. (1976). *Teaching styles & pupil progress.* London: Open Books.

Bennett, N. (1978). Recent research on teaching: A dream, a belief & a model. *British Journal of Educational Psychology, 48,* 127–47.

Bennett, N. (1982). Time to teach: Teaching–learning processes in primary schools. *Aspects of Education, 27,* 51–70.

Bennett, N. (1987) Cooperative learning: Children do it in groups – or do they? *Educational and Child Psychology, 3/4.* 7–18.

Bennett, N., Andreae, J., Hegarty, P. & Wade, B. (1980). *Open plan schools.* Windsor, England: NFER.

Bennett, N. & Carré, C. (Eds.). (1993). *Learning to teach.* London: Routledge

Bennett, N. & Cass, A. (1988). The effects of group composition on group interactive processes and pupil understanding. *British Educational Research Journal, 15,* 19–32.

Bennett, N. & Cass, A. (1989). *From special to ordinary schools: Case studies in integration.* London: Cassell.

Bennett, N. & Desforges, C. (Eds.). (1985). *Recent advances in classroom research.* Edinburgh, Scotland: Scottish Academic Press.

Bennett, N., Desforges, C. W., Cockburn, A. D. & Wilkinson, B. (1984). *The quality of pupil learning experiences.* London: Erlbaum.

Bennett, N. & Dunne, E. (1992). *Managing classroom groups.* London: Simon & Schuster.

Bennett, N., Dunne, E. & Austin, L. (1991). The impact of training on the quality of social interaction in cooperative groups. Paper presented at European Association for Research on Learning and Instruction conference, Turku, Finland.

Berliner, D. C. (1987). Simple views of effective teaching and a simple theory of classroom instruction. In D. C. Berliner & B. V. Rosenshine (Eds.), *Talks to teachers*. New York: Random House.

Best, R. (1991). Support teaching in a comprehensive school: Some reflections on recent experience. *Support for Learning,* 6(1), 27–31.

Biggs, J. (1990). Teaching for desired learning outcomes. In N. Entwistle (Ed.), *Handbook of educational ideas and practice*. London: Routledge.

Bikson, T. K. (1978). The status of children's intellectual rights. *Journal of Social Issues,* 34, 69–86.

Bissex, G. L. (1980). *Gnys at work: A child learns to write and read*. Cambridge, MA: Harvard University Press.

Black, H. D. & Dockrell, W. B. (1984). *Criterion referenced assessment in the classroom*. Edinburgh, Scotland: Scottish Council for Research in Education.

Blagg, N., Ballinger, M. & Gardner, R. (1988). *Somerset thinking skills*. Oxford, England: Blackwell/Somerset LEA.

Blenkin, G. & Kelly, A. (Eds.). (1983). *The primary curriculum in action*. London: Harper & Row.

Block, C. C. (1993). Strategy instruction in a literature based reading programme. *The Elementary School Journal,* 9(2), 139–152.

Bloom, B. S. (1956). *Taxonomy of educational objectives: The classification of educational goals. Handbook 1. Cognitive domain*. New York: Longmans, Green.

Bolton, N. (1989). Developmental psychology in the early years curriculum. In C. W. Desforges (Ed.), *Early childhood education*. Edinburgh, Scotland: Scottish Academic Press.

Booth, T, Swann, W., Masterton, M. & Potts, P. (Eds.). (1992) *Learning for all: Curricula for diversity in education*. London: Routledge.

Borg, W. R. & Ascione, F. R. (1982). Classroom management in elementary mainstreaming classrooms. *Journal of Educational Psychology,* 74(1), 85–95.

Bowles, S. & Gintis, H. (1976). *Schooling in capitalist America: Educational reform and the contradictions of economic life*. New York: Basic Books.

Boydell, D. (1975). Pupil behaviour in primary classrooms. *British Journal of Educational Psychology,* 45, 122–129.

Bradley, J. & Hegarty, S. (1981). *Students with special needs in FE*. London: FEU.

Brah, A. & Minhas, R. (1985). Structural racism or cultural difference. In G. Weiner (Ed.), *Just a bunch of girls*. Milton Keynes, England: Open University Press.

Brennan, J. & McGeevor, P. (1990). *Ethnic minority and the graduate labour market*. London: CRE.

Brennan, W. (1987). *Changing special education now*. Milton Keynes, England: Open University Press.

Brent, G. & DiObilda, N. (1993). Effects of curriculum alignment versus direct instruction on urban children. *Journal of Educational Research,* 86, 333–338.

Bricker, D. & Woods Cripe, J. (1992). *An activity-based approach to early intervention*. Baltimore: Paul Brookes.

Bristow, S. & Desforges, C. (1992). Working practices and children's application of subject knowledge in the primary school. Paper presented to the European Conference on Educational Research, Twente.

Broadfoot, P., Dockrell, W. B., Gipps, C., Harlen, W., & Nuttall, D. (1993). Policy issues in national assessment. *BERA Dialogues,* 7. Clevedon, England: Multilingual Matters.

Bronowski, J. (1973). *The ascent of man*. London: BBC Books.

Brophy, J. & Alleman, J. (1991). Activities as instructional tools in a framework for analysis and evaluation. *Educational Researcher,* 20(4), 9–23.

Brophy, J. & Good, T. (1974). *Teacher–student relationships: Causes and consequences.* New York: Holt, Rinehart & Winston.

Brown, A. & Reeve, R. (1987). Bandwidths of competence: The role of supportive contexts in learning and development. In L. S. Liben (Ed.), *Development and learning.* Hillsdale, NJ: Erlbaum.

Brown, A. L. & De Loache, J. S. (1978). Skills, plans and self-regulation. In R. S. Siegler (Ed.), *Children's thinking: What develops?* Hillsdale, NJ: Erlbaum.

Brown, G. & Wragg, E. C. (1993). *Questioning.* London: Routledge.

Brown, G., Cherrington, D. H. & Cohen, L. (1975). *Experiments in the social sciences.* London: Harper & Row.

Brown, G. & Desforges, C. (1979). *Piaget's theory: A psychological critique.* London: Routledge.

Brown, S., Collins, J. A. & Duguid, P. (1989). Situated cognition and the culture of learning. *Educational Researcher, 18*(1), 32–42.

Brown, S. & McIntyre, D. (1993). *Making sense of teaching.* Buckingham, England: Open University Press.

Bruner, J. (1966). *Towards a theory of instruction.* New York: Harvard University Press.

Bruner, J., Goodnow, J. J. & Austin, G. A. (Eds.). (1956). *A study of thinking.* New York: Wiley.

Bruner, J. & Haste, H. (1987). *Making sense.* London: Methuen.

Bullock Report. (1975). *A language for life.* London: HMSO.

Burgess, A. & Gulliver, J. (1989). Only chatter? Children talking and learning in primary schools. *English in Education, 22*(1).

Burt, C. (1955). The evidence for the concept of intelligence. *British Journal of Educational Psychology, 25,* 158–177.

Burns, R. B. (1984). How time is used in elementary schools: The activity structure of classrooms. In L. Anderson (Ed.), *Time and school learning.* Beckenham, England: Croom Helm.

Button, L. (1981). *Group tutoring for the form tutor: Vol. 1. The lower secondary school.* London: Hodder.

Button, L. (1982) *Group tutoring for the form tutor: Vol. 2. The upper secondary school.* London: Hodder.

Calderhead, J. (1984). *Teachers' classroom decision-making.* London: Holt, Rinehart & Winston.

Cambourne, B. (1988). *The whole story: Natural learning and the acquisition of literacy in the classroom.* Auckland, New Zealand: Ashton Scholastic.

Campbell, J., Emery, H. & Stone, C. (1993). The broad and balanced curriculum at Key Stage 2: Some limitations to reform. In BERA/ASPE policy paper: Research perspectives on the implementation of the National Curriculum at Key Stage 2.

Campbell, J., Evans, L., Neill, S. R. St J. & Packwood, A. (1991). *Workloads, achievement & stress.* Warwick: University of Warwick.

Campbell, J. & Neill, S. R. St J. (1992). *Teacher time and curriculum manageability at Key Stage One.* Warwick: University of Warwick.

Carlsen, W. (1991). Subject-matter knowledge and science teaching: A pragmatic perspective. In J. Brophy (Ed.), *Advances in research on teaching* (Vol. 2). Greenwich, CT: JAI Press.

Carpenter, B. (1992). The whole curriculum: Meeting the needs of the whole child. In K. Bovair & B. Carpenter, *Special curricular needs.* London: David Fulton.

Carpenter, P. T. & Moser, J. M. (1982). The development of addition and subtraction problem solving skills. In T. P. Carpenter, J. M. Moser & T. A. Romberg (Eds.), *Addition and subtraction: A cognitive perspective.* Hillsdale, NJ: Erlbaum.

Carraher, T. N., Carraher, D. W. & Schliemann, A. D. (1985). Mathematics in the streets and in schools. *British Journal of Development Psychology, 3*, 21–29.

Carré, C. (1993). Performance in subject matter knowledge in science. In N. Bennett & C. Carré (Eds.), *Learning to teach*. London: Routledge.

Carré, C. & Bennett, N. (1993). Subject matter matters. *Primary Science Review, 29*, 11–13.

Carré, C. & Ernest, P. (1993). Performance in subject matter knowledge in mathematics. In N. Bennett & C. Carré (Eds.), *Learning to teach*, London: Routledge.

Carré, C. & Ovens, C. (1994). *Science 7–11: Developing primary teaching skills*. London: Routledge.

Cato, V., Fernandez, C., Gorman, T. & Kispal, A. (1992). *The teaching of initial literacy: How do teachers do it?* Slough, England: NFER.

Central Statistical Office. (1990). *Social Trends 20*. London: HMSO.

Chapman, J. W., & Boersma, F. J. (1983). A cross-national study of academic self-concept using the Student's Perception of Ability Scale. *New Zealand Journal of Educational Studies, 18*, 69–75.

Chasty, H. (1993). A skills development approach to literacy. In *Proceedings of the British Dyslexia Association Conference, September 1993*. London: Hornsby International Centre.

Chi, M., Feltovich, P. & Glaser, R. (1981). Categorisation and representation of physics problems by experts and novices. *Cognitive Science, 5*, 121–52.

Chukovsky, K. (1963). *From two to five*. Berkeley, CA: University of California Press.

Clark, E. V. (1990). Children's language. In R. Grieve and M. Hughes (Eds.), *Understanding children*. Oxford, England: Blackwell.

Clark, M. M. (1976) *Young fluent readers*. London: Heinemann.

Claxton, G. (1984). *Live and learn: An introduction to the psychology of growth and change in everyday life*. Milton Keynes, England: Open University Press.

Clay, M. (1992). *The early detection of reading difficulties* (3rd ed.). London: Heinemann.

Clift, P. (1978). And all things nice . . . . Unpublished working paper, Open University.

Cobb, P., Wood, T. & Yackel, E. (1989). Young children's emotional acts while engaged in mathematical problem solving. In D. B. McLeod and V. M. Adams (Eds.), *Affect and mathematical problem solving: A new perspective*. New York: Springer-Verlag.

Cobb, P., Wood, T. & Yackel, E. (1991). A constructivist approach to second grade mathematics. In E. von Glasersfeld (Ed.), *Radical constructivism in mathematics education*. Dordrecht, Holland: Kluwer Academic.

Cockburn, A. D. (1986). An empirical study of classroom processes in infant mathematics education. Unpublished PhD. thesis, University of East Anglia.

Cockburn, A. D. (1992). *Beginning teaching*. London: Paul Chapman.

Cohen, D. (1983). *Piaget: Critique and reassessment*. London: Croom Helm.

Cohen, E. G. (1986). *Designing groupwork: Strategies for the heterogeneous classroom*. New York: Teachers College Press.

Cohen, M. (1980). Policy implications of an ecological theory of teaching: Towards an understanding of outcomes. In P. C. Blumenfeld et al. (Eds.), *Ecological theory of teaching*. Research report ETT 80–85. San Francisco: Far West Laboratory.

Connell, W. F., Stroobant, R. E., Sinclair, K. E., Connell, R. W. & Rogers, K. W. (1975). *Twelve to twenty*. Sydney, Australia: Hicks Smith.

Cooper, P. & Stewart, L. (1987). *Language skills in the classroom*. Washington, DC: National Education Association.

Cooper, P. & Upton, G. (1991). Controlling the urge to control: An ecosystemic approach to problem behaviour in schools. *Support for Learning, 6*(1), 22–26.

Coupe, J. & Porter, J. (1986). *The education of children with severe learning difficulties.* London: Croom Helm.

Cowie, H. & Rudduck, J. (1988). *Cooperative group work: An overview.* London: BP Educational Service.

Craig, I. (1990). *Managing the primary classroom.* London: Longman.

Craik, F. I. M. & Lockhart, R. S. (1972). Levels of processing: A framework for memory research. *Journal of Verbal Learning and Verbal Behaviour, 11,* 671–684.

Cruickshank, D. R. (1990). *Research that informs teachers and teacher educators.* Bloomington, IN: Phi Delta Kappa.

Damon, W. (1983). *Social and personality development.* London: Norton.

Davis, R. B. & McKnight, C. (1976). Conceptual, heuristic and S-algorithmic approaches in mathematics teaching. *Journal of Children's Mathematical Behaviour, 1,* 271–286.

Dean, J. (1983). *Organizing learning in the primary classroom.* London: Routledge.

DeCasper, A. & Fifer, W. (1980). Of human bonding: New-borns prefer their mothers' voices. *Science, 208,* 1174–1176.

deCharms, R. (1976). *Enhancing motivation: Change in the classroom.* New York: Irvington.

Deci, E. L. & Ryan, R. M. (1985). *Intrinsic motivation and self-determination in human behavior.* New York: Plenum.

Delamont, S. (1984). Sex roles and schooling. *Journal of Adolescence, 7,* 329–335

Delamont, S. (1990). *Sex roles and the school* (2nd ed.). London: Routledge.

Deliyanni-Kouimtzi, K. (1992). 'Father is out shopping because mother is at work': Greek primary school reading texts as an example of educational policy for gender equality. *Gender and Education, 4*(1–2), 67–80.

DeLoache, D., Sugarman, S., & Brown, A. (1985). The development of error correction strategies in young children's play. *Child Development, 56,* 928–939.

DES. (1975). *A language for life* (Bullock report). London: HMSO.

DES. (1978). *Primary education in England: A survey.* London: HMSO.

DES. (1984). *Middle schools.* London: HMSO.

Desforges, A. & Desforges, C. W. (1980). Number based strategies of sharing in young children. *Educational Studies, 6,* 97–109.

Desforges, C. W. (1993a). *Children as thinkers and learners.* London: British Association for Early Childhood Education.

Desforges, C. W. (1993). Children's learning: Has it improved? *Education, 3–13,* 1–8.

Desforges, C. W. & Bristow, S. (1993). Young children's procedures in using subject knowledge in maths and science. Paper presented at the Annual Conference of EARLI, Aix en Provence, August.

Desforges, C. W. & Bristow, S. (1995). Reading to learn in mathematics in the primary age range. In P. Ernest (Ed.), *Mathematics education and philosophy: On international perspectives (Vol. 2).* Lewes, England: Falmer Press.

Desforges, C. W. & Cockburn, A. D. (1987). *Understanding the mathematics teacher.* Lewes, England: Falmer Press.

Dewey, J. (1916–1964). The nature of subject matter. In R. Archambault (Ed.), *John Dewey on education.* Chicago: University of Chicago Press.

Dewey, J. (1938). *Experience and education.* New York: Collier Books.

DFE (1993). *Education Act 1993: Draft Code of Practice on the identification and assessment of special educational needs.* London: HMSO.

Dillon, J. (1988). *Questioning and teaching: A manual of practice.* London: Routledge.

Dillon, J. (1990). *The practice of questioning.* London: Routledge.

Dockrell, J. & McShane, J. (1992). *Children's learning difficulties: A cognitive approach*. Oxford, England: Blackwell.

Dockrell, W. B. (1988). *Achievement, assessment and reporting*. Edinburgh, Scotland: Scottish Council for Research in Education.

Donaldson, M. (1978). *Children's minds*. London: Fontana.

Donaldson, M. (1992). *Human minds: An exploration*. Harmondsworth, England: Penguin Books.

Doyle, W. (1977). Paradigms for research on teacher effectiveness. In L. Shulman (Ed.), *Review of research in education (Vol. 5)*. Itasca, TX: F. E. Peacock.

Doyle, W. (1980). *Student mediating responses in teacher effectiveness*. Denton, TX: North Texas State University.

Doyle, W. (1983). Academic work. *Review of Educational Research, 53* (2), 159–199.

Doyle, W. (1986). Classroom organisation and management. In M. C. Wittrock (Ed.), *Handbook of research on teaching*. New York: Macmillan.

Dreikurs, R., Grunwald, B. B. & Pepper, F. C. (1983). *Maintaining sanity in the classroom*. New York: Harper & Row.

Driver, R. (1983). *The pupil as scientist*. Milton Keynes, England: Open University Press.

Driver, R. (1989). The construction of scientific knowledge in school classrooms. In R. Millar, *Doing science: Images of science in science education*. Lewes, England: Falmer Press.

Driver, R. & Easley, J. (1978). Pupils and paradigms: A review of the literature related to concept development in adolescent science students. *Studies in Science Education, 5*, 61–84.

Driver, R., Guesne, E. & Tiberghien, A. (Eds.). (1985). *Children's ideas in science*. Milton Keynes, England: Open University Press.

Duffy, G. G. (1993). Teachers progress toward becoming expert strategy teachers. *The Elementary School Journal, 94*(2), 109–120.

Dunn, J. (1989). The family as an educational environment in the preschool years. In C. Desforges (Ed.), *Early childhood education*, Edinburgh, Scotland.: Scottish Academic Press.

Dunne, E. & Bennett, N. (1990). *Talking and learning in groups*. London: Macmillan.

Easley, J. & Easley, E. (1983). What's there to talk about in arithmetic? Paper presented to the Annual Meeting of the American Educational Research Association, Montreal, Canada, April.

Eccles, J. S., Midgley, C., Wigfield, A., Buchanan, C. M., Reuman, D., Flanagan, C. & MacIver, D. (1993). Development during adolescence: The impact of stage-environment fit on young adolescents' experiences in schools and in families. *American Psychologist, 48*, 90–101.

Edwards, A. & Westgate, D. (1987). *Investigating classroom talk*. London: Falmer Press.

Edwards, B. (1988). *Drawing on the artist within*. London: Fontana.

Edwards, D. & Mercer, N. (1987). *Common knowledge: The development of understandings in the classroom*. London: Methuen.

Elkjaer, B. (1992). Girls and information technology in Denmark: An account of a socially constructed problem. *Gender and Education, 4*(1–2), 25–40.

Ellington, H., Percival, F. & Race, P. (1993). *Handbook of educational technology* (3rd ed.). London: Kogan Page.

Englert, C., Raphael, T. & Andersen, L. (1992). Socially mediated instruction: Improving students' knowledge about talk and writing. *Elementary School Journal, 92*(4), 411–449.

Eraut, M. R. (Ed.). (1989). *The international encyclopaedia of educational technology*. Oxford, England: Pergamon Press.

Evertson, C. M. & Emmer, E. T. (1982). Effective management at the beginning of the year in junior high school classes. *Journal of Educational Psychology, 74* (4), 485–498.

Fagot, B. I. (1977). Consequences of moderate cross-gender behaviour in pre-school children. *Child Development, 13,* 166–167.

Feldman, D. H. (1980). *Beyond universals in cognitive development.* Norwood, NJ: Ablex.

Fisher, R. (1987). *Problem solving in the primary school.* Oxford, England: Blackwell.

Fisher, R. (1990). *Teaching children to think.* Oxford, England: Blackwell.

Fitzgibbon, C. T. (1992) Performance indicators. *BERA Dialogues 2.* Clevedon, England: Multilingual Matters.

Flavell, J. H. (1979). Metacognition and cognitive monitoring: A new area of cognitive-developmental inquiry. *American Psychologist, 34,* 906–911

Fogelman, K. (1978). School attendance, attainment & behaviour. *British Journal of Educational Psychology, 48* (2), 148–158.

French, J. & French, P. (1984). Gender imbalances in the primary classroom. *Educational Research, 26*(2), 127–36.

Froebel, F. W. (1887). *The education of man.* New York: Appleton.

Galloway, D. (1985). Pastoral care and school effectiveness. In D. Reynolds, *Studying School Effectiveness.* England: Falmer Press.

Galton, M. & Simon, B. (Eds.). (1980). *Progress and performance in the primary classroom.* London: Routledge.

Galton, M., Simon, B. & Croll, P. (1980). *Inside the primary classroom.* London: Routledge.

Galton, M. & Williamson, J. (1992). *Groupwork in the primary school.* London: Routledge.

Gardner, H. (1980). *Artful Scribbles.* London: Jill Norman.

Gardner, H. (1983). *Frames of mind: The theory of multiple intelligences.* New York: Basic Books.

Gardner, H. (1993). *The unschooled mind: How children think and how schools should teach.* London: Fontana.

Gelman, R. & Gallistel, C. R. (1978). *The child's understanding of number.* Cambridge, MA: Harvard University Press.

Gelman, R. & Shatz, M. (1977). Appropriate speech adjustments: The operation of conversational constraints on talk to two year olds. In M. A. Lewis & L. A. Rosenblum (Eds.), *Interaction, conversation and the development of language.* New York: Wiley.

Gersten, R., Woodward, J. & Darch, C. (1986). Direct instruction: A research based approach to curriculum design and teaching. *Exceptional Children, 53,* 17–31.

Gilbert, J. K. & Watts, D. M. (1983). Concepts, misconceptions and alternative conceptions: Changing perspectives. *Studies in Science Education, 10,* 61–98.

Gill, D. (1990). Response, on behalf of Hackney teachers to the National Curriculum History working Group Final Report. Unpublished submission to the DES.

Gipps, C. (1992). *What we know about effective primary teaching.* London: Tufnell Press.

Goldstein, H. (1987). Gender bias and test norms in educational selection. In M. Arnot & G. Weiner (Eds.), *Gender and the politics of schooling.* London: Hutchinson.

Golombok, S. & Fivush, S. (1994). *Gender development.* Cambridge, England: Cambridge University Press.

Good, T. L. (1981). Teacher expectations and student perceptions: A decade of research. *Educational Leadership, 38,* 415–422.

Good, T. L. (1983). Classroom research: A decade of progress. *Educational Psychologist, 18*(3), 127–144.

Good, T. L. & Beckerman, T. (1978). Time on task: A naturalistic study in sixth grade classrooms. *Elementary School Journal, 78*, 193–201.

Good, T. L. & Brophy, J. E. (1991). *Looking in classrooms* (5th ed). New York: HarperCollins.

Goodlad, J. (1984). *A place called school.* New York: McGraw-Hill.

Gorman, T., White, J., Brooks, G., Maclure, M. & Kispala, A. (1988). *Language performance in schools.* London: HMSO.

Gould, S. J. (1981–1992). *The mismeasure of man.* Harmondsworth, England: Penguin Books.

Graham, S. & Harris, K. R. (1993). Self-regulated strategy development: Helping students with learning problems develop as writers. *The Elementary School Journal, 94*(2), 169–182.

Graves, D. (1983). *Writing: Teachers and children at work.* Exeter, NH: Heinemann.

Gregory, E. (1993). What counts as reading in the early years' classroom? *British Journal of Educational Psychology, 63*(2), 214–230.

Groen, C. J. & Resnick, L. B. (1977). Can preschool children invent addition algorithms? *Journal of Educational Psychology, 69*(6), 645–652.

Grolnick, W. S. & Ryan, R. M. (1987). Autonomy in children's learning: An experimental and individual difference investigation. *Journal of Personality and Social Psychology, 52,* 890–898.

Gronlund, N. E. (1991). *How to write and use instructional objectives* (4th ed). London: Macmillan.

Grossman, P. M., Wilson, S. M. & Shulman, L. S. (1989). Teachers of substance: Subject matter knowledge for teaching. In M. C. Reynolds (Ed.), *Knowledge base for the beginning teacher.* New York: Pergamon.

Grugeon, E. (1993). Gender implications of children's playground culture. In P. Woods & M. Hammersley (Eds.), *Gender and ethnicity in schools: Ethnographic accounts.* London: Routledge.

Gulliford, R. & Upton, G. (1992). *Special educational needs.* London: Routledge.

Hadow Report on Primary Educatio. (1931). *Primary Education.* London: HMSO.

Haladyna, T. H., Nolen, S. B. & Haas, N. S. (1991). Raising standardized achievement test scores and the origins of test score pollution. *Educational Researcher, 20,* 2–7.

Hall, E. & Hall, C. (1988). *Human relations in education.* London: Routledge.

Hall, G. (Ed.). (1992). *Themes and dimensions of the National Curriculum.* London: Kogan Page.

Hall, N. (Ed.). (1989). *Writing with reason.* London: Hodder.

Halpern, D. F. (Ed.). (1992). *Enhancing thinking skills in the sciences and mathematics.* Hillsdale, NJ: Erlbaum.

Hargreaves, D. (1982). *The challenge for the comprehensive school.* London: Routledge.

Hargreaves, D. (1990). Making schools more effective: The challenge to policy, practice and research. *Scottish Educational Review, 22*(1), 5–14.

Hargreaves, D., Hester, H. K. & Mellor, F. J. (1975). *Deviance in classrooms.* Boston: Routledge.

Hargreaves, D. J. & Colley, A. M. (Eds.). (1986). *The psychology of sex roles.* London: Harper & Row.

Harris, S. & Rudduck, J. (1993). Establishing the seriousness of learning in the early years of secondary schooling. *British Journal of Educational Psychology, 63*(2), 322–336.

Hashweh, M. (1986) Toward an explanation of conceptual change. *European Journal of Science Education, 8*(3), 229–249.

Hashweh, M. (1987). Effects of subject matter knowledge in teaching biology and physics.

Teaching and Teacher Education: An International Journal of Research and Studies, 3(2), 109–120.

Hayes, N. (1984). *A first course in psychology.* London: Nelson.

Haylock, D. & Cockburn, A. D. (1989). *Understanding early years mathematics.* London: Paul Chapman.

Helmke, A. (1989). Affective student characteristics and cognitive development: Problems, pitfalls, perspectives. *International Journal of Education Research, 13*(8), 895–913.

Hertz-Lazorowitz, R. (1990). An integrative model of the classroom: the enhancement of cooperation in learning. Paper presented at the American Educational Research Association conference.

Hilsum, S., & Cane, B. (1971). *The teacher's day.* Slough, England: NFER.

HMI. (1978). *Primary education in England.* London: HMSO.

HMI. (1983). *9–13 middle schools: An illustrative survey.* London: HMSO.

HMI. (1989a). *Aspects of primary education: The teaching of mathematics.* London: HMSO.

HMI. (1989b). *The implications of the National Curriculum in primary schools.* London: HMSO.

HMI. (1991). *Six effective teachers.* London: HMSO.

HMI. (1992). *The new teacher in school.* London: HMSO.

Hoerr, T. (1992). How our school applied multiple intelligences theory. *Educational-Leadership, 50*(2), 67–68.

Holt, J. (1982). *How children fail* (Rev. ed.). New York: Delacort Press/Seymour Lawrence.

Houghton, S., Wheldall, K. Jukes, R. & Sharpe, A. (1990). The effects of limited private reprimands and increased private praise on classroom behaviour in four British secondary school classes. *British Journal of Educational Psychology, 60*(3), 255–265.

House of Commons. (1986). *ESAC third report: Achievement in primary schools* (Vol. 1). London: HMSO.

Hughes, J. N. & Hall, R. J. (1989). *Cognitive behavioural psychology in the schools.* London: Guildford Press.

Hull, R. (1985). *The language gap: How classroom dialogue fails.* London: Methuen.

Hunt, D. (1971). *Matching models in education.* Toronto, Canada: OISE.

Ingenkamp, K. H. (1977). *Educational assessment.* Slough, England: NFER.

Isaacson, Z. (1988). The marginalisation of girls in mathematics: Some causes and some remedies. In D. Pimm (Ed.). *Mathematics, teachers and children.* Sevenoaks, England: Hodder.

Jackson, P. (1968). *Life in classrooms.* New York: Holt, Rinehart & Winston.

James, W. (1899). *Talks to teachers.* London: Longman.

Jenkin, F. (1989). *Making small groups work.* Oxford, England: Penguin Educational.

Jenson, A. R. (1973). *Educational differences.* London: Methuen.

Johnson, D., & Johnson, R. (1975). *Learning together and learning alone.* Englewood Cliffs, NJ: Prentice Hall.

Johnson, D. & Johnson, R. (1985). The internal dynamics of cooperative learning groups. In R. Slavin (Ed.), *Learning to cooperate, cooperating to learn.* New York: Plenum.

Jones, A. (1993). Becoming a 'girl': Post-structuralist suggestions for educational research. *Gender and Education, 5*(2), 157–166.

Judson, H. F. (1980). *The search for solutions.* London: Hutchinson.

Kagan, S. (1985). In R. E. Slavin (Ed.), *Learning to cooperate, cooperating to learn.* New York: Plenum.

Kagan, S. (1988). *Cooperative learning: resources for teachers.* Riverside, CA: University of California.

Kail, R. (1984). *The development of memory in children* (2nd edn.). New York: Freeman.

Kameenui, E. J. & Griffin, C. C. (1989). The national crisis in verbal problem solving in mathematics. *Elementary School Journal, 89*(5), 575–593.

Kamii, C. K. (1985). *Young children reinvent arithmetic: Implications of Piaget's theory.* New York: Teachers College Press.

Kauffman, S. (1993). *The origins of order: Self-organisation and selection in evolution.* Oxford, England: Oxford University Press.

Kerry, T. (1993). Teachers learning differentiation through classroom questioning skills. *Journal of Teacher Development, 2*(2), 81–92.

King, R. (1978). *All things bright and beautiful?* Chichester, England: Wiley.

Klein, P. & Feuerstein, R. (1985). Environmental variables and cognitive development: Identification of potent factors in adult–child interaction. In Havel, S. and Anastasiow, N. (Eds.), *The at-risk infant: psycho-social-medical aspects.* Baltimore: Brookes.

Knight, B. (1989). *Managing school time.* Harlow, England: Longman.

Kohlberg, L. (1982). Recent work in moral education. In *The ethical dimension of the school curriculum.* Swansea, Wales: Pineridge Press.

Kohn, A. (1993). Choices for children: Why and how to let students decide. *Phi Delta Kappa, 75,* 9–20.

Kounin, J. S. (1983). *Classrooms: Individuals or behaviour settings.* Monographs in teaching and learning, No. 2. Bloomington, IN: University School of Education.

Kriegler, S. & Kaplan, M. (1990). Improving attention and reading in inattentive children through MLE: A pilot study. *International Journal of Cognitive Education and Mediated Learning, 1*(3), 185–192.

Kruger, C. & Summers, M. (1988). Primary school teachers' understanding of science concepts. *Journal of Education for Teaching, 14*(3), 259–265.

Kruger, C. & Summers, M. (1989). An investigation of some primary teachers' understanding of changes in materials. *School Science Review, 71*(255), 17–27.

Kruger, C., Summers, M. & Palacio D. (1990). An investigation of some English primary school teachers' understanding of the concepts force and gravity. *British Educational Research Journal, 16*(4), 383–397.

Kuhn, T. (1962–1970). *The structure of scientific revolutions.* Chicago: University of Chicago Press.

Kulik, C. C., Kulik, J. A. & Bangert-Drowns, R. L. (1990). Effectiveness of mastery learning programs: A meta-analaysis. *Review of Educational Research, 60*(2), 265–299.

Kulik, C. C., Kulik, J. A., Bangert-Drowns, R. L. & Morgan, M. J. (1991). Instructional effect of feedback in test-like events. *Review of Educational Research, 61*(2), 213–238.

Kutnick, P. & Jules, V. (1993). Pupils' perceptions of a good teacher: A developmental perspective from Trinidad and Tobago. *British Journal of Educational Psychology, 63*(3), 400–413.

Kyriacou, C. (1986). *Effective teaching in schools.* Hemel Hempstead, England: Simon & Schuster.

Kyriacou, C. (1991). *Essential teaching skills.* Hemel Hempstead, England: Simon & Schuster.

Kyriacou, C., and Wilkins, M. (1993). The impact of the National Curriculum on teaching methods at a secondary school. *Educational Research, 35*(3), 270–276.

Lane, C. (1990). Children's difficulties. In P. Pumpfrey & C. D. Elliot, *Reading, writing and spelling.* London: Falmer & Press.

Lather, P. (1991). *Getting smart: Feminist research and pedagogy within the postmodern.* New York: Routledge.

Lees, S. (1987). The structure of sexual relations in school. In M. Arnot & G. Weiner (Eds.), *Gender and the politics of schooling*. London: Hutchinson.

Leith, G. O. M. (1964). *A handbook of programmed learning*. Birmingham, England: Birmingham University, Educational Review Occasional Publications, No. 1.

Lemlech, J. K. (1988). *Classroom management*. London: Longman.

Levin, B. (1993). *Democracy and education, students and schools*. Paper presented to the Seven Oaks School Division Symposium Series, Winnipeg, Canada, January.

Licht, B. G. & Dweck, C. S. (1987). Sex differences in achievement orientations. In M. Arnot & G. Weiner (Eds.), *Gender and the politics of schooling*. London: Hutchinson.

Lipman, M. (1988). *Philosophy goes to school*. Philadelphia: Temple University Press.

Lipman, M. (Ed.). (1993). *Thinking children and education*. Cambridge, England: Cambridge University Press.

Lipman, M., Sharp, A. & Oscanyan, F. (1980). *Philosophy in the classroom* (2nd ed.). Philadelphia: Temple University Press.

Mac an Ghaill, M. (1988). *Young, gifted and black: Student–teacher relations in the schooling of black youth*. Milton Keynes, England: Open University Press.

Mac an Ghaill, M. (1993). Beyond the white norm: The use of qualitative methods in the study of black youths' schooling in England. In P. Woods & M. Hammersley (Eds.), *Gender and ethnicity in schools: Ethnographic accounts*. London: Routledge.

McCallum, B., McAlister, S., Brown, M. & Gipps, C. (1993). Teacher assessment at Key Stage one. *Research Papers in Education, 8*(1), 305–329.

Maccoby, E. M. & Jacklin, C. N. (1974). *The psychology of sex differences*. London: Oxford University Press.

McDiarmid, G. W., Ball, D. & Anderson, C. (1989). Why staying one chapter ahead doesn't really work: Subject specific pedagogy. In M. Reynolds (Ed.), *Knowledge base for beginning teachers*. Oxford, England: Pergamon Press.

Maclure, S. & Davies, P. (Eds.). (1991). *Learning to think: Thinking to learn*. Oxford, England: Pergamon Press.

McNeil, L. M. (1986). *Contradictions of control: School structure and school knowledge*. New York: Routledge.

Malcolm, N. (1964). Behaviorism as a philosophy of psychology. In T. W. Wann (Ed.), *Behaviorism and phenomenology*. Chicago: University of Chicago Press.

Markus, H. & Wurf, E. (1987). The dynamic self-concept: A social psychological perspective. *Annual Review of Psychology, 38*, 299–337.

Marsh, H. & Shavelson, R. (1985). Self-concept: Its multifaceted, hierarchical structure. *Educational Psychologist, 20*, 103–123.

Marshall, H. H. (1988). Work or learning: Implications of classroom metaphors. *Educational Researcher, 17*, 9–16.

Marx, R. W. & Winne, P. H. (1981). Students' views of how teachers want them to think. Paper presented at the annual meeting of the American Educational Research Association, New York, March.

Maslow, A. H. (1970). *Motivation and personality*. New York: Harper & Row.

Mayer, R. E. (1987). *Educational psychology: A cognitive approach*. Boston: Little, Brown.

Mead, G. (1934). *Mind, self and society*. Chicago: University of Chicago Press.

Meadows, S. & Cashdan, A. (1988). *Helping children learn: Contributions to a cognitive curriculum*. London: David Fulton.

Measor, L. & Sikes, P. J. (1992). *Gender and schools*. London: Cassell.

Mercer, N., & Fisher, E. (1992). How do teachers help their children to learn? An analysis of teachers' interventions in computer-based activities. *Learning and Instruction, 2*, 339–355.

Merrett, F. & Tang, W. M. (1994). The attitudes of British primary school pupils to praise, rewards, punishments and reprimands. *British Journal of Educational Psychology*, 64(1), 91–103.

Meyer, J. W., Kamens, D. H. & Benavot, A. (1992). *School knowledge for the masses: World models of national primary curricular categories in the twentieth century.* London: Falmer Press.

Millar, R. & Driver, R. (1987). Beyond processes. *Studies in Science Education, 14,* 31–62.

Milner, D. (1983). *Children and race: Ten years on.* London: Ward Lock Educational.

Montague, W. E. & Knirk, F. G. (1993). What works in adult instruction: Introduction. *International Journal of Educational Research, 19,* 333–344.

Montessori, M. (1912–1965). *The Montessori method.* New York: Schoken Books.

Montgomery, D. (1990). *Children with learning difficulties.* London: Cassell.

Moore, J. (1992). Good planning is the key. *British Journal of Special Education,* 19(1), 16–19.

Morgan, N. & Saxton, J. (1991). *Teaching, questioning and learning.* London: Routledge.

Mortimore, P., Sammons, P., Ecob, R. & Stoll, L. (1988). *School matters: The junior years.* Salisbury, England: Open Books.

Mortimore, P., Sammons, P., Lewis, D., Ecob, R. & Stoll, L. (1989). A study of effective junior schools. *International Journal of Education Research, 13*(7), 753–768.

Mortimore, P., Sammons, P., Stoll, L., Lewis, D. & Ecob, R. (1988). *School Matters.* London: Open Books.

Morrison, K. & Ridley, K. (1988). *Curriculum planning and the primary school.* London: Paul Chapman.

Munn, J. (1977). *The structure of the curriculum.* Edinburgh. Scotland: HMSO.

Munn, N. L. (1961). *Psychology: The fundamentals of human adjustments.* New York: Harrap.

Nash, S. C. (1979). Sex role as mediator of intellectual functioning. In M. A. Wittig & A. C. Petersen (Eds.), *Sex related differences in cognitive functioning.* Orlando, FL: Academic Press.

National Curriculum Council (NCC). (1989a). *Circular No. 6.* London: National Curriculum Council.

National Curriculum Council (NCC). (1989b) *English in the National Curriculum, Key stage one.* York, England: NCC.

National Curriculum Council (NCC). (1989c). *Interim whole curriculum committee report to the Secretary of State.* London: NCC.

National Curriculum Council (NCC). (1990). *Curriculum guidance No. 2: A curriculum for all.* York, England: NCC.

National Curriculum Council (NCC). (1991). *Curriculum guidance No. 3: The whole curriculum.* York, England: NCC.

National Curriculum Council (NCC). (1993). The National Curriculum at Key Stages 1–2. York, England: NCC.

National Oracy Project. (1990). *Teaching, talking and learning in Key Stage one.* York, England: NCC.

Neill, A. S. (1960). *Summerhill: A radical approach to child rearing.* New York: Hart.

Nias, J. (1989). *Primary teachers talking.* London: Routledge.

Nias, J., Southworth, G. & Yeomans, R. (1989). *Staff relationships in the primary school: A study of organizational cultures.* London: Cassell.

Nichol, J. & Mason, S. (1991). *Thinking history: Medieval realms.* Oxford, England: Blackwell.

Nicholls, J. (1979). Development of perception of attainment and causal attributes for success and failure in reading. *Journal of Educational Psychology, 71*, 94–9.

Nicholls, J. (1989). *The competitive ethos and democratic education*. Cambridge, MA: Harvard University Press.

Nicholls, J. & Hazzard, S. P. (1993). *Education as adventure: Lessons from the second grade*. New York: Teachers College Press.

Nickerson, R. S., Perkins, D. N. & Smith, E. E. (1985). *The teaching of thinking*. Hillsdale, NJ: Erlbaum.

Nisbet, J. & Shucksmith, J. (1986). *Learning strategies*. London: Routledge.

Nolen, S. B. (1988). Reasons for studying: Motivational orientations and study strategies. *Cognition and Instruction, 5*, 269–287.

Nolen, S. B. & Haladyna, T. M. (1990). Personal and environmental influences on students' beliefs about effective study strategies. *Contemporary Educational Psychology, 15*, 116–130.

Norman, K. (Ed.). (1992). *Thinking voices*. London: Hodder.

Norwich, B. (1990). *Re-appraising special needs education*. London: Cassell.

Notari, A., Cole, K. & Mills, P. (1992). Facilitating cognitive and language skills of young children with disabilities – the mediated learning programme. *International Journal of Cognitive Education and Mediated Learning, 2*(2), 169–179.

Nunes, T., Schliemann, A. D. & Carraher, D. W. (1993). *Street mathematics and school mathematics*. Cambridge, England: Cambridge University Press.

OFSTED. (1993a). *Curriculum organisation and classroom practice in primary schools: A follow-up report*. London: HMSO.

OFSTED. (1993b). *The teaching and learning of number in primary schools*. London: HMSO.

Oliver, M. (1993). Re-defining disability: A challenge to research. In J. Swain, V. Finkelstein, S. French & M. Oliver (Eds.), *Disabling barriers – enabling environments*. London: Sage.

Ornstein, A. C. (1990). *Strategies for effective teaching*. New York: Harper & Row.

Palincsar, A. & Brown, A. (1984). Reciprocal teaching of comprehension-fostering and comprehension-monitoring activities. *Cognition and Instruction, 1*, 117–175.

Parffrey, V. (1993). Exclusion: Failed children or systems failure? Paper presented at the annual conference of Educational and Child Psychologists, Torquay, British Psychological Society.

Peck, A. J. (1988). *Language teachers at work*. London: Prentice Hall.

Peterson, P. et al. (1984). *The social context of instruction*. New York: Academic Press.

Phoenix, A. (1987). Theories of gender and black families. In G. Weiner & M. Arnot (Eds.), *Gender under scrutiny*. London: Hutchinson.

Piaget, J. (1932). *The moral judgement of the child*. London: Routledge.

Piaget, J. (1959). *The language and thought of the child* (3rd ed.). London: Routledge.

Piaget, J. (1973). *To understand is to invent: The future of education*. New York: Grossman.

Pintrich, P., Cross, D., Kozma, R. & McKeachie, W. (1986). Instructional psychology. *Annual Review of Psychology, 37*, 611–651.

Pintrich, P. & DeGroot, E. (1990). Motivational and self-regulated learning components of classroom academic performance. *Journal of Educational Psychology, 82*, 33–40.

Plowdon Report. (1967). *Children and their primary schools*. London: HMSO.

Pole, C. J. (1993). *Assessing and recording achievement*. Buckingham, England: Open University Press.

Pollard, A., Broadfoot, P., Croll, P., Osborn, M. & Abbott, D. (1994). *Changing English primary schools*. London: Cassell.

Postlethwaite, T. N. & Ross, K. N. (1992). *Effective schools in reading*. The Hague, Holland: International Association for the Evaluation of Educational Achievement.

Prawat, R. S. (1989). Promoting access to knowledge, strategy and disposition in students: A research synthesis. *Review of Educational Research, 59*(1), 1–41.

Pressley, M., Goodchild, F., Fleet, J., Zajchowsky, R. & Evans, D. (1989). The challenges of classroom strategy instruction. *The Elementary School Journal, 89*(3), 301–335.

Pring, R. (1984). *Personal and social education in the curriculum*. London: Hodder.

Proctor, C. P. (1984). Teacher expectations: A model for school improvement. *Elementary School Journal*, 469–481.

Qualter, A., Strang, J., Swatton, P. & Taylor, R. (1990). *Exploration: A way of learning science*. Oxford, England: Blackwell.

Ramasut, A. & Reynolds, D. (1993). Developing effective whole school approaches to special educational needs: From school effectiveness theory to school development practice. In R. Slee (Ed.), *Is there a desk with my name on it? The politics of integration*. London: Falmer Press.

Raybould, T. & Solity, J., (1980). Teaching with precision: Special education. *Forward Trends, 9*(2), 9–13.

Reason, P. (1988). *Human inquiry in action*. London: Sage.

Resnick, L. B. (1987). Learning in school and out. *Educational Researcher, 16*(9), 13–20.

Reynolds, D. (1982). The search for effective schools. *School Organization, 2*(3), 215–237.

Reynolds, D. & Sullivan, M. (1987). *The comprehensive experiment*. Lewes, England: Falmer Press.

Rigby, C. S., Deci, E. L., Patrick, B. C. & Ryan, R. M. (1992). Beyond the intrinsic–extrinsic dichotomy: Self-determination in motivation and learning. *Motivation and Emotion, 16*, 165–185.

Rizvi, F. (1993). Critical introduction: Researching racism in education. In B. Troyna, *Racism and education*. Buckingham, England: Open University Press.

Robertson, J. (1981). *Effective classroom control*. London: Hodder.

Roehler, L. R. & Duffy, G. G. (1986). What makes one teacher a better explainer than another. *Journal of Education for Teaching, 2*, 273–284.

Rogers, C. (1983). *Freedom to learn for the '80s*. London: Merrill.

Rogers, P. (1979). *The New History: Theory into practice*. Teaching of history series, No. 44. London: Historical Association.

Rosenshine, B. (1987). Direct instruction. In M. J. Dunkin (Ed.), *The international encyclopaedia of teaching and teacher education*. Oxford, England: Pergamon Press.

Rosenshine, B. & Stevens, R. (1986). Teaching functions. In M. C. Wittrock (Ed.), *Handbook of research on teaching*. New York: Macmillan.

Rowntree, D. (1989). *Learning how to study* (3rd ed.). London: MacDonald.

Rutter, M., Maughan, B., Mortimore, P. & Ouston, J. (1979). *Fifteen thousand hours: Secondary schools and their effects on children*. London: Open Books.

Ryle, G. (1949). *The concept of mind*. Harmondsworth, England: Penguin Books.

Said, E. (1978–1991). *Orientalism: Western conceptions of the Orient*. Harmondsworth, England: Penguin Books.

Salame, P. & Baddeley, A. D. (1982). Disruption of short-term memory by unattended speech: Implications for the structure of working memory. *Journal of Verbal Learning and Verbal Behaviour, 21*, 150–164.

Säljö, R. & Wyndhamn, J. (1990). Problem solving, academic performance and situated reasoning: A study of joint cognitive activity in the formal setting. *British Journal of Educational Psychology, 60*(3), 245–254.

Sarup, M. (1986). *The politics of multiracial education*. London: Routledge.

Saunders, T. (Ed.). (1987). *Plato: Early Socratic dialogues*. Harmondsworth, England: Penguin.

Saxe, G. B. (1988). Candy selling and maths learning. *Educational Research, 17*(6), 14–21.

SCAA. (1993). *School Assessment Folder*. London: School Curriculum and Assessment Authority.

Schiefele, U. (1991). Interest, learning, and motivation. *Educational Psychologist, 26*, 299–324.

Schoenfeld, A. H. (1989). When good teaching leads to bad results: The disasters of 'well-taught' mathematics courses. *Educational Psychologist, 23*, 145–166.

Schwab, J. (1964). The structure of the disciplines: Meanings and significances. In G. Ford and L. Purgo (Eds.), *The structure of knowledge and the curriculum*. Chicago: Rand McNally.

Schwab, J. (1978). *Science, curriculum, and liberal education*. Chicago: University of Chicago Press.

Scott-Hodgetts, R. (1986). 'Girls and mathematics: The negative implications of success. In L. Burton (Ed.), *Girls into maths can go*. London: Holt, Rinehart & Winston.

Sellack, R. (1972). *English primary education and the progressives*. London: Routledge.

Serbin, L. A. (1978). Teachers, peers and play preferences. In B. Sprung (Ed.), *Perspectives in non-sexist early childhood education*. New York: Teachers College Press.

Sharron, H. (1987). *Changing children's minds: Feuerstein's revolution in the teaching of intelligence*. Bristol, England: Souvenir Press.

Shavelson, R. & Bolus, R. (1982). Self-concept: The interplay of theory and methods. *Journal of Educational Psychology, 73*, 3–17.

Shuell, T. J. (1988). The role of the student in learning from instruction. *Contemporary Educational Psychology, 13*, 276–295.

Shulman, L. (1986). Those who understand: Knowledge growth in teaching. *Educational Researcher, 15*(2), 4–14.

Shulman, L. (1987). Knowledge and teaching: Foundations of the new reform. *Harvard Educational Review, 57*(1), 1–22.

Shulman, M. (1991). *The passionate mind*. New York: Free Press.

Shultz, J. & Florio, S. (1979). Stop and freeze: The negotiation of social and physical space in a kindergarten/first grade classroom. *Anthropology and Education Quarterly, 10*(3), 166–181.

Siegler, R. S. (1978). The origins of scientific reasoning. In R. S. Siegler (Ed.), *Children's thinking: What develops?* Hillsdale, NJ: Erlbaum.

Siekerk, J. (1988). Teaching children to become autonomous learners. Unpublished manuscript, Arizona State University West, Phoenix, AZ.

Sikes, J. (1971). Differential behaviour of male and female teachers with male and female students. Unpublished doctoral dissertation, University of Texas at Austin.

Simon, B. & Willcocks, J. (Eds.). (1981). *Research and practice in the primary classroom*. London: Routledge.

Skinner, B. F. (1938). *The behavior of organisms: An experimental analysis*. New York: Appleton-Century-Crofts.

Skinner, B. F. (1964). Behaviorism at fifty. In T. W. Wann (Ed.), *Behaviorism and phenomenology*. Chicago: University of Chicago Press.

Slavin, R. E. (1987). Developmental and motivational perspectives on co-operative learning: A reconciliation. *Child Development, 58*, 1161–1167.

Slavin, R. E. (1991). *Educational psychology*. (3rd ed.). Boston: Allyn & Bacon.

Smith, M. L. (1992). Put to the test: The effects of external testing on teachers. Educational Researcher, 20(5), 2–7.

Smith, P. K. & Cowie, H. (1991). *Understanding children's development* (2nd ed.). Oxford, England: Blackwell.

Snow, R. E. (1989). Aptitude, instruction and individual development. *International Journal of Education Research, 13*(8), 869–881.

Soder, M. (1981). School integration of the mentally retarded. In CERI, *The Education of the Handicapped Adolescent*. Paris: OECD.

Soder, M. (1992). Disability as a social construct: The labelling approach revisited. In Booth et al. (Eds.), *Learning for all: Policies for diversity in education*. London: Routledge.

Sozniak, L. A. & Perlman, C. L. (1990). Secondary education by the book. *Journal of Curriculum Studies, 22*, 427–442.

Spender, D. (1980). *Man made language*. London: Routledge.

Spender, D. & Sarah, E. (1980). *Learning to lose: Sexism and education*. London: Women's Press.

Splitter, L. & Sharp, A. (in press). *The classroom community of inquiry: Teaching for better thinking*. Australian Council for Educational Research.

Springer, S. P. & Deutsch, G. (1981). *Left brain, right brain*. San Francisco: Freeman.

Stallings, J. A. (1975). Relationships between classroom instructional practices and child development. Paper presented at AERA Conference, Washington, DC.

Stanley, J. (1993). Sex and the quiet school girl. In P. Woods & M. Hammersley (Eds.), *Gender and ethnicity in schools: Ethnographic accounts*. London: Routledge.

Stanworth, M. (1983). *Gender and schooling: A study of sexual divisions in the classroom*. London: Hutchinson.

Steiner, R. (1926). *The essentials of education*. London: Anthroposophical.

Stobart, G., Elwood, J. & Quinlan, M. (1992). Gender bias in examinations: How equal are the opportunities? *British Journal of Educational Research, 18*(3), 261–276.

Stodolsky, S. S. (1981). Subject matter constraints on the ecology of classroom instruction. Paper presented to the annual meeting of the American Educational Research Association.

Stodolsky, S. S. (1988). *The subject matters: Classroom activity in math and social studies*. Chicago: University of Chicago Press.

Stone, M. (1981). *The education of black children in Britain: The myth of multiracial education*. London: Fontana.

Sugden, D. (1992). PE: Movement in the right direction. In K. Bovair, B. Carpenter & G. Upton (Eds.), *Special curricula needs*. London: David Fulton (NASEN).

Sulzby, E. (1988). A study of children's early reading development. In A. Pellegrini (Ed.), *Psychological bases for early education*. Chichester, England: Wiley.

Sutherland, P. (1992). *Cognitive development today: Piaget and his critics*. London: Paul Chapman.

Tann, C. S. (Ed.). (1988). *Developing topic work in the primary school*. Basingstoke, England: Falmer Press.

Task Group on Assessment and Testing (TGAT). (1987). *A report*. London: Department of Education and Science.

Thacker, J. (1993). A collaborative school culture in action. Unpublished internal report, University of Exeter, England.

Thacker, J., Stoate, P. & Feest, G. (1992). *Group work skills: Using group work in the primary classroom*. Crediton, England: Southgate.

Tharp, R. & Gallimore, R. (1988). A theory of teaching as assisted performance. In R. Tharp & R. Gallimore (Eds.), *Rousing minds to life: Teaching, learning and schooling in social context*. New York: Cambridge University Press.

Thickpenny, J. & Howie, D. (1990). Teaching thinking skills to deaf adolescents: The implementation and evaluation of instrumental enrichment. *International Journal of Cognitive Education and Mediated Learning, 1*(3), 193–210.

Thorkildsen, T. (1992). Establishing a moral atmosphere in school: Don't forget to listen! Paper presented at the annual conference of the Association for Moral Education, Toronto, Canada, November.

Thorkildsen, T. & Nicholls, J. G. (1991). Students' critiques as motivation. *Educational Psychologist, 26*, 347–368.

Thorkildsen, T., Nolen, S. B. & Fournier, J. (1994). What is fair? Children's critiques of practices that influence motivation. *Journal of Educational Psychology, 86.*

Thorndike, E. L. (1913). *The psychology of learning.* New York: Teachers College Press.

Tizard, B., Blatchford, P., Burke, J., Farquhar, C. & Plewis, I. (1988). *Young children at school in the inner city.* London: Erlbaum.

Tolman, E. C. (1932). *Purposive behavior in animals and men.* New York: Appleton-Century-Crofts.

Tomlinson, P. (1985). Matching learning and teaching: The interactive approach in educational psychology. In N. Entwistle (Ed.), *New directions in educational psychology: 1. Learning and teaching.* London: Falmer Press.

Topping, K. J. & Lindsay, G. A. (1992). Paired reading: A review of the literature. *Research Papers in Education, 7*, 199–246.

Torrey, J. W. (1973). Learning to read without a teacher. In F. Smith (Ed.), *Psycholinguistics and reading.* New York: Holt, Rinehart & Winston.

Treisman, A. M. (1964). Monitoring and storage of irrelevant messages in selective attention. *Journal of Verbal Learning and Verbal Behaviour, 3*, 449–459.

Troyna, B. & Hatcher, R. (1992). *Racism in children's lives.* London: Routledge.

Valencia, S. W. & Calfee, R. (1990). The development and use of literacy portfolios for students, classes, and teachers. *Applied Measurement in Education, 4*, 333–345.

Voss, J. F. (1987). Learning and transfer in subject matter learning: A problem solving model. *International Journal of Educational Research, 11*(6), 607–622.

Vulliamy, G. & Webb, R. (1993). *Teacher reseach and special educational needs.* London: David Fulton.

Vygotsky, L. S. (1962). *Thought and language.* Cambridge, MA: MIT Press.

Vygotsky, L. S. (1978). *Mind in society: The development of higher psychological processes.* Cambridge, MA: Harvard University Press.

Wade, B. & Moore, M. (1992). *Experiencing special education: What young people with special needs can tell us.* Buckingham, England: Open University Press.

Walkerdine, V. (1988). *The mastery of reason.* London: Routledge.

Walkerdine, V. (1990). *School girl fictions.* London: Verso.

Walklin, L. (1982). *Instructional techniques and practice.* Cheltenham, England: Stanley Thornes.

Wall, W. (1947). *The adolescent child.* London: Methuen.

Ward, G. & Rowe, J. (1985). Teachers' praise: Some unwanted side effects or 'praise and be damned'. *Society for the Extension of Education Knowledge, 1*, 2–4.

Warnock Report. (1978), *Report of the committee of enquiry into the education of handicapped children and young people* (Chairman: Mary Warnock). London: HMSO.

Watkins, C. (1992). *Whole school PSE: Policy and practice.* Coventry, England: National Association for Pastoral Care in Education.

Watkins, C. & Thacker, J. (1993). *Tutoring: INSET workshops for a whole school approach.* London: Longman.

Watson, B. & Konicek, R. (1990). Teaching for conceptual change: Confronting children's experience. *Phi Delta Kappan, 71*, 680–685.

Watson, J. B. (1913). Psychology as the behaviorist views it. *Psychological Review, 20,* 158–177.

Webb. N. M. (1982). Student interaction and learning in small groups. *Review of Educational Research, 52,* 421–445.

Webb, N. M. (1989). Peer interaction and learning in small groups. *International Journal of Educational Research, 13,* 21–39.

Webb, N. M. & Kenderski, C. M. (1985). Gender differences in small group interaction and achievement in high and low achieving classes. In L. C. Wilkinson & C. B. Marrett (Eds.), *Gender differences in classroom interaction.* New York: Academic Press.

Weinert, F., Schrader, F. & Helmke, A. (1989). Quality of instruction and achievement outcomes. *International Journal of Education Research, 13*(8), 895–914.

Wells, G. (1987). *The meaning makers.* London: Hodder.

Wheldall, K. (Ed.). (1987). *The behaviourist in the classroom.* London: Allen & Unwin.

Wheldall, K. & Glynn, T. (1989). *Effective classroom learning.* Oxford, England: Blackwell.

Wheldall, K. & Merrett, F. (1985). Reducing troublesome classroom behaviour in the secondary school. *Maladjusted Therapeutic Education, 3,* 37–46.

Wilkinson, L. C. & Calculator, S. (1982). Requests and responses in peer directed reading groups. *American Educational Research Journal, 19,* 107–20.

Williams, J. (1987). The construction of women and black students as educational problems: Re-evaluating policy on gender and race. In M. Arnot & G. Weiner (Eds.), *Gender and the politics of schooling.* London: Hutchinson.

Willis, P. E. (1977). *Learning to labour: How working class kids get working class jobs.* Westmead, England: Saxon House.

Wilson, S. & Wineburg, S. (1988). Peering at American history through different lenses: The role of disciplinary perspective in teaching history. *Teachers College Record, 89*(4), 525–539.

Wineburg, S. & Wilson, S. (1991). Subject-matter knowledge in the teaching of history. In J. Brophy (Ed.), *Advances in research on teaching (Vol. 2).* Greenwich, CT: JAI Press.

Wittrock, M. C. (Ed.). (1986). *Handbook of research on teaching.* New York: Macmillan.

Wolf, D. P. (1993). Assessment as an episode of instruction. In R. Bennett and W. Ward (Eds.), *Construction versus choice in cognitive measurement.* Hillsdale, NJ: Erlbaum.

Wolfendale, S. (1992). *Special needs in the primary school.* London: Cassell.

Wood, D. (1986). Aspects of teaching and learning. In M. Richards & P. Light (Eds.), *Children of social worlds.* Cambridge, England: Polity Press.

Wood, P. (1981). *International classification of impairments, disabilities and handicaps.* Geneva, Switzerland: WHO.

Wood, S. & Shears, B. (1986). *Teaching children with severe learning difficulties: A radical re-appraisal.* London: Croom Helm.

Woods, P. (1988). *How children think and learn.* Milton Keynes, England: Open University Press.

Wootton, M. (1992). *Explaining and questioning.* Upminster, England: Nightingale Teaching Consultancy.

Wragg, E. & Brown, G. (1993a). *Explaining.* London: Routledge.

Wragg, E. & Brown, G. (1993b). *Questioning.* London: Routledge.

Wray, D. & Medwell, J. (1991). *Language and literacy in the primary years.* London: Routledge.

Wright, C. (1987). The relations between teachers and Afro-Caribbean pupils: Observing multicultural classrooms. In G. Weiner & M. Arnot (Eds.), *Gender under scrutiny.* London: Hutchinson.

Young, P. & Tyre, C. (1992). *Gifted or able? Realizing children's potential.* Buckingham, England: Open University Press.

Zipes, J. (1983). *The trials and tribulations of Little Red Riding Hood: Versions of the tale in sociocultural context.* London: Heinemann.

Index

abstract problems, 67
academic learning time, 119–20
active learning, 83, 84–7, 129
active teaching, 115
adaptation, 19; accommodation and assimilation, 19
advanced organizers, 121
Ainscow, M. and Tweddle, D. A., 231
Alexander, R., 78–9, 264, 281, 283, 284, 285; et al., 79
alternative frameworks, 51
Alton-Lee, A. and Nuthall, G., 279, 283
Anderson, L. M., 125
Anderson, L. W., 117, 128; and Block, 119
anticipation, 186, 187
Aristotle, 39, 45
Arnot, M., 250; and Weiner, G., 244, 254
Aronson, E., 154
ARROW, 232
Aspy, D. N. and Roebuck, F. N., 257, 258
assessment, 4, 82, 292–3; assessing to a standard, 299–301; by teacher or external examination, 301–2; certifying and selecting, 293–4, 306; choosing the best, 297–9; content of, 295; continuous, 308–9; contribution of assessor, 295–6; diagnostic, 309, 311; domain, 295; in geography, 312–14, 315; in German, 315–16, 317, 318; influence of selection tests on, 299; for monitoring standards, 303–4; and non-academic outcomes of learning, 302–3; for planning, 304–5; summative, 291–2, 294, 306; techniques of, 311; uses of, 293, 305; valid, 294
assessment (formative), 294, 307–9, 321–2; of attitudes, 316, 318–20; in primary school, 309–11; school-based projects, 323; in secondary school, 311–14, 315–16; and use of summative examinations, 321
assimilation, 19
Associationism, 15
Atkinson, R. C. and Shiffrin, R. M., 25–6, 26
attitudes, 116; assessment of, 316, 318–20
Attwell, N., 204
Ausubel, D. P., 121; et al., 87
autonomy, 197–8, 213–14; defined, 209–12; establishing a social context for, 205–7; intellectual, 198–9, 202–3, 204, 206; of means, 199; moral, 207; perceptions of, 200–1; of purpose,